D0089002

Corporate Governance Failures

Corporate Governance Failures

The Role of Institutional Investors in the Global Financial Crisis

Edited by

James P. Hawley, Shyam J. Kamath,
and Andrew T. Williams

UNIVERSITY OF PENNSYLVANIA PRESS

PHILADELPHIA

Copyright © 2011 University of Pennsylvania Press

All rights reserved. Except for brief quotations used for purposes of review
or scholarly citation, none of this book may be reproduced in any form by any
means without written permission from the publisher.

Published by
University of Pennsylvania Press
Philadelphia, Pennsylvania 19104-4112
www.upenn.edu/pennpress

Printed in the United States of America on acid-free paper
10 9 8 7 6 5 4 3 2 1

Library of Congress Cataloging-in-Publication Data
Corporate governance failures : the role of institutional investors in the global
financial crisis / edited by James P. Hawley, Shyam J. Kamath, and Andrew T.
Williams.
ISBN: 978-0-8122-4314-7 (hardcover)
    p.   cm.
    Includes bibliographical references and index.
    1. Global Financial Crisis, 2008–2009   Congresses.   2. Financial risk—
Congress.   3. Corporate governance—Congresses.   4. Institutional
investments—Congresses.
HB3722.C696   2011
330.9'0511 22   2010053505

Library
University of Texas
at San Antonio

Contents

Introduction

James P. Hawley, Shyam J. Kamath, and Andrew T. Williams

Background

In late 2008 and early 2009, the subject of financial risk was widely debated and discussed among academics and practitioners, in the business press and on blogs, and among the general public, as well as in the U.S. Congress and parliaments abroad. Yet some of us were struck by how little serious attention (indeed, how little attention of any sort) was being paid to the relation of corporate governance to financial risk, especially the role (or lack thereof) of large institutional investors who have dominated corporate governance activities globally over the past two decades or so.

Institutional investors (public and private pension funds, mutual funds, and, in some countries, banks) have long since become the majority holders of not only public equity but other asset classes as well (e.g., bonds, hedge fund and private equity investments, real estate).[1] In prior work two of us (Hawley and Williams) have characterized these large investors as "universal owners" (UOs) because they have come to own a representative cross section of the investable universe, having broadly diversified investments across equities and increasingly all other asset classes.[2] One consequence of UOs dominating the global investment universe is that their financial and long-term economic interests come to depend on the state of the entire global economy. This contrasts with earlier periods of financial history (especially in common law countries where institutional investors were the rare exception rather than the rule prior to the 1970s) that were dominated by less diversified individual and family owners. Additionally, UOs have come to be the conduits for the majority of the working and retired populations' savings and investments in many countries, also a historically unprecedented development. Since UOs have broadly diversified financial and economic interests (and indeed, the majority of them are fiduciaries to individual pension fund beneficiaries and retirement investors), it would be logical and, in our view, a fiduciary obligation to closely monitor the behavior of the firms they own. During the past few decades such monitoring became more common of individual firms but of individual firms only. Such monitoring was especially directed at firms with poor corporate governance and poor (relative to their benchmarked peers) economic and financial performance.

In fact, growing corporate governance activism since the late 1980s and early 1990s by some UOs (mostly public pension funds, trade union funds, and some freestanding large investors, e.g., TIAA-CREF in the United States, USS and Hermes in the United Kingdom) has indeed led them to monitor and attempt to change the way in which firms operate (through focus on proxy voting processes, staggered boards of directors, division of CEO from board chair, top executive pay linked to clear performance standards). Varying by country, corporate governance activist UOs have achieved some significant reforms—putting a reform agenda both before the investing public and on the table of the political process while having some impact on how firms' governance structures operate.

In spite of this sea change in both ownership and firm-specific monitoring and corporate governance actions, missing was a program among almost all UOs prior to the financial crisis, and often in its early days as well, which would have monitored the various warning signs of financial danger and then developed actions to mitigate damage, both to their own portfolios and systemically. Additionally, the three editors of this volume came to ask ourselves whether, and if so to what extent, the various ways large UOs operated might have, unwittingly, contributed to the financial crisis itself, not necessarily as a primary cause, but as a potentially important factor. In our discussion with various UOs, with academics, policy analysts, and others, we concluded that the time was ripe for a candid discussion of these questions.

Thus, we organized a by-invitation-only meeting of academics, policy analysts, and UOs for a candid, off-the-record two-day conference entitled "Institutional Investors, Risk/Return, and Corporate Governance Failures: Practical Lessons from the Global Financial Crisis."[3] All but one of the chapters in this book are revisions of presentations at that conference. An additional chapter was solicited from a participant in the conference who has written widely on risk and who has had a long career as a self-described "risk quant" (Robert Mark).

We described the background of the conference as follows in our call for papers:

> The current financial crisis has, as part of its origins, a variety of corporate governance failures. Most obvious are misaligned compensation arrangements that incentivized extreme risk (while not punishing failure). Less examined is the role of large, supposedly sophisticated institutional investors (universal owners) in the crisis. Their role is likely one of unconscious commission as well as of omission. Commissions include, for example, both direct and indirect exposure to extremely complex financial instruments (e.g., credit default swaps) through investment in hedge funds and private equity funds, as well as more traditional equity investment in large financial institutions. In particular, the pursuit of "alpha" often coupled with leverage to magnify returns may have led institutional investors to pursue investment strategies that proved to be particular risky, and significantly contributed to the growth of these risky markets. Omissions include, for example, neither having nor considering having a risk monitoring system in place to monitor such investments based on what are now relatively well-established corporate governance principles and best practices.

The objective of the conference was to investigate the role of corporate governance failures, gaps, oversights, and missed opportunities leading up to and during the current global financial crisis as well as to consider and develop proposals to mitigate these failures in the future.

The problem may have been that institutional investors accepted high returns in the financial sector without adequately investigating the basis for the returns and asking the question about whether they were sustainable or might pose systemic risk. There may be an important parallel to the over-performers of the late 1990s, Enron, WorldCom, and so on, that were much admired for their performance, but where performance was built on an unsustainable business model, often not adequately transparent. Additionally, there has not typically been concern for systemic risk, which has resulted from the piling on of multiple firm, sector, and financial instrument risk.

Also, the apparent acceptance of a significant degree of lack of transparency, especially in the financial sector and among the majority of alternative investments, violated a core concept of corporate governance advocated by universal owners and others: that transparency is critical to accountability, which in turn is critical to a well-governed firm in relation to its owners. Transparency, accountability, and good governance generally add value. Lack of these was toxic.

In addition to considering the widespread failure of most mainstream investors, government agencies, and central banks to both foresee, and when warning flags were raised (e.g., by the Bank for International Settlements in 2006) to heed, these warnings, the conference focused specifically on what has become known as "responsible investment" (RI). Emerging in 2005–2006, RI brought together a variety of larger and smaller institutional owners, fund managers, and consultants under the umbrella of the Principles for Responsible Investment (PRI), a United Nations–initiated offshoot. As of February 2010, the PRI had nearly 200 end asset owner signatories (e.g., California Public Employee Retirement System or CalPERs) with a collective net worth of about $5 trillion, while total assets of all signatories (including almost 370 investment managers, e.g., TIAA-CREF, Blackrock) was about $21 trillion as of spring 2009. (With the growth of equity markets since then, the early 2010 value is likely about $23–24 trillion.) The key element of the PRI is that each signatory agrees to incorporate environmental, social, and governance (ESG) factors into their investment practices. This can take the form of negative exclusion from a fund's portfolio of firms that do not meet a fund's definition of ESG standards. It can also take the form of positive screening of a portfolio to include only or be weighted toward those investments that meet the fund's defined ESG standards. And finally, it can take the form of using various corporate governance tools and techniques to influence firms to report on and raise their environmental or social or governance standards. It can also include mixing these three forms of ESG monitoring, governance actions, and positive or negative screening.

What is striking about almost all PRI signatories is that none of them, either in private or in public as far as we know or could determine, prior to the global financial crisis had considered the issue of financial crisis any more than their mainstream counterparts. They had neither risk screens nor analysis nor corporate governance activities directed at the financial sector (including the shadow financial sector) that might have mitigated or signaled impending crisis. The conference, organized in coordination with some of the largest global PRI members and co-convened with the PRI, was an attempt to begin an examination of this huge gap in responsible investment theory and practice, one not captured by the ESG categories, yet obviously underlying any investment strategy and philosophy. If we had to sum up the point with one word, it would be "economic," specifically financial: thus, we might want to add to ESG an E for economic, making it EESG factors that need to be considered and integrated in investment and governance standards.

Prior to 2009, the critical missing element in almost all corporate governance practices, the practitioner and academic literature, various national corporate governance codes, law, and international corporate governance discussion forums (e.g., at the International Corporate Governance Network meetings) has been any link between governance and financial risk. Governance has been conceived too narrowly. Underlying this narrow conception was the fact that financial risk analysis itself had been relegated to the investment side of fund operations. Yet risk analysis has overwhelming viewed risk through the too narrow and established lenses of modern portfolio theory (MPT, of which more below) and macroeconomic general equilibrium theory whose models traditionally excluded financial (crisis) variables.

There was much discussion at the conference of what underlies financial sector and systemic risk, particularly MPT and its core assumption of the efficient market hypothesis (EMH). While there was no agreement as to what degree, if any, MPT—due to its widespread adoption—contributed to the financial crisis, there was agreement that once markets became stressed or failed, MPT ceased to work as understood, and may have had perverse consequences. Often discussed were three levels of risk: firm, sector, and system. Only firm-level risk has been addressed by corporate governance analysis and actions. There was general agreement that the failure to address sector (especially financial sector) and systemic risk had been a large failure and needed to be rectified.

The point was also made that the lessons of the turn-of-the-century

(Enron, WorldCom, the dot-com bubble) had not been fully or even partially learned from and acted on. There are a variety of similarities between the two crises, although the Enron bubble was far less systemically destructive. Foremost among the parallels are that gatekeepers were compromised and conflicted and massively failed to keep the gates closed. A major lacuna was that those supposedly sophisticated investors (UOs and other large institutional investors) did not recognize or act on gatekeeper failure; indeed, they relied on external gatekeepers (e.g., rating agencies) again in the second crisis. In addition to this failure, institutional investors engaged in a mostly illusory search for "alpha," achieving above-market returns over a sustained period without harming the majority of a UO's investment portfolio, including looking at the degree to which the alpha entities (e.g., hedge funds, private equity, real estate) and leveraged instruments (e.g., credit default obligations, credit default swaps) may have unwittingly contributed to crisis.

As of this writing, few UOs have made public statements about how they have corrected or are attempting to correct the mistakes of the past few years in terms of the relation between various levels of risk and corporate governance, although in private this discussion has occurred among at least some large institutional investors. There are some exceptions regarding public statements. For example, TIAA-CREF, the giant U.S. college teachers' pension and mutual fund, issued a statement in February 2010 stressing the importance of corporate governance in relation to assessing risk, and where appropriate and possible, its mitigation. In particular, the statement stressed the importance of effective monitoring, explicitly arguing that, "for universal owners, the 'Wall Street Walk' or simply selling stock in the face of inadequate performance is not the most attractive option." Long-term and diversified owners (UOs) "believe strong corporate governance helps reduce investment risk and ensures that shareholder capital is used effectively."[4]

There has been one notable exception worth highlighting concerning systemic risk among mainline global corporate governance activists: a focus on climate change as a major (albeit nonfinancial) systemic risk factor. Since about 2005 major governance activists have incorporated climate risk (and opportunity) into their corporate governance activities and, to a far more limited degree, into their investment activities, establishing, for example, "green-tech" subfunds.

In order to provide the proper frame of reference for the discussions, the questions, as laid out in our original proposal for the conference and discussed at the conference, were as follows:

1. *Corporate governance*: How did corporate governance failures (oversights, failure of risk analysis, etc.) contribute to the current global financial crisis? How much can realistically be expected from a robust form and execution of "good investment governance"? What specifically was and should be the role of large, universal-owner-type institutions in such governance?

- What is the role of governance in executive remuneration and compensation? Specifically, what are incentives for failure and short-term risk taking? How can misaligned compensation plans be corrected?
- What is the role of good investment governance in the investment decision and allocation process?
- What forms might good investment governance take?
- How might governance monitoring interact with investment decisions? Should they interact?

2. *Financial institutions*: Some financial institutions were deeply affected by the crisis (i.e., Citigroup and AIG) and others were less affected. Are there lessons to be learned by looking at their governance structures prior to the crisis and investigating their board and management responses to the crisis?

3. *Systemic risk*: Can and should institutional investors effectively identify and monitor for systemic risk?

- Can this role be played by institutional investors individually or is there need for some industry-wide entity that analyzes potential sources of systemic risk? What might entrepreneurial activity look like to provide value-added analysis? Is there a potential market for this? Is the early 1990s market in the U.S. for corporate governance analysis a parallel here?

4. *Alternative investments, alpha*: What role did the search for alpha play in the crisis and what role did institutional investors play in the pursuit of alpha? Did organizations monitor these investments on the governance side on the same basis as they did on the equity side? Should organizations? Can they?

- Were risks analyzed for various forms of securitization and collateralized debt obligations (CDOs)? What information was known, and what was asked for? What models were used to evaluate borrower-specific, sector-specific, and systemic risks?
- Were there failures in the governance structure of institutional investors themselves that might have prevented them from perceiving the housing and other credit bubbles or that prevented them from acting on their perceptions?
- Were outperforming investment sectors and specific investment entities subject to the same corporate governance standards that underperforming firms and sectors have been? (In other words, was there a corporate governance double standard in effect?)
- What was the role, if any, of endowments (e.g., Yale, Harvard, etc.) in pushing the envelope on returns? Are there different fiduciary standards and obligations between endowments, on the one hand, and pension funds and investment retirement accounts, on the other? Should there be?

5. *Alternative investments: Real estate, infrastructure, and commodities*: What role did the expansion of real estate, infrastructure, and commodity investment by large institutional owners play in the crisis? (See also question 4 above.)

6. *Role of gatekeepers*: What was the role of accounting, financial reporting, rating agencies, consultants, and regulation in the global financial crisis? What should have been the role of universal owners in relation to these gatekeeping functions? What should be changed going forward? Who watches the watchers remains a central focus.

- How much can be expected from institutional investors and corporate governance practices compared with governmental regulation? What should be the role of public policy advocacy on the part of institutional investors and owners?
- Can this advocacy role be played by individual institutional investors or should industry wide entities take on this task? Both?

7. *Responsible investment:* Do the perspectives of the movement for RI with its emphasis on corporate governance have roles to play in mitigating and minimizing the next crisis or in assisting the recovery from this one?

How can effective alignment of the long-term interests of most institutional investors and financial institutions be achieved? What should be the role of governmental regulation in this alignment and the prevention of such crises?

- What is or should be the role of ultimate beneficiaries and investors vis-à-vis universal owners and other institutional investors? How is or should this role be related to RI? What role could or should legal or regulatory changes have?
- Do the S (social) and E (environmental) factors in RI play a role in risk reorientation? If so, how and what does or might that role look like?

We elucidate the participants' discussions of these major themes and the major points that were raised in the presentations in the sections that follow.

Major Themes: Participants' Cross-Discussion

This section offers a brief summary of the major topics discussed at the conference after the presentations. Most of these themes are reflected in the chapters in this book. There was a range of opinion expressed regarding most of these issues, and there was a unifying sentiment that these topics are of utmost importance to the relation of corporate governance and risk. One of the goals of the conference was to pinpoint and highlight areas that participants thought needed additional research, which is mentioned in some of the theme summaries.

Modern Portfolio Theory (MPT)

As a paradigm, modern portfolio theory and its assumption of the efficient market hypothesis worked well to a point, but as MPT became the primary mode of operation in the economy, it created risk and undermined its own effectiveness. The logic is the fallacy of composition: if only some participants use MPT, it works well, but as more and more come to rely on it, it creates its own risks, its own tipping points. Some conference participants pointed out that MPT had never really worked well, as was demonstrated by rigorous statistical analysis and a number of recent studies in behavioral finance that pointed toward financial and other asset markets being inefficient.[5] While these points were long recognized in some of the academic literature critical of MPT, large investors, their advisers and fund managers mostly ignored this criticism (perhaps until well into the crisis).

There was general agreement that MPT doesn't work in stressed markets, but significant debate about whether (and if so, to what degree) it contributed to market stress by its widespread adoption. Some argued that it was necessary to fundamentally reconsider MPT; others wanted to understand its limits and how to make sure those limits are not exceeded in the future. They didn't want to throw the baby out with the bathwater. The discussion did not resolve how limits could and should best be accomplished.

A core question that most agreed was important was: what is the relation of MPT to corporate governance? Did it tend to create passivity in the face of rising asset prices because it didn't recognize bubbles in its models? Mostly, governance activists didn't engage with boards of directors of lending institutions such as the large lender and subprime originator Washington Mutual. (It was noted that there were a few exceptions such as the labor union SEIU [Service Employees International Union], which has also been a longtime governance activist. No nonunion funds engaged around risk issues with boards, although many voted in favor of proxy proposals on this issue once they were introduced.) One reason that almost no institution engaged with boards around risk was that MPT posits that the way to deal with risk is by diversification (typically no institution held more than a very small fraction of any firm's equity) and by hedging the portfolio. Both considerations suggest that no one needs to be monitoring such risk, and before the crisis all felt safe due to portfolio hedging as risk mitigation. This view is sharply at odds with the prevailing corporate governance view and practice that engaging with underperforming boards is a critical action that adds value to the portfolio.

The question thus is this: is MPT incomplete, is it perverse, or does it just not apply in a market breakdown? One participant argued the latter, regardless of whether it is incomplete or perverse. Most agreed a large unknown, when things break down, was what should or can be put in place of MPT. There is little or no good research on this, but it was agreed that it is a, if not the, crucial question.

Chasing Alpha and Universal Owners

A theme that ran throughout the conference was that of chasing "alpha." The search for above-market returns (alpha) has been in recent years a hallmark of the investment world. How *alpha* is defined varies, and its definitions are often vague and sometimes contradict one another. Widely discussed was how alpha is related to nonalpha investments. For example, ten to fifteen years ago, most large UOs' portfolios were overwhelmingly composed of equity and debt (bond) investments. Especially since the turn of the century (as equity market returns generally stagnated), the search for so-called alternative investments yielding higher (supposedly risk-adjusted) returns increased, in some cases dramatically. Whether these alternative investments were really a search for alpha is debatable, but the term was used increasingly loosely to mean above-equity-market returns. It could take the form of leveraged investments (in hedge funds and private equity, for example), as well as in "new" asset classes (for large investors), such as real estate, commodities (somewhat perversely including financial "commodities," e.g., structured products), and infrastructure. Clearly, the leveraged chase for alpha was a major contributor to the financial crisis, and UOs were major players on the investment side of this trend. A question most discussed was how much of this trend was attributable to MPT itself, or whether it was actually a distortion of MPT that suggests that at least for large investors it is not possible over the long term to beat the market. One of the key debates was whether UOs, as owners of a cross section of the whole economy, actually gained (over the long term and on a net basis) from alpha-type investments given how value destroying (as a whole) they were and the higher agency costs involved.

Is chasing alpha by some investors inherent to the adequate functioning of MPT as it is necessary to eliminate market imperfections by the seeking of arbitrage opportunities? This goes to core assumptions about how accurate or inaccurate the EMH is. If markets are not efficient (and perhaps grossly inefficient at certain times), can MPT function? If so, how many arbitrage-seeking opportunities need there be, and importantly from the UO perspective, which types of institutions should seek them? Closely related to this discussion was the topic of the degree to which especially equity markets need "price discovering" buyers and sellers who are not operating an indexed portfolio (itself rooted in MPT). A critical and debated issue here was who those players should be, and how many are necessary.

Modeling and Its Limits

A number of attendees, including those who had made a long career as risk "quants," noted that MPT should involve not only modeling the past but (perhaps more important) making informed judgments about the future. Models can't do this, it was argued; there has to be *ex ante* judgment by investors. The question was raised about what the role should be, if any, of government in this.

Environment, Social, and Governance Factors and MPT

It was noted in the discussion that there has been no attempt either empirically or theoretically to examine the relation between ESG factors and MPT. For example, how might (and can) climate change risk (and opportunity) be related to MPT? What can be said about the relation of corporate governance to MPT, as many noted that MPT tends to make institutional investors passive investors?

What is and should be the relation between the financial sector and broader interests of society? How can this be determined? This question was discussed in terms of a proposal to channel investment and closely define the appropriate social role of various asset classes (e.g., real estate and specifically "green" real estate).

What is the relation between government policies (e.g., tax and macroeconomic policies), growing inequality (over the past thirty-five years), and debt-financed consumerism? Specifically, the question focused on the means that households have used and to what degree in order to maintain their standards of living in the face of stagnating or declining real household income in the bottom three-fifths of income distribution. Can the housing bubble also be seen as households "chasing microalpha"?

Values

"Values" was considered a bad word among some strictly financial-bottom-line investors, but mentioned by those involved in socially responsible investment. The point stressed was that ESG is about social investing, connecting those who invest (ultimately, pension fund members and retirement investors/savers) with what their investments are doing and how funds are invested, and the world savers and investors (and their children and grandchildren) will inherit.

How to Get Risk/Return Right?

It has become widely accepted that almost all risk/return measures were inadequate to the challenges that became apparent in the global financial crisis. Yet there was skepticism about how to get it right going forward. What metrics should be used? Can any metric adequately capture risk, or is qualitative judgment additionally required? If so, how do the two become integrated? Who should be responsible for this risk-assessment function among UO-type investors?

Countervailing (Market-Based) Forces?

Most attendees agreed that significant government and regulatory reforms were needed to minimize future financial crises. Some felt that there is also an important role for market actors, especially UOs, to play. But the problem remained that UOs and others have been caught up in the search for alpha as a systemic destabilizing force. Reasons for this include the tendency of large institutions to benchmark their performance (and internally to benchmark their money managers) against similar institutions, creating ultimately destructive herding behavior, and providing incentives for some to seek greater leverage in the (perhaps illusory) pursuit of alpha.

Does Corporate Governance Become More Important During Financial Crises?

Based on the empirical evidence on U.S. real estate investment trusts (REITs) before and during the financial crisis, the role of corporate governance seemed not to matter much during boom periods but did matter considerably during the downturn. This supports the long-held idea that good governance is a form of insurance. Some argued this was the result of the more stringent payout rules for REITs making corporate governance by institutional investors less important during boom periods but requiring good governance when managerial discretion increased during the downturn and depreciation payments became important for cash retention for compensation and other insider purposes. The question was raised whether such rules may have something to offer for non-REITs, but there was debate about whether the special nature of REITS (e.g., they are mainly held for income purposes) made them different from industrial investments (e.g., in high-technology firms), where reinvestment and stock appreciation were critical. In any case, further evidence needs to be collected on these and other aspects of both REITS and other kinds of investments.

What Was the Role of Hedge Funds in the Crisis?

Participants argued that there is not yet a full understanding of the role of hedge funds (or some hedge funds) in the global financial crisis. They were big players as buyers of leveraged and complex financial products (e.g., collateralized debt obligations). Their role in leverage was important and had an impact on asset prices across the market. Thus, while they may not have caused the crisis, they may have contributed to it. Yet many hedge funds held assets (including equity) for longer than many mutual funds. It was pointed out that hedge funds are not all alike and generalization is difficult. In particular, some argued that it is one thing when investors use leveraged products to diversify portfolio risk while holding the underlying assets, but quite another when they do not hold the underlying assets and even worse when products are created (and held) that are entirely synthetic, second- and third-order creations (e.g., synthetic credit default swaps [CDS]).

What Is the Potential of In-House Hedge Funds and Private Equity?

Many participants were interested in further research on UOs creating in-house hedge funds or private equity firms. This has already been done by a number of large investors (e.g., the Ontario Teachers Pension Plan). Can these types of funds avoid the excesses and alleged abuses of external, more established funds? If so, how? How do they (indeed, do they) integrate ESG factors? Do they generate alpha, and if so how and over what time frame?

In what ways are they different from larger and more established hedge funds?

The "Do No Harm" Standard of Investing

Should there be a standard of "do no harm" for investing? What would it look like? Can markets or market institutions (e.g., stock exchange listing requirements, codes of good governance) enforce such a standard? If not, should government(s) define and enforce it?

Internally Versus Externally Managed Funds and the Problem of Politics

UOs often use external fund managers to manage all or part of their funds. How does a UO align the interests of beneficiaries and taxpayers (for public funds)? Do internally managed funds that reduce a layer of fees assist this, and if so, at what cost? The politics of such alignment are difficult since this often results in top management making more money than elected officials. It was pointed out that it is possible for large funds to work around this by a well-organized campaign to obtain support from key players (e.g., beneficiaries), as has occurred in California and Wisconsin.

Internal versus external management is part of the larger issue needing to be researched by focusing on the investment chain problem. While this issue is often talked about, participants felt there was an absence of good research, especially focused on long-term performance. This larger issue includes whether funds (whether managed internally or externally or typically both) can adequately account for risk. Do investors know how their various funds operate in terms of contributing to (systemic) or sector risk? It was widely agreed that few institutional investors track or conceptualize this.

Investment Chain ESG Issue

Another aspect of the investment chain is the role of investment consultants who advise large funds. It was suggested that it is critical for end-asset owners to mandate their own priorities, for example, on systemic financial risk issues about which most consultants know nothing, or concerning ESG issues where there are no more than perhaps twenty-five to thirty expert consultants worldwide in this area (e.g., at-large consultancies such as Mercer or Watson Wyatt).

Collective Corporate Governance Action Problem

On a topic partly related to herding dynamics, many participants felt that even the largest UOs cannot target more than ten or so firms a year for appropriate corporate governance actions. This was considered far too small a target universe to be effective. A number of organizations attempt to coordinate actions among UOs, such as the PRI Clearinghouse, the U.S. Council of Institutional Investors, and the National Association of Pension Funds in the U.K., but these efforts were also seen as inadequate. There is a need to both unify focus and divide up targets. Participants also felt that UOs and coordinating organizations need to develop their own compensation experts to counter firms' experts.

Because there is nothing like the U.K. Combined Corporate Governance Code in the U.S., the result is likely to be that private firms such as RiskMetrics and Glass Lewis will be the de facto standard setters, and given recent mergers there are fewer and fewer of them. It was pointed out that in Australia the procedure is to contract with, for example, RiskMetrics, but to mandate a fund's own, independent standards in addition.

Fiduciary Obligations and Duties

Regarding systemic risk a number of participants suggested that monitoring it is a fiduciary obligation while failure to do so would be a breech of fiduciary duty. Monitoring the so-called gatekeepers (e.g., rating agencies) and, where appropriate, considering actions to correct apparent failures and make improvements was seen as a duty of ownership. Quoting the well known corporate governance activist Robert Monks, one participant remarked that just as capitalism without owners will fail so, too, will property without adequate monitoring and stewardship.

During the discussion about climate change as a form of nonfinancial systemic risk and fiduciary duty, it was suggested that as conceived and practiced to date by most fiduciary attorneys and under much fiduciary law, fiduciary is a conservative concept. Some argued that this needs to be reformed by legislation (since the courts aren't likely to do it). In turn, this raised the issue of whether UOs should lobby for such reform as a prudential action. Because the herding effect is widespread among UOs, fiduciary legal reform needs to get the herd to run in a somewhat different direction.

An interesting and important research project suggested was to look at those interest groups that promoted MPT as part of fiduciary duty, including in the Employee Retirement Income Security Act (ERISA) and related legislation of the early 1970s. Related to this was a question about the scope of fiduciary duty: should it be (as currently) narrowly financial or more broadly economic? A number of examples of the financial versus economic issues were raised. One concerned the privatization of a school bus company whose employees' pensions prior to privatization were managed by a large public pension fund. The fund had invested in a private equity firm that planned to purchase the school bus franchise. The employees' pensions would be reduced under the purchase. What does fiduciary obligation dictate, a narrow investment focus, or a broader employee/beneficiary focus? The climate change issue presents questions focused on a very macro issue, while the school bus example is very micro. Yet both raise similar questions about the scope of fiduciary obligations, which in turn raise the issue of shareholder primacy (as U.S. law tends to emphasize) or the best interests of the company (which U.K. law focuses on). These issues are core to a UO perspective on investment since there is not a clear distinction in some cases between shareowners and stakeholders, as the school bus and the climate change cases suggest.

A long-established expert in fiduciary law made an additional point: the problem is that fiduciary lawyers tend to look at returns rather than risk-adjusted returns (as everyone else in business does). If risk-adjusted returns are combined with the too often forgotten fiduciary common law duty of impartiality (based on the law of trusts), this could go a long way toward addressing some of the systemic risk issues. For example, younger beneficiaries will bear the disproportionate outcomes of systemic risk, whether in terms of the economic consequences of financial collapse or those of climate change. This is in contrast to a focus on producing current, more narrowly defined financial returns. Thus there is an intergenerational equity issue. Were fiduciary law to clearly establish these principles, there is the truly vexing question of how to deal with conflicting fiduciary obligations.

The following section presents summaries of each chapter, emphasizing how each author(s) focused on the themes and questions addressed by the conference that resulted in the two days of cross-discussion among the participants, as outlined above.

Themes and Synopsis of the Chapters

In Chapter 2, Steven Lydenberg argues that today's dominant theory of investment, modern portfolio theory, is based on a definition of success that fails to acknowledge adequately the extent to which investments at the portfolio level can affect the overall financial market. In particular, the techniques—such as diversification, securitization, hedging, arbitrage, and leverage—used to control risks at the portfolio level while maximizing returns can create market-level risks that threaten financial and economic stability.

Thus, Lydenberg, cofounder and chief investment officer of the socially responsible investment fund Domini Social Investments, suggests that the portfolio-level benefits that accrue from this theory are, at best, part of a zero-sum game and at worst significantly contributed to the financial crisis. If there were gains, they were available to only a limited number of investors. In addition, in practice, the more investors who adopt these risk-control techniques, the less likely they are to succeed, especially in times of economic stress. Alternative theories of investment are needed that encourage assessments of the effects of portfolio-level decisions at a systemic level and define success in investment in ways that stabilize financial markets and increase the prospects of both portfolio-level and market-level returns. This chapter suggests that one such alternative definition of investment success derives from the observation that asset classes available to investors serve distinct and different societal purposes. Under governments' guidance, these asset classes have evolved to create a mosaic of complementary investment opportunities that can help in the creation of just and sustainable societies. Success in investment can therefore be defined as investors' skill in maximizing the societal benefits that each asset class naturally creates, while achieving competitive financial returns.

If Lydenberg argues that MPT may well have contributed to the financial crisis as it became widely adopted (and most all adopting it diversified into riskier and riskier assets in a search for alpha or in the name of hedging against portfolio risk), Robert Mark, a long-time quantitative risk analyst, risk manager, and author, argues in Chapter 3 that whatever the proximate causes of the global financial crisis, once it began, MPT (as well as the capital asset pricing model—CAPM) ceased to work as many expected it to and as advertised, and may well have exacerbated the crisis in ways he specifies. Mark outlines his view of risk management (and its limitations), focusing on a variety of risk areas, for example, model risk, credit risk, and operational risk. He argues that improved risk management within financial firms themselves is a necessary (although not sufficient) element in preventing or minimizing future crises. His chapter provides a detailed road map to various types of financial risk. He stresses the critical link between internal corporate governance structures in financial firms, and its relation to a variety of risk analyses and their management. He illustrates his key points with minicases of Long Term Capital Management's failure and a study of the current financial crisis, both focusing on internal governance failures of financial firms.

From a quite different perspective, Philip Augar, former U.K. investment banker, author, and financial journalist, argues in Chapter 4 that the pursuit of alpha (becoming a mania just before the financial bubble burst) was a major factor in the corporate governance failures in the U.K. Underlying those failures were policies of both the Conservative and Labour governments that promoted London as a global financial, relatively deregulated center, enabling alpha's global pursuit. Britain adopted a U.S.-style financial system after the Big Bang reforms of 1986 and became the premier international financial services capital over the next two decades. When the world's banking system unraveled between 2007 and 2009, Britain was more exposed to the consequences than most countries and the fate of its financial institutions was a microcosm of the global crisis.

Augar suggests the development of an ideological orthodoxy as an explanation for this failure. Its origins lay in the adoption of free market economics by the Conservative governments of 1979–1997. Eventually, in a dramatic reversal of its traditional socialist policies, Labour also embraced market capitalism and, after it was elected to office in 1997, implemented a series of pro-market reforms. The government cut tax rates for hedge and buyout funds and relaxed competition policy. Britain's financial services regulator was given a mandate to promote the City's global competitiveness and, in order to achieve this, relaxed supervision through light-touch regulation. As the financial services industry boomed, the government exulted in the City's success. Critical thinking about finance was marginalized and the City and Wall Street professionals were inducted in large numbers into Britain's government, civil service, and academic institutions. A new paradigm of derivatives-based risk transformation was proclaimed. Alternative ideas were dismissed out of hand; risk-averse managers and nonexecutives were told to "get with it" and were threatened by nonactivist investors. Bank executives faced the choice of chasing alpha or being forced out of office. Augar argues that an irresistible orthodoxy rather than more popular theories of greed and incompetence is a stronger explanation for the failure in governance during these years. In turn, deregulation of British financial markets was propelled by the firm, and he argues deeply misguided, belief in self-managing and self-correcting financial markets.

In Chapter 5, James Hawley (professor and director of the Elfenworks Center for the Study of Fiduciary Capitalism) raises the question of what UOs did and did not do and what they did or did not foresee in relation to the global financial crisis. He suggests that among almost all UOs, none had a robust model of financial risk, and few, if any, had developed alternative scenarios to the ones dominated by MPT. Nor did UOs, longtime and often-effective corporate governance activists, recognize on the corporate governance side of their organizations that risk went beyond firm-specific risk. Hawley suggests that there was a major disconnect between corporate governance practices and investment strategy, the latter directly and indirectly, although unwittingly, contributing to the global financial crisis. Well-established governance standards (e.g., accountability, transparency) were not applied to the growing area of alternative investments, nor were they adequately (and often not at all) applied to equity and debt investments in the financial and shadow financial sectors. These governance failures were a reflection of inadequate application of standard risk analysis, but more fundamentally were based on the uncritical acceptance of MPT, which itself contributed to the crisis as it became widely adopted by most large universal owners and others. This combined with the mostly illusory search for alpha in alternative investments negated and undermined corporate governance standards, especially in financial investments entities. He concludes that ESG and RI trends need significant self-reflection by UOs on these failures in order to move forward in the search for alternative governance directions as well as for UO-based investment strategies and risk analyses.

In Chapter 6, Kym Sheehan, Australian lawyer and academic legal scholar, traces the development of "say on pay" in Australia, which adopted that principle into law in 2005. The chapter presents a model of the regulatory framework for executive remuneration that examines the role of institutional investors as the key gatekeepers within this framework. Institutional investors, either individually or collectively, define standards of good practice, engage with remuneration committees to encourage compliance with the standards, and vote against company remuneration reports and binding remuneration resolutions. In terms of how much can be expected from institutional investors compared with government regulation of executive remuneration, there are great expectations of active involvement of institutional investors. That remuneration practices are now found to be wanting reflects past inconsistent efforts of institutional investors to enforce their own standards.

But it is not clear, Sheehan argues, that institutional investors are willing, able, and consistent gatekeepers, and this problem needs to be openly acknowledged by institutional investors and governments alike. If the regulatory framework relies on institutional investors being active in monitoring and enforcing good remuneration practices but investors are unwilling to do so, another regulatory framework with higher levels of government regulation is required. The difficulty for this regulatory framework is that governments must answer to the general public who elect them. That public sees executive remuneration as largely a quantum and distributive justice issue, whereas institutional investors are generally far less concerned about the quantum of remuneration, but very concerned that company performance is providing a positive return to shareholders. Sheehan concludes that shareowners (overwhelmingly institutional) have not made good use of say on pay provisions, thereby unwittingly contributing to an incentive misalignment in firms, including financial firms, which has been widely identified as an important factor in the global financial crisis.

Bruce Dravis, U.S. practicing corporate law attorney and former State of California official, in Chapter 7 looks at the role and limits of law in relation to asset bubbles. Existing laws on governance, he argues, are aimed at preventing managers from abusing the resources that investors have committed to business institutions, by requiring corporate processes intended to detect and prevent misuse of those resources. The law does not require managers to maximize corporate resources. The law does not, and cannot, dictate outcomes of management decisions. The law does not, and should not, make managers guarantors of results. But to investors who lost billions of dollars in the 2007–2008 financial crisis resulting from the sudden deflation of real estate prices, and to citizens who saw public wealth used to bail out failed companies, it is cold comfort to be told that the corporate managers did not abuse their positions and observed proper process. Investors who saw average portfolio declines of nearly 40 percent in 2008 probably would have argued that the process was inadequate to protect their interests.

Just two companies—American International Group (AIG) and Citigroup, Inc. (Citigroup)—accounted for approximately $800 billion of market capitalization losses and government bailouts. In the case of AIG, the market capitalization decline between January 1, 2008, and the end of the first quarter of 2009 was approximately $140 billion, and it had accepted $182.5 billion of additional government bailout funds. In the case of Citigroup, there was a market capitalization loss of roughly $140 billion over the same period, and Citigroup took $45 billion of government investment under the Troubled Asset Relief Program (TARP) program as well as an additional government guarantee of $300 billion on certain toxic assets. This chapter considers—in light of the examples of Citigroup and AIG— the limits on the ability to use the laws of corporate governance to generate positive results in the next financial bubble that will arise.

In Chapter 8, Nils Kok and his two coauthors, Piet Eichholtz and Erkan Yonder (all from the University of Maastricht, the Netherlands), analyze the role of corporate governance in real estate, specifically in U.S. REITs. Real estate was at the forefront of the financial crisis, with the lack of transparency of securitized products, such as mortgage-backed securities (MBS), collateralized MBS, and CDOs, playing a critical role. Real estate equity investments have received less attention during the crisis.

Listed property companies (REITs) offer an interesting perspective on the behavior of institutional investors in the real estate equity market. In this chapter, the authors study the influence of the recent crisis on the relation between corporate governance and the performance of listed property companies in the U.S. They first investigate the effect of corporate governance structures on abnormal stock returns during the pre-crisis period, and then address the effects of the financial crisis on this relationship. They find that firm-level corporate governance did not influence performance of real estate equity investments before the crisis, but the structure of corporate governance has become an important performance driver of real estate equity investments during and after the market downturn. Their conclusion supports one of the long-held beliefs among corporate governance practitioners and scholars, that good governance is a form of downside insurance. One interpretation of this downside insurance nature of corporate governance is that institutional investors just started to recognize the importance of transparency in real estate equity investments during the recent crisis, which is fully consistent with the herd investments in securitized debt products, where opacity of the investments was so blissfully ignored.

Chapter 9, by Jennifer Taub, former large-mutual-fund attorney turned academic legal scholar, explores how the overleveraging and collapse of the global financial system were related to legal and corporate governance acts and omissions that preceded the financial crisis. These acts and omissions enabled the boom and focused the pain of the bust disproportionately on the middle class while leaving many of the financial "middlemen," who were the perpetrators of the problems, untouched. This resulted in individuals being exposed to risky investments from which they should have been protected.

Even "sophisticated investors" such as U.S. mutual funds and public and corporate pension funds, who had pooled their assets, were exposed to these risky investments. The exemption of hedge funds and other collective pools of capital from the 1940 Investment Company Act caused investor protections and governance aspects of mutual fund regulation to be diminished even as the boom accelerated. As unregulated entities, these pools flourished by attracting more institutional assets and were not restricted in the use of derivatives, leverage, and illiquid securities. Another culprit was the Commodity Futures Modernization Act of 2000, which incubated and fostered the credit default swap (CDS) pandemic. A 2005 Bankruptcy Code change increased the supply of toxic assets by supporting unwise financing through housing overvaluation. When the bust occurred, middlemen received massive taxpayer-funded bailouts as CDS made commercial bankruptcy through Chapter 11 less viable. In addition, the change to Chapter 13 resulted in consumers not being able to downsize underwater mortgages. Finally, securities laws changes and legal doctrines shielded fiduciaries from liability and substantially eroded the ability of investors ultimately left holding the assets to seek redress.

The role played by investment consultants is examined in Chapter 10, by Eric R. W. Knight and Adam D. Dixon, the former an Australian attorney and Ph.D. candidate at Oxford University, the latter a lecturer at the University of Bristol in the U.K. Their chapter focuses on the role of investment consultants in advising the flow of capital from the world's largest institutional investors: pension funds. Using unique survey data from global investment consultants collected by the United Nations Environment Programme Finance Initiative, this chapter identifies the conflicted position of investment consultants as both thought leaders with direct access to trustee board decision making and also corporate followers who are servants to clients' short-term demands.

Developing a theoretical model to situate the consultant within the asset management chain, the authors argue that investment consultants have repeatedly failed to integrate corporate governance, social, and environmental considerations into their mainstream corporate valuation and advisory models. Although they do not claim that this was a proximate cause of the global financial crisis, the authors suggest that these cultural impediments create the conditions for mispricing long-term assets and that the global financial crisis represents one such example of this.

In their analysis, they identify three specific areas of conflict and discuss the nature of the current failure to incorporate such considerations at length. First, there is a lack of theoretical clarity within the investment community of the importance of long-term corporate governance, social, and environmental drivers in financial valuation. Second, there is a lack of training within the investment community, resulting in analysts lacking the appropriate skills to make this kind of valuation. Third, there are institutional barriers within the incentive structures of investment consultants. These include the prevalence of short-term time horizons, perverse short-term incentives structured into managers' remuneration, and the use of tracking error limits and index-referenced mandates which penalize portfolios that integrate long-term responsible investment themes.

In a somewhat related vein, Claire Woods, also an Australian attorney and Ph.D. candidate at Oxford University, in Chapter 11 examines the role of fiduciary law and pension fund trustees as each confronts another macro-risk: climate change. While financial crises and climate change are not related as such, Woods argues that they share some important common attributes in terms of how each may be viewed by current understandings and interpretations of fiduciary law. Woods begins by noting that pension funds control, on average, assets equivalent to 76 percent of the gross domestic product of their respective countries throughout the Western world. Their investments are colossal; as large shareholders, their potential to influence companies in almost all industries is profound.

Reflecting on the context of climate change and the global financial crisis, this chapter sets out to demonstrate the potential of pension funds to drive the reduction of firms' climate change impact, and to expose the institutional structures that stand in their way. The study examines why fiduciary duty is perceived as a barrier to change in investment practices by outlining recent legal developments in the area. It argues that, in theory, fiduciary duty should not be perceived as a legal barrier to pension funds' consideration of climate change impact: where corporate carbon footprint presents a financial risk in the context of climate change, the consideration of carbon footprint in investment decisions accords with the requirements of fiduciary duty. However, fiduciary duty is nuanced, and has both dynamic and static characteristics: just as the fiduciary standard has been flexible enough to evolve with social expectations in the past (and should be able to adapt to the increasing importance of climate change impact), it is also resistant to innovation in the investment context. The fiduciary's standard of prudence in the investment context is judged, in part, by reference to conventional investment decisions—courts have had the tendency to equate prudence with conventionality. The prudent course of action in this light becomes the status quo, limiting the potential for innovation in investment decision making. Therefore, this chapter argues that fiduciary duty both masks, and to some extent exacerbates, the real reasons for pension funds' slow reaction to climate change: ingrained institutional myopia regarding both financial performance and environmental impact, and practical shortcomings in techniques for measuring long-term risk. Finally, the chapter proposes a number of solutions for the problems set out.

The purpose of the conference as well as this volume is to raise what those participating in the conference, the chapter authors, and the editors consider critical strategic, theoretical, and empirical questions. While these chapters contribute to each of these areas, none has the last word on the problems they raise and analyze. Thus, we hope that this volume will encourage others to pursue and debate these and related issues and topics.

Chapter 2

Beyond Risk: Notes Toward a Responsible Investment Theory

Steve Lydenberg

Introduction

This chapter argues that today's dominant theory of investment, modern portfolio theory (MPT), is based on a definition of success that fails to acknowledge adequately the extent to which investments at the portfolio level can affect the overall financial markets. In particular, its techniques intended to control risks at the portfolio level while maximizing returns—such as diversification, securitization, hedging, arbitrage, and leverage—can create market-level risks that threaten financial and economic stability.

The portfolio-level benefits that accrue from this theory are by definition part of a zero-sum game at best and available to only a limited number of investors. In addition, in practice, the more investors adopt these risk-control techniques, the less likely they are to succeed, especially in times of economic stress.

Alternative theories of investment are needed that encourage assessments of the effects of portfolio-level decisions at a systemic level and define success in investment in ways that stabilize financial markets and increase the prospects of both portfolio-level and market-level returns.

This chapter suggests one such alternative definition of investment success. It derives from the observation that the asset classes available to investors serve distinct societal purposes. Under governments' guidance, these asset classes have evolved to create a mosaic of complementary investment opportunities that can help in the development of just and sustainable societies. Success in investment can therefore be defined as investors' skill in maximizing the societal benefits that each asset class is intended to create, while achieving competitive financial returns.

Why Modern Portfolio Theory Provides an Inadequate Definition of Success

The contemporary practice of investment is driven in large part by the basic principles of modern portfolio theory, which—in the wake of the financial crises of 2007–2009—has come under attack from various quarters. In particular, its techniques for risk management and the maximization of short-term returns are said to have contributed to the current financial crisis, which has brought the global financial system to the brink of collapse and triggered the worst global recession since the first half of the twentieth century.[1]

MPT was developed from approximately 1953 to 1972 through the work of academics who devised an elegant set of models of how the stock markets behave and how investors' success in investing at the portfolio level can be defined. The hypotheses developed during those two decades—many of which focus on the definition and management of risk—have provided the basis for MPT's influential theory of success in investing. Among its basic tenets are that

- Diversification reduces risk. Diversification offsets the risks of individual holdings and, properly managed, can increase rewards without increasing portfolio-level risks.
- Rewards and risks are related. The greater the risk taken by investors, the greater the rewards they should expect. Money managers can be deemed successful only if the returns they achieve are adjusted for the risks they take.
- Markets are efficient. Liquid and transparent markets reflect all information available at any given time and hence price securities traded in these markets appropriately.
- Options can be priced. Future rises and falls in the price of securities or markets can be hedged against by using options and other derivatives, for which accurate pricing models are available.[2]

These underlying principles—and their almost infinite and mathematically sophisticated variations—are among the cornerstones upon which MPT has been built. As a theory and practice, MPT was initially ignored by traditional money managers, for whom the relatively unsophisticated, but straightforward, definition of risk was something like "the chance that things could go wrong" and the definition of prudence in investment was generally speaking preservation of capital.[3] By the 1980s, the contributions of MPT's progenitors became widely recognized, and several were awarded the Nobel Prize in economics. By the 1990s, major institutional investors in substantial numbers had begun to adopt its practices. By the turn of the century, it was increasingly applied to all asset classes.

The primary contribution of MPT to the theory of investment is that it conceived of investment, and addressed the question of risk management, at a portfolio level—not, as had been previously done, at the individual security level. At the portfolio level, most simply put, MPT defines success in investment in relation to risks taken and measures that success in one of two ways—beating the market or matching its returns at the lowest possible cost.

Beating the market involves using a series of techniques—including diversification, securitization, and hedging—to control the risks and increase rewards of the overall portfolio relative to benchmarks that represent the market. These techniques have the virtue of allowing investors to purchase individual securities that have relatively high levels of risk that can be offset in various ways and therefore don't increase their portfolios' overall risk. Because riskier securities generally provide greater returns, these risk-control techniques increase a portfolio's returns without increasing its overall risk. Those who adopt this strategy are often referred to as active investors, and when they achieve greater returns than their peers without taking greater risks, they are, according to MPT, successful.

A second definition of success is constructing a portfolio that matches market risks and rewards while keeping costs at a minimum. This is generally called passive or index investing—a financial index being a benchmark that captures the risk/reward characteristics of an asset class or market. Indexing is simplicity itself: the investor buys securities that capture the characteristics of the asset class in question and holds them forever. Because no further research or transaction expenses are involved once the securities are purchased, this strategy assures low costs. MPT considers matching market returns at the lowest possible cost a success because it has shown that most active managers don't consistently outperform these index benchmarks, and their high fees are therefore a wasted expense and a long-term drag on performance.

While MPT's assertion that active managers can beat the markets appears to contradict its contention that passive managers should behave as if they cannot, the two assertions can coexist relatively comfortably because MPT holds that, although most active managers don't beat the markets consistently, some do some of the time. If you happen to be one of the happy few, then active management is an attractive choice.[4]

Despite its broad acceptance among institutional investors, MPT has come under a variety of attacks. Behavioral economists have attacked MPT's assumption that investors in practice always act rationally—that is, make choices that are in their short-term self-interest. Practitioners and statisticians have attacked MPT's assertion that stock returns always behave as if randomly distributed—that is, fall in a classic bell curve with "fat tails" of only insignificant consequence. Liberal economists have questioned the view that markets can correctly price securities and efficiently allocate assets—that is, are fundamentally more reliable than government in laying the foundations of a sound economy. Proponents of MPT themselves have also acknowledged that their theories may not work in practice due to the actual costs of doing business—that is, transaction costs make certain theoretically attractive techniques impractical.[5]

Recently, critics have laid responsibility, or at least partial responsibility, for the 2007–2009 collapse of the worldwide financial markets and its devastating economic consequences at MPT's door. They have variously argued that MPT's innovations have been abused by unethical practitioners in the financial community, introduced excessive risk into the financial system, are useless in times of crisis, or are inherently flawed.[6]

This chapter does not elaborate on these numerous, thoughtful critiques. They are in essence correct. Markets do not always behave rationally. Government is essential for the maintenance of a stable, transparent, and honest financial system. The mainstream financial community has been riddled with unethical and unprofessional behavior. Today's financial practices have put our global markets in jeopardy through misuse and abuse.

This chapter instead focuses on one particular criticism of MPT—its assumption that portfolio management techniques do not affect market-level risks and returns. This criticism is important because it implies that the responsibilities of investors cannot be neatly contained at the portfolio level, but must include their decisions' implications at a market and societal level.

MPT is called modern *portfolio* theory for good reason: it defines success in investing at a portfolio level. The risk-control techniques that lie at its core address what it refers to as "unsystemic risk"—that is, risk and reward at the portfolio level. It generally ignores the possibility that investors may negatively or positively affect "systemic" risk—that is, risk and reward at the market level. If the market as a whole goes down, managers should not be blamed, nor should they take credit if it goes up. They should only be praised or blamed for what they can control—the performance of their portfolios relative to that of the overall market.

As Harry Markowitz, one of the founding fathers of MPT, put it in an article in *Investment Professional*: "Systemic risk, due to beta, does not diversify away; unsystemic risk does. . . . This does not mean that individual securities are no longer subject to idiosyncratic risks. It means, rather, that the systemic risk swamps the unsystemic risk during [a crisis]. . . . MPT never promised high returns with low risk. You pays your money and you takes your choice."[7] MPT assumes that investors essentially operate in a portfolio-level world that is disconnected from the risks and rewards that arise at the market level. Investors behave as if their investment decisions individually and cumulatively do not influence the market. It is one of the paradoxes of MPT that it assumes that portfolio decisions operate independently of the market, but that it does not recognize that, should all investors apply the tools that MPT provides, they will become the market they are theoretically operating independently from.

This assumption of independence from the broader market simplifies the theoretical tasks of MPT. It is simpler to understand the relationship between investors' choices and portfolio returns than it is to understand the relationship between portfolio choices and the markets' returns. However, adverse consequences can result when the question of the relationship of portfolio-level investing to the markets and society as a whole is left unexamined.[8]

MPT's inclination to disassociate investment performance from market performance can be illustrated in graphic form by looking at the bell curve upon which one of MPT's fundamental assertions rests: the returns of stock prices are essentially random, with extreme variations happening relatively infrequently. Such distributions result in a Gaussian bell curve that looks like Figure 2.1. This bell curve represents the percentage price change of

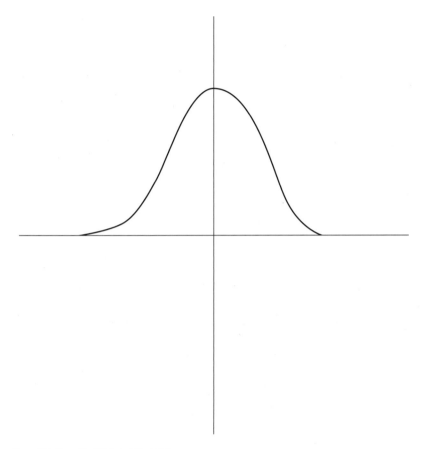

Figure 2.1. Normally Distributed Stock Return

stocks, or a single stock, which over time is randomly distributed around a mean that represents its expected return. This chart says that the prices of stocks are as likely to go up as they are to go down, and more likely to go up or down a little than a lot. This is sometimes referred to as a random walk.

One of the implications of this theory is that investors who are actively trading are as likely to lose as to win in the long run and in the aggregate. The stock market therefore looks like a zero-sum game, a view that has led many institutional investors to adopt index investing. If, as active traders, they are as likely to win as lose in the long run, the best thing to do is to keep costs as low as possible by trading as infrequently as possible.

Participants in a truly zero-sum game are essentially gamblers, and not just gamblers, but losers in the long run. They gamble that they will be on the right side of the curve earning above-normal returns and that they will be there consistently. The law of averages, however, says that ultimately everyone ends up in the middle—and because there are transaction costs to investing, the more actively investors trade the more they lose.

If MPT assumes that markets are really a zero-sum game, it is reasonable to ask why investors play the markets at all. The answer to this theoretically puzzling question is rather straightforward. They invest because in the end the stock market as a whole goes up more than it goes down. It is generally a rising tide, although one on which some ships randomly rise faster than others. The reason for this rising tide is growth of the overall economy. Investors invest in stocks because they assume the economy will grow.

As Peter Bernstein puts it: "[Investing] has to be a positive-sum game to some extent, or else no one would play. . . . But where does that positive sum come from in the first place? From the growth of the economy itself, whose fruit must accrue to someone, somewhere, some time."[9] Investors may behave as if the market is a zero-sum game, seeking to beat their peers or minimize their costs, but they are really in it because, independent of the daily games they play, they benefit from the overall growth of the market and the economy as a whole. Again, this assumes that investors' choices do not affect the basic performance of the market.

Figure 2.2 then is a more complete representation of what the bell curve for stock market returns looks like according to MPT. The bell curve is here positioned to the right of a vertical axis that can be thought of as representing a stock market return of zero—that is to say, the stock market in a truly zero-sum game. The distance between that zero-sum-game axis and the axis around which stock market returns are distributed represents an expected positive return to the stock market as a whole and this expectation is the reason investors, according to MPT, invest. This ability of the stock market as a whole to produce a positive return should be one of responsible investors' most important concerns, or even their most important concern. The further the bell curve falls to the right the better off investors are as a whole.

For MPT to ignore the question of whether their investments affect the growth of the economy positively or negatively—that is to say, the distance to the right of this axis that the bell curve falls—may simplify its tasks, but

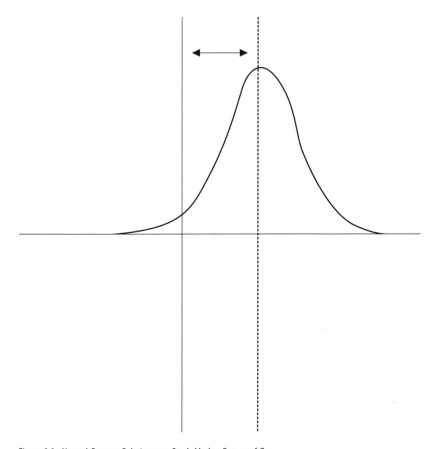

Figure 2.2. Normal Returns Relative to a Stock Market Return of Zero

it leaves unexamined several important possibilities. Among them is the possibility that MPT's risk-control and return-enhancement techniques when widely used actually cause the bell curve to shift to the left—that is to say, hurt the financial markets and the economy. It similarly ignores the possibility that when investments are aligned with their natural societal functions, they could push this axis toward the right, to the benefit of all.

It may seem counterintuitive to argue that risk-control techniques increase risk. However, they can do so in theory and in practice if, instead of being disconnected from the systemic risks of the market, they increase these risks by increasing the demand for, and the supply of, risky products.

The risk that was in the markets prior to the credit crisis of 2007–2009 was due in part to excessive leverage (debt) and poor lending decisions—in effect, irresponsible risk taking and poor implementation of risk-control techniques. The argument here, however, is that these abuses were exacerbated by the more fundamental problem of the proliferation of risky products in the marketplace driven by investors' increased "appetite for risk," to use a favorite phrase of financial journalists.

It can be argued that the 2007–2009 credit crisis illustrates just such an effect. The collapse of the housing-price bubble in the United States that led ultimately to a global financial and economic crisis can be directly tied to the demand for high-risk, high-return securitized mortgage-backed securities. This demand was legitimized by MPT's various risk-control techniques—that is, investors believed that they could diversify or hedge away the risks inherent in these products. The demand was then augmented by financial theory's claims that portfolio returns could be enhanced by increasing the proportion of high-risk securities with their higher returns in portfolios. Then leverage was added to the mix in part because of the belief that the bets taken were essentially riskless. It is not surprising that this heightened demand for risky products, combined with various abuses, increased the chances of a financial meltdown.

With high levels of risk spread across all asset classes and all regions, catastrophe in any segment of any of these markets could cascade throughout the system in ways that were next to impossible to control. Although MPT's risk-control techniques allowed investors to increase their portfolios' returns while controlling particular risks, the general levels of risk they externalized onto the world's financial markets turned out to be disastrous to the whole of the financial system and global economy.[10]

This spreading of increased risk throughout the markets that has been the consequence of MPT's risk-control and risk-enhancement techniques is a phenomenon that has been widely noted. Here are four of the many recent critical commentators on the subject.

> Financial products that purport to reduce the risks of investing can end up actually magnifying those risks. . . . We are now seeing the destructive results of structured finance products that disguised the real risks of subprime mortgage loans as low-risk, high-return investment opportunities.[11]

Hedge funds, though seeming like a niche activity for the rich, inject massive risk and instability into the entire system—but monopolize the rewards for their investors.[12]

While the system now exploits the risk-bearing capacity of the economy better by allocating risks more widely, it also takes on more risks than before. . . . Moreover, the linkages between markets, and between markets and institutions, are now more pronounced. While this helps the system diversify across small shocks, it also exposes the system to large systemic shocks.[13]

What neither we [pension fund trustees] nor our advisors noted was that given the tremendous growth in pension fund assets, these actions in the aggregate contributed to the exponential growth in importance of private equity and hedge funds (replete with high fees, little to no regulatory oversight, inadequate transparency, high levels of leverage and illiquidity) that helped generate greater market volatility and a new set of risks to the pension funds and the financial system.[14]

The direct result of this increased level of risk in the markets is that the chances of what are sometimes referred to as fat-tail events occurring increase. In the language of statistics, a fat-tail event is an event of substantial magnitude that arises at the end—or "tail"—of a bell curve. It is a statistical anomaly that falls outside the expected normal distribution.

In the financial markets, these fat-tail events are crashes, burst bubbles, panics, and other crises. Although panics and bubbles seem to be an inevitable part of the workings of a capitalist economy, it is possible, or even likely, that increasing the demand for and supply of risky products in these markets increases the chances of such fat-tail events occurring and the severity of the disruptions they cause.

Among MPT's techniques that have increased risks in the financial markets are:

- Securitization and the selling off of risky loans
- Hedging strategies that create liquidity problems when used simultaneously by numerous market participants

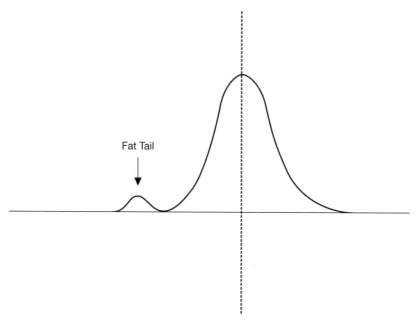

Figure 2.3. Normal Returns with a Fat Tail

- Deregulation of financial services that results in unregulated "shadow" financial systems
- Correlation of risks that trigger the failure of one financial product when another fails

In addition, by defining success in investing as the beating of benchmarks and simultaneously asserting that risks can be controlled, MPT has encouraged the taking on of high levels of debt to enhance returns.

On the bell curve, fat tails may appear small, because their occurrence is infrequent, as Figure 2.3 shows.

Their effect on the market, however, is large. As Taleb puts it, they are not like the random occurrence of an eight-foot-tall man, a statistical anomaly of anecdotal interest to a student of human height.[15] When fat tails occur in the financial world, they affect the market profoundly and can hurt the returns of all investors. A world where fat tails are likely to happen with frequency might be represented by Figure 2.4.[16]

Figure 2.4 illustrates the point that fat-tail events can influence the risk/

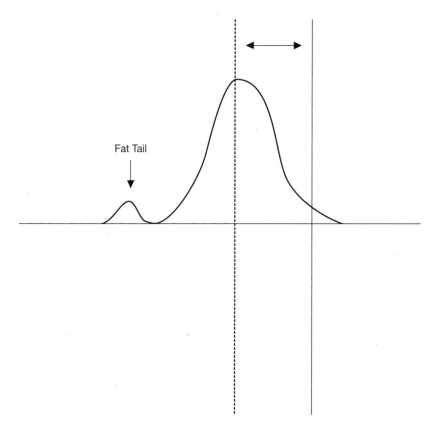

Figure 2.4. Influence of Fat-tail Events on the Risk/Reward Characteristics of the Market as a Whole

reward characteristics of markets as a whole by moving the median return to the left, rather than to the right.

In addition to the challenges created by MPT's assumption that its practices are unrelated to market returns, additional problems arise because both on theoretical and practical levels MPT's risk/reward techniques work only for some of the investors some of the time.

Active managers who strive to beat the market are sometimes known as "alpha chasers"—*alpha* being the name MPT gives to the value managers add to their portfolios once various levels of risk are taken into account relative to their returns. Chasing alpha is by definition a zero-sum game, because for every winner there is a loser in the market. Still, some do win. As the economist Paul Samuelson describes it: "Modern bourses display what I like to call Limited Micro Efficiency. So long as a minute minority of investors, possessed of considerable assets, can seek gain in trading against willful uninformed bettors, the Limited Efficiency of Markets will be empirically observable. The temporary appearance of aberrant price profiles coaxes action from alert traders who act gleefully to wipe out the aberration."[17] In other words, a small number of smart investors can beat the markets when fools make bad bets. These gains are available only to the happy few.

At best, alpha chasing corrects temporary aberrations in market price—arguably a minor contribution to the financial well-being of society. At worst, it encourages excessive risk taking and market abuses, creates more volatile financial markets, and encourages short-termism and asset bubbles. Moreover, it is reasonable to ask whether a marketplace in which only a few have access to the information and technology that allow consistent profit taking is the kind of broad-based and transparent market that society should encourage.

Just as active management cannot benefit all, neither can indexing, at least in theory. On a theoretical level, by definition it cannot be used by everyone in the market. Were everyone to index, there would be no one in the market to set prices, which would then freeze and never change.

Although the likelihood of such a scenario occurring is nil, the question points to one of the weaknesses of indexing as an investment philosophy. That is, index investors abdicate responsibility to set prices in the marketplace. This abdication of responsibility—which ultimately finds its justification in the efficient market hypothesis's assertion that stocks are priced correctly by markets—undercuts one of the basic purposes of public exchanges, which is to provide management of companies with investors' feedback on the value of their firms. The more investors who index, the fewer there are to provide this valuable feedback.

This raises the interesting question of how many market participants are necessary to provide adequate feedback to corporations and to set prices in such a way that speculation doesn't dominate the markets. Given the fact that the stock markets in the decade from 1999 to 2009 were subject to two major speculative booms and busts—not to mention bubbles in real estate and commodities during that same period—it is reasonable to ask if in fact the speculative element has dominated in recent years and whether there are now a sufficient number of market participants with a long-term perspective to accurately value securities of all sorts.

It is only logical to assume that as more institutional and retail investors choose to index, as has been the case since the 1990s, the greater the domination of speculators in the markets will be. Effectively by definition, speculators don't index—they wouldn't be speculators if they did. Similarly, indexers are not, by definition, speculators. As more and more investors have chosen to index—index funds were introduced only in the late 1970s—the proportion of speculators setting prices in the markets will have necessarily increased.

Index investors do little more than amplify whatever the characteristics of the market are at a given time. Although indexers often portray themselves as long-term investors because they buy and hold stock, this is not exactly the case. Indexes are a reflection of whatever the market is at any given time. If the market is overpriced because of a valuation bubble, indexers are investors in, and contributors to, that bubble. If the market is short term they are short term. As Simon Zadek of AccountAbility once put it, "When pension funds say they are long-term investors, what they mean is that they have rolling investments in largely indexed linked funds. To speak accurately this makes them *perpetual investors* making short-term investments, forever."[18] Put differently, if society is concerned about short-termism in the markets, it cannot look to indexers to provide a countervailing force.

In addition, many of the techniques advocated by MPT work only if relatively few investors use them. These are generally techniques that depend on hedging. If used by many, they collapse in times of crisis because they cause liquidity problems—that is to say, various hedging programs will all try to make the same trades at the same time, freezing the markets because there is not enough product to execute all the trades. This phenomenon has been a concern since 1987 when, during the October market collapse, a type of hedging technique known as portfolio insurance not only failed to protect portfolios from loss of value but actually exacerbated the market declines.[19]

In confining itself to the question of the relationship of investment to portfolio returns, MPT has made a contribution to portfolio management that has taken financial markets beyond the relatively simple, but conservative, practices of earlier years. However, by ignoring the question of the relationship between portfolio investment and market-level returns, it has also unintentionally introduced more risky products into these markets, increased the role of speculators, and heightened markets' sensitivity to the short term, while benefiting only a few and costing the financial system in the collapse of asset-class bubbles and economic destabilization.

Broader lessons need to be drawn from the current financial debacle if we are to avoid similar crises. A definition of success in investment that simply manages risk or costs is not sufficient to the task of creating stable financial markets that enable the generation of long-term wealth. We should demand a theory of investment that not only controls risk and cost at a portfolio level but also generates systemwide rewards with broad societal benefits. How to envision such a system is the question that this chapters turns to next.

Notes Toward an Alternative Theory of Investment

The best-recognized theories of finance today appear to work satisfactorily for some of the people some of the time on a portfolio level, but not for all of the people all of the time on a market level. Modification of this system is necessary to assure that investments realize their potential to create positive returns for both investors and society. Reconsidering today's all-pervasive definition of success as risk-adjusted, portfolio-level returns is challenging given its widespread acceptance as the measure of man in the investment community, but it is a question that needs to be addressed.

Clearly, financial returns—making money—are a crucial part of any definition of success in investing. Investors, after all, want a satisfactory return for the risks they take. MPT has developed sophisticated tools for measuring appropriate returns and for determining when Investor A is making more money than Investor B. These tools will continue to be useful. But a comprehensive theory of investment should also be able to tell us when Market A or Asset Class A is successful and whether it is more or less successful than Market B or Asset Class B. Beating risk-adjusted returns at the portfolio level does not help measure market-level or asset-class-level success since risk is defined in relationship to the characteristics of the market or asset class itself. Contemporary investment theory provides no measuring stick against which the risks or rewards of a market or asset class itself can be measured.

In other words, markets should have a more ambitious goal than simply "making money" for their participants. Market-level success and that of investments in general should also include in their definition an assessment of the rewards and benefits that society has empowered these investments as a whole to produce. We need to think about investments assuming that we care about their intended results.

This essay outlines one such expanded means of measuring the success of financial markets. It argues that ultimately the purpose of financial markets as they have evolved is to support governments in the task of creating just and sustainable societies. Their success can best be measured by assessing how well investors within these markets use particular asset classes to realize these goals while earning reasonable financial returns.

The ideas explored here are not the only possible approach to an expanded and refined definition of success in investment. Among the alternative conceptions of how investors ought to behave are the theories of the universal owner and fiduciary capitalism as expounded by James Hawley and Andrew Williams,[20] among others; and the principle of increased integration of environmental, social, and governance (ESG) factors into mainstream investment practices as laid forth in the United Nations Global Compact's Principles of Responsible Investment.

This chapter proposes an approach complementary to these other important efforts. Universal investors could consider the economic implications of their investments through the lens of asset-class characteristics; ESG concerns could be incorporated into analyses of different asset classes in their own particular ways. How these ideas can be fully integrated into a theory and practice of finance that works at a market level, not just at a portfolio level, remains to be seen. The hope is that this chapter will be useful in provoking further debate and discussion on this question.

Need for an Alternative Theory

Contemporary theories of finance vacillate between attempts at describing how markets behave as independent phenomena that can be objectively observed and described and whose behavior can be predicted, and assertions that markets are man-made artifacts designed and shaped to serve society and tailored to specific practical and normative functions.

This chapter starts from the latter position, assuming that theories of finance influence the markets and societies within which they operate. It asserts that financial markets—as expressed in asset classes—ought to provide maximum benefits not only to investors but to the societies on whose well-being these investors ultimately depend for their long-term returns. It is based on a normative theory of finance.

This view of finance derives from two fundamental observations: (1) the asset classes in which investments are made have distinct and natural societal and financial characteristics, and (2) these asset classes differ from one another because they have evolved and been shaped by societies over time for distinct purposes. It combines these observations with the assumption that the goal of legitimate governments is the creation of just and sustainable societies and that these governments make use of regulated financial markets to support that goal.[21]

Building on these observations and assumptions, this chapter defines success in the financial markets as *investment managers' skill in maximizing the societal benefits that asset classes have evolved to create while achieving competitive financial returns* and makes three assertions.

1. Individual asset classes have different societal functions, each with its own intended benefits.
2. Successful investment is best defined as enhancing these intended benefits while earning competitive returns.
3. Successful investments in asset classes help enhance overall market-level stability and returns.

These assertions are elaborated here to suggest the direction in which full development of this definition of success in investment might be taken.

Individual Asset Classes Have Different Societal Functions, Each with Its Own Intended Benefits

It is in some senses self-evident that asset classes differ in their financial and societal characteristics. Cash obviously isn't the same as stocks; stocks differ from bonds; bonds don't serve the same function as real estate.

These differences are not accidental, but arise from the distinct societal functions that these asset classes serve. A brief survey of six asset classes commonly used by institutional investors—cash, fixed-income securities, public equities, real estate, venture capital, and commodities—highlights these different societal functions and suggests that, in a properly functioning society, these different asset classes contribute benefits that are mutually supportive and complementary. Together they form a mosaic, the pieces of which work together to help create a flexible and dynamic society that can be steered toward justice and sustainability. Currently, contemporary finance all too often views these asset classes as abstract financial benchmarks of interest solely for their risk and return characteristics and tends to ignore their intended and interrelated functions.

Cash consists essentially of deposits in lending institutions and the various treasury functions of organizations. Among its intended societal benefits are the preservation of capital ("saving for a rainy day"), the creation of a capital base for lending institutions, and the facilitation of commerce. It is perhaps simplest to say that the natural function of cash is *promoting community economic development.* Properly used, cash helps ensure financial and economic stability at a local level.

Fixed income securities consist primarily of bonds issued by governments and large corporations to fund, respectively, public works and capital-intensive investments with long-term returns. Since governments issue the vast majority of these bonds, it is perhaps simplest to say that fixed income's natural function is *promoting the creation of public goods* such as infrastructure, transportation, health, social security, local and national security, and judicial and other regulatory regimes. Although fixed-income products run the gamut from short to long term, they are particularly well suited to fund long-term, publicly oriented investments in the infrastructure of our society.

Public equities consist primarily of the stocks of large corporations traded on liquid exchanges. They are both a means of raising capital for large-scale enterprises and of imposing financial and societal discipline on these corporations. It is perhaps simplest to say that this asset class's natural function is *promoting feedback between large-scale private enterprises and society.* In particular, equity investments—through an elaborate system of transparency and disclosure—can help impose incremental change on mature commercial and industrial institutions.

Real estate makes up the physical environment in which we live and work. It consists primarily of housing, as well as industrial, office, commercial, and agricultural properties. It is perhaps simplest to say that its natural function is *creating livable communities and environments.* Real estate defines the physical world that surrounds us daily and that influences for decades our sense of community, who we are, and how we live.

Venture capital makes speculative bets on start-up businesses, many of which break new technological ground. Most of these investments fail, but some that succeed produce revolutionary changes in technology and business practices. It is perhaps simplest to say that this asset class's natural function is *promoting revolutionary change in how business is conducted.* In recent decades venture capital has funded breakthroughs in information technology, Internet communications, and health care, and is currently investing heavily in clean technology and alternative energy.

Commodities exchanges were originally created to protect farmers and natural-resource-related firms from unanticipated swings in prices and to help overcome the limitations of pricing in local markets. Their virtue and primary function is to *protect producers and consumers from undue market fluctuations and distortions.* A large portion of the commodities markets relates to natural resources and the environment.

These asset classes work together in society to address a variety of complementary goals. Their differing inherent functions balance the needs in society for stability and at the same time for dynamic change, for incremental progress in business and at the same time for revolutionary disruptions, for the creation of public goods and at the same time for private wealth. Government permits and encourages the continued existence of each separate asset class because each fills a specific function. If they fail to satisfy that need or no longer work together in harmony, a properly functioning society will modify the structure of these asset classes or even do away with them entirely.

Successful Investment Is Best Defined as Enhancing Asset Classes' Intended Societal Benefits While Earning Competitive Returns

Successful investments in asset classes should fulfill a dual purpose. They should allow investors to earn a competitive return and should fulfill the societal functions for which the asset classes have evolved and are designed. Conversely, they should not lose money or be used in ways that undercut the financial markets or the goals of society as a whole.

This chapter argues that, in addition to the basic goal of achieving competitive financial returns, the appropriate use of asset classes can achieve three broader goals, each of which simultaneously strengthens financial markets and the fabric of society. It can encourage:

- Productive financial innovation
- Prudent financial decision making
- Effective measurement of long-term wealth creation

Productive financial innovation. In the wake of the financial crises of 2007–2009, the former chairman of the Federal Reserve, Paul Volcker, suggested that, despite the much vaunted vitality and creativity of our financial engineers on Wall Street, the only useful financial innovation in recent years had been the ATM machine.

Implicit in this assertion is the fact that many of the sophisticated financial innovations and money-management techniques that have swept the financial markets since the early 1990s—collateralized debt obligations, structured investment vehicles, auction-rate securities, credit default swaps, to name just a few—exacerbated the instability of financial markets, precipitated the downfall of some of our largest financial institutions, and derailed economic progress.

By contrast, during this same period, some particularly productive and socially beneficial innovations in asset classes evolved outside of our mainstream financial community. For example:

- In the asset class of cash, one of the most significant innovations of the past three decades has been the emergence of microfinance—small loans made to economically disadvantaged individuals not previously served by mainstream finance. It took a banker from Bangladesh and the work of nongovernmental organizations serving the world's poor to understand how to serve this new market.
- In real estate, the U.S. Green Building Council understood that it is in society's long-term interest that buildings be environmentally sustainable. Its development of the LEED standards for new and refurbished buildings has created competition within the real estate industry to achieve sustainable development and created responsible investment opportunities not previously available.
- In commodities, without persistent government action a market for carbon credits would not have been possible. This innovative market holds the promise of using the mechanisms of commodities trading to help address climate change, one of the most serious and difficult environmental challenges of our time.

Wall Street's excessive focus on the maximization of short-term, portfolio-level returns not only prevented the mainstream financial community from recognizing these opportunities but steered it toward innovations that contributed to our current crises.

Prudent financial decision making. It can also be argued that attention to the proper function of asset classes can help prevent behavior that destabilizes financial markets and economic systems and at the same time can help stabilize and enhance them.

That inattention to basic asset-class-related fundamentals can be destructive is clear. For example, when investors from the United Kingdom and the Netherlands blindly chased unbelievably high returns on cash deposits offered by the largest banks in Iceland, they not only lost billions of dollars but contributed to the virtual bankrupting of that nation. Many of these investors were theoretically sophisticated institutions, but their failure to understand and assess the primary purpose of the asset class in which they were investing—that is to say, local economic development—caused them to make investments that were both financially disastrous and societally detrimental.

By contrast, responsible investors are naturally led to engage with those providing investment opportunities to enhance their prudent behavior. For example, in the asset class of publicly traded stocks, responsible investors often work with the companies in which they invest for incremental changes that help minimize their societal and environmental risks. In the United States, responsible investors have recently worked with management of the Gap to encourage it to adopt an industry-leading set of monitoring and reporting practices for its vendors; with Yahoo and other Internet providers to develop a code of conduct for operations in countries where censorship is a challenge; and with Kimberly-Clark to implement sustainable forestry practices.

Effective measurement of long-term wealth creation. Measuring returns from investments in asset classes in more than financial terms helps resolve some of the dilemmas created by measurements made simply against benchmarks—such dilemmas as those between short-term and long-term investment goals and between the duties of fiduciaries to enhance their beneficiaries' financial status and to protect their beneficiaries' best long-term interests.

There is a short-term-versus-long-term dilemma that money managers face when their success is measured only in terms of price at a portfolio level.[22] As Alain Leclair, president of the French Association of Financial Management, has put it: "We face a dilemma. . . . In practically all aspects [of investing], although everything ought to direct us to adopt a long-term approach, we are forced to measure and act in the short term."[23]

This dilemma arises because once the societal functions of asset classes are ignored and returns are defined only in relation to price at the portfolio level, the short term inevitably predominates. If returns take into account the specific purpose of each asset class, then their measurement can accommodate both financial results—short term and long term—and the success of investments in stabilizing financial markets and realizing appropriate societal benefits. In addition, when the intended purposes of asset classes are taken into account, an artificial distinction between financial and non-financial returns, which often creeps into discussions of responsible investment, disappears.

Accounting for the intended purposes of various types of investments also helps address a dilemma related to the definition of fiduciary duty. As long as fiduciary duty is defined exclusively as maximizing the risk-adjusted returns of portfolios, money managers have difficulty taking into account the implications of their investment decisions on other aspects of their beneficiaries' lives.

Amy Domini highlights this issue when she writes that "while looking after the best interest of the beneficiaries and their dependants sounds like a noble goal, this section [of the Employee Retirement Income Security Act governing fiduciaries of certain pension funds], which has come to be known as the 'exclusive benefit' section, has created an understanding that *nothing but making money* can enter into the mind of the fiduciary. But the language of the law, and I would argue the intent of the law, is not stated that way. The language directs the fiduciary to think of nothing but 'the benefits.' We need clarification as to the meaning of benefit."[24] Understanding that asset classes provide particular benefits to society as a whole helps clarify the meaning of benefit. With a proper understanding of both the financial and social benefits of asset classes, fiduciaries can be permitted to address issues that are not strictly related to portfolio-level returns but clearly harm or clearly benefit their beneficiaries' well-being. For example, in a stock portfolio, a manager might contend with the fact that certain companies available for investment pollute the air their beneficiaries breathe or unreasonably drive up their health-care costs or, on the positive side, create affordable and energy-efficient housing.

Successful Investments in Asset Classes Help Enhance
Overall Market-Level Stability and Returns

In addition to helping spur productive financial innovation, prudent investment decision making, and broad-based measurement of long-term wealth creation, investors who take an asset-class approach can help minimize investments that destabilize financial markets and maximize investments that contribute to these markets' stability.

To begin with, understanding the intended purposes of an asset class helps investors avoid complex investment innovations that, when they malfunction, destabilize financial markets. For example, structured investment vehicles and auction-rate securities were products designed for sophisticated institutional investors to help them beat benchmarks for returns on cash. During the crisis of 2007–2009 these complicated products played a major role in the financial turmoil, cost investors heavily, and contributed to the destabilization of the markets in general. Had institutional investors sought cash investments with competitive returns that directly supported local community economic development through well-run, federally insured banks, savings and loans, or credit unions, such investments as structured investment vehicles and auction-rate securities might not have found such a ready market.

Similarly, the complexity of financial derivatives in general makes them susceptible to overuse and abuse. Gao Xiqing, the president of the China Investment Corporation, China's sovereign wealth fund, while acknowledging the limited usefulness of financial derivatives in general, has expressed strong reservations about the effect these products have on the financial markets as a whole. As he put it in an interview with James Fallows, when asked about the usefulness of derivatives: "If you look at every one of these [derivative] products, they make sense. But in the aggregate they are bullshit. They are crap. They serve to cheat people."[25]

What he means here is that they are sold, and bought, as "insurance" at the portfolio level, but they are no such thing, in that they can encourage unrealistic risk taking and help destabilize whole markets in times of crisis. If, in 1987, sophisticated institutional investors had concentrated less on beating stock indexes while supposedly insuring their gains by purchasing "portfolio insurance" and more on investing in appropriately valued stocks, the crash of October of that year might have been avoided. If, in 2006 and 2007, sophisticated institutional investors had concentrated less on enhancing their returns with risky investments of collateralized debt obligations supposedly "insured" by credit default swaps and more on investments in mortgages backed by responsible borrowers building strong communities, we might have avoided at least part of the credit bubble that burst in 2008.

Moreover, derivatives and other complex financial risk-control products are capable of such infinite variations and complications that it is almost impossible for most institutional investors of reasonable sophistication to keep up with the newest offerings. The temptations that this complexity offers to game the system are too great for the unscrupulous to resist and their traps are too many for the sophisticated to avoid.

Another advantage of taking this approach that assesses investments in asset classes relative to their intended purposes is that it can help minimize exposure to investments that are simply unproductive. Financial services companies that earn their profits primarily from transaction fees rather than lending to socially productive projects, or credit card companies that aggressively work to create a citizenry crippled by debt, may beat a financial benchmark of their peers, but they function in society more as wealth extractors than wealth creators. It is in the nature of the responsible investor who understands the purpose of public equities as an asset class to contend with these difficult problems, rather than to ignore or even to encourage them.

Put positively, an asset-based approach is likely to encourage good investments in the sense that it calls attention to what John Maynard Keynes describes as investments that constitute "enterprise." Keynes defines enterprise as investment for productive purposes, distinguishes it from speculation, and points to the importance of enterprise for the economy as a whole. "Speculators may do no harm as bubbles on a steady stream of enterprise. But the position is serious when enterprise becomes the bubble on a whirlpool of speculation. When the capital development of a country becomes a by-product of the activities of a casino, the job is likely to be ill-done."[26] Encouraging investors to look through investment opportunities to their actual purpose and to align that purpose with the purposes of specific asset classes makes their decisions more likely to result in investments aligned with the productive goals of society.

Furthermore, a system of investment based on the proper use of asset classes has the potential to encourage investment decisions by multiple investors that will work in complementary ways to create additional value and stability at a market level. For example, assuming one reasonable goal of society should be to use energy as efficiently as possible, one investor may use venture capital to fund revolutionary technologies more efficient at generating electricity; a second may press publicly traded companies to use the energy they purchase more effectively; and a third may use real estate investments to create walkable cities where transportation costs decrease and greenhouse gas emissions are sharply reduced. Together, their investments have complementary societal goals that reinforce the benefits of each and cumulatively enhance total returns.

Finally, proper respect for the appropriate use of asset classes would represent a positive cultural change. The 2007–2009 financial and economic crises have sprung in part from a belief that "greed is good"—the assumption that the financial markets and any product that can be sold into these markets will produce the greatest good in the best of all possible worlds. A cultural change is necessary to reform these beliefs. A proper respect for risk is essential. Contemporary financial engineers have ignored the dictum that if you open a thousand doors, a tiger will eventually jump out. A theory of investment that more deeply understands and respects the risks implicit in investment, the limits of greed to do good, and the long-term societal benefits of properly conceived investments is needed.

By promulgating a definition of success in investment that includes tangible societal benefits along with competitive financial performance, the financial community can identify for praise and emulation those who make use of investments in ways that stabilize markets and build long-term societal wealth. Creating a culture in which those who succeed in this challenging task are singled out for praise can be a powerful tool for cultural change. As Adam Smith points out in *The Theory of Moral Sentiments,* there is "in the desire of praise-worthiness, and in the aversion to blame-worthiness" as powerful a motivator of human behavior as in the desire for financial gain or aversion to financial loss.[27]

We should not forget that it was not so long ago that, as responsible investors, fiduciaries were restricted in their investments in risky assets. For example, the pension funds of the State of California were not permitted to invest more than 25 percent of their assets in the stock markets until 1984, when a statewide referendum was passed to allow them to expand their exposure to this class previously deemed too risky to be overweighted by fiduciaries of retirement assets.[28]

The point here is not that past days were better than our own. Rather, it is that a culture of respect for risk and for the intended societal purposes of investment is a thing to be greatly desired. Treating asset classes and their risks and rewards with proper respect is not so difficult. Investment theory and practice are normative societal constructs reflecting conscious decisions. Investing today is what we have chosen it to be. If it has led to destabilized financial markets and economic crises in the past, it is now time to consider what simple steps can be taken to make investment more reasonable and to better align it with the goals of a just and sustainable society.

Conclusion

The choices that investors make matter to markets and to society as a whole. Aligning investments with societal goals by using assets classes for their intended purposes is certainly as straightforward a task as manipulating assets to maximize portfolios' risk-adjusted returns, and it leads down a road that is in the long run surely more productive. We must move forward from where we now stand into this underresearched territory or the next financial and economic crises, driven by appetites for risk and outsized returns without regard for societal benefit, will be even more severe than the ones with which we must contend today.

Chapter 3

The Quality of Corporate Governance Within Financial Firms in Stressed Markets

Robert Mark

Introduction

The recent financial crisis has caused internal and external corporate stake-holders to increase their scrutiny of the quality of corporate governance within financial firms in stressed markets. This scrutiny includes examining the impact that financial models, financial products (e.g., credit default swaps), and business operating styles (e.g., the amount of financial leverage) have on managing and hedging risk.[1] The financial crisis has also raised issues on how the individual objectives of firms on Wall Street are harmonized to achieve broader societal goals (e.g., increased home ownership).

The risk governance objective of a chief risk officer (CRO) in financial firms is to guide management toward controlling the amount of risk through ensuring measures of risk are reasonably accurate and assigning risk limits based on a clearly articulated set of corporate objectives. The risk governance objectives of the CRO are also designed to protect the firm from excessive losses in stressed markets. The objective of a corporate treasurer is to generate gap revenue[2] within interest rate risk governance limits assigned by the CRO. Financial firms rely on highly analytical financial models to guide the firm toward achieving clearly articulated risk-adjusted return on capital (RAROC) objectives (see the Appendix for an explanation of RAROC).

A significant challenge for regulators is to tie the deployment of financial models within the firm to the amount of risk generated external to the firm. Typically the internal risk governance objective of financial firms is neither designed to enhance the health of Main Street nor harmonized to achieve societal goals in stressed markets. For example, the objective of a trader is to generate trading revenue within trading risk governance limits assigned by the CRO. Risk governance to control model risk within financial firms is typically not designed to reduce external systemic risk across the financial markets in stressed markets. Systemic risk refers to the risk of a systemwide financial crisis caused by the contemporaneous failure of a substantial number of financial markets, institutions, or both.

Sophisticated financial theories are analytically elegant, but over and over again the shock of extremely volatile markets has demonstrated that the application of financial theories that either guide portfolios toward optimal solutions (e.g., making investment decisions based on using modern portfolio theory [MPT]) or link return with risk (such as based on using the capital asset pricing model [CAPM]) is a double-edged sword.

Financial firms that understand the inherent risk of marketing and trading financially engineered products (e.g., interest rate caps) have implemented risk governance policies that enable them to understand the limitations of financial models. Sophisticated financial firms that deploy leading-edge risk governance practices are able to slice and dice their risk as well as append warning labels to dashboards that serve to highlight the amount of risk in stressed markets. On the other hand, if financial firms fail to implement best-practice risk governance through well-designed risk-management programs, then many of these firms will be in danger of experiencing dramatic losses due to model risk in the so-called highly improbable stressed markets.

There has been a relentless increase in the complexity of financial models and the associated valuation theories since 1973, with the publication of the Black-Scholes and the Merton models.[3] The fixed-income instrument market, and the derivatives markets more generally, provide the most striking examples. Throughout the 1970s, the market risk of bonds was assessed using a simple duration-based measure, with or without an adjustment for convexity.[4] As securities increased in sophistication to include features such as embedded options, valuation came to be based on complex models. The models work well in normal markets but tend to break down in stressed markets.

The pace of model development accelerated through the 1980s and 1990s to support the rapid growth of financial innovations such as caps, floors, swaptions, spread options, and other exotic derivatives. Product innovations (e.g., credit default swaps) were themselves made possible by developments in financial theory that allowed analysts to capture many new facets of financial risk. The models could have never been implemented in practice, or have come to be so well accepted, had the growth in computing power not accelerated dramatically.

Financial innovation, model development, and computing power have engaged in a game of leapfrog. Financial innovation calls for more model complexity, which in turn requires greater computing power. The proliferation of highly complex financial instruments contributed to the recent financial crisis since the risks of many of these complex financial products at the transaction level were not very well understood (e.g., collateralized debt obligations [CDOs] of an asset-backed security [ABS]).

Models are utilized to calculate the economic value added (EVA)[5] of business strategies, as well as to examine the impact of these strategies on standard profitability measures of performance[6] in normal markets. A critical success factor toward simultaneously achieving firm-specific business strategies such as evaluating loans to achieve superior risk-adjusted returns on capital (see the Appendix for a numerical example) and the broader societal objectives of Main Street (e.g., reduced home foreclosures) is to find financial models that are capable of being utilized for best-practice internal risk management as well as for reducing external systemic risk across the financial system.

Financial models can be deployed to link the impact of superior corporate governance on managing risk at both the transaction level and at the value-of-the-firm (V) level. For example, let WACC represent the weighted average cost of capital, as well as let Rs represent the cost of stock (S) and Rd the cost of debt (D). Further, let Ws and Wd represent percentages of the firm that are financed respectively with stock and debt.

The traditional measure for the value of the firm can be calculated through discounting FCF (free cash flows) where WACC = Ws Rs + Wd Rd. If we let V equal the sum of discounted cash flows over the projected

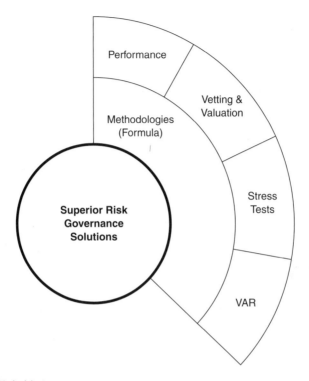

Figure 3.1. Methodologies

life of the firm, then a particular challenge is to increase V through superior governance while reducing the volatility of V.[7]

$$V = \sum_{t=1}^{T=n} \frac{FCF_t}{(1 + s\ WACC)^t}$$

Characteristics of Superior Internal Risk Governance within Financial Firms

Characteristics of methodologies at the core of superior risk governance within financial firms (as illustrated in Figure 3.1) contain the idea that measures of risk in normal markets (such as value-at-risk [VAR])[8] and stress test methodologies are *predictive of the actual losses* and integrated across all risks and all books of business.

A particular risk governance challenge is that most measures of risk break down in markets under stress. Further, the use of financial models to achieve stated risk and revenue objectives should be vetted and positions should be properly independently valued. An important part of risk governance is to ensure that an independent third party performs the vetting. It is essential that the models used to control risk (e.g., credit risk) are integrated into well-designed risk governance approaches.[9] These risk governance approaches should be designed to meet firm-specific as well as broader external systemic objectives. Collectively, the use of these analytical models should be utilized for such things as computing the amount of required *economic capital*, as well as measuring risk-adjusted performance (e.g., calculating RAROC).

There are a series of multidimensional measures of risk (Figure 3.2) that should be used in assessing the amount at risk.

The risks shown in Figure 3.2 are particularly damaging in stressed markets. Significant practical and analytic progress has been made in measuring credit and market risk on an integrated basis. Funding-liquidity risk was a particularly damaging risk in the recent financial crisis.

Measuring operational risk remains a significant challenge. For example, a key operational risk is making business decisions based on faulty data. Many mortgages (such as those associated with "no documentation/low documentation" mortgages) were underwritten with faulty data (e.g., the income of the mortgage holder and the value of homes were overstated). The lack of due diligence on assessing the data contributed to the recent financial crisis. Key model risk challenges for measuring operational risk include accounting for long modeling time horizons, a significant divergence of expert opinion with respect to self-assessment, and lack of uniform global regulatory standards.

A key challenge has also been to secure adequate levels of good-quality internal and external loss data to calculate the amount of business risk, reputational risk, and strategic risk. The lack of data has led practitioners to construct a variety of key risk indicators that are utilized to signal a rising (or falling) amount of risk.

A firm can have great policies and methodologies but will be unable to reap their benefits without a superior risk governance infrastructure. Characteristics at the core of a superior risk governance infrastructure (as illustrated in Figure 3.3) include the idea that the appropriate proactive risk and corporate governance teams are in place with the right quantitative

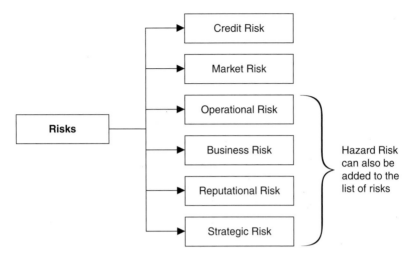

Figure 3.2. Types of Risks

Counterparty credit risk (CCR) is risk that a change in the credit quality of a counterparty will affect the value of a security or a portfolio. It includes the probability of default (PD), loss given default (LGD), and exposure at default (EAD). See M. Crouhy, D. Galai, and R. Mark, ``A Comparative Analysis of Current Credit Risk Models,'' *Journal of Banking and Finance* 24 (1–2) (January 2000), pp. 59–117.

Market risk (MR) consists of interest rate risk, the risk that the value of a security will fall as a result of an increase in market interest rates; equity price risk, the risk associated with volatility in stock prices; foreign exchange risk, which arises from open or imperfectly hedged positions in a particular currency; and commodity price risk, which differs considerably from interest rate and foreign exchange risk, since most commodities are traded in markets in which the concentration of supply in the hands of a few suppliers can magnify price volatility.

Operational risk (OR) refers to potential losses resulting from inadequate systems, faulty data, management failure, faulty controls, fraud, human error, and so on. For example, the Basel II±defined taxonomy of operational risk includes (1) internal fraud, (2) external fraud, (3) employment practices and workplace safety, (4) clients, products, and business practices, (5) damage to physical assets, (6) business disruption and system failure, and execution, and (7) delivery and process management.

Business risk (BR) refers to such things as uncertainty about the demand for products.

Reputation risk (RR) is one of the most important risks and also one of the most difficult to protect. Reputation risk is the potential for negative publicity regarding business conduct or practices which could significantly harm the institution (e.g. materially and adversely affect business operations or financial conditions).

Strategic risk (SR) refers to the risk of significant investments for which there is uncertainty about success and profitability.

Hazard risk (HR) refers to classic property and casualty exposures as well as highly specialized coverage for professionals, products, employment practices, workers compensation, pandemic, intellectual property, the environment, surety, natural catastrophe, reinsurance, and more.

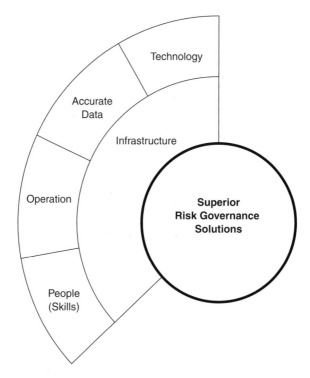

Figure 3.3. Infrastructure

financial skills. Also, a superior risk governance infrastructure calls for an integrated operational, risk software, and technology environment that integrates data management, risk analytics, and reporting in a flexible manner.[10]

A superior risk governance infrastructure provides the risk governance teams as well as their business partners with the appropriate tools to accomplish its mandate. Organizations that have an integrated risk-data infrastructure are able to obtain a competitive advantage. For example, there is significant value to having timely access to market data, transaction data, and legal data.

Characteristics of policies at the core of a superior risk governance solution include the idea that the tolerance for risk is integrated and consistent with business strategies and vice versa in both normal and stressed markets (as illustrated in Figure 3.4). Policies should also call for risk measures to

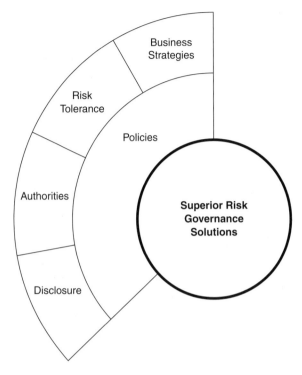

Figure 3.4. Policies

be back tested. It is also essential that policies call for limits on the amount at risk to be *expressed in meaningful* terms and reflect a desired tolerance for firm-specific as well as systemic risk. Finally, policies should call for the amount at risk to be properly *disclosed* internally and externally on a granular and integrated portfolio management basis.

A key aspect of policy and infrastructure related to risk governance is ensuring that roles and responsibilities are clearly spelled out and integrated with one another.

Illustrative Roles and Responsibilities Within a Financial Firm

The chief executive officer (CEO) is typically responsible for ensuring that all of the operations of the firm are carried out with due consideration of the risk appetite of the organization and that the accompanying risks are understood and taken into account in the trading room. The CEO communicates the objectives of the firm and the rules and boundaries that have been established for pursuit of those objectives.

The CRO is responsible for (1) determining the risk appetite of the organization and then implementing this throughout the organization, through the risk-management infrastructure, (2) ensuring that the reporting of risk- and governance-related matters is produced in a timely and accurate manner, (3) helping line leaders to understand the cost of risk capital and (4) working to ensure a risk-aware and risk-appreciating culture in the organization via education, models, and technology.

The chief financial officer (CFO) must ensure that all of the risks associated with the key processes that contribute to the financial reporting of the organization have been identified and that effective controls are in place to mitigate these risks to an acceptable level. The CFO must accurately represent the financial condition of the company to both internal and external parties and must ensure the company has sufficient financial resources to pursue its market risk objectives.

Business heads (mini-CEOs) are responsible for the effective use of scarce market risk capital in pursuit of trading objectives and fully accountable for gains and losses in the trading room.

The general counsel is responsible for the legal affairs of the organization and communication with key external regulatory bodies related to risk. The chief technology officer is responsible for the integrity of the firm's technological infrastructure related to risk). The chief information officer is responsible for the integrity of the firm's risk data.

The chief audit officer (CAO) must maintain appropriate assurance measures to ensure that the risk framework of the organization is effective and, if any shortcomings are discovered, to escalate these shortcomings to the appropriate organizational levels so that remedial action can be taken in a timely manner. The CAO assesses the general controls of the company regarding compliance with the risk policies and procedures of the organization.

Model Risk

Model risk has increased due to the proliferation of highly complex financial instruments. The many significant advances in financial models and financial theory (such as MPT and CAPM)[11] are vulnerable to model risk in stressed markets. I have found it useful to categorize model risk into those caused by *model error* and those caused by *implementing a model incorrectly*.

Model error refers to the case where the model might contain mathematical errors or, more likely, be based on simplifying assumptions that are misleading or inappropriate. *Implementing a model incorrectly* refers to doing so either by accident or as part of a deliberate fraud. The most frequent error in model building is to assume that the distribution of the underlying asset is stationary, when, in fact, it changes over time. For example, practitioners know that volatility is not constant, as is typically assumed in the application of many financial models (e.g., Merton Model or MPT).

Practitioners find themselves engaged in a continual struggle to find the best compromise between complexity (to better represent reality) and simplicity (to improve the tractability of their modeling). For example, practitioners who apply MPT often assume that rates of return are normally distributed (i.e., bell shaped). However, it is well known that empirical evidence often points to the existence of "fat tails." Unlikely events are, in fact, much more common than would be the case if the distributions were normal. Extreme events have also become more likely and therefore are not well described by a normal distribution.

The application of complex financial models (such as models to price exotic derivatives) can be oversimplified by underestimating the number of risk factors that must be taken into account. Further, model risk arises because financial models are typically derived under the assumption that perfect capital markets exist. The lack of liquidity in turbulent markets, where liquidity dries up and correlations move toward 1, is a major source of model risk. Most financial models are ill equipped to capture liquidity risk. It is necessary to complement these models by using coherent scenario analysis that incorporates macroeconomic scenarios and stress testing.

A model developed and approved for one product may be inappropriately used for another product (e.g., a bond with embedded options is erroneously priced with a plain vanilla bond pricing model that does not account for its optionality). Even if a model is correct and is being used to tackle an appropriate problem, there remains the danger that it will be incorrectly implemented. For example, some implementations rely on numerical techniques that exhibit inherent approximation errors and limited ranges of validity. In models that require a Monte Carlo Simulation[12]

(MCS), large inaccuracies in prices and hedge ratios (while easy to correct) can creep in if insufficient simulation runs or time steps are implemented.

An important component of model risk associated with the application of financial theories (such as MPT) is the failure to get the input data right. The lack of proper input data results in the classic "garbage in, garbage out" phenomenon. For example, the input data utilized to select the risk model that best fits the data may be incomplete. Further, the input data to estimate model parameters of the risk model (such as volatilities and correlations) may be invalid.

An important question, then, is how frequently should input data be refreshed? How should the adjustments be made in stressed markets? Should the adjustments be made on a periodic basis, or should they be triggered by an important economic event? Should parameters be adjusted according to qualitative judgments, for example, or should these adjustments be purely based on statistics? The statistical approach is bound to be in some sense backward looking, while a human adjustment can be forward looking, that is, it can take into account a personal assessment of likely future developments in the relevant markets, including a host of potential human foibles.

The process for measuring contamination risk in stress markets should become standardized. The financial industry should develop a standardized set of models that work well in stressed markets in order to review the performance of a firm-specific portfolio or business in extreme markets. The deployment of models that work in stressed markets should also be encouraged by regulators in order to forecast potential future systemic losses across the financial system caused by extreme market conditions.

Dynamic stress scenario models that incorporate an allowance for management action can avoid significant losses in market conditions such as those that occurred in the recent financial crisis. Financial firms need to ask themselves a series of tough questions in terms of how each element of the risk governance framework would perform in stressed markets. Firms need to continually ensure that risks in extreme markets will be properly disclosed, made transparent, and understood.

Financial firms need to ask how well their risk governance approach served the organization in stressed markets. For example, did the firms' risk-measurement models predict the amount at risk in stressed markets? The tolerance for risk in stressed markets should follow directly from the financial firm's business strategy. A best-practice policy calls for the active management of the risk limits in stressed markets. For example, an analysis of market conditions should prompt a firm's risk committee to slow down some of the firm's businesses in stressed markets, such as by reducing risk authorities. Firms should also ask how well did their infrastructure work in stressed markets. For example, did a firm's risk-management staff, as well as its systems, serve it well in extreme markets?

Modern Portfolio Theory

Harry Markowitz introduced the foundations of MPT[13] in 1952. Markowitz did not fully consider the impact of stressed markets. He pointed out that rational investors select their investment portfolio using expected profit and risk.[14] The usefulness of MPT is diminished in stressed markets, since the behavior of rational investors in normal markets is quite different from their behavior in stressed markets.

"Profit" is measured in terms of the average (mean) rate of return. "Risk" is measured in terms of how much returns vary around this average rate of return. The approach used to predict the amount of risk in stressed markets is substantially different from those used in normal markets. The greater the variance of the returns, the riskier the portfolio. When building a portfolio, investors like to reduce variance as much as possible by diversifying their investments.

According to MPT, investors select financial assets for their portfolio based on each asset's contribution to the portfolio's *overall* mean and variance. The risk of a single investment can be measured in the terms of its own variance, as well as in terms of its interaction (i.e., correlations) with other assets in the portfolio. Investors can dilute the risk that is specific at virtually no cost. If assets are selected carefully, then diversification can allow investors to achieve a higher rate of return for a given level of risk.

Investors can construct an *efficient frontier*, represented by the curved solid line in Figure 3.5. A particular challenge is to forecast the behavior of portfolios on the efficient frontier in stressed markets. The efficient frontier contains all portfolios of assets such that there are no other portfolios (or assets) that for a given amount of risk (in terms of standard deviation of rates of return) offer a higher expected rate of return.

The measures of risk embedded in MPT are not typically stable in

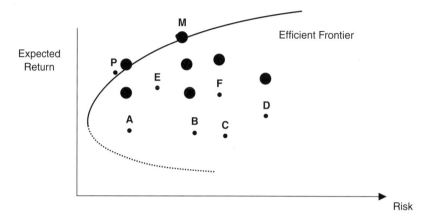

Figure 3.5. The Efficient Frontier of Markowitz

stressed markets. Portfolio P in Figure 3.5 has slightly less risk than port-folio A, but portfolio P has a substantially higher expected return. There is no portfolio in Figure 3.5 with the same amount of risk as P that also exhibits a higher expected rate of return than P. Portfolios in stressed mar-kets can quickly deteriorate and migrate on a path toward increased risk accompanied by declining expected returns (e.g., migrating from being on the efficient frontier at P toward E to F to D) or migrating from below the efficient frontier at A toward B to C.

If a portfolio contains only assets that are on the efficient frontier, a higher expected return can be achieved *only* by increasing the riskiness of the portfolio. Conversely, a less risky portfolio can be achieved *only* by reducing the expected return on the portfolio. The lower part of the fron-tier, which contains all the inefficient assets and portfolios, is represented by a dotted line. It indicates the most inefficient combinations of assets with the lowest possible expected return for a given level of risk and therefore the assumption underlying MPT breaks down.

If the market is in equilibrium, then portfolio M, the market portfolio, will include all risky assets in the economy, each entering the portfolio in a proportion equal to its relative market value.[15] For example, an imperfect but often useful proxy for all the risky equity assets in the economy of the United States is the S&P 500 index. In this market portfolio, the power of diversification means that the specific, or idiosyncratic, risk of a security is not taken into account by the market in its pricing of a security. A particular challenge is that if a financial institution deploys a deeply analytical approach to its investment decisions (such as MPT), it may work well in normal markets but fail to work well in stressed markets, which in turn may exacerbate systemic risk. Further, there are alternate investment strategies to MPT that could result in different choices that might provide superior results in stressed markets.[16]

The Capital Asset Pricing Model (CAPM)

A key tenet of CAPM[17] is that the risk of an individual asset can be decomposed into two portions. The first component is that there exists a portion of risk that can be neutralized through diversification (called diversifiable or specific risk). The second component is that there exists another portion of risk that cannot be eliminated through diversification (called systematic risk). A key assumption is that the investor can choose to invest in any combination of a risk-free asset and a market portfolio. The market portfolio includes all the risky assets in an economy. Investors therefore weight their personal portfolios as a combination of these two investment vehicles, in various proportions based on their risk appetite. A particular challenge is that the CAPM measures of risk are not stable in stressed markets and therefore the assumptions underlying CAPM often break down.

Investors demand a premium for taking on the risk of the market portfolio (M). This "market risk premium" is simply the difference between the expected rate of return on the risky market portfolio and the risk-free rate. The market risk premium can be calculated by subtracting the interest rate on an asset that is free of default risk (such as, say, a U.S. Treasury bill) from the expected return on a market index (the S&P 500). Estimates of the market risk premium tell us how much investors have to be paid to take on some notional "average" amount of market risk generated by the complete market portfolio.

According to CAPM, this contribution is accounted for by a beta (β)[18] that contains the components utilized to calculate systematic risk. A particular challenge is to ask how the price of a given asset will reflect the relative contribution of that asset to the total risk of the market in a stressed market.

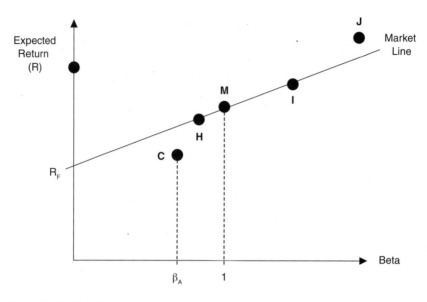

Figure 3.6. The Market Line

Beta represents that portion of an asset's total risk that cannot be neutralized by diversification in a portfolio of risky assets, and for which some compensation must be demanded. We can think of this expected return as consisting of the interest on the riskless asset (invested over the same period as the holding period of the asset) plus the market risk premium multiplied by the adjusted beta, but its components often become unstable in stressed markets. Beta is an important component of calculating the expected return on an individual asset. In other words, in Figure 3.6, the *market line shows* the linear relationship between the expected rate of return on any asset and risk as measured by beta.

In Figure 3.6, the intersection with the vertical axis yields the risk-free interest rate, R_F. This rate of return reflects the yield on an asset with beta of 0. Assets that lie on the market line (e.g., H, M, and I) are said to be market efficient. I is riskier than H, and therefore is expected to yield a higher return than M. The market portfolio has a beta of 1. Asset C is inferior since it lies under the market line, meaning that another asset (or a portfolio of assets) can be found with the same amount of beta risk but with a higher expected rate of return. Asset J is superior since it is expected to yield more in relation to its risk than assets on the market line. If participants in the financial market realize that J is superior, then they will increase the demand for J which in turn will put pressure on its price. As the price of this asset rises, its rate of return can be expected to fall until J lies on the market line.[19]

Firms that utilize MPT and CAPM[20] to make their investment decisions run the risk that their analytic approach sends the wrong signals due to the breakdown of key assumptions embedded in MPT and CAPM in stressed markets. For example, correlations tend to become unstable in stressed markets, assets tend to collectively deteriorate in value, and the probability distributions of returns migrate toward fat tails.

The Corporate Governance of Model Risk

Model risk is a significant issue in stressed markets especially for illiquid products (as well as for products that are embedded within complex strategies). In relatively efficient and liquid securities markets, the market price is, on average, the best indicator of the value of an asset. Theoretical valuation models have to be used to mark to model a position as well as to assess the risk exposure in terms of the various risk factors, and to derive the appropriate hedging strategy in stressed markets where you find the absence of liquid markets and price discovery mechanisms.

Losses arising from model risk in stressed markets can be quite large and might force institutions to restructure or disappear (e.g., Bear Stearns). Models are susceptible to many sources of error. These include incorrect assumptions about price dynamics and market interactions, estimation error with regard to volatilities and correlations (and other inputs that are not directly observable and so must be forecasted), the implementation of valuation models, and so on. Most models are derived under the assumption of perfect capital markets but, in practice, market imperfections in stressed markets lead to substantial and persistent differences between the way markets behave and the results generated by models. In many instances, too much faith in models has led institutions unknowingly to take large bets on key parameters such as volatilities or correlations. The fact is that these parameters are difficult to predict and can be shown to be unstable over time.

A vital way of reducing model risk is to establish a governance process for independent vetting of how models are both selected and constructed. The role of vetting is to offer assurance to the firm's management that any model for the valuation of a given security proposed by, say, a trading desk is reasonable. In other words, it provides assurance that the model offers a reasonable representation of how the market itself values the instrument, and that the model has been implemented correctly. Vetting should consist of the components discussed in the following sections.

Document the Model

The vetting team should ask for full documentation of the model, including both the assumptions underlying the model and its mathematical expression. This should be independent of any particular implementation[21] and should include such things as an explicit statement of all the components of the model (including stochastic variables and their processes, parameters, equations, and so on) as well as the calibration procedure for the model parameters in both normal and stressed markets.

Verify Model Soundness

The model vetter needs to verify that the mathematical model is a reasonable representation of the instrument that is being valued. At this stage, the risk manager should concentrate on the finance aspects and not become overly focused on the implementation of the mathematics.

Ensure Independent Access to Financial Rates

The model vetter should check that the middle office has independent access to an independent market-risk-management financial rates database (to facilitate independent parameter estimation).

Benchmark the Model

The model vetter should develop a benchmark model based on the assumptions that are being made and on the specifications of the deal.

Health Check and Stress Test the Model

The vetter should make sure that the model possesses the basic properties that all derivatives models should possess, such as put-call parity and other nonarbitrage conditions. Finally, the vetter should stress test the model.[22]

Provide Education Programs on Model Risk

Financial institutions are increasingly partnering with academic institutions to train the next generation of financial engineers, so that they are able to communicate the strength and limitations of these quantitative approaches throughout the organization. For example, one such program is the master's in financial engineering program.

Offering risk governance education programs to key stakeholders is an integral part of managing risk. Stakeholders who attend these risk governance educational sessions will gain a deeper insight into risk-management practices, as well as the ability to add significant business value to their organization, Specifically, these stakeholders will gain the practical skills and knowledge necessary to identify, analyze, and respond to key risks, which in turn will allow them to contribute toward improving the return-to-risk dynamics of their organizations.

Firms would benefit from offering targeted educational programs on stress testing. Integrated stress testing is a key part of the overall risk governance framework. Stress testing has become a required component of risk management because of the highly violent fluctuations in financial markets as well as the increase in regulatory scrutiny of stress-testing practices. For example, topics might include (1) a detailed exposition of theory and practice of stress testing, (2) how to design integrated stress tests that cover different types of risk, (3) developing stress tests either through a top-down approach or bottom-up approach, and (4) how to translate stress-testing results into actions and communicate them to senior management. Analyzing stress-test case studies should be included in the educational program.

Conferences (such as the one held at Saint Mary's College of California called "Institutional Investors, Risk/Return, and Corporate Governance Failures: Practical Lessons from the Global Financial Crisis") add value through encouraging and sharing a deeper understanding of the role corporate governance plays in controlling model risk in stressed markets.[23]

Build a Formal Treatment of Model Risk into
the Overall Risk Governance Process

The vetter should periodically reevaluate models, as well as reestimate parameters using best-practice statistical procedures. Experience shows that simple, but robust, models often tend to work better than more ambitious, but fragile, models. It is essential to monitor and control model performance over time.

Crisis Case Studies of Model Risk in Stressed Markets

Case Study: Long Term Capital Management (LTCM)

LTCM is a classic case study of an environment where the very best financial models and well-designed trades collapsed in stressed markets. LTCM was engaged primarily in *convergence* and *relative-value* strategies. Both types of strategy involved taking long and offsetting short positions in instruments that were close substitutes. For example, recently issued (so-called on-the run) U.S. Treasury bonds typically trade at slightly lower yields (higher prices) than comparably mature but older (so-called off-the-turn) Treasury bonds. If this spread was sufficiently wide, LTCM might purchase the off-the-run bond, and sell short the lower-yielding on-the-run bond. If the bonds are held to maturity and attractive financing rates are assumed, then this position would make money. The position also makes significant profits if the yield spread (and hence the value differential) narrowed.

LTCM used the term *convergence trade* when there was a specifiable future date by which convergence in the value of the positions should occur. Such trades usually involved instruments such as bonds and derivative instruments, which had near- to medium-term fixed maturities. With *relative-value* trades, convergence was expected but not guaranteed except perhaps over a very long horizon.

LTCM also engaged to limited extent in *directional trades*. These directional trades were positions such as an unhedged long position in French government bonds that was exposed to broad market movements.

LTCM had a strong preference for strategies that exposed the fund to little or no default risk. The firm therefore generally avoided outright long positions in high-yield corporate bonds or emerging-market sovereign

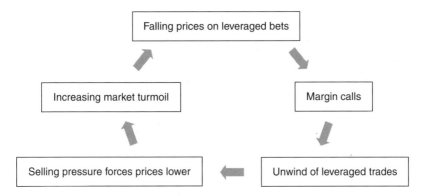

Figure 3.7. Market-induced Selling Pressure in Stressed Markets

debt. However, LTCM did have some relative-value trades that included these instruments, such as being long the debt and short the equity of a particular corporation. Falling prices in stressed markets may lead to market-induced credit problems as a result of margin calls.

For example, LTCM was exposed to funding-liquidity risk,[24] which in turn ultimately drove LTCM toward the risk of default, as illustrated in Figure 3.7.

LTCM believed that most of its trading opportunities arose as a result of dislocations in the financial markets caused by institutional demands The firm would build models to find mispricings created by such demands, but would also identify the reason for the mispricing before initiating a trade.[25] Nevertheless, LTCM's financial models broke down and its positions suffered from substantial losses in stressed markets, as illustrated in the chronology of events described in Figure 3.8. LTCM would have benefited from building one set of risk models to be deployed during normal market conditions and another set to be deployed in stressed markets. The LTCM arbitrage models that worked well in normal markets did not capture the risk associated with the rapid increase in risk premium for bonds worldwide. For example, the crisis in Russia in 1998 made many investors fear that other nations might follow Russia's lead and that there would be a general dislocation of financial markets. The Russian crisis triggered a "flight to quality," and investors fled to the liquid and safe haven of the U.S. and German governments' bond markets.

Risk governance at LTCM included relying on a traditional VAR model.

1. May and June—Salomon unwinds their proprietary trading positions. This caused prices to drop and caused LTCM heavy losses amounting to 16% of their asset base.
2. August 17—Russia announced it was restructuring its bond payments—a de facto default. The losses forced many investment banks, hedge funds and other institutional investors to reduce their positions en masse.
3. August 21—Swap spreads moved 21 basis points.LTCM's losses were breathtaking. On August 21 alone, the firm lost $550 million. LTCM decided to stick to their strategy, but losses kept growing.
4. End of August—capital was down to $2.3 billion. The fund had lost over half of the equity capital (its asset base was about $107 billion, so its leverage ratio had climbed to over 45 to 1—a very high ratio by any standards, but especially in that volatile environment.
5. September 21—The firm's Net Asset Value (NAV) dropped to $600 million, with total assets above $100 billion. The firm was leveraged more than 100 to 1. A rescue package was put together.

Figure 3.8. LTCM Chronology of Events

According to LTCM, the fund was structured so that the risk of investing in it should have been no greater than investing in the S&P 500. The average annual volatility of the S&P 500 served as a poor proxy of the eventual losses that LTCM experienced. Assumptions that are usual in VAR calculations were not realistic for LTCM in stressed markets. For example, VAR calculations are not usually designed to capture the breakdown of correlation and volatility patterns that had been observed in the past.

VAR models assume that normal market conditions prevail and that these exhibit perfect trading liquidity. Liquidity risk is not typically factored into traditional VAR models. LTCM used too short of a time horizon for the VAR clculation in stressed markets. For example, if a crisis hits the financial markets, then trading liquidity dries up for a period that is longer than the normal VAR calculation. Highly leveraged institutions (such as LTCM) cannot expect to gain access to fresh funds in such an environment. LTCM required cash to meet its margin calls during market turmoil; positions were unwound at fire-sale prices, and liquidity dried up.

The LTCM approach to stress testing its trading positions was limited. For example, LTCM did not simulate an extreme flight to quality across multiple scenarios, under which correlation patterns would break down, credit spreads would widen, and volatility would increase greatly. Something was clearly wrong in the way the firm was modeling risk. LTCM partly recognized liquidity in its stress testing by using correlations that were greater than historical correlations. Nevertheless, it underestimated the impact of its competitors who adopted similar trading strategies and therefore, by their herd behavior, amplified price movements.

An appropriate set of stress scenarios for LTCM would have tested for the impact on LTCM's portfolio of a systemic flight to quality that in turn would have caused significant losses in LTCM's portfolio. For example, an appropriate stress test would have examined the impact of lenders to LTCM demanding significantly more collateral. The demand for more collateral would call for LTCM either to abandon its arbitrage plays or to raise money for the margin calls by selling other holdings at fire-sale prices. If all this resulted in spreads widening, then the gains a trader might make on short positions are not always enough to offset the losses on the long positions. In some instances, both sides of the LTCM relative trades could end up losing money.

In short, risk governance at LTCM underestimated risks and incurred substantial losses because of the size of its positions and high leverage. LTCM would have benefited from deploying trading and risk-management models that worked to anticipate the vicious cycle of losses that occurred when volatilities rose dramatically, liquidity dried up, and correlations among markets and instruments moved closer to 1.

Case Study: The Recent Financial Crisis

The recent financial crisis is another case study where financial models collapsed in stressed markets. It was an accident waiting to happen. We saw an overreliance on unrealistically simple risk models, that is, models that were not designed to deal with the complexity of structured credit products, and incorrect ratings from rating agencies.

The foundation of modern risk analysis contained in CAPM and Markowitz's principles of portfolio selection broke down in the recent financial crisis. For example, assumptions that capital markets are frictionless and that liquidity is stable broke down. The idea that a rational investor behaves in a way that is consistent with a stable mean and variance for the rate of return cannot be relied on in stressed markets.

MPT suggests that the specific risk of a single security (i.e., the elements of its risk profile that it does *not* share with other investments) arising from volatile returns can easily be diversified away and eliminated at virtually no cost. Unfortunately, specific risk cannot easily be offset against the returns of other securities in stressed markets. A key aspect of MPT is that a security should be evaluated only in the context of the portfolio of investments to which it belongs, through its contribution to the mean and variance of the portfolio. In other words, the risk of a single investment should be measured in terms of the covariability, but measures of covariability break down in stressed markets.

The trigger for the financial crises was a series of events that appeared to strike out of the blue. In June 2007, Bear Stearns attempted to bail out two hedge funds hurt by subprime mortgage losses. Merrill Lynch's effort to liquidate some of the funds' assets revealed how illiquid the market for such securities had become. In July, we saw the first bailout by German regulators of IKB. In July, BNP Paribas also froze three investment funds with assets of 2 billion euros because the bank could not value the subprime assets in the funds. It seems that all of a sudden the market realized that mortgage-backed securities (MBS), CDOs of ABS, and other structured products were mispriced. As a consequence, during July and August 2007, lenders and investors began to worry not only about risk in mortgage-related securities but also about the extent of the subprime exposure of banks and other financial institutions.

This led to problems with information and problems with liquidity that helped cause the markets for important securities to "freeze up" and models to fall apart.

Assessing the potential amount of information risk in stressed markets is an important component of superior risk governance. Information problems during the financial crises included: (1) inadequate information about the underlying mortgage loans and the borrowers, especially for subprime mortgages and affordability products ("liar loans"); (2) loss of confidence in the accuracy of credit ratings from Moody's and Standard and Poor's; (3) market prices that became unavailable or unrealistic for many securities, including those rated AAA; and (4) lack of knowledge about what positions and liabilities the major banks and other players had.

An important element of model risk governance during the recent financial crisis was a failure related to acquiring quality input data to adjust the parameters of risk models during stress periods. Well-designed, integrated risk governance applications enable businesses to know how frequently their data should be refreshed across all risks. For example, businesses can adjust their parameters periodically after an important economic event based on a blend of quantitative and qualitative judgments.

Financial firms should be well aware of the quality of their data infrastructure. Faulty data (e.g., erroneous stated income and home valuations on mortgage applications) were a significant factor that led to poor business decisions during the recent financial crisis. As noted earlier, the lack of proper input data creates a classic "garbage in, garbage out" dynamic. Using input data to estimate the parameters of the risk model (such as volatilities and correlations in stressed markets), for instance, may be invalid.

Information interacts with risk-management policies, methodologies, and infrastructure in subtle ways. It is imperative to assess information risk in a structured, methodical way as with any other operational risk. The crisis revealed that many firms failed to have the necessary policies on data for superior risk governance. Firms need to carefully describe the data elements necessary to avoid significant risk in stressed markets. For example, from a risk-disclosure perspective, firms should have a policy that prescribes the necessary data to generate the information to be provided in a risk dashboard. The risk dashboard should serve to provide significant value-added insight beyond the obvious. A tailored dashboard can be provided on a regular basis to the board, showing a variety of drill-down risk disclosures against limits.

Further, from a methodology perspective, firms should ask how well their data enable them to calculate risk such as the probability of default (PD). Firms should also ask how well their data enable them to stress test risk (e.g., the PD), as well as how well their data enable them to slice and dice and attribute and aggregate the various types of capital such as regulatory capital, economic capital, and book capital. Book capital is the actual amount of capital on the balance sheet. Regulatory capital is the amount of capital required to meet minimum regulatory standards of capital adequacy. Economic capital is the capital cushion required by the institution's actual risk profile. A challenge is that the economic capital measure of risk may be more than the regulatory capital measure of that same risk.

The quality of data can be benchmarked from multiple factors. These include such factors as integration, integrity, completeness, accessibility, flexibility, extensibility, timeliness, and auditability. *Integration* refers to the ability to adequately capture relevant data relationships. For example, does the information about insurer-wrapped CDO tranches link to information about the insurer, including current ratings information? Data *integrity* refers to the idea that position data reconcile with financial statements. *Completeness* is another important attribute since it refers to the ability to adequately capture all exposures across the organization. *Accessibility* refers to the ability of users to access current and historical data in any form they require within limits set by security requirements. There must also be enough *flexibility* to ensure that users are able to analyze data across any dimension, including the ability to filter or summarize information. *Extensibility* refers to the ability to bring into the environment new types of data for valuing instruments with relevant links and the appropriate level of data quality. The *timeliness* of information, also crucial, refers to how data (deal information, market data, revaluations, etc.) are available after the occurrence of the relevant business event. And last but not least, *auditability* refers to the idea that data must be easily traceable from reports back to their source.

Liquidity problems included the following: (1) Home buyers could not refinance their loans as they had expected, and they could not make the required payments when their mortgages reset to much higher interest rates. (2) Hedge funds could not roll over the financing of their leveraged positions, their investors tried to withdraw capital at the same time, and primary dealers were asking for more collateral. (3) Special investment vehicles (SIVs) could not roll over asset-backed commercial paper—sponsoring banks bailed out their SIVs and took over their liabilities. (4) Some investors, like money market funds, may only hold AAA-rated securities; when those securities were downgraded, they were forced to sell.

Banks experienced huge amount of losses and write-downs far in excess of what pricing models, rating models, and risk models would have predicted as more and more securities (MBS, CDOs of ABS, etc.) and monolines were downgraded. Risk-measurement models totally underestimated the risks, and many risk managers didn't see the crisis coming. In a context where there were no reliable data to calibrate the models, risks were massively underestimated. The reliance on oversimplified models did not capture the full dimensionality of the risk being undertaken.[26]

Static model parameters (such as volatilities and correlations) failed to realistically assess losses in the recent financial crisis. Firms that utilized a "black box" analytical engine to value structured products exposed them-selves to significant model risk due to a lack of transparency associated with their models. Historical or hypothetical stress scenarios at many firms failed to capture the snowball effects of macroeconomic and market-specific events on correlations between risk exposures

Many firms failed to estimate future potential losses using forward-looking economic scenarios that incorporate extreme events. These extreme events should include behavioral patterns that lead to adverse market dy-namics (e.g., dramatically widening credit spreads). Firms that avoided model risk during the crisis reviewed combinations of many smaller events that had the potential to lead to catastrophic losses.

Firms that performed a variety of stress tests benefited from having placed limits on potential losses based on the outcome of a dynamic set of stress scenarios. Dynamic stress tests can identify hidden pockets of risk that arise from a mismatch in repricing of assets and liabilities as well as increased illiquidity in complex and structured products. These include the inability to roll over maturing debt or a sudden increase in refinancing costs. These scenarios incorporate a combination of market moves (e.g., shocks in market volatility) that can cause insolvency. This would include unique risks such as examining the impact of a firm's inability to raise cash in stressed markets. This would also involve analyzing basis risk in hedging strategies to evaluate the impact of stressful paths.

Firms should incorporate their specific objectives into the construction of an efficient frontier in stressed markets and select an appropriate level of risk on the efficient frontier. Firms should develop internal protocols to incorporate their risk-mitigation strategies into the business decision proc-ess. Management should design a risk-mitigation strategy that takes into consideration systemic risks and market shocks. This would include design-ing optimal strategic hedges that reduce risk, with a focus on how these hedges perform in stress scenarios. Also, firms need to analyze financing decisions that optimize liquidity position and capital needs. Moreover, it is important to provide transparency into the overall amount of firmwide risk for both internal and external stakeholders.

Summary Comments

Superior corporate governance within financial firms needs to include well-defined risk policies as well as robust risk methodologies and a flexible

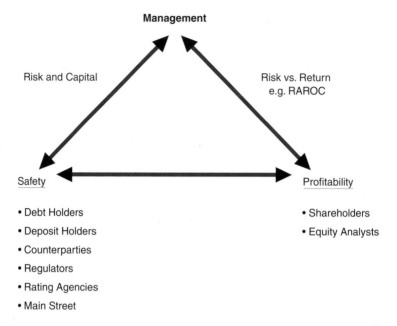

Figure 3.9. Balancing the Desires of Stakeholders

infrastructure that enable the firm to control risk as well as reach its corporate objectives. There have been useful studies that examine the linkage of superior corporate governance and firm performance[27] (e.g., the linkage between corporate governance and equity prices).[28] The recent financial crisis has revealed that a corporate governance program that was adequate in normal markets may not work well in stressed markets.

Superior risk governance in financial firms calls for balancing trading off safety (for debt holders, deposit holders, etc.) versus profitability consideration (for shareholders and equity analysts), as shown in Figure 3.9. The superior risk governance process should establish the strategy for how business should be conducted in stressed markets. The CRO within financial firms provides a framework for evaluating related risks and monitoring whether the organization is operating within that framework during stressed markets. As noted, risk is a common factor for both safety and profitability.

As discussed, there are a variety of risks (see Figure 3.2) that drive the amount of risk taken and that need to be considered in assessing the quality of corporate governance in stressed markets. Risk models need to properly measure the amount of systematic risk in stressed markets. The correlation of changes in the value of an asset with changes in value of the market portfolio is a key measure of the amount of systemic risk. Correlation models typically failed to measure systematic risk in the recent subprime financial crisis.[29]

Stress testing and scenario analysis are a necessary complement to the use of internal VAR models that measure risk in normal markets. Stress testing and scenario analysis help analyze the possible effects of extreme events that lie outside normal market conditions.

Best-practice stress tests combine periods of projected normal market conditions with periods of market crises characterized by large price changes, high volatility, and a breakdown in the correlations among the risk factors. A stress test should be dynamic to account for long time horizons. The purpose of stress testing and scenario analysis is to determine the impact (though not the frequency) of potential losses related to specific scenarios. The selection of an appropriate scenario is largely based on expert judgment. The scenario should consist of the result of extreme changes in the value of a risk factor (interest rate, exchange rate, equity price, or commodity price).

One of the key corporate governance challenges in financial firms is to work out a rigorous way of applying different kinds of stress scenarios to uncover model risk across the firm in a consistent manner. For example, the stress methodology might incorporate a variety of stress categories corresponding to various risk categories.[30] For each stress category, the worst possible stress shocks that might realistically occur in the market are defined. We can think of the stress envelope itself as the change in the market value of a business position in a particular currency or market in response to a particular stress shock. A scenario can then be created using a combination of several stress shocks.

Risk authorities should be developed to limit overall risk exposure in stressed markets as well as limit overall exposure by asset class (e.g., the subprime mortgage asset class). Recall that risk authorities are intended to ensure that the firm maintains a control on risk in stressed markets as well as reduces business unit risk authorities in stressed markets.

A firm's policies should call for a full daily disclosure of risks through the publication of a variety of risk reports in stressed markets. These should be circulated from the bottom of the house (trading desk level) to the top of the house (management committee level). Stress scenarios can be reviewed and disclosed at the weekly review of risk by both the risk committee and the management committee. In times of difficult markets, the firm should hold more frequent meetings, since the frequency and quality of risk communication in stressed markets is crucial. Written reports are not enough. Meetings should involve the most senior management.

The firm's daily VAR report should compare the firm's actual financial performance to its daily VAR limit. Firms should also publish a daily stress test report, which shows the results of a series of relatively extreme (although realistic) worst-case stress tests over a period (e.g., one week, one month, and one quarter). Reports should also include a weekly summary of significant risks that ranks these risks from high to low in stressed markets. In addition, the firm should produce a report that shows projected RAROC performance in stressed markets.

Superior risk governance provides the structure through which the risk and returns objectives of a firm are set, and the means of attaining those objectives. Superior corporate governance at a firm should provide proper incentives for the board and management to pursue objectives that are in the interests of its shareholders and should facilitate effective monitoring of the risk. The presence of an effective risk governance system, within a firm and across an economy as a whole, helps to provide a degree of confidence that is necessary for the proper functioning of a market economy in stressed markets.

Appendix: Risk-Adjusted Return on Capital (RAROC) Calculations

The numerator (N) of the RAROC calculation includes ER (expected revenues, of a product or activity) and C (costs, the direct expense associated with running the activity—e.g., salaries, bonuses, infrastructure expenses). The numerator of RAROC also includes EL (expected losses, e.g., the expected loss from a default on a loan). A variety of credit models have been designed to predict EL, which in turn is used to forecast the loan loss reserve.[31]

Risk capital needs to be allocated to each risky activity. It is generally assumed that this risk capital is invested in risk-free securities such as government bonds. The numerator also includes T (transfers), which corresponds to transfer pricing mechanisms, primarily between the business unit and the Treasury group.[32] It also includes overhead cost allocation from the head office. RAROC includes a TR (tax rate) that is the expected effective tax rate of the company. The EC (economic capital) is in the denominator of the after-tax RAROC equation. In short, for a financial asset, $RAROC = (ER - C - EL + RORC - T) \times (1 - TR)/(EC)$. We want RAROC to be greater than a hurdle rate.[33] Most firms use a single hurdle rate (H) for all business activities, which is based on the after-tax weighted average cost of equity capital, where $H = (CE \times Re + PE \times Rp)/(CE + PE)$. CE and PE denote the market value of common equity and preferred equity, respectively. Re[34] and Rp[35] are the cost of common equity and preferred equity, respectively.

Example: RAROC Analysis of a Loan

Let's first plug in numbers to obtain the baseline RAROC calculation for a $1 billion corporate asset that offers a headline return of 9 percent, then run a scenario analysis to examine the performance of the baseline RAROC calculation in stressed markets.

Assume that the operating cost is $9 million per annum and that the effective tax rate is 30 percent. We also assume that the portfolio is funded by $1 billion with an interest charge of 6 percent. The risk capital associated with the portfolio is $75 million (i.e., 7.5 percent of the asset amount). The risk-free interest rate on government securities is 7 percent. The expected loss on the asset is 1 percent per annum (i.e., $10 million).

The RAROC for this loan portfolio is 15.2 percent.[36] This number can be interpreted as the annual after-tax expected rate of return on equity needed to support this loan portfolio.

Best-practice risk governance calls for analyzing the potential impact of a stress test on RAROC (Table 3.1). This includes running several scenarios. For example, assume Scenario 1 calls for a drop of the asset return from 9 percent to 8 percent. Assume Scenario 2 calls for interest rates to rise by two hundred basis points (bps). Also assume that Scenario 3 calls for credit losses to rise due to deteriorating economic conditions. Further assume that Scenario 4 calls for a combination of scenarios 2 and 3.

Table 3.1: Stress Testing RAROC

	ER	EL	RORC	Risk-Free Securities (%)	Interest Expense	Funding (%)	EC	RAROC (%)	Change (%)
Baseline[a]	90	10	5.25	7	60	6	75	15.2	
Scenario 1	80	10	5.25	7	60	6	75	5.8	−61.5
Scenario 2	90	10	6.75	9	77	8	75	7.2	−96.3
Scenario 3	90	12	5.95	7	60	6	85	12.3 −	18.8
Scenario 4	90	12	7.65	9	70	8	85	−0.4	−102.7

Notes: ER = expected revenues; EL = expected losses; RORC = return on risk capital; RAROC = risk-adjusted return on capital
[a] The baseline loan portfolio excludes (for illustrative purposes) consideration of operational risk.

Chapter 4

Chasing Alpha: An Ideological Explanation of the Catastrophic Failure in the U.K.'s Financial Services Industry

Philip Augar

Introduction

"Alpha" is shorthand in the City of London for supercharged profit, and "chasing alpha" is what Britain's bankers, investors, and corporate chief executives did in the last two decades of the twentieth century and the opening years of this millennium, culminating between 2003 and 2007 in an orgy of leverage and reckless growth plans.

But to most participants and observers, the years 1997–2007 seemed to show that chasing alpha worked. By the year 2007, the U.K. had come to play a pivotal role in the global financial services industry. The financial districts of London—the Square Mile around the Bank of England in Threadneedle Street, the soaring towers of Canary Wharf in Docklands, and glitzy hedgefundland in St. James's and Mayfair, collectively known as the "the City"—claimed to rival New York as the world's international financial services capital. New York's city fathers were sufficiently concerned by the City's rapidly increasing market share that in 2007 they commissioned the consulting firm McKinsey to address the issue.[1] The statistics were indeed impressive. London's share of the global over-the-counter derivatives market exceeded 40 percent, over 20 percent of the world's hedge fund assets were managed in London, and Europe, principally the City, accounted for 63 percent of global IPOs in 2006. By this time, Europe, at one time an afterthought for the big American investment banks, contributed nearly half of their total revenues.[2]

The City's success helped to transform Britain's ailing manufacturing economy into a modern knowledge-led economy. Financial services' share of national output rose from 5 percent in 2001 to 8 percent in 2007, the industry contributed a trade surplus of nearly £40 billion, provided more than one million jobs, and accounted for almost 14 percent of the total tax collected by Her Majesty's Revenue and Customs.[3] Much of this success had been achieved during Gordon Brown's record-breaking time as chancellor of the exchequer between 1997 and 2007 and he regarded the City as a role model for the rest of the country, once telling an audience of bankers: "What you have achieved for the financial services sector we, as a country, now aspire to achieve for the whole of the British economy."[4]

The Turnaround

It had been a sudden turnaround. London's mercantile traditions went back to the fifteenth century but for many years the City was a closed shop, clubby and inward looking and not especially hard working. Entrepreneurialism was strongest in the eponymous merchant banks founded by European émigré families such as the Rothschilds and the Warburgs, but their development was hindered by banking rules and regulations that restricted their involvement in capital markets. Between the end of the Second World War and 1979, as the Labour and Conservative parties took turns holding power, the City lumbered on, distrusted by the former, left to its own devices by the latter, and not regarded as critical to national prosperity by either party.

Things changed for Britain and the City in 1979 when Margaret Thatcher's Conservatives won power. Vigorous free market economics replaced a postwar muddle as the guiding ideology. Industry was deregulated and competition policy was relaxed, opening the way for industrial restructuring and a wave of mergers and acquisitions. Legislation was introduced to break the power of the trade unions, which for three decades had held the country in their palm. One of the first acts of the Thatcher government was to abolish foreign exchange controls, removing a forty-year-old constraint that had discouraged British investors and industrialists from investing abroad. Publicly owned utilities such as the gas, electricity, and telecommunications industries were deregulated and privatized, exposing strategic parts of the economy to market forces for the first time.

Deregulation was extended to the financial services industry itself through the Big Bang reforms of 1986, which opened the stock exchange to competition and introduced the American model of integrated investment banking. U.S. banks and investment banks moved into London, using their superior managerial skills, more rigorous work ethic, and the superprofits earned on Wall Street to squeeze out the British competition. Between 1986 and 1997, the year that New Labour came to power, the City was transformed as the likes of Goldman Sachs, Merrill Lynch, and Morgan Stanley appeared at the top of the investment banking league tables and corporate executives and institutional investors learned to live with big business U.S.-style.

Becoming Number One

By 1997, London was on the way to becoming the world's financial services capital but this was in spite of rather than because of the domestic institutions. Between 1995 and 1997, U.K.-owned and managed investment banks such as Warburg, Kleinwort, and Smith New Court sold themselves to overseas rivals and the large U.K. banks NatWest and Barclays were forced by shareholders to scale down their investment banking ambitions. Commentators likened the City to the Wimbledon tennis tournament, an event that is held in London but where the best players usually come from abroad.

Other sectors of the financial services industry were in equal disarray. The U.K.'s asset management industry was embarrassed by poor investment performance and a series of high-profile gaffes that suggested the industry was out of control. The corporate sector was gripped by scandal such as the Guinness affair, in which the company's chief executive and several senior City men were sent to jail for their part in an illegal share support operation, and by the looting of pension funds belonging to the Maxwell group of companies. The reputation of Britain's regulators was sullied by the collapse of Barings, a venerable City institution brought down by a part-qualified young trader whose activities were missed by management and regulators alike. The Lloyds insurance market ran up heavy losses and its management was accused of "negligence, fraud, complacency and sardonic uncaringness" by the novelist Julian Barnes.[5] Another writer, the journalist Will Hutton, proclaimed in *The State We're In,* his best-selling treatise of Britain in the last days of the Conservatives: "The City of London has become a byword for speculation, inefficiency and cheating."[6]

When New Labour swept to power in 1997 after eighteen years of unbroken Tory rule, the City did not know what to expect. Would Prime Minister Tony Blair and Chancellor Gordon Brown agree with Hutton's damning analysis and revert to the party's anti-City roots—in 1989 Brown had penned a radical critique titled *Where There Is Greed*—or would it live up to its more recent pro-markets rhetoric? The outcome exceeded the City's best expectations. A series of policy measures created the most favourable environment imaginable for the U.K.'s financial services industry and a string of government appointments gave the City more influence over a British government than had ever been seen before.

The timing could not have been better. The world economy was in good shape and markets boomed. Cross-border trade flourished as the emerging economies of South America and Asia matured and seamless twenty-four-hour trading developed in equities, debt, currency, commodities, and derivatives. The City was in dreamland. Building on the advantages it already possessed as a result of its location in the right time zone between Asia's closing and America's opening bell, its well-established cluster of supporting professional services companies, its large financially literate and numerate work force, and the fact that it spoke English, the international language of finance, the City entered a golden age that lasted until 2007.

The Labour government introduced three key policy initiatives that helped the City. Less than a week after Labour was elected to power in 1997, Chancellor Gordon Brown announced that he was handing over responsibility to set interest rates to the Bank of England. This change had symbolic and practical significance. Investors liked the idea that economists, not politicians, would control interest rates and this underpinned markets for the next few years.

The second initiative came a fortnight later when the Bank of England, which was delighted by its new independence in monetary policy, received less welcome news. Along with the eight other U.K. bodies involved in financial regulation, its powers in this area were to be taken over by a new superregulator, the Financial Services Authority (FSA). The FSA became one of London's key competitive weapons in the fight for global market share. It regulated by means of principles rather than setting a rule for every eventuality and this was widely admired, not least by McKinsey, which in its report for New York sang the praises of "high-level, principles-based standards set by a single regulator for all financial markets."[7]

The new regulator's terms of reference were extraordinary. The Financial Services and Markets Act of 2001 gave it a remit that reads more like a mandate to protect the U.K.'s financial services industry than to regulate it. It was to facilitate innovation, avoid erecting regulatory barriers, and consider "the desirability of maintaining the competitive position of the UK."[8] The FSA certainly got the message and prioritized persuasion above compulsion: "our preference is for working with the industry to find solutions to market failures and to intervene only where the benefits of doing so are likely to outweigh the costs."[9] Senior FSA executives such as Hector Sants, who later became the organization's chief executive, took a constructive view of practitioners, stating that "the vast majority of firms are run by decent, honest people,"[10] and the industry reciprocated with equally warm words. The CEO of one U.S. securities firm said, "The FSA is open to discussing issues constructively and resolving problems quietly."[11] The founder of one of London's leading hedge funds described the FSA as "a pleasure to work with"[12] and the global head of compliance at one of the big investment banks spoke of "a very close and personal relationship with the FSA. I would not dream of going to the US regulators to discuss an issue without taking a lawyer with me; in the UK it is a very different environment."[13]

Labour's next helping hand came in Gordon Brown's second budget in 1998, which contained the single measure that was to guarantee the City's place as Europe's financial services capital. This was the reduction in the capital gains tax from 40 to 10 percent on business assets held for a short qualifying period. It provided a stimulus for hedge and buyout funds and ensured they would not be tempted to move their businesses overseas. According to one hedge fund manager, "With ten per cent taper relief it became possible for a new generation of entrepreneurs . . . to set up on their own and basically risk their careers but possibly make a fortune. The pay-off slope changed. The tax situation meant that the threshold hurdle for taking risks came down."[14] This change was allied with a decision to retain low tax rates for high earners and tax breaks for nondomiciled residents of the U.K. The consequence of this was that the City became a magnet for European financiers. As one European banker put it: "If you want a Greek quant, you'd look in London not Athens."[15]

As the Labour government settled in, it grew increasingly comfortable with the City, endorsing it with personal appearances. Prime Minister Blair headlined an event organized by Goldman Sachs, Chancellor Brown opened Lehman's new offices at Canary Wharf, and Economic Secretary Ed Balls eulogized about the City's success at a Bloomberg meeting. City grandees were consulted at breakfast meetings in Downing Street and were invited to join the advisory councils that were set up to discuss issues of national importance.

A two-way street opened between Westminster and the City. In 2002, James Sassoon, a former investment banker with S. G. Warburg, took office as managing director of finance and regulation at the Treasury, becoming its most senior outside recruit in decades. In December 2005, he was appointed as the Chancellor and Treasury's representative for promotion of the City, a part-time role in which he championed internationally the interests of the U.K.'s financial and business services firms and markets. Sassoon was eventually knighted for his services to the finance industry and for public service.

The career of Jeremy Heywood spoke volumes for the City's newly found influence and gravitas. Heywood was a career civil servant who had held a variety of positions at the Treasury, including time as principal private secretary to three chancellors of the exchequer (including Gordon Brown) and as head of the team that oversaw the regulation of financial markets. In 2003, he took unpaid leave from the civil service to become a managing director at the U.S. investment bank Morgan Stanley and then, in June 2007, he switched back to the public sector as head of domestic policy and strategy in the Cabinet Office.

The Precipitating Factors

The City's newfound status was partly attributable to global developments in risk management. The financial services industry claimed that derivatives had taken the risk out of banking. Old-style banking involved banks taking deposits from some customers and lending to others, paying careful attention to ensure that they did not lend out more than they received from their savers. New-style originate-and-distribute banking, developed in the second half of the 1990s by derivatives experts at JP Morgan and other investment banks, enabled banks to originate loans and sell on the risk to others. Lower-risk banking, supporters said, cut the cost of debt for borrowers and enabled governments to plan for a smooth economic cycle without the kind of banking crises that had spattered the twentieth-century landscape.

The chief proponent of this system was Alan Greenspan. He was so widely admired in Britain that three-quarters of the way through his nineteen-year spell as chairman of the U.S. Federal Reserve he was knighted. He used that visit in 2002 to extol the virtues of the new banking model. "The broad success of that paradigm," he told an audience at Lancaster House in London, "seemed to be most evident in the U.S. over the past two and a half years. Despite the draining impact of a loss of $8 trillion of stock market wealth, a sharp contraction in capital investment and, of course, the tragic events of September 11 2001, our economy held firm. Importantly, despite significant losses, no major U.S. financial institution was driven to default."[16]

Britain's Chancellor Gordon Brown was one of Greenspan's most ardent disciples, as was made clear at a speech he gave in 2006 at London's Mansion House, one of the showpiece occasions in the British financial calendar. Brown delivered a eulogy to globalization, free markets, and the British economy, working in references to Greenspan and Adam Smith, the eighteenth-century Scottish philosopher whose treatise on free trade was the market economists' bible. As a result of following free market principles and prioritizing monetary and fiscal stability through an independent Bank of England, Brown was able to boast that "government debt in Britain is lower than France, Germany, Italy, America and Japan" and that growth in Britain was "expected to be stronger this year than last and stronger next year than this."[17]

Chancellor Brown's speech that evening had the bankers purring as he lavished praise on them. They were told that they had helped to secure "London's position of global pre-eminence not only as the international financial centre of the world but of global pre-eminence: London the 2012 Olympic city." What clever fellows they all were: "London has enjoyed one of its most successful years ever, for which I congratulate all of you here on your leadership skills and entrepreneurship." Their "dynamism has led

London to innovate" some of "the most modern instruments of finance." Brown quoted a raft of figures, which he said showed that "London, like New York, is already the capital market place of the world." Brown did not believe this had happened by accident: "The message London's success sends out to the whole British economy is that we will succeed if like London we think globally . . . and nurture the skills of the future, advance with light touch regulation, a competitive tax environment and flexibility."

It was a revealing summary of New Labour's economic philosophy. Globalization was good and free markets were better. Taxation was a competitive weapon, not just a means of raising revenue. "Light-touch regulation" was as much as a way of making progress as a means of prudential supervision.

And this was the prevailing orthodoxy in the U.K. for most of the decade leading up to 2007. It was supported by leading business publications such as the *Financial Times* and the *Economist* and was accepted without question by both of Britain's major political parties. Critics were rare and found little support in the U.K. as was evident at a debate in Cambridge in 2005 between the Nobel Prize winner Joseph Stiglitz and the *Financial Times* writer Martin Wolf, where the former's skepticism was received coolly by a mixed audience of business people and academics. When my own first book, *The Death of Gentlemanly Capitalism*, was published in 2000 and raised doubts about the way the modern financial services system was evolving, I was told by bankers that the world had moved on and to "get with it." Will Hutton, whose ideas about stakeholder value, not just shareholder value, challenged one of the key principles of the market economy, was quietly dropped as a mainstream influence on Labour Party policy: "One minute the then-editor of the *Observer* [Hutton] was sitting in Blair's kitchen watching Tony Blair push down the plunger on his cafetière as he said 'Will, stakeholding is going to be our Bible.' . . . Just six weeks later Hutton found his idea had been dropped."[18]

The Chicago school of free market economics had evidently ousted the social market. Shareholder value had trumped stakeholder value. For the corporate sector, the message was clear. Creating shareholder value was the sole criterion by which they would be judged. The fate of underperforming companies would be left to market forces. Wider concepts such as national interests, customer service, relationships with suppliers, and the considerations of employees were subsidiary to this overarching goal. They were of interest only if they were a means to the end of increasing shareholder value by raising earnings, dividends, and the share price.

Chasing Alpha

Banking was one of the few industries where Britain was globally competitive and banking chiefs were judged by global standards. They were under intense pressure from institutional investors who were caught up in their own chase for alpha and there were plenty of examples of what happened to banks and bankers that failed to please their shareholders. In February 2000, NatWest, one of Britain's largest banks, was taken over by a smaller rival, the Royal Bank of Scotland (RBS), its management having lost the support of shareholders as a result of a failed investment bank and unpopular diversification strategy. In 2005, Philip Purcell, Morgan Stanley's global chief executive, was forced from office by a group of disaffected shareholders who wanted the bank to take more risk in its business. In 2007, just before the credit crunch took hold, an activist shareholder owning just 0.3 percent of the bank's total share capital attacked Britain's largest bank, HSBC. Criticism centered on the composition and structure of the board, corporate pay policies, and the positioning of some of the bank's global businesses.

Against this globally competitive background, banking chiefs had little alternative but to attempt to please the crowd. In the decade up to 2007, this usually involved leveraging their balance sheets, squeezing operational efficiency, and seeking to achieve scale through acquisition if necessary. The chief executive of RBS, Sir Fred Goodwin, was admiringly known as "Fred the Shred" for his ability to strip costs out of existing and newly acquired banks. In the end, he did a deal too far, paying a top-of-the-market price for ABN AMRO's investment banking division. The leveraging of the British banks' balance sheet was even more ambitious. In 2000, the British banks only lent out what they held in deposits. There was no leverage in the industry's balance sheet and no funding gap. But then the banks got originate-and-distribute religion. They used securitization to slice and dice their debt and move it off the balance sheet. They believed they lived in a risk-free world and they were emboldened to drop their credit standards, lend more aggressively to personal and corporate borrowers, and take proprietary positions in their own and other institutions' securitizations. Just seven years later, the British banks' funding gap had risen to an astronomical £500 billion.

The Causes of the Fall

The global credit crisis of 2007–2008 showed that this business model was high risk and unsustainable. The U.K.'s eighth largest bank, Northern Rock, had to be nationalized. Britain's largest mortgage lender, Halifax Bank of Scotland (HBOS), had to be rescued by a rival and the state ended up as the majority owner of two of the country's top four banks, the Lloyds Banking Group and RBS, as well as running an insurance scheme for banking assets.

The executives at the head of Britain's banks have been heavily criticized for greed, incompetence, and hubris, creating, according to the U.K.'s influential Treasury Select Committee, "an environment rich in over-confidence, over-optimism and the stifling of contrary opinions" in which "bankers have made an astonishing mess of the financial system."[19] These characteristics were certainly present but can best be understood in terms of the ideological orthodoxy that became all pervasive during these years.

Greed is the easiest charge to make and the hardest to evaluate. According to John McFall, chairman of the House of Commons Treasury Committee, "Bonus-driven remuneration structures led to a lethal combination of reckless and excessive risk-taking. The design of bonus schemes was not aligned with the interests of shareholders and the long-term sustainability of the banks and has proved to be fundamentally flawed."[20] Senior bankers admit that their objective was to get their share price up but say that this was because that was what shareholders expected of them rather than being driven by personal financial considerations.[21] FSA chairman Lord Turner, himself a former banker, also believes that the issue was more complex than greed alone, arguing that "a reasonable judgement is that while inappropriate remuneration structures played a role they were considerably less important than other factors already discussed—inadequate approaches to capital, accounting and liquidity."[22]

Hubris—excessive pride and self-confidence—played a part in the misjudgments that were made. Bankers' language during the bubble years suggests that they had got carried away with themselves. Citigroup boss Chuck Prince's comment that "as long as the music is playing, you've got to get up and dance"[23] was matched by the rhetoric of Britain's bankers. In March 2007, just months before the investment-banking sector began to unravel, Johnny Cameron, head of RBS's markets division, looked back on record results and boasted: "That is a huge number. It is bigger than Coca-Cola's profits! Compared to other banks it is, for example, twice the size of Bar-Cap—we make more or less twice as much money as BarCap with just over half as many people."[24] Another senior British banker, James Crosby, formerly chief executive of HBOS, had doubled the bank's profits between 2001 and 2005, and was knighted for his work in the financial services industry. After he left in 2006, he looked back on his time and said: "Now I know what I know, I wish I'd been bolder."[25]

Their self-confidence was born out of their experience. As Alan Greenspan had noted at Lancaster House, the new business model seemed to work.[26] The years of the great moderation produced steady growth, low inflation, low interest rates, and healthy corporate profits. The global economy seemed to be able to absorb all kinds of shocks and banking crises seemed to be so twentieth century. The banks had been successful for so long that they believed they were infallible. The last time that the capital markets had faced meltdown was during the oil crisis of 1973–1974, before the careers of most twenty-first-century bankers, fund managers, and chief executives had begun. The senior British journalist Christopher Fildes defined the moment of maximum danger as the point at which the last person to have lived through the last recession retires, a telling description of the situation in the opening years of the twenty-first century.[27] Financial services practitioners, nonexecutive directors who sat on their boards, and regulators forgot that liquidity is what keeps markets going. They were blinded by their own genius. It is significant that two of the banks that survived the crisis best were JP Morgan and Goldman Sachs, two banks that were hit heavily in the bond market crash of 1994 and learned the lessons by introducing strong risk-management systems and analytics.

As we have seen, British bankers worked in a country that had convinced itself about a new orthodoxy. The upper echelons of the British public and private sectors were full of people who believed in the rule of markets, and they formed an elite that was closed to those with different views. For thirty years, British governments of the left and right listened far too much to investment bankers and not enough to people in other industries. They also listened too much to extreme economic liberals and not enough to writers such as Will Hutton, John Kay, and John Plender, all of whom warned of the risks of relying too heavily on markets well in advance of the crisis.

The Perpetrators

In the private sector, chief executives pumped up on the doctrine of shareholder value and under pressure from institutional investors surrounded themselves with those of a similar view. A case in point was Northern Rock, victim of the first run on a British bank since the nineteenth century and the first financial institution to fall in the crisis. Its chief executive, Adam Applegarth, had a reputation for being difficult to challenge and insiders said: "Any rival plan or idea was rejected by those close to him on the basis that 'Adam wouldn't like it.' He had an iron grip on the company. There was no feedback. He surrounded himself with 'yes men' who worked their way up the company and who were dependent on him."[28]

Northern Rock's nonexecutives were drawn from the same pool. Dr. Matt Ridley had been chairman since 2004. He was an Old Etonian with a first-class degree and a doctorate from Oxford and like his predecessor, Sir John, the thirteenth Baronet Riddell, was a member of Northumberland's upper crust. He worked for the free market magazine the *Economist* between 1983 and 1992 and had a family connection to Northern Rock as his father, the fourth Viscount Ridley, was a previous chairman. Five of the company's six other nonexecutives had backgrounds in or experience of the financial services industry. Sir Ian Gibson, the company's senior independent director, had been on the board since 2002 and had been a member of the Court of the Bank of England from 1999 to 2004. Nicola Pease, a nonexecutive since 1999, had the financial services industry in her blood. Her father was chairman of Yorkshire Bank, her husband, Crispin Odey, was a successful hedge fund manager, her brother-in-law John Varley was chief executive of Barclays, and Nicola and her brother were fund managers.[29] Two nonexecutives were appointed in 2005. Rosemary Radcliffe had been chief economist at Northern Rock's accountants, a situation that left her vulnerable to criticism. Michael Queen was director of the private equity group 3i. The nonexecutive quota was completed by Derek Wanless, appointed to the board in 1999 soon after resigning as chief executive of NatWest during its battle for independence. Wanless chaired the Risk Committee, which also included Radcliffe, Gibson, and the executive directors, and Pease sat on the Audit Committee.

The background of these nonexecutives meant that they were far too close to the financial services industry to challenge the executives' key assumption that financial markets worked and that securitization was a repeatable process. Ridley had written for a pro-free-market magazine. The Bank of England during Gibson's time supported the growth of a market economy and Pease and her relatives made a living from it. Radcliffe had worked for an organization that lubricated the system and Queen for one that relied on it. Wanless had been chief executive of one of the U.K.'s major players in debt trading.

This elite was replicated at British bank after British bank and it determined the environment in which the chief executives worked. A case in point is Andy Hornby, the much criticized chief executive of the failed bank HBOS from 2006 to 2008 and a man I have never met, spoken to, or dealt with in any way. Hornby is the son of a Bristol headmaster, had a distinguished academic career at Oxford and the Harvard Business School, and was considered to be a rising star during his time at the retail company Asda and by his bosses at HBOS after he moved there in 1999. As the retail director, he played his part in growing HBOS's consumer lending business and was appointed chief executive in a raging bull market for housing in which HBOS was the market leader. Now, he might have said to shareholders and the board: "wait a minute, this money market funding thing could disappear and the housing market could slump. I am going to shrink market share, build up deposits and earnings per share will halve. Is that OK?" But if he had, he would probably have got a pretty rude answer. This young man in his first chief executive's job would have needed to turn the world on its head and tell the market "you are all wrong." Adam Applegarth at Northern Rock had had longer at the top of his organization but he could advance similar arguments. This was not the failure of a handful of individual executives motivated by greed, it was a systemwide failure of ideologically based conventional wisdom.

It was of course a major error of judgment for the bankers to have allowed their companies to become so vulnerable to market liquidity but they were products of their age. They had grown up in a system that was sweeping all before it. Presidents and prime ministers, regulators and the regulated, central bankers and investors, the Left and the Right all agreed that markets were the way forward. The investment banks had the resources to employ the best people and the best machines to dream up sophisticated products and had an army of talented, persuasive individuals to sell them to customers. The pressure to be part of the trading set was enormous. A whole range of customers from the treasurer of Orange County, California, who was sold inappropriate products by Bankers' Trust derivatives salesmen in the 1990s, to the wide-eyed and innocent board of Northern Rock a decade later were swept away by the current.

The Lessons

The banking crisis of 2007–2008 has lessons for all parts of the social, economic, and political system. Thought leaders are reassessing their interpretation of free market theories. If markets cannot be left to their own devices, how much state intervention is appropriate and what form should it take? Regulators, central bankers, and governments have realized that banks are part of society's infrastructure and cannot be allowed to fail. What protection should the state take against this in limiting the systemic risk of failing banks? Financial institutions are revising their governance arrangements, reviewing the role of nonexecutive directors, and strengthening the committees that oversee risk and remuneration. Shareholders are asking themselves and being asked by others what they should be doing to engage responsibly with the companies in which they hold shares. There is a new focus on the quality of earnings as well as their quantity. Banking executives are trying to walk the narrow line between risk aversion and risk awareness as they seek to keep their shareholders happy.

It will take some time to absorb all of these lessons but there is one conclusion that stands out already. Whenever consensus becomes orthodoxy, stakeholders should be prepared to speak up and challenge conventional wisdom. They should remember the nineteenth-century fairy story "The Emperor's New Clothes," about two fraudulent cloth makers who promised an emperor a new suit.[30] The clothes were imaginary, but assured of their finery by the makers, the emperor paraded naked, and his subjects, through fear, flattery, and delusion, professed admiration. It took a child to point out what was really going on, at which point the scales fell from everyone's eyes.

Chapter 5

Corporate Governance, Risk Analysis, and the Financial Crisis: Did Universal Owners Contribute to the Crisis?

James P. Hawley

Background and Context

My colleague Andrew Williams and I ended our book on fiduciary capitalism (published in 2000) by suggesting that a critical element in corporate governance was "who will watch the watchers?"—who will monitor the monitors? In light of the 2007–2010 financial and economic crises we should have added, "and for what will they monitor?" This chapter argues that overwhelmingly large institutional investors, including those centrally involved in "responsible investment" developments (most of which are universal owners—UOs),[1] failed to implement well-established corporate governance principles in most alternative investments (especially those directly and indirectly in the financial sector), and did not integrate governance with risk analysis, the latter itself being inadequately conceived.[2]

Risk analysis as most large institutional investors practiced it was inadequate to both foresee the financial crisis early on and mitigate or stop it once under way, on both an individual portfolio level and on a systemic level. Indeed, paradoxically, its widespread acceptance was a contributing factor to the financial crisis itself in two dimensions. First, on its own terms it either ignored or denied the likelihood of a systemic financial crisis because it was focused on "beta," tracking risks within a given portfolio. Based on modern portfolio theory (MPT), this focus was seen as fulfilling the fiduciary duty of prudence and care. (This approach resulted mostly from various hedging strategies intended to minimize portfolio-wide risk but contributed to systemic risk.) Second, and more fundamentally, risk was not seen in relation to the fiduciary duty of loyalty to the end-asset owner/investor or pension fund beneficiary, together the vast majority of investors that various types of institutional investors are supposed to serve to fund their retirement. Retirement accounts compose the vast majority of investments (e.g., 401k's in the U.S.).

This chapter delineates three types and levels of risk from a corporate governance perspective.[3] The first is firm risk that has been the relatively successful level on which corporate governance activists have focused using techniques running from quiet, behind-the-scenes negotiations to proxy actions to public shaming and naming in the media. The foci have been on firms' financial and economic underperformance, especially when these foci are combined with a focus on firms with poor corporate governance structures (e.g., staggered boards of directors, pay misaligned with performance, CEO and chair of the board the same person).

The second level of risk is portfolio-level risk, which prior to the financial crisis of 2007–2010 has not been in the purview of governance activity or analysis. That risk is portfolio tracking error risk, which MPT, as discussed below, has argued can be hedged (thereby minimizing tracking error).[4] The reason this should be a concern for governance analysis (and other risk analysis) is that once both MPT and hedging portfolio risk are widely adopted and practiced, hedging (and other activities) may result in systemic instability, undermining the purpose and effectiveness of hedging risk on a portfolio level in the first place. Another way to conceptualize portfolio-level risk as a governance concern is to look at this as sector (specifically financial sector) risk. Thus, there are two elements in financial sector risk: the consequences of widespread hedging to minimize portfolio risk and the riskiness of individual financial actors held in a portfolio (e.g., Washington Mutual's actions in subprime lending as firm-specific risk).[5]

In turn, these two types of financial sector risk lead to a third level of risk: systemic risk. Widely discussed and debated as a result of the financial crisis, systemic risk, I ague below, is also a concern of corporate governance analysis as it most obviously impacts financial performance.

During the 1990s and especially since the Internet bubble and Enron-type collapses at the turn of the century, various alternative responsible investment (RI) trends have developed and made their presence felt to mainstream investors. While there are significant differences among RI institutions, all paid inadequate attention, prior to the 2007–2008 meltdown, to issues of financial stability and systematic risk. These RI institutions and trends go under various names, varying time and location (e.g., socially responsible investment, responsible investment, sustainable investment, a focus on environmental, social, and governance—ESG—factors). None of them to my knowledge has paid attention (until very recently) to the relation between governance and potential financial instability. Much discussion within responsible investment circles has been primarily focused on E and S, with G being mostly seen as a means to an E and S end, although longtime governance activists (e.g., CalPERS, CalSTRS, Hermes, USS, TIAA-CREF, FRR, Norway Pension Fund-Global) continued to pursue an active governance agenda. (The important exception among some responsible investment participants regarding financial issues has been in the formation of the online, virtual Network for Sustainable Financial Markets.)[6] In governance circles (which long predate the terms and programs of ESG, RI, and sustainable investment), academic and practitioner governance literature had as well been too little concerned with financial risk, in spite of its long-established focus on the economic and financial performance of firms. Indeed, the raison d'être of corporate governance has been viewed as superior long-term performance.[7] There were exceptions, but on the whole responsible investment organizations and discussions did not consider issues of the financial crisis much more than their heretofore-mainstream counterparts.[8] In short, there has been a black hole in theory and practice regarding governance actions and engagement by end asset owners (e.g., CalPERS) and asset managers (e.g., TIAA-CREF) in relation to financial sector risk and systemic risk. (In the standard risk literature there has been a long-standing emphasis on internal firm governance and financial risk, primarily focusing on the role and structure of the board of directors in relation to top managers. There is little discussion of the role of the owners of these firms, which are overwhelmingly UOs.)[9]

A similar conclusion is reached regarding institutional investors in general by the U.K. Treasury's "Walker Report": There was "widespread acquiescence by institutional investors and the market for gearing up of banks' balance sheets as a means of boosting returns on equity." The report observes that institutions were "slow to act where issues of concern were identified in banks in which they were investors, and of limited effectiveness in seeking to address [them] either individually or collectively."[10]

How Much Self-Reflection by Universal Owners?

As of this writing there has been precious little public self-examination in the U.S., or examination by others, of whether large institutional investors (mostly UOs) considered the possibility of the financial crisis in their risk analysis. Even postcrisis, there have not been attempts to critically examine their own roles looking for strengths, weaknesses, or errors. Nor have public authorities in the U.S. called attention to this lack, as has occurred in the U.K. A notable, recent exception is that of TIAA-CREF's statement on "Responsible Investing and Corporate Governance." However, this report is not an analysis, but rather a direction for what TIAA-CREF believes should occur going forward to minimize weaknesses of the past.[11]

More typical of avoiding (a public) analysis is the congressional testimony of Joseph A. Dear, chief investment officer of CalPERS. While urging some significant regulatory changes and reforms, he defended investments in hedge funds and private equity as core elements of CalPERS's investment strategy, which together composed about 14 percent of CalPERS's asset allocation in mid-2009. Dear argued that these alternative investments are critical, as their total return since 1999 has been a thousand basis points above global equity. He did not raise the question of how they might fare going forward, post-2007. Abuses of hedge funds and private equity occurred, according to Dear, because there was an absence of regulation allowing them to operate in the shadows away from effective oversight. Missing from Dear's statement is any questioning of how certain types of hedge funds and private equity may, in the search for alpha, harm other, nonalternative investments of a universal owner such as CalPERS. That is, there needs to be some recognition of how one's actions in one sector may impact other sectors, some form of holistic, portfolio-wide analysis that would include how such alpha-seeking investments may serve as a catalyst to systemic risk. Absent, too, was an articulation of whether these investment vehicles should conform to CalPERS's corporate governance principles, and if they do not, how they should be treated. Both of these elements go to the core of the relation between the obligations of owners as stewards of their investments and risk management.[12]

Nonetheless, in response to the financial crises CalPERS, along with other major U.S. institutional investors, has been an early and articulate supporter of a variety of regulatory financial reforms, most importantly focusing on proxy access, executive compensation, systemic risk, and regulatory oversight for private pools of capital, derivatives, and credit rating agencies, in addition to increased consumer protection reforms.[13] Yet none of these proposals goes to the heart of questioning whether, and if so how, CalPERS's and other UOs' investment strategies might have contributed to systemic risk. In turn, this question goes to the heart of investment strategies based on modern portfolio theory, as discussed below. In late 2009 Joseph Dear did raise the prospect of a more introspective look at CalPERS's risk models, mentioning that the institution is "developing new internal risk models that account for non-quantitative market factors," while also "realigning" its relationships with private equity and hedge fund managers "to improve fee structures, transparency and better control our committed capital."[14] It is not yet clear to the outside observer exactly what these initiatives were and what they might really mean in terms of risk analysis.

An interesting contrast from a different UO is Hermes Equity Ownership Services' document *The Way Ahead*, based on a meeting in London in late 2008, which included a number of U.S. attendees in addition to others from six countries. According to this document the most important directions for the way ahead included the aim of seeking to "understand and define the limits of financial product innovation" and the contention that "pension funds should use their power as major clients of the investment industry to demand products that are appropriate to their needs." Proposals for regulatory reform included a specific call for "banks to behave more like utilities," while also asking for investment consultants to be "clearly aligned and consistent with their clients' needs and interests," including pension funds aligning with the "long-term interests of beneficiaries."[15]

These examples are not a comprehensive survey of ways UOs have defined the significance of the financial crisis for themselves and for regulatory and legislative reforms, but they suggest two quite different approaches. Generally, leading U.S. institutional investors have avoided the larger issues of examining implications of unimpeded financial innovation, and many of the assumptions underlying it. They have not focused on the specifics of banking reform (the "too big and interconnected to fail" issues). In contrast, Hermes, more in line with U.K. official reports (i.e., the Walker and Turner reports), has suggested an examination of more fundamental issues.

A major unexplored area is to understand how large institutional end-asset owners and asset managers (mostly universal owners) understood sector and systemic risk prior to the crisis; to understand what role, if any, corporate governance played (or might have played) in relation to risk analysis (mostly carried on by the investment side within the institutions); and, most important, looking forward, to suggest directions for change. I believe the next phase of responsible investment, and of corporate governance in particular, needs to focus on the relatively unexplored relation between established corporate governance standards and practices, on the one hand, and UO *investment strategy*, and systemic risk analysis, metrics, and their parameters, on the other.

Risk and the Search for Alpha: Threatening Beta?

In an oft-cited work Frank Knight in the 1920s made the distinction between risk and uncertainty.[16] Risk was calculable; uncertainty was not. The growth of highly sophisticated mathematics when combined with near-real-time massive computer power (beginning in the 1980s) tended in the minds of theoreticians and practitioners alike to obliterate this important distinction, whether by omission or commission.[17] One important practical implication is that as the view that "all that could be quantified" is only what effectively matters came to dominate, systemic risk, because it couldn't be quantified, was not and could not have been built into risk models and mind-sets.

Specifically I argue that the search for alpha (perhaps too often confused with "yield," but which is more likely "alternative beta") contributed to the financial crisis.[18] An empirical investigation into this argument would include examining how various alternative investments, which increasingly grew as a proportion of portfolios during this period, were vetted for risk, as well as how investments in equities of the financial sector (both official and shadow) were examined in terms of risk. For example, the U.S. Washington State Investment Board in mid-2009 had 28 percent of its assets in private equity, "innovation," and real estate. One investigation suggests that the board had developed a new risk and benchmarking system for its alternative investments in terms of net return but as far as can be gathered, there was no discussion of the systemic relation of various types of alternative investments to overall portfolio or macroeconomic risk.[19]

Even robust risk monitoring on the portfolio level is no panacea. Crouhy et al. note that "risk management has not consistently been able to prevent market disruptions or to prevent business accounting scandals resulting from breakdowns in [a firm's internal] corporate governance. In the case of the former problem, there are serious concerns that derivative markets make it easier to take on large amounts of risk, and that the 'herd behavior' of risk managers after a crisis gets underway . . . actually increases market volatility." They add: "There is no single solution to the problem of how we measure credit risk—no Holy Grail of credit modeling. . . . There are a variety of approaches. . . . Modelers have not found any easy way to integrate market risk and credit risk . . . [because each disregards the other]."[20]

Additionally, while portfolio risk in terms of beta was modeled and monitored by many if not most universal owners, it was in general not coordinated or integrated with corporate governance, which has, or should have, as a main task the monitoring of how individual firms (or perhaps all firms within a sector) conduct their internal risk assessment. This is an essential and critical function of the board of directors. Thus, the massive failure by CEOs, CIOs, and boards of directors in the financial sector to adequately assess risk to their own firms is a corporate governance issue on two levels. The first is the adequacy of firm-level internal (board and top management) risk assessment. The second, and a critical failure, is the adequacy of monitoring the internal firm governance by financial institutions' owners, that is, by UOs.

Thus, on the one hand, there were relatively well-developed corporate governance practices, strategies, and philosophies, and on the other hand, there was the absence of applying those practices, strategies, and beliefs to the public equity and alternative investment sides of portfolios vis-à-vis firm, sector, and system financial risk.

To this end, what is necessary is a conceptual model of UO risk management that stresses monitoring of both under- and hyperperformance for firms individually, but also for sectors (in this crisis, the growth of the financial sector relative to all others specifically). Governance activities (engagement, proxy actions, etc.) directed at underperformers have been well established over the last two decades, and have been quite effective. Governance activities that focus on apparent hyperperformers (e.g., Enron, Citigroup) have been extremely rare if not nonexistent. The financial crisis raises the question of whether even the largest UOs acting collectively (a generous assumption) are capable of effectively minimizing and mitigating sector, most importantly and specifically financial sector, and systemic risk. That is, can governance actions impose a degree of self-regulation on individual sectors? If they cannot, what are the implications for UO governance and investment activities in relation to public policy advocacy and actions?[21]

I hypothesize that these gaps and failures to adequately monitor occurred because institutions did not take into account and apply across the investment spectrum basic corporate governance principles: specifically transparency, monitoring, and accountability. In turn, this contributed, albeit unknowingly, to the financial crisis when combined with the large institutional capital flows into (some or many, depending on the specific institutional investor) alternative investment vehicles, along with the indirect investment in various structured investment products by equity investment in the financial sector itself (e.g., Citigroup, GE). In the case of hedge funds, for example, Brown, Goetzmann, Liang, and Schwarz studied a comprehensive sample of due diligence reports, finding that in 21 percent of the sample there was misrepresentation about past legal and regulatory problems, while in 28 percent there were incorrect or unverifiable claims regarding other material topics. Additionally, they found that due diligence reports were typically issued just after high-return periods as well as during the point of highest cash inflow into funds. (Compounding the problem in terms of herd behavior is that large institutional investors tended to be hedge fund chasers at peak periods.)[22]

To state the obvious, many alternative assets (hedge funds and private equity in particular, but some commodity investments as well) were far less transparent (and accountable) to owners than is public equity. How do governance principles on the public equity side apply on the alternative investment side? What can be truly verified? What are the implications for risk and monitoring in the absence of basic corporate governance principles?

Corporate Governance and Financial Market Instability

Rodney Sullivan, an official of the CFA Institute, in a *Financial Times* article argues that a distinction should be made between corporate governance failures (especially compensation alignment issues in the financial sector) and the more general issue of market failures and financial instability.[23] He argues that the two are not linked, and further that the failure of governance does not prove inherent market financial instability. He concludes: "The current crisis can be best understood as a crisis of governance rather than an inherent failure of markets or of capitalism itself."[24] Pursuing the theme of internal (that is, firm-specific) governance failure, Grant Kirkpatrick in an essay for the Organisation for Economic Co-operation and Development (OECD) examines in detail widespread financial failures of internal governance, from boards to top executives to inadequate monitoring of top traders.[25] He argues that OECD guidelines and other (e.g., Treadway Commission) standards were not followed by boards and top executives. While the OECD guidelines are quite abstract, principle VI.D 2 does assert, for example, that a board function should be "monitoring the effectiveness of the company's management practices and making changes as needed." This includes "monitoring of governance by the board and also includes continuous review of the internal structure of the company to ensure that there are clear lines of accountability for management throughout the organization." Kirkpatrick makes the important point that such monitoring should have occurred given the official warnings about financial dangers issued in 2006–2007 by the International Monetary Fund, Bank for International Settlements, OECD, Bank of England, Financial Services Authority, and others but were greeted "with mixed reactions by financial institutions."[26]

This is the context for Chuck Prince, CEO of Citigroup, famously saying with regard to "froth" in the leveraged home loan market that "as long as the music is playing, you've got to get up and dance"; that is, in order to maintain at least short-term market share a firm has to participate. Here, then, is the link between internal firm governance failures, and market failures and instability. Internal governance was, on the whole and with some exceptions, shown to be inadequately robust when confronted with the music of the market. The repeated tendency of most financial institutions to follow the herd ("dance to the music") is due to the commodity-like nature of most financial products. Kirkpatrick's analysis of internal financial institutional governance failures is good, but limited as he appears to assume that governance is solely an internal affair. He does not look at who's monitoring the (failed) board monitoring, or who should have been. This is to say that he does not look at governance from an owner's perspective.[27] Institutional owners should have been monitoring the monitors, as they have long since owned the vast majority of large financial institutions' equity (and debt).

Bebchuk and Spamann convincingly show that risks taken by top management (and top traders) of financial institutions that might reasonably threaten a bank's existence and have previously benefited shareowners are a rational if long odds bet given past (hyper) performance. Self-preservation (along with the "reputational risk" of the firm in the financial sector) does not mitigate this risk since the risk is to the firm while the potential benefit is to the individual. (Consider Alan Greenspan's mea culpa as a classic and tragic commentary, as he had always believed that reputation risk to the individual top managers would prevent "betting the bank.") Yet failure and collapse comes at the expense of debt holders specifically, and with systemic implications. Since UOs own both debt and equity, as well as face massive systemic losses by definition given broadly invested portfolios, their failure to be adequate external monitors of the internal monitors (boards, top executives) was critically important. The restricted and immediately self-interested rationality of boards and top management could not be relied upon to preserve the institution. Too much had already been earned by most of these individuals to prevent future increasingly risky behavior. Individual risk/reward calculations skewed toward ever-higher risk as past high earnings offset future risky rewards, of both top management *and* for shareowners.[28]

The corporate governance implications of this for financial institutions, *and for them alone*, are profound. No longer is shareowner/top manager alignment the goal; indeed, as the two studies cited suggest, it became perverse in terms of systemic, sector, and firm risk (as only financial institutions have the ability by themselves to cause systemic risk), and thereby for a UO, a risk to its entire portfolio. Bebchuk and Spamann argue that in order to reward top financial managers (and board members), firms should not tie their compensation solely to firm share price (or bank holding company share price) even over the long term but rather to a basket of instruments including equity and debt. For institutional owners, financial sector risk and rewards therefore must also be calculated in terms of a basket of holdings on the debt *and* equity side of each specific entity, in addition to the possibility of system failure devaluing all other nonfinancial sector holdings. This means that governance should not be solely governance based on equity ownership, but must be more inclusive across the investment portfolio.[29]

A number of empirical questions for future research arise from this. Were any UOs tracking financial institutional and financial sector risk from this perspective? If so, which ones, how, and what actions did they take? If not, looking forward, how can and should this perspective be integrated into risk assessment? Clearly VAR (value-at-risk) models cannot do this.[30] What should be the role of the governance side? For example, should share owners engage with financial firms to radically restructure compensation package benchmarks, not only for the long(er) term but in order to align compensation with UO financial interests, which are broader than just their share ownership interests since they include debt and other assets, particularly alternative assets? What is or should be the role of regulators and regulatory regimes? To ask these questions is to immediately suggest that self-governance, at least in the financial sector, cannot occur. It necessitates a robust governmental (and intergovernmental) regulatory regime.[31]

Financial crises are fundamentally about asset inflations of one sort of another (historically from tulips to housing to oil and energy to land speculation). This raises an important issue of what role UOs should take upon themselves if and when they and others see asset bubbles forming. This falls in the areas of both risk analysis and corporate governance, as UOs likely own a significant proportion (indeed, collectively often a majority) of many players in "frothy" markets. But it also calls into question whether, absent a significant regulatory regime change, they are able to do this.

A Case in Point: Can and Should a UO Try to "Prick a Commodity Bubble"?

Lord Desai in a 2008 *Financial Times* article[32] argues that the price of oil during that year's oil run-up does not reflect end-use underlying supply and demand factors (however much those have changed in a secular manner in the last five to ten years), but rather to some debated but significant degree reflects speculation. The exact nature of this speculation has been much discussed. Was it a hedge against global inflation? A hedge against the then-declining dollar or simply the placing of a put on rising oil and commodity prices themselves? Or did it reflect the move by large institutional investors in "alternative" assets since the Enron scandals using commodity indexes?[33] Desai argues that speculation was responsible for commodity markets bubbles in the oil market (and commodities markets generally), posing a systemic risk financially, as well as causing damage to the real economy. Specifically, commodity index funds treat oil as an asset to be bought and sold, which is not the case with nonindex speculators. This is what Michael Masters calls physical commodity traders contrasted with index commodity traders.[34] Desai's proposal is to require a lower margin from "regular" physical traders while raising the margin for index traders to nearly 50 percent (from its current 7 percent).

Whether this and numerous other proposals were adequate or, indeed, whether the analysis underlying various restrictive proposals is in fact correct in whole or part is beyond the present scope. Rather my purpose (being a nonexpert in the areas of commodity trading and investment generally, and oil in particular) is to raise a question for institutional investors who compose the vast majority of what Masters calls index speculators. By this he means large institutional investors in the commodity markets who allocate a proportion of their portfolio (alternative investments) to the futures and derivatives markets and in his view behave very differently than "traditional speculators." They are typically indexed distributing their investment using indexes such as S&P, Dow Jones–AIG commodity index, and the like. The major investors are sovereign wealth funds, corporate and government pension funds, university endowments, and institutions, most of which are UOs. Additionally, index investments aimed at the retail market are using exchange-traded funds. (For example, Masters calculated that index speculators held long 47 percent in the heating oil market; 39 percent in gasoline; 28 percent in natural gas; 31 percent in West Texas intermediate crude oil, etc., in mid-2009.)[35] These investments have occurred mostly since 2001.

These are large numbers that, if correct, impact the price of "real" goods and commodities as the futures markets set the world price for commodities. Two key elements distinguish index speculators from traditional ones: the former tend to be price insensitive, thereby augmenting the impact on commodity markets. That is, an investor will allocate a given amount to invest in a commodity index, regardless of price. Additionally, this kind of investor tends to hold long term.[36] (Masters suggests that due to a regulatory loophole, index speculators are not subject to position limits if they use commodity index swaps with banks, as most do.)

The point of this all-too-brief summary is that these markets have immediate and long- term impact on all sectors of the economy. As institutional investors search for alpha (e.g., through alternative investments directly in commodity markets, but indirectly as well in some of their hedge fund and private equity investments), the collective impact of individual institutional decisions may well have had and continues to have an impact on all sectors of the economy. This is perhaps another example in which the search for alpha may harm absolute market returns in the longer run.

As large institutional investors are mostly universal owners, it would be a reasonable and prudent action to consider whether this collective "rush to alpha" is in fact hurting market values as a whole, thereby making alpha a temporary (bubble?) phenomenon, and rendering the search for alpha at best somewhat illusory, and at worst significantly destructive of the value of the whole portfolio.[37] If there was a significant possibility that this might be the case, would it not be prudent to find ways to evaluate whether this is in fact a risk? If it is or might reasonably be, then the question becomes whether it is possible, given the huge collective action problem endemic to this situation, to contain or minimize the negative impact (what we can call intraportfolio negative externalities) of a bubble or potential bubble market.

This is why Desai (and some others) have called for pricking the bubble or other actions.[38] Could the search for alpha in commodities be its own worst enemy when considered systemically and holistically (that is, inclusive of feedback loops)?

It is likely well beyond the collective agreement capacity of institutional investors, including those interested in or committed to sustainable finance, to solve this collective action problem. If this is the case, then various public policies (regulatory, listing, legislative) should be considered as a part of fiduciary duty, much as adequate climate change legislation is now considered within the legitimate purview of fiduciary duty. In this case, the sustainable institutional investor might consider developing a public policy position and considering what actions might promote it. This in effect asks the state to save us from ourselves as competitive dynamics lead to herd-like behavior. One critical element in this dynamic is benchmarking to peers, which ultimately drives herd behavior when done *absent a holistic (interactive) portfolio risk analysis*, as noted above. Alternatively, seeking absolute rather than relative, benchmarked returns (again on a portfolio-wide holistic basis) avoids these problems of tracking error and index-referenced mandates and benchmarking.[39]

Conceptual Underpinnings of Failure: Collectively Creating One's Own Negative Financial Externalities

Along similar lines Steve Lydenberg, in the conference presentation on which his chapter in this volume is based, argues that the main techniques for improving portfolio returns (e.g., diversification, securitization, hedging) "when widely adopted can actually increase market risk."[40] MPT limits its risk scope to the single portfolio, rather than looking at its possible contribution to cumulative and systemic effects if widely adopted. Single portfolio risk is measured in terms of how much returns vary around an average/mean rate of return.[41] While it is well understood that MPT cannot deal with marketwide risk, Lydenberg suggests that under certain conditions widespread adoption of MPT contributes to, rather than is a passive recipient of, market-systemic disruption or failure. Lydenberg is not alone in this line of analysis. For example, Justin Fox suggests that the paradox of so-called portfolio insurance (that is, using various forms of derivatives) as a means of minimizing portfolio risk is that as it becomes widely adopted it creates new and systemic risks.[42] Such feedback loops, as Fox points out, make sense, as the behavior of investors (especially large institutional investors, run by professional managers) reflects similar and often identical investment strategies and behaviors. Thus, the widespread adoption of the capital asset pricing model investment strategies in the 1980s undermined the model's prior predictive power.[43]

Professional money managers dominate both end-asset-owning and fund management institutions (e.g., corporate and local government pension funds, mutual/unit funds) and throughout the investment chain (e.g., advisers, consultants, secondary investment managers). The significance of this lies in their relation with their clients as they manage other people's/institutions' money. Thus, making contrarian investments, for example, risks their (usually short-term, quarter-to-quarter) benchmarks, risking individuals' compensation as well as their organization's competitiveness. This reinforces herding behavior and has the perverse consequence of increasing systemic risk while seemingly protecting individual compensation, measured against relative benchmarks.[44]

A UO perspective on ESG, in particular a focus on externalities (E and sometimes S), necessitates what I have called holistic portfolio monitoring. That is, analyzing the interactive effects of the behavior of one firm or sector on other firms and sectors held in the portfolio.[45] Previously I have argued that this is and should be a prudent and indeed fiduciary duty for a universal owner. This holds true not just for public equity but also for activities in all asset classes. To the degree that UOs invested in, for example, hedge funds, private equity, and real estate entities, which facilitated and drove financial risk (e.g., through massively increased leverage, second-

and third-degree securitization creating synthetic collateralized debt obligations [CDOs], etc.), the systemic result was to massively increase both individual portfolio risk and systemic risk. MPT simply does not examine such interactive effects; it assume a static, unchanging, and in this sense simple and stable environment, as the efficient market hypothesis (EMH)/rational actor model would suggest. The pursuit of alpha may have increased marketwide risk because MPT does not take into account possible marketwide consequences of its own widespread adoption, either for systemic risk or even for single portfolio risk. Thus, for example, as greater and greater use is made of CDOs as "insurance," the result is not more hedged risk but given leverage, the greater possibility of systemic crisis. The consequence is a "fat-tail" event.[46]

A variety of theories and perspectives have long pointed this out. For example, Soros calls this "reflectivity,"[47] while Allen and Snyder suggest that a better alternative to a general equilibrium model is complexity theory, based on the biological model, which they term, in relation to financial markets, "complex adaptive systems." At root is the commonsense idea that, as they write is, "an economy . . . is composed of agents who both perceive their situation and are capable of changing their behavior [in relation] to it." In such a system the highest level is where mental models interact with each other, each agent (not necessarily fully "rational") attempting to imagine what other agents are attempting to imagine and to act on that, in a potentially infinite regression.[48] Such a formulation is similar to Keynes's famous description of the stock market, where there are multiple equilibria points since each actor attempts to gauge and act on the average opinion of the average opinion, again to a potentially infinite regression.[49]

The implication of this very brief and oversimplified summary of longstanding formulations for UOs is that especially given their participation across all or most assets markets, it should have been incumbent on them to consider two factors. First were the dissenting critiques of the EMH on which MPT is based. Because they were major MPT actors (indexation playing an important part in their portfolio construction), playing out different scenarios would have seemed prudent. Second, because they were large actors, especially large actors as a collectivity whose portfolios more or less mirrored each other, consideration of the actual or potential impacts of their own actions on market behavior would, again, have been prudent risk management. They would have had to undertake both not only in

terms of their own direct investments but in regard to the investment behavior of other institutions as well—that is, in monitoring and analyzing,
for example, the growth of the "shadow" financial system (e.g., CDOs,
credit default swaps).

For a UO, this is conceptually similar to the failure to conduct interactive monitoring for environmental externalities. What one sector or firm
does is internalized in varying degrees within the portfolio as a whole. The
same is true for financial products and firms. Monitoring is essential, but
not (only) within the confines of a MPT perspective but in terms of the
interactive (and cumulative) effects of various financial products and entities. This is a major challenge for both risk analysis and corporate governance.

What can various forms of corporate governance do in these circumstances or is this beyond the effective reach of even highly coordinated
governance coalitions? Apparently little was done prior to the financial crisis using governance and engagement to attempt to minimize risk. For example, in the public equity space it would have been possible to raise in a
variety of ways (including in public fora and the media) the risks that most
firms in the financial sector were running, given leverage ratios, warnings
of subprime problems, and the like. With few exceptions to my knowledge,
little was done. An important element, still unknown, is what occurred in
private discussions on the governance or the investment or the risk operations sides in large UOs.[50] There is a legitimate question of what possible
impact these activities might have had even had they been used. If, that is,
corporate governance is inadequate to the task, then a UO has a fiduciary
obligation to consider other means, the most obvious and important being
public policy advocacy and mobilization.[51]

Lydenberg suggests that a beginning point for an alternative theory to
MPT is a UO perspective (which includes considerations of ESG and a
sustainability approach). In part this implies that fiduciary obligation
means not simply the risk-adjusted beating of benchmarks but rather looking at the "prudent enhancement of asset-class opportunities." (This gets
into the meaning of the "exclusive benefit" rule—the Employee Retirement
Income Security Act in the U.S.—which has typically been interpreted as
meaning the financial benefit, even at the possible cost to other elements of
retirement benefits, that is, well-being, e.g., oil investment returns at the
cost of global climate change, pharmaceuticals profits at the cost of higher
medical care.)[52]

Risk must be conceptualized and metrics developed in relation to the ultimate purpose(s) of an investment or an investment institution (e.g., defined-benefit pension plans or defined-contribution 401k-type investment plans in the U.S.). Thus, fiduciary duty needs to be aligned with this long-term goal. For example, climate change is a legitimate (indeed necessary) risk/opportunity factor to consider as it will affect not only the value of various investments but also both present and future ones (and present and future generations of beneficiaries and investors, by definition). This raises the duty of impartiality (as developed mostly in common law, especially trust law) as a hugely important and mostly overlooked third element of fiduciary duty in addition to the duties of loyalty and care. That is, fiduciary obligation cannot favor present retirees or investors over future ones. Thus the scope and definition of risk needs to be broadened to align with savings' and investments' ultimate goals. While many institutional owners have come to see climate change as such a risk factor, in principle the same applies to financial risk, reasonably reconceptualized.

As a consequence, "outperformance" and benchmarks should not be the indicator of long-term investment success (chasing alpha/harming markets as a whole), but rather absolute long-term returns based on real productivity increases (reasonably distributed across the socioeconomic spectrum) need to be the indicator of a UO's success.[53] Such a profound change in investment philosophy, strategy, and operations is a massive challenge. An obvious corollary is that a UO's remuneration policies must align the incentives of its managers with those of pension fund beneficiaries and retirement investors (e.g., in 401k mutual funds) whose well-being depends on long-term return, not on quarterly or even annual returns. As Taub (quoting Coffee) argues, fund managers tend to herd because they find it more damaging to their careers "to be individually wrong than collectively wrong." Benchmarking is thereby reenforced and perpetuated.[54]

Conclusion: The "Sophisticated Investor"?

Institutional investors, according to the U.S. 1940 Investment Company Act, are considered "sophisticated investors." It is time to rethink this definition. For too long institutional investors, including UOs, have depended mostly on gatekeepers and the supposed checks and balances (e.g., credit rating agencies, banks as monitors, trading counterparties, self-preservation instincts of financial firms, assumptions of rational actors, efficient markets, and the investment chain of consultants and money managers) to ensure, benchmark, if not create "sophistication." Few UOs and other large institutional investors actively sought out minority views on financial risk or built alternative scenarios that would consider the possibility that the financial system might be significantly fragile and crisis prone. Even after the near systemic disaster that came with the 1987 collapse of Long Term Capital Management, there was little effective concern with asset inflation and leverage built up. In addition to "sophisticated investors" having learned too little from the Internet bubble and the subsequent Enron-type collapses, one must question their ability or willingness to protect their own interests. This is closely related to the benchmarking problem. If gatekeepers are necessary but not sufficient, as is increased disclosure and transparency, then the only prudential recourse would be what Taub calls "substantive investment and operations restrictions" on various types and classes of investment.[55]

Thus the network of nongovernmental gatekeepers and the supposed monitoring of investment and corporate governance risk by end-asset owners (including most likely the majority of those that have adopted RI principles) failed, for a complex matrix of reasons only alluded to in this chapter. Sophisticated investors failed the monitoring test. Either they have not been particularly sophisticated or if sophisticated they have been apparently incapable of monitoring adequately and effectively. If the former, a new regulatory regime and standards are called for. If the latter, a radical reconsideration of the relation of corporate governance to investment strategies, and to risk analysis and monitoring, is called for. It is likely that important elements of each are necessary.

Chapter 6

Great Expectations: Institutional Investors, Executive Remuneration, and "Say on Pay"

Kym Sheehan

Introduction

The year 2009 was a watershed for the regulation of executive remuneration. Around the world, governments considered how best to regulate in light of evidence from the global financial crisis of a link between certain remuneration structures and excessive risk-taking.[1] Two clear categories of regulatory response emerge from this latest crisis. First, there is the local adoption of the Financial Stability Board's *Principles for Sound Compensation Practices.*[2] Governments are translating these principles into national standards and allocating the monitoring task typically to the prudential regulator (the regulator with primary responsibility for ensuring financial stability).

The second pattern of regulatory responses targets executive remuneration practices in public or listed companies more generally. These initiatives can include what is known as a "say on pay": a rule that gives the company's shareholders an annual vote on executive remuneration, either as a binding vote (for example, the binding vote on remuneration policy in the Netherlands) or an advisory-only vote (for example, the annual advisory vote on the remuneration report, as in the U.K. and Australia). This last type of vote has existed in the U.K. since 2003 and Australia since 2005 and is attracting increasing attention from researchers[3] and politicians (for example, in the U.S. the Dodd-Frank Wall Street Reform and Consumer Protection Act of 2010, H.R.4173). However, before introducing a say on pay, governments should pause to consider how institutional investors can use this "say" to ensure companies adopt appropriate executive remuneration practices.

The evidence of poor remuneration practices in a number of financial institutions in the FTSE 100[4] confirms that the vote has not invariably ensured appropriate remuneration practices. A number of financial institutions subject to either full nationalization (for example, Northern Rock) or some partial intervention (for example, the Royal Bank of Scotland, and the merger between HBOS and the former Lloyds TSB, now the Lloyds Banking Group) were required to prepare a remuneration report and to put that report to an annual advisory vote. By and large, shareholders in these companies did not signal that they were displeased with the practices disclosed. For example, the lowest level of support received by the Royal Bank of Scotland for its remuneration report was 84 percent in 2003, followed by 85 percent in 2005. In all other years (2004, 2006, 2007, and 2008), the remuneration report has received over 90 percent of votes cast in favor of the resolution to adopt it. Institutional investors in U.K.-listed financial institutions collectively failed to ensure that good executive remuneration practices were adopted. Hence institutional shareholders have to accept some responsibility for these practices: to extend the sentiments expressed by the United Nations Environment Programme Finance Initiative,[5] the failure by institutional investors to collectively challenge financial institutions' remuneration practices meant the practices remained.

Understanding how the "say on pay" regulates executive remuneration demonstrates the "elements" that must exist if the say is to be effective. This chapter contributes to this understanding by presenting a model of the regulatory framework for executive remuneration in the U.K. and Australia. The next section presents a holistic model of the regulatory framework for executive remuneration applicable in Australia and the U.K., known as the regulated remuneration cycle.[6] Closer inspection of the four activities in this cycle (practice, disclosure, engagement, and voting) highlights the three important roles institutional investors play in this framework. First, institutional investors act as rule makers by issuing statements of best practice on executive remuneration. Second, institutional investors engage with remuneration committees on the remuneration practices the committee discloses in the remuneration report. Finally, institutional investors vote on remuneration-related resolutions, including the advisory vote on the remuneration report. In other words, say on pay is not just about governments legislating to give shareholders the right to vote on remuneration. Its effectiveness depends on the quality of shareholders' actions in the three roles identified, and the synergy between these roles.

The chapter then examines the expectations on institutional shareholders to "do something" about executive remuneration. Both government and institutional investors expect that institutional investors will actively monitor executive remuneration. Governments will legislate to give shareholders additional voting rights such as a mandatory annual say on pay, but government expects shareholders to exercise these rights to screen out poor remuneration practices. In this context, "poor remuneration practices" are not only those that encourage excessive risk taking, they are also those structures that simply pay out too much. In other words, it is the quantum of remuneration that concerns the government, whereas it is the alignment of executive interests with shareholder interests that draws shareholder attention to remuneration structures.

The third section considers institutional investors as the "gatekeepers" of reasonable remuneration payments. It argues that institutional investors are not necessarily gatekeepers. Unlike auditors or credit rating agencies, institutional investors' interests in the company are primarily financial through the ownership of and trading in equities. Even when institutional investors do monitor remuneration, they are not always effective in identifying in a timely manner inappropriate practices. The limits on shareholders' willingness and ability to use the say on pay to achieve government policy goals need to be explicitly acknowledged. If governments want to see different executive remuneration practices from those that shareholders want, alternative models of regulation that address the public interest could prove to be more appropriate legislative initiatives.

The chapter concludes by examining prudential supervision of remuneration practices in financial institutions as an alternative to shareholder monitoring. While this might prove effective for what is ultimately a small group of companies, its costs might prohibit the broader adoption of this model. Governments may wish to recalibrate their expectations of what can

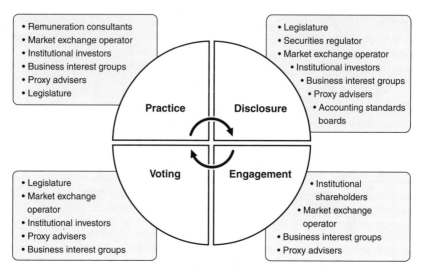

Figure 6.1. The Regulated Remuneration Cycle

be achieved via a say on pay, and consider it as one of a number of initiatives that could be introduced to deal with egregious remuneration practices.

Regulatory Framework for Executive Remuneration

The regulatory framework for executive remuneration in Australia and the U.K. can be conceived of as a regulatory space[7] in which various actors (the remuneration committee, institutional shareholders, proxy advisers, stock exchange operators, securities regulators) share authority with a number of other actors (the board of directors, remuneration consultants, individual directors, institutional shareholders). The regulated remuneration cycle consists of four separate activities: remuneration practice,[8] disclosure of that practice,[9] engagement with shareholders on practice as disclosed,[10] and shareholder voting on practice.[11] This cycle is illustrated in Figure 6.1.[12]

This figure illustrates some of the important aspects of the regulatory framework for executive remuneration in Australia and the U.K. First, there are four distinct activities to be regulated: practice, disclosure, engagement, and voting. Second, authority is shared in this regulatory space, with a

Table 6.1: Rule Styles and Regulators for Executive Remuneration in Australia and the United Kingdom

Rule	United Kingdom	Australia
Legislation	U.K. Parliament	Federal Parliament
Regulations	DTI/BERR/BIS	ASIC, Treasury
Market exchange rules	FSA	ASX, ASIC
Codes of best practice	Financial Reporting Council	ASX Corporate Governance Council
Accounting standards	Accounting Standards Board	Australian Accounting Standards Board
Practice statements	Institute of Chartered Secretaries and Administrators	AICD, Chartered Secretaries of Australia
Practice guidance	ABI, NAPF, Institutional Shareholders' Committee (ISC)	ACSI, IFSA
Voting guidance	IVIS (ABI), RiskMetrics, PIRC[a]	CGI Glass Lewis, RiskMetrics[b]

[a]The NAPF's corporate governance statements also give an indication of voting intentions and thus can also provide voting guidance on some practices.
[b]Both CGI Glass Lewis and RiskMetrics issue annual updates on remuneration practices that can be either practice guidance (a preferred practice is identified by the rule) or voting guidance (a rule that specifies the voting recommendations, given a particular practice exists).

variety of organizations acting as a regulator: the legislature, the executive (in the form of the securities regulator or some other government agency or department), the accounting standards maker, the market exchange operator, the industry body, even the individual investor and the individual firm. Examining this cycle more closely in the U.K. and Australia reveals the many different rule types that exist within it: legislation and regulations made pursuant to legislative powers, codes of best practice,[13] market exchange rules, accounting standards, shareholder practice guidance,[14] business interest group statements,[15] and voting guidance.[16]

Given this broad variety of rule-making styles, it is clear that a number of different regulators are also involved in the framework. Table 6.1 sets out the relevant regulators for Australia and the U.K., based on the style of regulation. The development of a regulatory framework that includes the legislature as only one of many regulators might reflect a manipulative process on the part of the government. By making facilitative rules but not content rules,[17] government allows the tension between institutional investors and remuneration committees on the company's remuneration practices to exist. It will step in to alter the balance of power between these two groups via content rules where necessary to further its own policy objectives.[18] Hence the introduction of a say on pay, a content rule, is best thought of as a mechanism to further *government* policy objectives.

Role of Institutional Investors in the Regulated Remuneration Cycle

In this market-based approach to the regulation of remuneration, institutional investors in Australia and the U.K. play a key role in three activities: practice, engagement and voting. This section examines each of these activities to illustrate the importance that all three play in the regulated remuneration cycle.

Rule Making on Remuneration Practice

Table 6.3 and Table 6.4 in the appendix to this chapter set out the framework of rules for remuneration practice in the U.K. and Australia respectively. While institutional investors also make rules about remuneration disclosure (in the form of best practice guidance), regulating disclosure is largely the domain of legislation and regulations made by parliaments[19] and government agencies, as well as accounting standards. These will prevail over shareholder guidance because they have legislative support. By issuing guidance on remuneration practices,[20] institutional investors act as "norm entrepreneurs" for executive remuneration.[21] That is, underpinning the rules found in shareholder guidance is a set of norms about what is the purpose of executive remuneration and what is "performance." Institutional investors promote these norms in competition with other rule makers on remuneration practice, such as market exchange operators, who sanction norms found in the "code" of corporate governance.[22] This rule making by institutional investors is a crucial role within the regulated remuneration cycle. In those instances where the shareholder guidance is adopted by proxy advisers as the relevant screen to rate remuneration reports, it will guide shareholders' engagement and voting practices.[23] A further justification for the rule-making activities of institutional shareholders is the need to counterbalance the views of remuneration consultants' advice. While remuneration consultants are widely used in the U.K.[24] and in Australia,[25] remuneration consultants are perceived to be not sufficiently independent from management to provide robust advice.[26] Without institutional investors' statements of good practice, companies are relying on their remuneration consultants for guidance on what are appropriate remuneration practices.

To date, more attention has typically been given to the codes of corporate governance practice as *the* source of rules on remuneration practice. Yet these "codes" largely focus upon the structure and tasks of the remuneration committee, rather than provide guidance on the intricacies of remuneration practices. Any guidance the codes give for remuneration structures and payments tends to be at a high level of abstraction. As a principles-based approach, the U.K.'s *Combined Code* has not operated as intended, partly because institutional investors have adopted a "box-checking" (or, as it is known in the U.K. "box-ticking") approach, but also because companies adopt boiler-plate disclosures.[27] Regulating remuneration practices via codes that contain very high level principles is not ideal. Complying with guidance, as in Australia, that says "Companies should ensure that the level and composition of remuneration is sufficient and reasonable and that its relationship to performance is clear"[28] gives companies a lot of discretion to set high levels of remuneration or to have a relationship with performance that does not promote shareholders' interests, but is merely clear. "Sufficient" can be interpreted as "sufficient to retain, attract and motivate suitable candidates," while "reasonable" can be interpreted as "reasonable in all the circumstances." If company performance is strong, this guidance suggests it is acceptable to pay high levels of remuneration, "provided its relationship to performance is clear."

Hence before legislators introduce a say on pay, it is important to check whether institutional shareholders are currently undertaking this rule-making role. If they are, there are further questions to consider: who makes the rules (is it a committee of recognized experts from the industry or is it developed by the executive management of a professional body)? What rules are made? What forms do the rules take (high-level principles or more detailed statements of requirements—a combination is required)? How often are these updated and when are the updates released? To ensure quicker adoption of revised guidance, the updates should be timed to coincide with remuneration committee decision making, rather than shareholder voting decisions. Ideally there is a synergy between the rules and shareholders' engagement and voting practices. Without this synergy, the imperative for remuneration committees to follow these rules diminishes.

Engagement and Voting

The ability of one individual institutional shareholder to change remuneration practices in an investee company is limited, so changing remuneration practices requires continuing and consistent efforts from many investors. This means, first, monitoring executive remuneration disclosures, then engaging with remuneration committees in an effort to improve remuneration practices, and finally voting on remuneration-related resolutions. While voting is important, it is not the only activity that matters: influence via dialogue (engagement) to change remuneration practices is critical when the say on pay is to adopt the remuneration report. Voting alone will not change practice because the vote against the *remuneration report* does not give a sufficiently clear signal of why the report was rejected, only that it was rejected by a number of investors represented by the votes cast against the resolution, as well as votes withheld. Companies depend on shareholders communicating the exact issues of concern via engagement.

Decisions as to the appropriate application of remuneration principles devised by shareholders for an individual firm are settled by engagement between shareholders and the company. Engagement is a "regulatory conversation"[29] in which shareholders seek to establish how the rules on remuneration practice apply to this company. They can ask for further information that might explain company performance or the remuneration practices. Indeed the decision by both the U.K. and Australia governments to enact an advisory vote on the remuneration report was to give an opportunity for shareholder voice (Australia)[30] and to foster shareholder engagement (U.K.).[31] Recent reports from both jurisdictions confirm increased engagement and dialogue on remuneration practices has followed.[32] However, more engagement does not ensure better remuneration practices. As Deborah Gilshan and PIRC Ltd. note, engagement and voting are not substitutes, but complements.

When engagement occurs is pivotal to its impact. Anecdotal evidence suggests engagement by institutional investors may not occur until after the annual general meeting, to avoid intense lobbying by companies to change the voting intention. In other instances, shareholders do not communicate the reasons for voting against the remuneration report at all. Remuneration committees are starting to seek out opportunities to engage with institutional investors rather than waiting for institutional shareholders to approach them. My own interview research in the U.K. and Australia shows that companies are indeed frequently initiating dialogue with their key institutional shareholders outside the peak annual general meeting season. Dialogue is seen as a critical activity of companies seeking to engage with major shareholders.[33] However, this process allows the company, not shareholders, to set the agenda for discussion. More engagement does not necessarily equate with dialogue on issues of concern to shareholders, or better outcomes.

To summarize, the role of institutional shareholders within the regulated remuneration cycle is not just about voting on remuneration. Say on pay relies on standards of practice developed by institutional investors that are accepted by remuneration committees as valid (so who makes the code is important),[34] proxy advisers that carefully scrutinize remuneration reports with valid criteria for endorsing or rejecting practices, institutional investor engagement with investee companies on remuneration practices, and active use of voting rights. If any part of the regulatory framework is absent or shareholders are not diligent in undertaking these activities, say on pay does not offer a magic solution to poor remuneration practices. In fact, it can encourage poor practices by seemingly sanctioning such practices. This can occur when there is private engagement without public shaming of the conduct in question.[35] Private engagement might reflect a cultural preference to avoid conflict.[36] Hence a further preliminary consideration before introducing a say on pay is the current style of engagement practices in the jurisdiction, and the evidence of shareholders' willingness to vote against management.

Enforcement of Good Remuneration Practices

While voting alone cannot change remuneration practice, neither can mandatory disclosure. A regulatory regime that relies solely on disclosure as a regulatory strategy yet seeks to change practice is unlikely to be successful. With no sanctions for wrong practice in the disclosure-based rules, only a sanction for nondisclosure, the result can be "creative compliance"—the

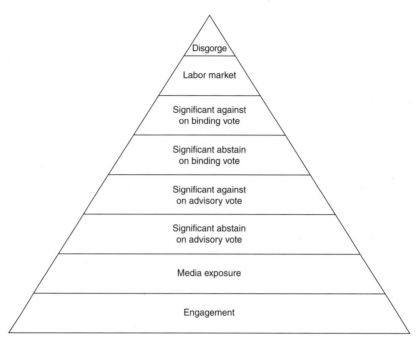

Figure 6.2. The Enforcement Pyramid for Executive Remuneration Practice in the U.K. and Australia

disclosure is there in fulfilment of the black letter law but the spirit of the disclosure regime has been successfully avoided.[37] Thus an important element of the regulation of remuneration practice via disclosure is to ensure that the sanction for wrong practice exists in some other part of the regulatory framework and via a nongovernment mechanism,[38] given that governments do not see it as their role to decide what remuneration a listed firm should pay its senior executives. Who enforces sanctions against companies with poor remuneration practices?

Figure 6.2 sets out the enforcement pyramid for remuneration practice in Australia and the U.K. While this resembles the enforcement pyramid devised by Ayres and Braithwaite,[39] one key difference is that the enforcement strategies shown do not belong to any one regulator of remuneration practice.

The main enforcers of good remuneration practice are shareholders, through their engagement with companies who undertake to change their remuneration practices and through voting. The media too has a role to play here in drawing attention to particular companies whose remuneration practices are likely to attract shareholder wrath.[40] The securities regulator has limited scope to take action in relation to actual remuneration practices, although it plays a part in enforcing compliance with the mandatory rules for disclosure and voting. There is also the issue of how motivated securities regulators are to act on executive remuneration issues, given the other regulatory objectives set out in the relevant enabling legislation.[41] The labor market sanction is likely to be directed at the nonexecutive directors on the remuneration committee rather than at the executive accepting the excessive remuneration.[42]

In the U.K. and Australia, few legal sanctions exist to prevent a particular remuneration payment occurring. Shareholder approval of a resolution that is binding on the board/company is required for four different payments: termination payments,[43] related party transactions,[44] issues of securities to a director (Australia only),[45] and approval of an employee incentive scheme.[46] The top enforcement option shown in the pyramid will require the executive director to return any payments received in breach of some, but not all, of these particular resolution rules.[47] Should a company pay excessive remuneration, the available enforcement options lie toward the middle to lower end of the pyramid: engagement, publicity, and advisory voting. The legal sanctions for errant remuneration practices are thus very limited.

Expectations for Institutional Investors

The respective U.K. and Australian governments' policy goals for legislating resulted in laws that create the conditions for the shareholder sanctions highlighted in Figure 6.2 to occur. From the government's perspective, shareholders need to be given voting rights on executive remuneration to hold boards accountable for their executive remuneration decisions.[48] This is achieved by laws that mandate disclosure and voting on remuneration reports, and attach legal sanctions to a failure to disclose and a failure to conduct the advisory vote. How effective this legislation is in terms of achieving good remuneration practice must be considered within the overall regulatory framework for remuneration practice, disclosure, engagement, and voting, explained above. The disclosure and voting rules do not mandate that shareholders must read the disclosure, engage with companies on the remuneration practices as disclosed, or vote on the remuneration report. Thus one may ask: is merely creating the conditions for shareholders to act sufficient to achieve the ultimate goal of better remuneration practices?

The regulated remuneration cycle relies heavily on shareholder involvement and there are great expectations of active involvement by shareholders in regulating executive remuneration. At an international level, the United Nations Environmental Programme Finance Initiative (UNEPFI) and the International Corporate Governance Network (ICGN) have issued statements that set out various expectations on institutional shareholders.[49] The ICGN statement on remuneration explicitly links executive remuneration with the fiduciary responsibilities and economic interests of institutional investors, while implicitly urging engagement: "the guidelines serve as a *communication tool* from investors to companies."[50] Its statement of institutional investor responsibilities calls for the responsible exercise of ownership rights. It exhorts institutional investors to maintain dialogue with investee company boards on governance policies and to work with other shareholders, particularly when dialogue does not appear to be working.[51] The goal of this activity is to generate value for beneficiaries, because shareholders can "help investee companies make sound decisions and manage risks to deliver sustainable and growing value over time."[52]

The *UN Principles for Responsible Investment* (UN PRI) provides framework principles for signatories to fulfil their fiduciary duties by monitoring environmental, social, and governance issues (ESG) in investee companies. Principle 2 of the UN PRI indicates that active ownership including engagement capabilities and voting actions can achieve better portfolio performance and may lead to a closer alignment between investor objectives and *broader societal objectives*. Curbing excessive executive remuneration might be one such broader societal objective, although the UN PRI itself does not identify clearly what these broader societal objectives are or might be. An indication of the types of "broader societal issues" can be inferred from the ESG issues addressed in the engagement initiatives of UN PRI signatories either directly or through their service providers in 2009. "Benefits and compensation" is one of thirteen categories identified in the self-reporting survey of signatories, but ranks behind labor issues, environment, governance, and climate change as an issue of concern.[53] The mission of the UNEP itself is "to provide leadership and encourage partnership in caring for the *environment*" while the UNEPFI has as its mission "to identify, promote and realise the adoption of best *environmental and sustainability practice* at all levels of financial institution operations."[54] In other words, based on the pattern of signatories' behaviors and mission statements of the UNEP and UNEPFI, the key broader societal objectives of interest are those linked with the environment. It is difficult to see the explicit link between executive remuneration and these societal objectives.

However, the institutional investors undertaking these activities argue they are doing so to fulfil the fiduciary responsibilities imposed by law, not necessarily to achieve particular social ends or social benefits.[55] The pursuit of high standards of governance in investee companies is part of a fiduciary responsibility that is defined to include a responsibility *to generate sustainable and growing value for beneficiaries.*[56] Furthermore, it has recently been suggested (in Australia at least) that government cannot use the superannuation system to achieve other policy objectives.[57] The decisions to undertake engagement and voting activities made by individual fund managers and by pension and superannuation trustees are to achieve their differing goals, not societal goals. Hence there is an immediate disconnect between the government policy goals behind introducing a say on pay (accountable boards of directors that make "better" remuneration decisions, where "better" equates with "not excessive" levels of remuneration) and the reasons institutional investors undertake engagement and voting activities (to increase shareholder value).

Additionally, the ICGN and UN PRI guidelines are both self-regulatory initiatives.[58] A global regulatory initiative such as the UN PRI is said to result from actor design: "mechanisms are used by actors either unilaterally or in cooperation with others *in order to achieve their goals and plans.*"[59] Yet within the broad umbrella group defined as "institutional investors," there are differences between the goals of fund managers and pension and superannuation fund trustees. Fund managers' goals are centered on attracting funds for investment from pension and superannuation trustees and profiting from the receipt of fees. By becoming a signatory to the UN PRI, fund managers are seeking to attract funds from those clients who themselves are responding to "external pressures" to adopt these guidelines. The pension and superannuation trustee signatories may have different goals and plans from those of fund manager signatories. A superannuation fund will be more concerned about ensuring the future lifestyles of members.[60]

In other words, the tension between the short-term horizon of fund managers (whose performance is typically reported on a quarterly basis) and the long-term horizon required by pension and superannuation funds is likely reflected in a differing view of which ESG issues are of most concern. If institutional shareholders seek to achieve better investment terms over a particular time frame, it is likely that any engagement and monitoring efforts will focus on the issues they believe contribute to and, conversely, detract from the achievement of this aim. The level of ongoing interest in executive remuneration that is needed to make a say on pay work cannot be guaranteed if institutional investors do not truly believe that it either contributes to or detracts from the achievement of good investment returns.

Furthermore, there does not appear to be a public interest group that has set its agenda *exclusively* on changing executive remuneration practices. Public interest groups can position themselves to exert influence over institutional investors as the regulated and governments as the regulator to force regulation that responds to the public interest groups' agenda.[61] The most likely activists in this regard are unions. In the U.S., the American Federation of Labor–Congress of Industrial Organizations (AFL-CIO) has for many years published an analysis of executive pay practices.[62] A say on pay fits the social agenda of these unions and like organizations, although it is not their primary social objective.[63] While the say on pay creates the opportunity for voice, it leaves the role of institutional shareholders to develop statements of good remuneration practice intact. Union and other organizations interested in the levels of executive remuneration should step back and consider whether their social objectives are aligned with institutional investors' statements of good remuneration practice.

To summarize the above: there is an expectation that institutional investors will be both active and responsible investors, although being active on executive remuneration issues—a subset of the "G" in ESG—is likely to be a lower engagement priority than engagement on environmental, social, and broader corporate governance issues.

Willing and Able "Gatekeepers"?

Coffee's work on gatekeepers notes:

> Put simply, one cannot be a credible gatekeeper without significant reputational capital. Because new entrants typically lack such capital,

they thus face a high barrier to entry. This, in turn, implies a tendency for such markets to be concentrated and even oligopolistic in character. . . . In such a concentrated market, *gatekeepers can collude, or at least engage in consciously parallel behaviour*, that subordinates the protection of reputational capital to other goals. *Rather than compete to enhance their reputations, they may quietly permit their reputations to become noisy and indistinct*, so long as entry to new firms into the market is restricted.[64] (Emphasis added)

What "reputational capital" is at stake for institutional investors to motivate them to undertake the role of executive remuneration gatekeeper? It is difficult to know what, if any, aspects of remuneration matter to the investment decision.[65] While pension and superannuation funds may set out guidelines for remuneration or adopt the statements issued by their representative organization (such as the National Association of Pension Funds [NAPF] or Australian Council of Superannuation Investors [ACSI]), it is not clear that they necessarily drive the voting decision or any decision to engage on remuneration. It is not clear which aspects of executive remuneration will tip the report from a vote for to a vote against. Members of pension/superannuation funds are not able to easily monitor the engagement and voting performance of institutional investors on remuneration issues because of a lack of access to disclosure of the voting and engagement records of the fund managers. Furthermore, the reluctance of beneficiaries to switch their investments to a different pension/superannuation fund[66] that has a beneficiary-preferred position on executive remuneration means little market pressure exists to encourage institutional investors to become active rule makers and engaged shareholders on executive remuneration issues. The role of gatekeeper of executive remuneration practices might actually be played by proxy advisers,[67] yet even this is unclear. Typically the decision to engage a proxy adviser is a decision to outsource the task of reviewing the remuneration report and making a recommendation. Therefore the responsibilities for monitoring still rest with institutional investors. *Monitoring* is also rather different from *a policing function* that has been associated with the task of gatekeeping.[68]

Comparing the role and regulation of auditors, a recognized gatekeeper, with that of institutional investors highlights the fundamental problem in seeking to formally assign the role of executive remuneration practice gatekeeper to institutional investors. It is not their primary purpose or raison d'être. Unlike auditors who are appointed by a company and owe duties to a company to undertake the audit of the financial statements and report to the company on their findings, institutional investors become associated with the company via the investment decision and do so for expected financial gain for their beneficial owners. That is, the purpose of institutional investors is primarily to invest, which may involve some monitoring activities; whereas the purpose of auditors *is* to "gatekeep" by auditing a company's financial accounts and records and producing a report. While both auditors and institutional investors are subject to a level of government regulation, the purpose of regulating audit is different from the purpose of regulating fund managers and pension/superannuation funds. Davies notes the purposes of audit regulation include regulating the auditing process (for example, how to conduct a sampling process to verify the underlying transactions reported in the financial statements).[69] The situation with institutional investors is more complex. While a license is typically required, and the activities may be also subject to conduct and disclosure regulation and/or prudential supervision,[70] such regulation is not strictly about the process of investment (for example, how to select companies to invest in or the proportion of investment that should be made in each company).

Willing Gatekeepers?

Even if institutional investors could be anointed as the gatekeepers of executive remuneration practices in investee companies, they may be unwilling to undertake this role in the way government might wish. Governments and the broader community are concerned about the overall levels of executive remuneration: these levels are not invariably of concern to institutional shareholders themselves. This does not mean that institutional investors are totally unconcerned about the levels of executive remuneration. Institutional shareholders appear concerned about excessive termination payments that reward failure, but not necessarily when the payment is for a successful executive upon retirement or resignation, or when an annual bonus payment reflects a good year of performance. In other words, the expectation for institutional investors *to do something* to hold boards of directors accountable for the level of remuneration payments[71] is unrealistic.

This is confirmed by institutional investor guidelines for executive remuneration. The reward-for-failure concern is reflected in detailed provisions on termination payments.[72] In a sense this is an easy position for shareholders to adopt: a contractual term is either for twelve months or it is for some other period; the unvested share-based incentives either lapse on termination or they do not. As the disclosure of termination payments can be delayed by up to fifteen months after the executive has left, the time to influence what should happen has long passed. Issues about the overall size of executive remuneration payments or "distributive justice," that is, how fair executive remuneration payments are when compared to ordinary workers' wages,[73] are not reflected in institutional investor guidelines.

Able Gatekeepers?

Shareholders seem better equipped to monitor simple remuneration aspects and enforce compliance with these requirements[74] than a more nuanced concept of pay reflecting performance. However, given the lead time in executive remuneration decision making where a long-term incentive plan has a three-year period before paying out, poor remuneration outcomes today reflect the policies and decisions taken over the previous one to three years. Particularly with long-term incentive schemes, it is difficult for shareholders to know how much the scheme will pay out in the future, even though the performance criteria are clearly identified (and meet shareholders' specific requirements) and the number of performance awards initially allocated and potentially available is known. If short-term incentive schemes are poorly disclosed (as they typically are),[75] it is difficult for shareholders to know how much short-term incentive pay is appropriate for the performance criteria set. It is difficult to assess whether the performance criteria are indeed valid, as companies hide behind "commercial-in-confidence" disclosure carve-outs in legislation, even for disclosure expost.

However, even when disclosure fully complies with the legislative requirements, shareholders may be unable to understand the disclosures and identify, in advance, those policies that are likely to lead to egregious future payments. Two remuneration decisions that attracted widespread condemnation in 2009 (Royal Bank of Scotland PLC in the U.K. and Qantas Airways Ltd. in Australia) illustrate the problems shareholders encounter in interpreting remuneration disclosures. Both instances confirm the importance of monitoring executive remuneration over a longer time frame than simply the year-to-year comparison that attracts proxy adviser and media attention.

Royal Bank of Scotland PLC

There was widespread condemnation in 2009 of the accumulated "pension pot" of £16 million to be paid to Sir Fred Goodwin on his early retirement from the bank, following its partial nationalization the previous year and the posting of a record loss of £24 billion. Reviewing the annual reports for 2006 and 2007 confirms that the pension benefits were disclosed in the annual accounts as required, and that both the accrued entitlement per annum plus a transfer value were disclosed. For the year to December 31, 2007, the relevant accrued entitlement (the estimated annual pension) was £579,000 per annum (transfer value of £8.37 million), up from the 2006 accrued entitlement of £510,000 (with a transfer value of £7.043 million).[76] The difference in the 2008 accrued entitlement of £693,000 per annum (and the associated transfer value of £16.63 million)[77] is that by the time the 2008 accounts were released, Sir Fred's employment had ceased and a definite value could be attributed in the accounts for this benefit. How did shareholders miss the fact that Sir Fred's pension benefits, irrespective of when he retired, were going to be sizable? An *annual* pension payment of £579,000 as disclosed in 2007 seems incredibly generous. Did shareholders in early 2008 not care about this issue? Or did they simply not understand how to interpret the pension information the company disclosed?

Granted, it is difficult to see the relationship between annual remuneration (something that institutional investors and proxy advisers might examine) and the potential pension payment that can be made in a defined-benefits scheme. Table 6.2 sets out actuarial estimations of the annual contributions toward executive directors' pensions made by FTSE 100 companies, expressed as a percentage of base salary.[78]

While contributions by the company to the executives' defined-contribution scheme contributions are clear from the remuneration disclosures, contributions toward a defined-benefit pension scheme (such as Sir Fred's) are not. Shareholders might be making assessments on the size of the annual executive remuneration and the termination provisions in a contract, without appreciating the potential size of the pension payments and the importance of assessing all the benefits payable on termination. This perhaps explains the surprise when the time arrived to quantify Sir Fred's pension payment: until then, it might have simply escaped shareholder attention. Shareholders may have taken a different view of Sir Fred's annual

Table 6.2: Estimates of Pension as a Percentage of Annual Salary: FTSE 100

	Defined-Benefit Pension Schemes Value of Contribution as a Percentage of Base Salary			Defined-Contribution Pension Schemes Value of Contribution as a Percentage of Base Salary		
	Lower quartile (%)	Median (%)	Upper quartile (%)	Lower quartile (%)	Median (%)	Upper quartile (%)
2003	27	42	**63**	15	28	40
2004	18	30	**40**	15	31	40
2005	30	43	**70**	15	29	39
2006	30	43	**67**	20	25	39
2007	37	51	**70**	20	26	35

fixed remuneration of £1.2 million in 2006, and £1.3 million in 2007 (annual pension of £579,000) had they truly appreciated the extent of the pension benefits that were also "fixed" in the sense of being unrelated to performance, and the size of contribution the company would need to make to fund this level of benefit.

Qantas Airways Ltd.

Even quite simple and straightforward disclosures can be overlooked when analyzing a company's remuneration policies. In 2009, the media expressed dismay[79] that Geoff Dixon, the retiring CEO of Qantas, received $11.5 million for the financial year ended June 30, 2009 (for nine months of this twelve-month period), including $3 million in compensation for an unfavorable and retrospective change in superannuation legislation.[80] Yet shareholders should not have been surprised about this payment, given previous disclosures made in respect of Dixon's remuneration. The 2005 annual report revealed that Dixon had generous end-of-service payments of 37.2 months' fixed annual remuneration plus $500,000, an amount equal to *$7.2 million* (based on his 2005 fixed annual remuneration of $2.16 million).[81] In 2006 these arrangements were amended when Dixon signed a new employment contract. The 2006 disclosures showed that Dixon received a payment of *$7.6 million* on signing his new contract, to be taken as a superannuation contribution.[82] Given that his fixed annual remuneration increased to $2.3 million in January 2006, the $7.6 million is roughly equivalent to the 37.2 months' fixed annual remuneration plus $500,000. In other words, the termination benefit in the 2005 annual report morphed into a superannuation contribution in the 2006 annual report.

It might be expected that shareholders identified the change of policy in 2006 and responded to it via the advisory vote. The proxy results suggest otherwise and confirm that support for the Qantas remuneration report waned only in 2008, not earlier when the original change of policy in respect to Dixon's termination payments was disclosed. The vote in favor of the remuneration report was 98 percent in 2005, 2006, and 2007; the vote in 2008 was only 59 percent in favor.[83] Even then, RiskMetrics recommended a vote against the Qantas remuneration report in 2008 on a different issue (pay for performance concerns).[84] Where were shareholders' questions about the changes made in 2006? Australian law does not require disclosure of the full service agreement; thus it is not possible to know whether Qantas had previously agreed to make additional payments to Dixon in the event of negative tax treatment, although this practice has been observed in other companies.[85] It was a reasonable question to ask in 2006; posing this question in 2009 was too late.

Conclusion

These two case examples indicate that institutional shareholders with an advisory vote on remuneration are not necessarily able keepers of executive remuneration practices because they appear to overlook certain disclosures in choosing to focus on others, and hence miss the overall picture. That shareholders miss what their own guidance flags as important (both of these examples relate to payments made on termination) not only calls into question the ability of shareholders to take on the role of gatekeeper of investee company practices for broader social concerns. It also suggests that expecting shareholders to undertake this role is a misjudgment. This relates to the reputational capital for institutional investors as gatekeepers for listed company executive remuneration practices. Are institutional investors competing for funds based on their reputation as governance monitors and gatekeepers or on their investment performance capabilities, which include governance monitoring and gatekeeping? Are institutional investors—fund managers and pension/superannuation funds—clear about their activities in these areas, or do they allow their reputation in these areas to become noisy and indistinct, so that it is not possible to assess who is a good gatekeeper of executive remuneration and corporate governance practices and who is not? The relevant regulatory mechanisms to ensure institutional investors play their role in the regulatory framework are not clear[86] or, in the case of investment mandates issued by pension and superannuation fund trustees to fund managers, not public. At the time of writing, both the Stewardship Code in the U.K. and how the Financial Reporting Council will monitor its uptake remain unresolved.[87] While the need for some form of external monitoring of the engagement and voting activities of institutional investors is acknowledged, only time will tell whether this initiative will prove effective.

Alternative Models of Regulation

If shareholders are unable or unwilling to undertake the three key roles assigned to them in the regulated remuneration cycle noted above, but the public interest demands that someone monitor executive remuneration and enforce good remuneration practices, some alternative form of regulation, with a greater level of government involvement, is necessary. One example of an alternative model to the regulatory framework outlined above can be found in the recent approaches of various governments in adopting the Financial Stability Board's *Principles for Sound Compensation Practices.*

Prudential Supervision

In the U.K. and Australia, prudential regulators will from 2010 undertake monitoring of remuneration practices within financial institutions under their supervision. The content of the Australian Prudential Regulatory Authority (APRA) Governance Standard and the Financial Services Authority's (FSA) Remuneration Code provides a set of rules around remuneration practice, but sets different disclosure requirements from those found in the corporate law for remuneration reports. Both sets of rules have the flexibility to demand additional disclosures, whereas institutional investors are not able to command better disclosures than the company law itself requires. The enforcement strategies open to these regulators will include the ability to penalize breaches of the relevant remuneration standards;[88] institutional investors can only penalize a "breach" of their remuneration standards by voting against the remuneration report. Hence, as regulators,

APRA and the FSA have different sanctions with legal backing they can deploy when compared with institutional investors.

Consider an authorized deposit-taking institution (e.g., a savings bank) regulated by APRA as an example; its board will have to attest annually to the procedures, controls, and oversight that exist to ensure the remuneration requirements under *Prudential Standard APS 510—Governance* are complied with as part of the annual risk management declaration. Should the bank fail to comply with the prudential standards (which include the remuneration provisions),[89] APRA can issue a direction to comply with the standard. Failure to follow the direction constitutes an offense.[90] In the U.K., breach of the remuneration code principles in the *Senior Management Arrangements, Systems and Controls Sourcebook* issued by the FSA is evidence of noncompliance with the general requirement to establish, implement, and maintain remuneration policies, procedures, and practices that are consistent with and promote effective risk management, required under the relevant FSA handbook.[91] Furthermore, the FSA has advised it will factor remuneration risk into its risk-assessment process and other supervisory programs.[92]

Thus it is clear these types of initiatives create incentives to comply with the relevant guidance. Moreover, in the first instance, APRA and the FSA are likely to deploy engagement strategies in an effort to achieve voluntary compliance with the relevant guidelines rather than resort to more formal mechanisms, consistent with their style of supervision.[93] Given uncertainty as to how various firms will respond to the new requirements, together with the inexperience of prudential regulators in monitoring remuneration, a period of adjustment is necessary. It may take some time to tweak the various disclosure requirements to ensure they receive appropriate information.

A model of this regulated remuneration cycle is shown in Figure 6.3. This regulatory framework largely resembles the regulated remuneration cycle shown in Figure 6.1, except that engagement might be optional and enforcement is by exception only. Engagement on remuneration practices in listed companies now appears to be happening in the U.K. and Australia as a matter of course, even if only with key institutional shareholders and notwithstanding some evidence of remuneration committees seizing the upper hand and setting the agenda. Additionally, voting on the remuneration report happens annually as a matter of course. For the cycle in Figure 6.3, enforcement may occur after a second cycle of practice and disclosure/

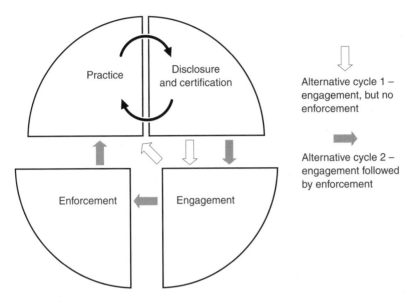

Figure 6.3. The Regulated Remuneration Cycle

certification, rather than on the initial cycle, where regulators are likely to try persuasion to encourage compliance.

Notably, these reforms do not seek to limit what is paid,[94] but how it is paid. Therefore the quantum issue that has persisted with a shareholder-focused regulatory framework is likely to persist with these frameworks, notwithstanding statements that suggest it should not do so.[95]

Conclusion

In say on pay jurisdictions such as Australia and the U.K., institutional shareholders are the primary rule makers and enforcers of good executive remuneration practices in listed companies. With evidence from the global financial crisis of poor remuneration practices in many listed financial institutions, it is clear that institutional shareholders cannot shift the blame for poor remuneration practices onto remuneration committees alone. Furthermore, government intervention into setting standards for remuneration practice has not really occurred, despite policy pronouncements that it might. Thus institutional investors are the gatekeepers for executive remuneration in listed companies. It is not clear that institutional investors necessarily accept this role, despite statements of intent in relevant principles. In part this is a definitional issue: are shareholders really gatekeepers in the sense commonly understood? The shareholder's relationship to the company is ownership, not merely contractual, such as an auditor's contractual relationship to provide a service for reward. It is also clear that the reason for appointing an institutional shareholder (either a fund manager or a pension/superannuation fund) to undertake the investment is primarily to achieve financial benefits.

More significantly, there appears to be a gap between what governments want executive remuneration to look like (not excessive, especially not in the current economic climate) and what shareholders are able to monitor effectively via ex ante disclosures, engagement, and ex post voting on the practices disclosed. Shareholders' own statements of preferred remuneration practices are not specific on the size of remuneration payments that are acceptable, given good firm performance, only specific on the size of the payment when performance is so poor that the executive's employment has been terminated. Are institutional shareholders unable or unwilling to say to successful companies, "Actually, that's too much"?

These great expectations of institutional investor interest in, and active monitoring of, executive remuneration in listed companies might not lead to better remuneration practices if the expectations remain unfulfilled. Before any further initiatives are contemplated, consideration should be given to whether institutional investors are truly ready, willing, and able rule makers and enforcers, if not gatekeepers, of good executive remuneration practices in listed companies.

Appendices

Table 6.3: Regulatory Framework for Executive Remuneration Practice: United Kingdom

Aspect of Practice	Regulator					
	Legislature	Securities Regulator (FSA)	Market Exchange Operator (FSA)	Business Interest Groups	Institutional Investors	Proxy Advisers
RemCo exists			CG code (C/E)	Practice statement (V)	Practice guidance (V) Voting guidance (V)	
Structure of RemCo			CG code (C/E)		Practice guidance (V) Voting guidance (V)	
Tasks or activities			CG code (C/E)		Practice guidance (V)	
Use of remuneration consultants			CG code (C/E)		Practice guidance (V)	
Remuneration policy			CG code (C/E)		Practice guidance (V)	Voting guidance (V)
Remuneration contract				Practice statement (V)	Practice guidance (V) Voting guidance (V)	
Base pay					Practice guidance (V) Voting guidance (V)	
Annual bonus/ short-term incentives			CG code (C/E)		Practice guidance (V) Voting guidance (V)	
Long-term incentive schemes			CG code (C/E)		Practice guidance (V) Voting guidance (V)	
Share-based remuneration	Listing Rules (M)		CG code (C/E)		Practice guidance (V) Voting guidance (V)	

Table 6.3: (Continued)

| | | | | Regulator | | |
Aspect of Practice	Legislature	Securities Regulator (FSA)	Market Exchange Operator (FSA)	Business Interest Groups	Institutional Investors	Proxy Advisers
Performance criteria			CG code (C/E)		Practice guidance (V) Voting guidance (V)	
Pension	Pension laws (M) Taxation laws (M)		CG code (C/E)		Practice guidance (V)	
Termination provisions	Company law (M)				Practice guidance (V) Voting guidance (V)	
Share holdings			CG code (C/E)		Practice guidance (V)	Voting guidance (V)
Share transactions		Listing Rules (M)		Practice statement (V)		
Loans	Company law (M)					

Key to codes used in this table: FSA = Financial Services Authority (U.K.); RemCo = Remuneration committee; CG code = *The Combined Code*; C/E = comply or explain noncompliance (compliance with the guideline is voluntary but the company must disclose whether it complies or else explain in its disclosure why it does not comply with the guideline); Practice statement = business interest group practice statement; V = voluntary; Practice guidance = shareholder practice guidance; Voting guidance = guidance to shareholders on what voting response particular remuneration practices will attract; it can be issued either by a proxy adviser (the main source) or by an institutional investor; M = mandatory.

Table 6.4: Regulatory Framework for Executive Remuneration Practice: Australia

Aspect of Practice	Legislature	Securities Regulator (ASIC)	Market Exchange Operator (ASX)	Regulator — Business Interest Groups	Institutional Investors	Proxy Advisers
RemCo			CG code (INWN)	Practice statement (V)	Practice guidance (V)	
Structure			CG code (INWN)	Practice statement (V)	Practice guidance (V)	Voting guidance (V)
Tasks or activities			CG code (INWN)	Practice statement (V)	Practice guidance (V)	
Use of remuneration consultants			CG code (INWN)	Practice statement (V)	Practice guidance (V)	
Remuneration policy			CG code (INWN)	Practice statement (V)	Practice guidance (V)	Voting guidance (V)
Remuneration contract			CG code (INWN)	Practice statement (V)	Practice guidance (V)	
Base pay			CG code (INWN)		Practice guidance (V)	
Annual bonus/short-term incentives			CG code (INWN)		Practice guidance (V)	

Table 6.4: (Continued)

		Regulator				
Aspect of Practice	Legislature	Securities Regulator (ASIC)	Market Exchange Operator (ASX)	Business Interest Groups	Institutional Investors	Proxy Advisers
Long-term incentive schemes			CG code (INWN)		Practice guidance (V)	Voting guidance (V) Practice guidance (V)
Share-based remuneration			CG code (INWN) Listing Rules (M)	Practice statement (V)	Practice guidance (V)	Voting guidance (V) Practice guidance (V)
Performance criteria			CG code (INWN)	Practice statement (V)	Practice guidance (V)	Practice guidance (V)
Superannuation	Superannuation laws (M) Taxation laws (M)					
Termination provisions	Company law (M)		CG code (INWN) Listing rules (M)	Practice statement (V)	Practice guidance (V)	

Share holdings				Practice guidance (V)	Practice guidance (V)
Share transactions		CG code (INWN)			
Loans	Company law (M)		Practice statement (V)	Practice guidance (V)	Practice guidance (V)
Margin loans		CG code (INWN)		Practice guidance (V)	
Hedging positions		CG code (INWN)		Practice guidance (V)	

Notes: Key to codes used in this table: ASIC = the Australian Investments and Securities Commission; ASX = Australian Securities Exchange; RemCo = Remuneration committee; CG code = ASX Corporate Governance Council, *Corporate Governance Principles and Recommendations*, 2nd edition (2007); INWN = if not, why not (compliance with the guideline is voluntary but the company must disclose whether it complies or else explain why it does not comply); Practice statement = business interest group practice statement (issued by the Australian Institute of Company Directors, the Business Council of Australia, or the Chartered Secretaries Association); V = voluntary; Practice guidance = shareholder practice guidance (for example, that issued by the Australian Council of Superannuation Investors Inc., or by the Investment and Financial Services Association); Voting guidance = proxy adviser voting guidance (for example, that issued by RiskMetrics [Australia] Pty. Ltd.).; M = mandatory.

Chapter 7

Against Stupidity, the Gods Themselves Contend in Vain: The Limits of Corporate Governance in Dealing with Asset Bubbles

Bruce Dravis

Introduction

Existing laws on governance are aimed at preventing managers from abusing the resources that investors have committed to business institutions, by requiring corporate processes intended to detect and prevent misuse of those resources. The law does not require managers to maximize corporate resources. The law does not, and cannot, dictate outcomes of management decisions. The law does not, and, for the policy reasons discussed in the extensive case law precedents on the business judgment rule, should not, make managers guarantors of results.

But to investors who lost billions of dollars in the 2007–2008 financial crisis resulting from the sudden deflation of real estate prices, and to citizens who saw public wealth used to bail out failed companies, it is cold comfort to be told that the corporate managers did not abuse their positions and observed proper process. Investors who saw average portfolio declines of nearly 40 percent in 2008 would not have been arguing that the process was adequate to protect their interests.

Just two companies—American International Group (AIG) and Citigroup, Inc.—accounted for approximately $800 billion of market capitalization losses and government bailouts. In the case of AIG, the market capitalization decline between January 1, 2008, and the end of the first quarter of 2009 was approximately $140 billion, and it had accepted $182.5 billion of additional government bailout funds.[1] In the case of Citigroup, there was a market capitalization loss of roughly $140 billion[2] over the same period, and Citigroup took $45 billion of government investment under the Troubled Asset Relief Program (TARP) as well as an additional government guarantee of $300 billion on certain toxic assets.[3]

In the wake of the financial crisis, some commentators and policymakers suggested that a corporate governance failure was to blame for the financial crisis.[4] Various governance changes relating to corporate evaluation of risk have been advanced (e.g., risk committees),[5] and enacted into law (Emergency Economic Stabilization Act [EESA] and the The Dodd-Frank Wall Street Reform and Consumer Protection Act [Dodd-Frank][6] and SEC rules on disclosing the relation of compensation to risk).[7]

This chapter posits that:

(a) the nature of asset bubbles is that holders of the "bubbled" assets bear risk, regardless of whether those parties actively contribute to forming the bubble, and regardless of the strategy adopted to deal with the bubble;

(b) the goal of corporate law is rightfully to protect directors who undertake proper processes, and not to make directors guarantors of results; and

(c) any rational response to an asset bubble by a corporate board using proper process will be protected, whether the response generates gains or losses to the company;

therefore,

(1) improved corporate process might affect an individual company's outcomes, but should not be relied upon to prevent the formation of asset bubbles; and

(2) prevention of asset bubbles requires regulation of the market environment, rather than regulation of the motivations of the players in the market.

This chapter is intended as a response to the reflexive reactions that improvements to governance processes will prevent future asset bubbles, but it does not attempt a mathematical or case history proof of its conclusions. The examples of Citigroup and AIG presented in the chapter are intended to be illustrative of the complex factual situations facing corporate boards assessing risk and facing judges reviewing the actions of corporate decision makers after the fact.

The "Business Judgment Rule" Is Not the "Good Judgment Rule"

The failures of 2008 notwithstanding, American capitalism has a historic record of producing individual and social wealth on a scale unrivalled by any other nation. No small part of that record can be attributed to the flexibility and freedom provided by the laws relating to the control of private enterprise, and the allocation of rights and powers, and remedies, among investors, boards of directors, and management.

In her 1995 book *Ownership and Control*, Vanderbilt University law professor Margaret Blair aptly and succinctly summarized the context in which an evaluation of corporate governance must take place: "Corporations are legal devices for assembling and organizing capital, labor, and other resources to produce and sell goods and services. . . . The central problem in any corporate governance system is how to make corporate executives accountable to the other contributors to the enterprise whose investments are at risk, while still giving those executives the freedom, the incentive, and the control over resources they need to create and seize investment opportunities and to be tough competitors."[8]

Investors who put resources into the control of managers and boards of directors want the law to protect them from management abuse. Directors and managers want the law to protect them from being personally liable if a business strategy fails, notwithstanding their informed and good faith efforts.

Corporate governance is primarily state law, although increasingly it is becoming federalized, at least with respect to publicly traded corporations.[9] The leading state law on corporate governance is the law of Delaware. Case law developed by the Delaware Chancery Court and Supreme Court consistently reflects a high level of thoughtfulness regarding the policy implications of judicial decisions.

The key doctrines in Delaware corporate law relate to the duties of directors as fiduciaries, and the protection of directors under the "business judgment" rule. The essence of the business judgment rule is that directors can be liable for business decisions that are not made in a considered and unbiased fashion, but not on the basis of the contents of that decision.

What should be understood, but may not widely be understood by courts or commentators who are not often required to face such questions, is that compliance with a director's duty of care can never appropriately be judicially determined by reference to *the content of the board decision* that leads to a corporate loss, apart from consideration of the good faith *or* rationality of the process employed. That is, whether a judge or jury considering the matter after the fact, believes a decision substantively wrong, or degrees of wrong extending through "stupid" to "egregious" or "irrational", provides no ground for director liability, so long as the court determines that the process employed was either rational or employed in *a good faith* effort to advance corporate interests. To employ a different rule—one that permitted an "objective" evaluation of the decision—would expose directors to substantive second guessing by ill-equipped judges or juries, which would, in the long-run, be injurious to investor interests. Thus, the business judgment rule is process oriented and informed by a deep respect for all *good faith* board decisions.[10]

The business judgment rule reflects a recognition that business entails risk, and a board that feared liability would be averse to taking even reasonable risks—even for ventures that would be highly profitable to the company.

It is almost impossible for a court, in hindsight, to determine whether the directors of a company properly evaluated risk and thus made the "right" business decision. In any investment there is a chance that returns will turn out lower than expected, and generally a smaller chance that they will be far lower than expected. When investments turn out poorly, it is possible that the decision-maker evaluated the deal correctly but got "unlucky" in that a huge loss—the probability of which was very small—actually happened. It is also possible that the decision-maker improperly evaluated the risk posed by an investment and that the company suffered large losses as a result.[11]

It also recognizes that a legal system that permitted review of the content of business decisions could unfairly subject directors to "hindsight bias"—the tendency "for people with knowledge of an outcome to exaggerate the extent to which they believe that outcome could have been predicted" or controlled.[12] "There is a substantial risk that suing shareholders and reviewing judges will be unable to distinguish between competent and negligent management because bad outcomes often will be regarded, ex post, as having been foreseeable and, therefore, preventable ex ante. If liability results from bad outcomes, without regard to the ex ante quality of the decision or the decision-making process, however, managers will be discouraged from taking risks."[13]

As a matter of Delaware law, the business judgment rule "is a presumption that in making a business decision the directors of a corporation acted on an informed basis, in good faith and in the honest belief that the action taken was in the best interests of the company."[14]

Litigants challenging the directors' decision must rebut this presumption by showing that the decision was tainted by self-interest or disloyalty to the corporation, or that the board decision was not "the product of a rational process [in which] the directors availed themselves of all material and reasonably available information."[15]

Under a line of cases commencing with *In re Caremark* the Delaware courts have also considered the question of potential director liability for a failure to monitor liability-creating activities of management.

> *Caremark* articulates the necessary conditions predicate for director oversight liability: (a) the directors utterly failed to implement any reporting or information system or controls; *or* (b) having implemented such a system or controls, consciously failed to monitor or oversee its operations thus disabling themselves from being informed of risks or problems requiring their attention. In either case, imposition of liability requires a showing that the directors knew that they were not discharging their fiduciary obligations. Where directors fail to act in the face of a known duty to act, thereby demonstrating a conscious disregard for their responsibilities, they breach their duty of loyalty by failing to discharge that fiduciary obligation in good faith.[16]

While directors of Delaware corporations have a duty to implement and monitor a system of oversight, that obligation does not eviscerate the core protections of the business judgment rule. "Accordingly, the burden required for a plaintiff to rebut the presumption of the business judgment rule by showing gross negligence is a difficult one, and the burden to show bad faith is even higher."[17]

In sum, because Delaware courts do not want to create timid, risk-fearing boards or subject directors to unfair hindsight judgments, they do not (1) second-guess good faith and informed business decisions of boards or (2) hold directors liable for failing to oversee employees, absent compelling facts showing that directors failed to establish controls over employees, or consciously ignored risks or problems.

Within that legal framework, boards and managers must make real-time decisions, based on the information that they are able to develop, on behalf of companies that find themselves dealing with the development and ultimate crash of an asset bubble, such as the real estate bubble that preceded the 2008 financial crisis.

Following the discussion below on the historically predictable course taken by asset bubbles—from formation to exuberance to crash—this chapter offers the illustration of the actions of the directors and managers of Citigroup and AIG that resulted in the tremendous losses in the financial crisis.

The Rational, Self-Maximizing Bubble

> Against stupidity, the very Gods Themselves contend in vain.
> —Friedrich Schiller, quoted by John Kenneth Galbraith in *A Short History of Financial Euphoria*[18]

The story of the financial crisis is one of "intelligent businessmen rationally responding to their environment yet by doing so creating the preconditions for a terrible crash."[19] In the wake of the financial crisis, Alan Greenspan noted that he was surprised that the executives in the financial institutions did not, in accordance with the free market, moderate their appetite for risk. As he acknowledged in testimony before the House Committee on Oversight and Government Reform in October 2008, "Those of us who have looked to the self-interest of lending institutions to protect shareholders' equity, myself included, are in a state of shocked disbelief."[20]

This apostasy by one of the greatest adherents of the free market was not singular. Another advocate of limits on market regulation, Judge Richard Posner, observed following the financial crisis that the "economists and eventually the politicians who pressed for deregulation [of the financial industry] were not sensitive to the fact that deregulating banking has a macroeconomic significance that deregulating railroads or trucking or airlines or telecommunications or oil pipelines does not"[21] and that the financial fallout from the crisis "is the result of normal business activity in a laissez faire economic regime. . . . Bankers and consumers alike seem on the whole to have been acting in conformity with their rational self-interest throughout the period that saw the increase in risky banking practices, the swelling and bursting of the housing bubble and a reduction in the rate of personal savings combined with an increase in the riskiness of those savings."[22]

Galbraith observes that financial bubbles—the inflation of valuations of an asset class, followed inevitably by a crash—are with us forever, in forms that we never recognize until after the fact.[23] History offers no shortage of examples: tulips in seventeenth-century Holland, radio stocks in the 1920s, real estate in the 1980s, dot-com stocks in the 1990s, or real estate in the 2000s, to name a few.

As the price of an asset class is bid up, there are two types of participants—those who truly believe that a new paradigm has been established and that the asset bidding-up process represents a fundamental store of value, with assets that can be purchased today and be worth more tomorrow, and the speculators who want to take the ride up and optimistically believe that they can get off before the crash.

The crash at the end of the bubble is another inevitable feature of financial bubbles. After the top has been reached and prices begin to decline, speculators and true believers alike rush for the exits, generating a surplus of sellers and precipitous price declines.

Another dependable feature of financial bubbles is that those who argue against the bubble are dismissed as not understanding the new forces at work in the economy, or as envious, or as enemies of the market itself. Those who benefit in the short term are getting rich, and as Galbraith observes, no one "wishes to believes that this is fortuitous or undeserved; all wish to think that it is a result of their superior insight and intuition."[24]

With respect to assessing the risks in a bubble, modeling for prediction of risk in asset bubbles is fraught with peril. Modeling economic behavior over a short time requires assuming that the near-term future will be like the near-term past, and trying to create a model that goes back to the crash of 1929 means modeling an economy in which so many variables have changed that the model is dubious. Posner identifies a different culprit where failures in risk prediction are concerned: "It was the failure to heed warning signs, and thus search out the necessary data, rather than the failure of model design, that caused the failure of prediction."[25]

Finally, even if a crash of an asset bubble market is inevitable, the timing of the crash is unknowable, and short sellers who bet against a bubble can be right on the merits, yet experience significant economic losses by betting too early.[26] Reduced to essentials, corporate decision makers dealing with an asset bubble have four basic models (with innumerable subvariations) on how to respond:

1. Go all in.

Embrace the bubble as a paradigm shift that is permanent or at least long-lasting enough to be stable, and invest resources on that basis. This behavior would capture the full gains available during the bubble period. The optimum outcome for an individual player is to be the first participant to exit, at exactly the top of the market, capturing all of the gains and suffering none of the losses. The risk in this strategy is the failure to exit the market ahead of the crash, incurring losses when the values start collapsing.[27]

2. Play cautiously.

Develop a thesis that the bubble represents a temporary change in assets values, and invest resources to capture the temporary gains, but limit participation or invest resources in risk mitigants. This response would capture gains, and limit downside risk. This approach also entails the risk that the smaller gains resulting from a smaller level of participation or the cost of risk mitigants provides a competitive advantage (near or long term) to more fully invested players. It is also possible that the mitigants adopted are insufficient to shield the company from the entire risk.[28]

3. Don't play.

This strategy involves forgoing the gains that the bubble produces over the short term. While this approach eliminates the risks of investing in inflated assets, it simultaneously results in exposing the company to the risks that its more aggressive, or reckless, competitors are able to make use of the short-term gains to drive the company out of the market, or that investors will go where returns are higher.

4. Bet against the bubble.

This strategy puts resources at risk away from the prevailing wisdom. It entails the risk that the analysis is wrong, or that the timing of the counter-investments is wrong, such that the investments go bad before the bubble bursts.[29]

All of these strategies relate to the means by which an individual company can maximize gains or minimize losses in a bubble environment.

Goldman Sachs, the investment bank, did not suffer as greatly as other major financial institutions in the crisis. It pared back its exposure to real-estate-related investments beginning in 2007.[30] Lloyd C. Blankfein, Goldman's chairman and chief executive officer, in a 2009 speech to the Council of Institutional Investors, offered his analysis of the underlying causes of the real estate and related financial bubble of the 2000s, and a relatively blunt assessment of how he saw Goldman's involvement.[31]

His analysis was that strong economic growth, low real interest rates, and huge pools of capital resulted in pressure on investors to find a successful market. Real estate drew that investment because of its historic stability, government support and subsidy for home ownership, and "flexible and varied mortgage products [that] attracted even more capital in search of higher returns." The resulting housing bubble was not confined to the United States, but involved run-ups in residential real estate in the U.K., Ireland, Spain, and France as well.

Blankfein acknowledged that Goldman, like other participants in the financial mania, made "rationalizations [to justify] the downward pricing of risk. . . . While we recognized that credit standards were historically lax, we rationalized the reasons with arguments such as: the emerging markets were more powerful, the risk mitigants were better, there was more than enough liquidity in the system. . . . We rationalized because *our self-interest in preserving and growing our market share,* as competitors, sometimes blinds us—especially when exuberance is at its peak" (emphasis added).[32]

His observation that Goldman could not preserve or grow its market share by remaining out of the irrationally exuberant market encapsulates a key challenge for investors and managers regarding financial bubbles. As Posner noted, "The most aggressive players in the financial sandbox would ramp up the riskiness of their lending or other investing, and this would increase their returns, at least in the short term. Their timid competitors would be forced to match the daring ones' strategy, or drop out of the competition."[33]

In such circumstances, participation in a financial mania is a rational, and perhaps even necessary, strategy to be adopted by an informed board of directors, acting without self-interest and with due consideration, within the protection from liability afforded by the business judgment rule.

The Citigroup and AIG Financial Crisis Litigation

Both AIG and Citigroup directors have been sued for failures of governance in connection with the financial crisis. The Citigroup case was brought in Delaware as a case based on the *Caremark* precedent. The AIG case is being conducted in federal court in New York as a securities law case, but raises factual issues relating to governance.[34]

The Citigroup case was dismissed in February 2009, in favor of the directors.[35] As of February 2010, the AIG case was ongoing, with significant battling on procedural matters, as a result of which AIG had not filed its formal answer to the initial complaint.

Citigroup

In the case of *In Re Citigroup Inc. Shareholder Derivative Litigation* (*In Re Citigroup*) shareholders claimed that the directors were liable to the corporation for losses arising from Citigroup's exposure to the subprime lending market, claiming that the directors had breached their fiduciary duties by failing to properly monitor and manage the risks in the subprime lending market.[36] The shareholders claimed that the board ignored extensive red flags warning of problems in the real estate and credit markets in the pursuit of short-term profits and at the expense of the company's long-term viability.

Citigroup had significant exposure to the subprime lending market through collateralized debt obligations (CDOs), which were repackaged pools of lower-rated securities that Citigroup created by acquiring asset-backed securities, including residential-mortgage-backed securities (RMBS). Citigroup sold rights to the cash flows from the securities in classes, or tranches, theoretically with different levels of risk and return. Some Citigroup CDOs included a "liquidity put" that permitted CDO purchasers to require Citigroup to repurchase the instruments at the original price.

The suit related to $55 billion of Citigroup subprime exposure, in the form of $11.7 billion of securities tied to subprime loans in awaiting packaging into CDOs, and $43 billion of supersenior securities, which were portions of CDOs backed in part by RMBS collateral.

From 2007 onward, these securities generated significant losses to Citigroup, and investors were repeatedly subjected to bad news:

- *October 2007*: Citigroup announced a $1.4 billion write-down of highly leveraged finance commitments, and announced that earnings were 57 percent lower than in the prior year.
- *November 2007*: Citigroup announced that it estimated additional write-downs of the $55 billion U.S. subprime-related direct exposures would be between $8 and $11 billion, and that Citigroup had provided $7.6 billion of emergency financing to the seven off-balance-sheet vehicles (structured investment vehicles, or SIVs) operated by Citigroup that had been unable to repay maturing debt.
- *December 2007*: Citigroup bailed out seven affiliated SIVs by bringing $49 billion in assets onto its balance sheet.
- *January 2008*: Citigroup announced it would take an additional $18.1 billion write-down for the fourth quarter 2007 and reduced its dividend 40 percent, to $0.32 per share.
- *March 2008*: Citigroup announced the layoff of two thousand employees, bringing to six thousand Citigroup's total layoffs since the beginning of the financial crisis.
- *July 2008*: Citigroup announced it lost $2.5 billion in the second quarter, with $7.2 billion of write-downs of mortgages and other loans.

Citigroup was not an incautious speculator caught up in the real estate mania. It had procedures and controls in place that were designed to monitor risk. It had in place an Audit and Risk Management Committee (ARM Committee), which was intended to assist the board in fulfilling its oversight responsibility relating to policy standards and guidelines for risk assessment and risk management.

The ARM Committee was tasked with (1) discussing with management and independent auditors the annual audited financial statements, (2) reviewing with management an evaluation of Citigroup's internal control structure, and (3) discussing with management Citigroup's major credit, market, liquidity, and operational risk exposures and the steps taken by management to monitor and control such exposures, including Citigroup's risk-assessment and risk-management policies. The ARM Committee met eleven times in 2006 and twelve times in 2007.

Nonetheless, the shareholders pointed to a series of publicly known events that they claim should have put management on notice that the real estate market, and the market for related investments, was in trouble. The list started with the May 27, 2005, *New York Times* column by economist Paul Krugman arguing that "America's housing market, like the stock market at the end of the last decade, is approaching the final, feverish stages of a speculative bubble." The list continued with a list of bankruptcy filings by subprime lenders through 2006 and 2007, and the 2007 rating agency downgrades of instruments secured by real estate.

The court noted that the shareholders' claim was a variation of the *Caremark* theory that a board could be liable for failure to monitor liability-creating activities of management. Rather than claiming that failure to monitor employees resulted in a violation of law, the Citigroup shareholder "*Caremark* claims are based on defendants' alleged failure to properly monitor Citigroup's *business risk*, specifically its exposure to the subprime mortgage market" (emphasis in the original).[37]

The court was having none of it. While the case was "framed by plaintiffs as *Caremark* claims, plaintiffs' theory essentially amounts to a claim that the director defendants should be personally liable to the Company because they failed to fully recognize the risk posed by subprime securities. . . . What is left appears to be plaintiff shareholders attempting to hold the director defendants personally liable for making (or allowing to be made) business decisions that, in hindsight, turned out poorly for the Company."[38]

Chiding the plaintiffs, the court noted that "to the extent the Court allows shareholder plaintiffs to succeed on a theory that a director is liable for a failure to monitor business risk, the Court risks undermining the well settled policy of Delaware law by inviting Courts to perform a hindsight evaluation of the reasonableness or prudence of directors' business decisions."[39]

The court acknowledged that Citigroup suffered large losses and that there were certain warning signs that could or should have put defendants on notice of the business risks related to Citigroup's investments in subprime assets.

The court was not willing to agree with the plaintiffs that since the board had failed to prevent the losses, the directors must have consciously ignored these warning signs or knowingly failed to monitor the company's risk. "The warning signs alleged by plaintiffs *are not evidence* that the directors consciously disregarded their duties or otherwise acted in bad faith"[40] (emphasis added). The court further noted that the plaintiffs did not allege specific acts by the directors pointing to such misconduct. In light of the multiple ARM Committee meetings, such a showing was likely impossible to make.

In dismissing the claims, the court contrasted Citigroup claims with those in the *American International Group, Inc. Consolidated Derivative Litigation*,[41] which grew out of the AIG accounting misstatements in the years 2000–2005, and not the 2008 financial crisis. That case was a better candidate for a failure-of-oversight claim, since it involved specific claims there had been "pervasive, diverse, and substantial financial fraud involving managers at the highest levels of AIG."[42]

In short, Citigroup had made overwhelmingly poor choices, but there was nothing the shareholders could do about it, at least in terms of seeking remedy from the directors.

The AIG Financial Crisis Litigation

Unlike Citigroup, AIG's primary exposure to the sub-prime market did not come from lending or from ownership of real-estate-related mortgage instruments.[43] Instead, AIG's chief exposure arose from its creation and sale of credit default swaps (CDS) in connection with CDOs. By the end of 2005, AIG had approximately $80 billion of risk based on its insurance, through the sales of CDS on CDOs in the subprime market.

The CDS were created by an AIG subsidiary, AIG Financial Products (AIGFP). AIGFP was begun in 1987 as a joint venture, established with former Drexel Burnham Lambert personnel.[44] A former Drexel employee, Joseph Cassano, became AIGFP's chief executive officer in 2001. CDS can be created with respect to various instruments, including municipal debt, corporate debt, or packaged instruments such as CDOs. Credit default swaps act like insurance policies for debt securities instruments. In exchange for premiums, the party writing the CDS agrees to pay the par value of the underlying instrument if there is a default. The value of obtaining the CDS to the debt issuer is that it can tell its investors that their investment is secure.[45] However, over time some CDS, including some written by AIG, were created between parties who were not owners of the underlying securities—in other words, such CDS (called "naked" credit default swaps) acted as a side bet on the performance of the referenced security.[46]

Through 2004, AIGFP had written 220 CDS agreements. In 2005 alone, it wrote approximately 220 CDS agreements, primarily on mortgage CDOs. By the end of 2005, however, AIGFP stopped writing CDS on mortgage securities. Cracks in the housing market were already beginning to become visible. AIG's response to its exposure to long-term downside risk in the housing market was schizophrenic. It stopped writing CDS on CDOs, but it did not hedge its exposure on the CDS it carried on its books. An AIG operation that underwrote mortgage loans stopped making loans. At the same time, AIG increased is investments in mortgage instruments in order to increase yields on cash that had been provided to AIG as collateral.

With respect to the CDS on CDOs, the firm recognized that its financial models of the CDO market no longer reflected the reality of the mortgages that had been pooled in the underlying CDO instruments because of the deterioration of the mortgage market. After leaving the mortgage CDS field at the end of 2005, AIGFP continued to write CDS on other instruments in 2006 and 2007. At the end of 2007, the aggregate notional CDS value was $527 billion, and for the year AIGFP generated profits for AIG (for 2007, AIGFP's contribution to AIG's $6.2 billion reported profit was $210 million).[47]

AIGFP's profitability was not a small matter to Cassano and other executives within AIGFP itself, whose bonuses were dependent on reported profitability. Hedging AIG's exposure to the CDS market would have meant incurring the expense of purchasing default swap coverage, reducing the profitability of AIGFP. At a minimum, there was a strong financial incentive by AIGFP management to avoid harming the profitability.

AIG was exposed to three types of financial risk to the mortgage market through the CDS and its investments in mortgage instruments. First, AIG was exposed to the risk that if there was a default under the stated terms of the CDS, it would be required to make the required payment. Second, there was an accounting risk, or valuation risk, since the CDS were themselves financial instruments carried on AIG's books at management's estimates of "fair value" under GAAP. A declining market meant that the value of the CDS would decline, putting AIG in a loss position on those instruments.

Finally, and in the end fatally, there was a liquidity risk created by the obligation to post collateral if the CDOs declined in value or if AIG's financial rating slipped. The CDS agreements provided that under certain circumstances, AIG would be required to post collateral as an assurance it would be able to perform if there was a default. Collateral would be required if the credit rating of the underlying CDO or of AIG itself declined. Even without a default, AIG was exposed to the risk that it would have to come up with billions in cash for collateral postings if the underlying CDOs declined in value in a housing market decline.

Because derivative products depend on complex mathematical models, AIGFP was originally the province of "quants," individuals with academic and mathematical backgrounds, who undertook ongoing valuations of the exposure that the instruments were creating. Cassano, who had a finance background but was not a quant, did not conduct such ongoing valuations and his handling of the accounting and financial models of AIGFP has generated substantial questions after the fact.

AIG was rocked in the early part of the decade by an accounting fraud problem that ultimately resulted in the removal of Hank Greenberg, its longtime CEO, and the payment of multimillion dollar fines and penalties to the SEC. AIGFP activities had contributed to the fraud, which involved creating artificial transactions for an AIG client to hide some of that client's financial problems. The settlement of the SEC enforcement action in 2005 required AIG to establish internal financial controls to better detect and prevent such fraud from recurring. In June 2006, AIGFP retained Joseph St. Denis, a former SEC accountant, as assistant vice president to assist in establishing and operating the financial controls system.[48]

In August 2007, Goldman Sachs made a collateral call on AIG under the terms of the CDS. St. Denis learned of the collateral call in early September 2007 and was alarmed. "I was gravely concerned about this, as the mantra at AIGFP had always been (in my experience) that there could *never* be losses on the [specific CDS]."[49] St. Denis learned that he was being deliberately excluded from AIGFP valuation discussions by Cassano. St. Denis attempted for several weeks to resolve the problem, but resigned in early October 2007, and brought the reasons for his resignation to the attention of AIG's general counsel, the chair of the audit committee, and the outside auditor.

In November 2007, the auditor warned AIG management that there were issues relating to the internal financial controls. During the fourth quarter of 2007, AIG announced that it was adjusting the valuation of its portfolios downward by about $1 billion, but after year-end announced that the proper valuation was about $4 billion even lower.

Cassanno was terminated from AIGFP in January 2008, but retained on a $1 million per month consulting agreement. By February 2008, AIG issued a statement notifying the market that the auditor had concluded AIG's financial controls were inadequate, but then filed its annual report with the SEC asserting that its valuations were sound. AIG established internal committees to evaluate risk and liquidity issues. In May 2008, AIG raised $20 billion of additional capital, to "fortify [AIG's] fortress balance sheet." AIG simultaneously declared a 10 percent increase in its dividend.

However, by June, following the news that Cassano was being investigated for fraud, the AIG board of directors removed the company's CEO, Martin Sullivan. By September, the financial situation at AIG had deteriorated to the point where it took the first installment of what was ultimately $189 billion of bailout funds from the U.S. government.

In roughly one year, AIG had gone from believing that it could contain the damage to its financial position from the real estate collapse to capitulation. At each stage of the process, management was provided with information that it used to assess and mitigate risk. It is possible to attribute the judgments made at AIG to bad faith rather than optimism that the worst of the financial crisis was past. However, assuming that AIG's board acted in good faith throughout, AIG provides an excellent test case for the policies underlying the business judgment rule.

After the fact, the failures in performance by AIG management are numerous. AIG's assumptions concerning the pricing of CDS premiums, the risk of default on CDS, valuation risk, and liquidity risk were massively wrong. In its SEC filings in the years prior to the financial crisis, AIG reported that it was exposed to no substantial risk of default "even under severe recessionary scenarios" and it repeated that claim in the form 10-K filed in February 2008, following the auditor's warnings on its financial controls.

- AIG modeled its financial exposure in the CDS based on whether the default rates in the underlying CDO pool would hit the point triggering a payment by AIG, but AIG did not model its exposure to collateral calls, or to default rates that might trigger a revaluation of the CDS on AIG's books on a fair-value basis.

- From what is currently known, it appears that Cassano was able to deliberately prevent transparency into the AIGFP operation. It is not clear whether there were failures of internal reporting that meant Cassano's actions were not brought to management's attention, or whether management knew and circumvented the internal controls in support of Cassano.

After settlement of its early 2000s accounting scandals, AIG installed, or was in the process of installing, financial controls to prevent a recurrence of the financial and operational problems that gave rise to the restatements and forced departure of Hank Greenberg. In such circumstances, one would presume that reviewing AIG's financial statements would have been akin to flying the day after an airplane crash—the level of vigilance should have been extraordinary.

AIG personnel reviewed the company's financial exposures. The failures in the economic assumptions, or the failures to recognize the potential liquidity problems in extreme financial crisis scenarios, are obvious after the fact, and yet highly intelligent, highly trained, and highly compensated personnel did not recognize them in advance. Moreover, as Goldman's Blankfein noted, all market participants were caught unawares by the illiquidity of hedging products in the financial crisis. The circumstance had not arisen before. Parties who had assumed they had taken adequate financial protections found that they had not.[50]

It is fair to ask what more the Audit Committee or the board of directors could have done. After 2005, it had replaced management, it had required the creation of improved financial controls, it had auditor attestation (prior to 2007) of the adequacy of the controls, and it had installed a former SEC accountant in a significant operational and oversight role.

Excluding the question of whether the actions of Cassano or his supervisors were culpable, which is not yet resolved, as a matter of Delaware law or the business judgment rule, it is hard to imagine that there was a failure of attention or care by the board on the basis of the facts known to date.

The Limits of Governance

The courts reviewed the performance of the board in the Citigroup massive failure, and found no culpability.[51] Additional facts may come to light about

AIG management, and whether management was culpable in causing the AIGFP risks to be either concealed or undetected. In all events, from the record generated to date it is not clear what additional processes the board could have undertaken to prevent the harm that was caused.[52]

With the benefit of hindsight, it is clear that investors would have been better served had Citigroup and AIG avoided the subprime real estate markets entirely.

Yet had they done so in a competitive environment, when money was being made at the time that the market was on the way up, it is worth considering whether the boards would have been congratulated for their foresight and wisdom in passing up the short-term profits or investors would have put cash into companies that were harvesting the short-term gains, regardless of the long-term risks.

The law is capable of protecting investors in the cases of deliberate or reckless misfeasance. But the law is a blunt instrument, as likely to create harm as benefit if it is used to dictate highly detailed requirements for the conduct of business under the assumption that all requirements fit all companies in all circumstances.

Since the time of the financial crisis, additional corporate governance legislation and regulation has been implemented or recommended, addressing such issues as proxy access, executive compensation, and the formation of risk committees.[53] These initiatives are almost certainly well intended and some of them may even be useful.

The simplicity of the term "corporate governance" belies the complexity and nuance of the rules and practices affecting the relationships among the players involved in the ownership and operation of corporations. The term can refer to the command and control of the internal corporate decision-making and reporting processes, including internal financial controls, directed by executives.[54] It can refer to the oversight and direction supplied to executives by the board of directors, and to the compensation practices of the board.[55]

It can refer to the gatekeeper functions supplied by outside professionals, such as attorneys and accountants who assist the board and management in complying with law and with accurately reporting the corporation's financial position, both for the benefit of investors and for the corporation's own understanding of its operations.[56] It can refer to the process by which shareholders elect directors, as well as to the process by which shareholders can be involved in nomination of director candidates.[57]

It can refer to rules respecting how and when information about the corporation is disseminated to shareholders and to the market at large.[58] In practice, the limits of corporate governance law are also affected by the insurance coverage provided to officers and directors, since the insurance policy is often the asset from which recovery is sought in litigation.[59]

All of these functions, company by company, manager by manager, and investor by investor, can benefit from careful attention. Without the changing of liability standards, or the policies underlying the business judgment rule, thoughtful and deliberate governance can improve corporate performance.[60]

There is no end of recommendations on potential improvements in corporate decision-making processes[61] and corporate personnel processes[62] to improve corporate performance. There is no doubt that successfully implemented—in a particular company, in the context of its industry, in the right circumstances, in light of the talents and weaknesses of its management and employees—some or all or those recommendations would be appropriate and effective. Governance law, however, only describes the boundary conditions for implementing operational improvements. Implementing improvements is an art, not a science, and merely performing within the legal boundaries will not provide safe outcomes for investors.

Improvement in individual corporate performance is not the same as preventing formation of or problems with asset bubbles. "[Each historic asset bubble] began as a sensible bet on a bright though uncertain future; it continued to expand, even as fears began to be voiced that it might indeed be a bubble (that is, that the rising price did not reflect a change in fundamentals); and it burst when the market realized that the expectation of a new era had once again been mistaken."[63]

Implicit in Alan Greenspan's "shocked disbelief" that the independent and individual decisions of free market actors had not prevented the financial crisis was the concession that government regulation—which in the best case represents the transformation of one generation's bad experience into the accumulated wisdom of future generations—is needed to ensure that the game of capitalism is played within bounds.

There is support for the argument that executive compensation incentives played a role in the formation of the financial crisis asset bubble, a factor that could be affected by corporate governance improvements. However, executive compensation is not being argued as the sole cause of the crisis.[64] This does not mean that there is nothing to be done to prevent future asset bubbles from arising, particularly in the financial services industry.

Targeted regulation of the financial services industry (which is appropriately considered as a special case where regulation is concerned),[65] which has a known history of excesses, should enhance competition, by placing risky strategies or markets out of bounds. A regulated environment would permit all players to proceed with strategic decisions knowing that their competitors would not attempt to improve competitive position by using riskier strategies such as riding an inflating asset bubble. During the financial bubble, there were reportedly instances of companies attempting to use the regulators to referee the game, to prevent them from being required to respond to aggressive competitors with aggressive strategies of their own.[66]

There has been the suggestion that all substantial pools of capital become subject to regulation—including existing hedge funds and private equity pools.[67] Just as the antitrust laws measure industry concentration for purposes of evaluating potential anticompetitive impacts of a merger, it could be possible to evaluate whether an organization had become so large that its economic failure posed a threat to society at large, and mandate additional controls to limit the risks of such failure.

Some commentators have suggested examining—with regard to the financial services industry particularly—the reinstitution of Glass-Steagall or a "Glass-Steagall Lite" to separate the "utility" function of the financial system from the "casino" function.[68] There is considerable discussion among commentators and policymakers that the economy does not benefit from having companies that are "too large to fail."[69] Addressing such issues requires legislation, rather than individualized company-by-company decisions by corporate managers.

While an ideologically driven deregulation of the financial industry was a key factor in the development of the financial crisis, there is no reason to think that an immediate and unconsidered reregulation of the financial marketplace that does not reflect the economics and practices of the twenty-first century would be an effective solution.[70]

In May 2009, in the Fraud and Enforcement and Recovery Act of 2009, the bipartisan Financial Crisis Inquiry Commission was created to investigate the sources of, and responses to, the financial crisis, and that body had only begun its work in the summer of 2009.[71] Through 2010, the commission was conducting hearings and preparing reports on the events that led up to the financial crisis and the performance of the participants—

including the government—in the crisis, but as of September 2010 the commission had not completed its work.

Policymakers did not wait for the Financial Crisis Inquiry Commission report before adopting some remedial legislation in the form of Dodd-Frank. Dodd-Frank addressed a significant number of structural and regulatory elements in the financial system, as well as providing some corporate governance changes. It is possible that additional insights provided by the work of the Financial Crisis Inquiry Commission could result in additional legislation.

Chapter 8

Real Estate, Governance, and the Global Economic Crisis

Piet Eichholtz, Nils Kok, and Erkan Yonder

Introduction

The real estate market played an important role in the current economic crisis. Investors' bullish perspectives regarding the residential and commercial property markets not only allowed borrowers access to cheap and almost unlimited credit but also offered the possibility of raising large amounts of equity on the public capital markets. However, when the property boom eventually came to an end, this changed the situation with regard to these investments rapidly and fundamentally.

In retrospect, the recent crisis is to a large extent a governance crisis, in which the lack of transparency of securitized products, such as mortgage-based securities (MBS), collateralized mortgage-based securities (CMBS), and collateralized debt obligations (CDO), played a crucial role. However, this lack of transparency seems to be mostly associated with the securitized debt products created to finance real estate investments. On the real estate equity side, transparency seems to be less of a problem, thanks to the global rise of the real estate investment trust (REIT).[1]

This REIT market has become of major importance for institutional investors. The REIT structure was primarily created as an avenue for retail investors to gain exposure to (commercial) real estate investments. In the past two decades, however, institutional investors in many countries shifted their property exposure from direct real estate holdings into listed and private property companies. As a result, REITs have become the key vehicle for real estate investments of institutional investors, who are now the dominant holders of REIT shares. For example, more than 60 percent of the property allocation of Dutch pension funds is now invested through private or public property companies.

With property investments mostly allocated to intermediate property vehicles, the governance structures of these vehicles are of real importance to key players in the global capital market—pension funds and insurance companies. The governance structures and their implications for the performance of equity investments in real property are difficult to observe in the market for private funds, but the listed property sector offers a laboratory as to how real estate capital providers integrate and evaluate corporate governance in real estate investment decisions.

Interestingly, where many articles have shown the importance of firm-level governance for common equity investments (see the next section for a detailed review of the literature), the evidence shows that governance has less influence on the performance of REITs.[2] The distinct legal setting and organizational structure of REITs—U.S. law requires a 90 percent mandatory payout of net earnings—fundamentally changes the traditional principal-agent setting. The free-cash-flow problem is of less concern for REIT investors, as the legal distribution requirement limits the opportunities for managerial entrenchment.[3] Thus, the restricted setting in which managers of REITs operate offers an interesting natural experiment to test the relationship between governance and performance. Under the substitution hypothesis, the legal restrictions that apply to REITs mitigate the need for strong firm-level corporate governance mechanisms.[4] Governance may therefore be less important to investors. On the other hand, REIT managers can freely decide on how to use the free cash flow that remains after the mandatory payout. As the depreciation expense is sizable for property companies, the discretionary cash flows can still be substantial. Under the complement hypothesis, it can therefore be expected that the relation between corporate governance and performance, which has been documented in the finance literature, holds for U.S. REITs as well.

Moreover, corporate governance is likely to play a more critical role during the current global financial crisis, as the expected return on investment for managers declines during such crises.[5] As a result, managers may become more entrenched during the crisis, in order to compensate their losses. Rajan and Zingales have documented how investors shunned Asian markets at the beginning of the Asian crisis, since the legal environment did not sufficiently protect them from losses or downright expropriation.[6] And the role of institutional ownership may also change during a crisis. Mitton finds that institutional ownership positively affected returns during the Asian crisis, which was not the case before the market downturn.[7]

We analyze the impact of the strength of corporate governance on the performance of equity investments in property during the most recent boom and bust in the real estate market. Our analysis covers U.S. equity REITs, which we study on a yearly basis from 2003 through mid-2009. From 2003 through 2006, the REIT market was booming, and attracted large inflows of capital from both retail and institutional investors. In the real estate frenzy that preceded the current financial crisis, investors may well have invested in REITs regardless of their governance structure. The investigation for the remaining period—from 2007 through mid-2009—examines how corporate governance affected stock performance during the market downturn, when well-governed REITs may have had an edge over their less transparent counterparts.

To investigate whether there are significant performance differences between well-governed and poorly governed REITs, we exploit the corporate governance quotient (CGQ) index. First, we perform a two-step cross-sectional analysis on the sample of equity REITs. We then replicate the process for two subperiods, in the rising market before the crisis and in the market downturn.

Our results show that the effects of corporate governance on REIT performance differ markedly between the two subperiods. In the boom period, we do not find any significant relationships between corporate governance structures of real estate equity investments and their abnormal returns. One of the interpretations of this finding is that (institutional) investors did not incorporate extrafinancial information on the corporate governance structure of REITs in their investment decision-making process. Contrasting the precrisis results, we document that the governance structure of property companies is positively associated with abnormal returns during the downturn, especially where related to board composition and audit quality.

We also address the degree of ownership concentration of institutional investors and executives. We find a convex relationship between abnormal returns and the share ownership of executives. Up to a threshold, insider ownership negatively affects stock performance, but above that threshold, stock performance is positively related to insider ownership. Our results also show that the size of shareholdings of block holders has a positive relationship with abnormal returns. Thus, even though real estate holdings of institutional investors are mostly indirect, large shareholders can still have a direct impact on the performance of their real estate equity investments.

The rest of this chapter is organized as follows: in the next section, we briefly address the literature on corporate governance, performance, and listed property companies. The third section provides an explanation of our main data set: the Institutional Shareholder Services (ISS) corporate governance index. This section also provides the descriptive results of the portfolio analysis, comparing the performance of portfolios of badly governed REITs with those of well-governed ones. In the fourth section, we analyze the relationship between corporate governance and equity performance in light of the changing investment climate surrounding U.S. listed property companies. We investigate the effect of corporate governance determinants on equity performance from a cross-sectional perspective. The chapter ends with conclusions and practical implications for institutional investors and policymakers.

Literature Review

The seminal work of Gompers, Ishii, and Metrick documents that stock returns are positively related to the structure and strength of corporate governance.[8] An investment strategy that buys a portfolio of well-governed companies and sells a portfolio of poorly governed companies generates abnormal returns of 8.5 percent. Following this article, a new stream of literature has emerged, studying different markets and different periods.

For instance, Drobetz, Schillhofer, and Zimmermann perform a similar portfolio analysis on German companies.[9] Their investment strategy, which takes a long position in companies with high governance quality and a short position in poorly governed companies, earns abnormal returns of 12 percent. They explain this finding by unexpected agency costs, the closing of the value gap, and a noise effect. If investors do not identify the corporate governance differentials immediately, and they eventually do, this is corrected by paying a premium for well-governed companies. Alternatively, it is possible that correcting a poor governance structure creates value, and consequently causes a value gap between the fair market value and actual market value of companies. The adjusting of stock prices then closes this value gap. Last, there may be a sudden improvement in the governance structure, leading to a noise effect that produces higher stock returns.

The literature regarding the relationship between stock returns and corporate governance for other countries than the U.S. and Germany generates similar findings. Bauer, Guenster, and Otten find that good governance portfolio returns are higher than returns for bad governance portfolios by around 7 percent for U.K. companies, but much smaller for similar continental European portfolios.[10] For Japan, Bauer et al. show that well-governed companies exhibit annual excess abnormal returns of up to 15 percent compared to poorly governed companies.[11]

The governance anomaly seems to be at least partially driven by the ignorance of governance issues by investors during the early days of the bull market in the 1990s, as the results disappear in studies using more recent samples.[12] Indeed, after adjusting firm returns by industry returns, Johnson, Moorman, and Sorescu find that the abnormal returns obtained from the difference portfolio in the 1990s disappear.[13]

The importance of corporate governance has also been investigated for investments in real estate equities—or REITs. To gain their tax-exempt status, REITs are required to generate at least 75 percent of their income from real-estate-related projects and are required to distribute 90 percent of net income to shareholders. However, net income excludes depreciation, which can generate substantial discretionary cash flows for managers of property companies. Additionally, the five largest shareholders cannot hold more than 50 percent of the shares outstanding. These requirements may affect the need for corporate governance structures for REITs, and the restricted legal setting surrounding REITs makes this market an interesting laboratory for analysis.

Several studies have addressed the distinct governance setting in REITs. Han investigates the effect of insider ownership on REIT share performance, and finds a positive, but nonlinear, relationship.[14] Hartzell, Sun, and Titman conclude that higher institutional ownership makes REITs more active in exploiting the investment opportunities surrounding them.[15] Ghosh and Sirmans and Feng, Ghosh, and Sirmans study the impact of board structure on stock performance.[16] Both studies document a positive impact of outside directors on performance. Hartzell, Kallberg, and Liu analyze corporate governance in the initial public offerings (IPOs) of REITs.[17] They find that REITs with better governance structures at the IPO stage have higher operating performance.

In an article that is most closely related to this study, Bauer, Eichholtz, and Kok test the relationship between corporate governance and operating performance in U.S. REITs, using a broad range of indicators for governance quality.[18] Contrasting the evidence for the general stock market, they do not find a relation between the strength of company-specific corporate governance structures and firm valuation or operating performance. The authors explain the lack of this relationship for REITs as a "REIT effect": REITs operate under such specific legal obligations that managerial freedom is structurally curbed and the agency conflict thereby reduced. However, their analysis is performed in a booming market, and one could argue that investors are less critical with respect to the quality of corporate governance when the market participants are bullish, as the majority of investors in real estate markets were until early 2007. The remainder of this chapter aims to analyze this puzzle in more detail.

Data and Descriptive Statistics

This section describes the data used in this study and the descriptive statistics of the data sets.

The Corporate Governance Quotient

There are several frequently used proxies for the quality of corporate governance. We employ the corporate governance quotient (CGQ) index, provided by Institutional Shareholder Services. The CGQ index is based on publicly disclosed documents and distinguishes sixty-one different governance mechanisms in four sets of items: board of directors, charter and bylaw provisions, antitakeover provisions, and executive compensation. Using an internal scoring system, the index calculates ratings for each company.[19] What distinguishes the CGQ index from other measures of corporate governance is its relative setting, which ensures cross-sectional variability in the corporate governance scores within an industry.

In addition to the overall governance rating, four different subscores are assigned to each company. These subscores provide information on four specific governance areas: the board of directors, takeover defenses, executive and director compensation and ownership, and auditing. While the overall CGQ index ranges between 1 and 100, the scores on the four subindexes range from 1 to 5. In all cases, a high score represents a governance structure that is favorable to shareholders.

The CGQ database starts in 2002, but we restrict our analysis to the 2003–2009 ratings, as data on subindexes are not or only partially available before 2003. We use only the governance scores of equity REITs.[20] We match the list of equity REITs in the CGQ database to the list of constituent companies in the National Association of Real Estate Investment Trusts (NAREIT) Equity index.[21] This creates an initial equity REIT sample of 144 companies in January 2003, increasing to 152 in 2005, and subsequently decreasing to 112 property companies in May 2009.

We collect data on executive and institutional stock ownership from the SEC proxy statements (item Def. 14-A) for each REIT. To obtain financial information, we match the REIT information in the CGQ database with the Center for Research in Security Prices data on stock prices. After this matching exercise, we end up with 131 publicly traded equity REITs in January 2003, increasing to 139 REITs in 2005, and then falling to 112 REITs by May 2009.

Table 8.1 presents the descriptive statistics for the sample of equity REITs. Panel A shows that the average CGQ ratings increase by some 10 points from 2003 to 2004. The average governance scores persistently decline afterward. An explanation may be the privatization of well-governed REITs during that period. During the turn of the market in 2007, the ratings decrease by another 7 points.

The subcategories of the governance index in panel A, governance quality related to board structure and executive compensation, show a downward trend after 2004. Conversely, governance quality related to takeover defenses increases until 2007, but experiences a sharp decline in 2008. This may be a reaction to the high number of acquisitions in 2007: around 20 REITs disappeared from the market. The annual averages for governance practices related to auditing do not show a clear trend before the crisis, but the strength seems to increase during the downturn, which suggests that equity REITs improve their auditing structures. The average leverage ratio is slightly increasing before the crisis, and increases more rapidly with the

Table 8.1: Descriptive Statistics for Governance Scores and Firm Characteristics

| | Panel A. Descriptive Statistics Annual Averages | | | | | | |
	2003	2004	2005	2006	2007	2008	2009 (Q2)
CGQ index	59.08	69.73	66.18	64.31	57.69	58.42	55.97
Board index	3.21	3.69	3.65	3.56	3.41	3.41	3.34
Compensation index	3.82	3.86	3.66	3.64	3.31	3.42	3.26
Takeover defenses index	2.58	3.46	3.55	3.67	3.70	2.94	3.05
Audit index	3.41	3.67	3.35	3.75	3.66	3.73	3.87
Number of equity REITs	131	127	139	133	114	113	112
Size	1582.74	2159.51	2212.24	2954.60	2501.92	1558.28	1389.46*
Leverage	50.72	51.46	53.32	52.71	54.91	55.74	—

Panel B. Sample Trends

Removals from the sample	2004	2005	2006	2007	2008	2009 (Q2)
Number of removals	12	11	16	22	6	1
			Average Governance Score of Previous Year			
CGQ index	59.69	79.14	73.35	61.69	55.48	37.30
Board index	3.50	4.27	3.94	3.59	4.00	3.00
Takeover defenses index	3.33	3.55	3.13	3.95	3.00	5.00
Audit index	4.17	4.09	3.44	3.82	2.67	2.00
Compensation index	2.67	4.55	3.94	3.18	2.50	2.00

Additions to the sample	2004	2005	2006	2007	2008	2009 (Q2)
Number of additions	8	23	10	3	6	0
			Average Governance Score			
CGQ index	88.85	69.93	63.88	52.50	49.32	—
Board index	4.50	4.13	3.50	3.67	3.00	—
Takeover defenses index	4.00	3.70	3.90	4.33	3.00	—
Audit index	3.88	3.17	3.70	4.33	2.33	—
Compensation index	3.88	2.87	3.30	3.33	3.33	—

Note: Indexes listed other than CGQ index are subcategories of that index.

start of the crisis. This may be explained by the sudden decrease in the market value of assets, relative to a more stable level of debt.[22]

Panel B shows the average governance scores of the companies that are delisted and the companies that are first listed during the sample period. The delistings include REITs that were acquired, were voluntarily delisted, or went bankrupt.

We observe that, before the crisis, the average governance score of delisted companies is higher than the average governance score of all REITs in the same year. In other words, well-governed companies were taken private while more poorly governed REITs were floated. However, during the crisis, the situation reverses: delisted companies have CGQ scores that are lower than the annual average of all listed property companies.

The Crisis: A Structural Break in the Listed Property Market

The upward trend in the listed property market ended abruptly in early 2007. Figure 8.1 illustrates how the NAREIT Equity index and the S&P 500 index performed from January 2003 through June 2009. The cumulative return to the NAREIT Equity index corresponds to 191 percent from January 2003 through January 2007, the top observation in the NAREIT index, while it lost 68 percent from January 2007 through February 2009. In the same period, the S&P 500 index increased by 68 percent and then decreased by 49 percent. The figure shows that the NAREIT index experienced sharper upward and downward trends during the sample period compared to the S&P 500 index. Moreover, we do not observe a break point in the broader stock market index that is as clear as the break point observed for the property share index (Figure 8.1).

To determine the beginning and the end of the crisis, we perform an endogenous break-point test, as developed by Zivot and Andrews.[23] We assume that the structural break occurs in the trend term, since the market moves from an upward-sloping trend to a downward-sloping one. First, using the NAREIT index from January 2003 to December 2009, we determine the beginning of the crisis, which is February 2007. We then replicate the test from that month to the end of the data set, December 2009, to determine the end of the REIT crisis. The second break point is in May 2009. These break points are consistent with the top observation of the series and the end of the downturn in the market.

Figure 8.1. Time Patterns of the NAREIT Equity Index and S&P 500 Index, January 2003 through December 2009. The beginning of the series is rescaled to 100.

REIT Returns, Corporate Governance, and the Global Financial Crisis

This section provides a detailed investigation of the relationship between REIT returns and the various indexes of corporate governance before and during the financial crisis.

Portfolio Analysis

To analyze the impact of corporate governance on REIT equity returns, we construct two mutually exclusive, value-weighted equity portfolios: the "good governance" portfolio, which includes the companies that represent the top 30 percent of CGQ-rated REITs, and the "bad governance" portfolio, which includes the REITs in the bottom 30 percent of CGQ scores. Then, we construct a difference portfolio by subtracting the monthly return of the bad governance portfolio from the good governance portfolio, which resembles a trading strategy buying stocks with a high governance rating and shorting stocks with a low governance rating. We rerank the portfolios annually using the year-end data sets published by ISS, and we obtain end-of-month value-weighted portfolio returns for seventy-seven months, from January 2003 through May 2009. Companies that no longer appear in the database are excluded.

Panel A of Table 8.2 shows the annual average governance scores of the good governance and the bad governance portfolio. In the rising market (until 2006), we find that the average score of companies in the good governance portfolio is around 89 and relatively stable compared to the average governance score of the companies in the bad governance portfolio. In the market downturn, the average governance rating of the good governance portfolio increases to around 91, again relatively stable within the subperiod.

The annual average CGQ score of the bad governance portfolio is striking, increasing year by year during the crisis. It seems that poorly governed companies gradually improved their governance structure after the financial crisis began. (However, this could also imply that poorly governed companies may have gone out of business during the crisis.)

Panel B presents some descriptive statistics on the returns of the good governance and bad governance portfolios. In the first subperiod, both portfolios generate positive returns, but a trading strategy taking a long position in stocks with a high governance rating and shorting stocks with a low governance rating would not have performed very well, ending up with an average negative monthly return of 0.11 percent. During the crisis, both good governance and bad governance portfolios exhibit negative returns, although the difference portfolio return yields an average positive return of 1.07 percent. The cross-sectional variation within the good governance portfolio is substantial, and the positive performance of the difference portfolio seems to be driven by a few firms with a very high positive return.

In general, the first descriptive statistics suggest that the change in the economic conditions affects the governance structures of REITs, and the stock returns related to those governance structures.

We further observe the effect of the changing investment climate on the returns of the good versus the bad governance portfolio in Figure 8.2. The graph shows the annual returns of the respective portfolios. During the rising market, the outperformance of the portfolios is mixed, with poorly governed REITs outperforming their better-structured counterparts in

Table 8.2: Sample Statistics: Good and Bad Governance Portfolios

Panel A. Governance Score Mean

	2003	2004	2005	2006	2007	2008	2009
Good governance	88.91 (7.22)	89.73 (6.58)	89.52 (6.28)	89.28 (6.54)	91.18 (5.37)	91.20 (5.46)	91.05 (5.25)
Bad governance	21.73 (11.83)	30.17 (12.53)	24.20 (11.64)	25.11 (11.59)	23.81 (11.69)	27.63 (13.39)	30.58 (13.68)

Panel B. Monthly Portfolio Returns

	January 2003–January 2007			February 2007–May 2009		
	Mean	Max	Min	Mean	Max	Min
Good governance	2.27 % (0.61)	8.20%	−13.60%	−0.99% (3.19)	53.7%	−37.58%
Bad governance	2.38 % (0.63)	7.96%	−15.74%	−2.06% (2.11)	26.52%	−26.83%
Difference portfolio	−0.11 % (0.31)	5.84%	−6.11%	1.07% (1.47)	35.28%	−10.75%

Note: The sample statistics use CGQ industry ratings. The difference portfolio is established with a trading strategy that buys the good governance portfolio and shorts the bad governance portfolio. The values in parentheses are standard deviations.

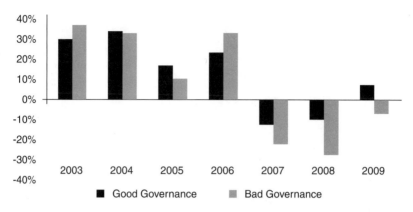

Figure 8.2. Annual Average Returns of Governance Portfolios. The good governance portfolio includes the companies that represent the top 30 percent of CGQ industry ratings, and the bad governance portfolio includes the companies that represent the bottom 30 percent of CGQ industry scores provided by Institutional Shareholder Services.

some years. However, during the crisis, well-governed companies consistently outperform poorly governed companies, on average.

Abnormal Returns and the Structure of Corporate Governance

To investigate the effects of corporate governance on the returns of equity REITs in more detail, we follow a two-stage approach. In the first stage, alpha is calculated for each company by employing the four-factor model proposed by Fama and French[24] and Carhart:[25]

(1) $\quad R_{ti} = \alpha_i + \beta_{0i}(R_m - R_f)_t + \beta_{1i}(SMB)_t + \beta_{2i}(HML)_t + \beta_{3i}(MOM)_t + \epsilon_{ti}$

where
SMB = the monthly return on a small minus big factor portfolio in month t
HML = the monthly return on a high minus low book-to-price portfolio in month t
MOM = the monthly return on a past month's winners minus past month's losers portfolio in month t

The risk factors used in this model have been previously applied to explain returns on REIT stocks.[26] Although there is an ongoing discussion whether the factors used in Carhart's model are risk proxies, we avoid discussion of this issue and view it as a method of performance attribution.

Thus, can be interpreted as the return in excess of what could have been achieved by means of passive investment in the factors. The individual company alphas are calculated for the subperiods from January 2003 through January 2007 and from February 2007 through May 2009, representing the boom period and the crisis period, respectively. We use the NAREIT index[27] as a proxy for the market return and the *SMB*, *HML*, and *MOM* factors from the Kenneth French Data Library.[28]

In the second stage, the generated alphas are regressed on corporate governance characteristics and company characteristics, using Equation (2), which is estimated using ordinary least squares (OLS), while correcting for heteroskedasticity.[29]

(2) $\quad \alpha_i = \delta_0 + \delta_1 G_i + \delta_2 \text{ DEBTRATIO }_i + \delta_3 FFO_i + \vartheta_i$

where

G = a vector of governance characteristics of equity REIT i
DEBTRATIO = leverage ratio of equity REIT i
FFO = funds from operations over total assets of equity REIT i

In Table 8.3, we provide the results of the cross-sectional estimation of Equation (2) for the precrisis period.[30] We use the annual averages of the governance scores and financial firm determinants. The explanatory power of the models is low, and we do not find a statistically significant relation between governance and performance. This may be attributed to the very limited managerial discretion in cash-flow spending of REIT management teams, due to the institutional framework surrounding U.S. REITs.[31]

Alternatively, these findings may indicate that (institutional) investors did not attribute any value to the particulars of REIT governance structures in the boom period that preceded the crisis. This irrational behavior would be fully consistent with the herd investments in securitized debt products, such as CDOs, where the opacity of the investments was so blissfully ignored.[32]

In Table 8.4, we estimate the effect of governance scores on abnormal returns during the crisis period, again applying Equation (2).

Contrasting findings for the precrisis period, the results show that governance matters for stock performance of REITs during the crisis, *even in the very strict legal setting in which REITs operate*. These findings are in line with Mitton.[33] The coefficients for "Board" and "Audit" scores are

Table 8.3: Cross-Sectional Regression of Pre-Crisis Abnormal Returns on Governance Scores

	(1)	(2)	(3)	(4)	(5)
			Coefficient x 100		
CGQ index	−0.010 [0.005]				
Takeover defenses index		0.050 [0.084]			
Audit index			−0.214 [0.109]		
Board index				−0.006 [0.119]	
Compensation index					−0.241 [0.126]
Debt ratio	0.003 [0.007]	0.002 [0.007]	0.004 [0.007]	0.002 [0.007]	0.001 [0.007]
Funds from operations	−0.000 [0.000]	−0.000 [0.000]	−0.000 [0.000]	−0.000 [0.000]	−0.000 [0.000]
Constant	0.774 [0.412]	0.001 [0.004]	0.878* [0.430]	0.288 [0.519]	0.011* [0.005]
N	133	133	133	133	133
Adjusted R^2	0.01	0.02	0.01	0.02	0.03

Note: The OLS regression is obtained from Equation (2). In the first stage, alpha is calculated for each company applying the four-factor Carhart model (1997) from January 2003 to January 2007. In the second stage, those alphas are regressed on company corporate governance characteristics, leverage, and funds from operations over total assets. White's (1980) heteroskedasticity-robust standard errors are in brackets.
* Indicates significance at the 5 percent level.

significantly positive in the regressions, and the overall CGQ score is significantly positive at the 5 percent significance level. There is no significant effect of the quality of compensation structure on abnormal returns.

We can explain this in three ways. First, the "REIT effect" may be diminished during the crisis. REITs have to distribute 90 percent of income. However, this excludes depreciation. In times of crisis, the property portfolio of REITs will likely drop in value, so marking the value of the property

Table 8.4: Cross-Sectional Regression of Crisis Abnormal Returns on Governance Scores

	(1)	(2)	(3)	(4)	(5)
		*Coefficient. x 100*			
CGQ index	0.011 [0.006]				
Takeover defenses index		0.188 [0.152]			
Board index			0.265* [0.128]		
Audit index				0.270* [0.127]	
Compensation index					0.081 [0.115]
Debt ratio	−0.011 [0.011]	−0.004 [0.011]	−0.010 [0.011]	−0.009 [0.011]	−0.007 [0.012]
Funds from operations	0.229** [0.072]	0.269** [0.071]	0.233** [0.070]	0.253** [0.069]	0.247** [0.068]
Constant	−0.955 [0.558]	−1.4* [0.7]	−1.260* [0.568]	−1.537* [0.663]	−0.870 [0.570]
N	112	112	112	112	112
Adjusted R^2	0.13	0.13	0.14	0.13	0.11

Note: The OLS regression is obtained from Equation (2). In the first stage, alpha is calculated for each company applying the four-factor Carhart model (1997) from February 2007 to May 2009. In the second stage, those alphas are regressed on company corporate governance characteristics, leverage, and funds from operations over total assets. White's (1980) heteroskedasticity-robust standard errors are in brackets.
* Indicates significance at the 5 percent level. **Indicates significance at the 1 percent level.

holdings to market will imply a depreciation that is far more severe than the depreciation in normal periods. Since the depreciation expense is deducted from taxable income, this means that less cash has to be distributed to shareholders, leaving more free cash flows to the discretion of the managers, thereby increasing the need for good governance. In effect, the crisis makes REITs more like regular corporations and diminishes the REIT-effect that results from the otherwise strong governance setting. This explanation is in line with a finding by Bauer et al., who show that the REIT effect is stronger for cash-constrained REITs and weaker for those REITs that have abundant free-cash flows.[34] This may also explain why the quality "Audit" especially is a significant and valuable aspect of corporate governance during the crisis.

A second explanation for the finding that firm-level corporate governance matters during the crisis is that the expected returns to managers decline, since executive payment packages are likely to include bonuses that are based on absolute stock performance. That means executives may be more likely to become entrenched compared to the precrisis situation.[35]

Third, it may well be that (institutional) investors in real estate equities did not take corporate governance structures into account before the market collapsed. Corporate governance seemed to be ineffective in the listed real estate market and investors unrealistically revalued the stock price of the poorly governed companies. This implies that poorly governed companies were overvalued relative to well-governed property companies. The crisis led to investors scrutinizing their securitized real estate holdings more intensively. As investors recognized the influence of corporate governance on REIT management and operational performance, a difference in share returns developed, related to the underlying corporate governance structure of property companies.

We observe that there is a time-specific effect in the relation between abnormal returns of real estate equity investments and governance structures: the effect of governance on stock performance changes in direction and significance during the crisis. Overall, our results show that the relationship between abnormal returns and corporate governance is sensitive to time and the investment climate. These findings support the ideas of Gompers, Ishii, and Metrick[36] and Core, Guay, and Rusticus[37] that the relationship may be time specific and depends on the (irrational) exuberance of the investors. Additionally, and most important, the results for the crisis period show that corporate governance may become more important in a market downturn. The quality of governance matters during a crisis.

Abnormal Returns and Ownership Structure

For a more thorough understanding of the importance of governance during the crisis, we also investigate how ownership concentration influences share performance after January 2007. If internal governance mechanisms are complemented by external governance mechanisms, such as block holdings by institutional investors, the outperformance of well-governed companies strengthens, according to Cremers and Nair.[38] We address the ownership concentration separately for share ownership of executives and institutional ownership concentration.[39] We exploit a similar econometric setup as in the previous analysis, but we now use ownership concentration data from the annual reports of the REITs, instead of the CGQ data, as the main explanatory variable. We again control for annual financial characteristics.

The results are presented in Table 8.5. Model 1 analyzes the effect of executive ownership concentration on abnormal returns of real estate equities. However, as it is unlikely that executive stock ownership has a simple linear relation with stock performance, Model 2 includes the square of executive ownership. We find a convex and statistically significant relationship. At first, executive stock ownership affects abnormal returns negatively, which is in line with Ghosh and Sirmans, who document that CEO ownership negatively affects REIT performance.[40] This may be explained by executive stock ownership increasing executive power at the cost of the other shareholders (a "power effect"), which leads to increased entrenchment and could negatively affect operational performance. On the other hand, executives who own company stocks also directly feel the financial pain of weak stock performance. It may that the power effect plays a dominant role at low degrees of executive share ownership, while if executives have a lot invested in the company, underperformance would hurt them more than the possible benefits of expropriation. Indeed, executive stock ownership seems to have a negative performance effect up to a certain threshold, and a positive effect thereafter. It seems that beyond a certain level of insider ownership concentration, the interest of managers aligns with that of the existing shareholders. This is an important finding for (institutional) investors in property companies.

In Models 3 and 4, we document that larger concentration of institutional stock ownership positively affects performance of property companies. The monitoring effect of institutional ownership over managers seems to be effective during the crisis. So institutional investors in REITs seem to be able to influence the operations of these property companies. However, these results mainly hold if there is at least one large shareholder in the investor base. For total institutional ownership, the results are economically less powerful and only statistically significant at the 10 percent level. These results are consistent with the findings of Mitton.[41]

Table 8.5: Cross-Sectional Regression of Crisis Abnormal Returns on Ownership Concentration

	(1)	(2)	(3)	(4)
	Coefficient x 100			
Executive ownership	−2.345*	−6.637*		
	[1.127]	[2.568]		
[Executive ownership]^2		6.971*		
		[0.297]		
Largest blockholder Ownership			0.140**	
			[0.016]	
Total blockholder ownership				0.001
				[0.000]
Debt ratio	−0.008	−0.003	−0.007	−0.004
	[0.011]	[0.011]	[0.010]	[0.010]
Funds from operations	0.215**	0.235**	0.256**	0.263**
	[0.066]	[0.069]	[0.067]	[0.068]
Constant	−0.014	−0.142	−0.675	−0.850
	[0.662]	[0.680]	[0.565]	[0.573]
N	112	112	112	111
Adjusted R^2	0.14	0.16	0.13	0.11

Note: The OLS regression is obtained from Equation (2). In the first stage, alpha is calculated for each company applying the four-factor Carhart model (1997) from February 2007 to May 2009. In the second stage, the estimated alphas are regressed on corporate governance and financial characteristics of the company. The ownership concentration data are the last available observations before the crisis. White's (1980) heteroskedasticity-robust standard errors are in brackets. * Indicates significance at the 5 percent level. ** Indicates significance at the 1 percent level.

Concluding Remarks and Practical Implications

Real estate has been at the forefront of the financial crisis, but thus far, investment research has mostly focused on the transparency and perform-ance of securitized debt products, such as CMBS and CDOs. Listed prop-erty companies (REITs) offer an interesting insight about the role of transparency in the performance of real estate equity investments and the behavior of investors therein. Previous evidence has shown that the agency conflict between managers and investors is reduced in REITs, as managerial freedom is curbed following legal requirements regarding obligatory payout and investment strategies. This may substitute for the need for alternative corporate governance mechanisms and raise industry-wide governance standards. However, the limited effect of company-specific governance structures on the corporate performance of REITs has only been documented in a rising/booming market, and under bullish market conditions, governance may well receive less attention from investors.

Starting in 2007, the property market shifted from boom to distress, with a very distinct break point. The legal restrictions regarding REIT cash flows might not be sufficient to decrease agency conflicts during the market downturn. In other words, under crisis circumstances, corporate governance may again become of importance to investors. Our results seem to suggest that the structure of firm-level corporate governance mechanisms became more critical during the crisis.

Using a sample of U.S. equity REITs during the 2003–2009 period, we find that governance practices did not significantly affect abnormal stock returns during the market boom. But during the crisis, the relation between governance and performance in REITs rapidly became positive and significant. Our results show that the results are mostly driven by the quality of corporate governance that is related to board composition and audit quality. Additionally, we document a positive, convex relationship between abnormal returns and executive ownership concentration during the crisis period. Insider ownership affects stock performance negatively below a threshold and positively above that threshold. Our results also show that abnormal returns are positively affected by the ownership concentration among the largest institutional shareholders during the crisis.

The previously documented REIT effect, resulting from the strong industry-wide governance framework, seems to disappear during the crisis. We explain this by the fact that the crisis increases depreciation in REITs, thus reducing the required cash distribution, and leaving more cash at the discretion of management. The second explanation is that the crisis decreases managers' performance-based compensation, thus increasing the incentives for entrenchment. As a result, the effectiveness of the governance setting surrounding REITs is weakened, and REITs more closely resemble regular corporations in the importance of firm-level governance for share performance. Third, these findings may indicate that (institutional) investors did not attribute any value to the governance structure of REITs in the boom period that preceded the crisis. This irrational behavior would be fully consistent with the investments in securitized debt products, such as CDOs, where opacity of the investments was also ignored.

An important implication of our findings concerns the possibility for mandatory payout rules and other institutional limitations on managerial discretion. Our precrisis results support the earlier findings of Bauer et al., suggesting that the institutional design of REITs alleviates the need for company-specific governance measures.[42] This may be viewed as an argument to introduce such measures in a wider set of industries. However, we have some serious doubts as to whether the lessons from the REIT market can simply be applied to other industries.

First, the real estate industry is all about income, but many other industries are not. In high-tech sectors, for example, dividend payment is rare. Shareholders accept low or no dividend payments, since they may regard the internal reinvestment of retained earnings as a value enhancer in the long run. Introducing mandatory payout to these industries would probably do more harm than good. Second, our empirical results for the crisis suggest that the manner in which the payout rule is defined is not crisis proof. It may be better to set the payout requirements relative to the free cash flow rather than the income, leaving less discretionary cash for managers. This would diminish the importance of depreciation and decrease the possibilities of agency problems and earnings management. Last, the payout rule was never designed as a governance mechanism, but as a guarantee that the tax authorities would get their taxes, if not at the corporate level, then at the shareholder level. This may imply that mandatory payout may be accepted as a quid pro quo for a zero corporate tax rate.

Our results also have important implications for institutional investors that invest in real estate equity via intermediate property companies. In "normal" times, investors can rely on the beneficial governance setting derived from the institutional framework surrounding REITs. Attention regarding firm-level governance may be of less importance under these circumstances, which is one of the main benefits of investing in REITs as compared to investing directly in real property or in private property funds, where governance is a far more problematic issue.[43] This implies that the costs of monitoring REIT portfolios are far lower compared to those of portfolios of directly held real estate. This is illustrated by the fact that the number of people required for the portfolio management of the REIT assets is substantially smaller than for the management of a portfolio of real property, even if the actual property management is outsourced.

However, our results also suggest that the quality of firm-level governance matters, especially during times of crisis. These periods are arguably the times that investors most care about, especially from a risk-management perspective. This implies that institutional investors should always focus on the quality of the firm-level corporate governance of the REITs they invest in, regardless of the economic circumstances. This ensures the best all-weather approach toward real estate equity investments.

Chapter 9

The Sophisticated Investor and the Global Financial Crisis

Jennifer S. Taub

> We want the sophisticated investor to protect himself, but we also want a system
> that identifies crooks and comes down like the wrath of God on them. We need
> both.
> —Charles Munger, vice chairman of Berkshire Hathaway
>
> And here I think what's intriguing is we have a failure of both.
> —Joseph Grundfest, Stanford Law School professor

Introduction

The financial instruments and risky practices that caused the global financial crisis of 2008 were enabled by decades of deregulation and anemic
government enforcement efforts. The elements that combined to create the
crisis were subprime mortgage securities, credit default swaps, highly leveraged hedge funds, and excessive short-term borrowing at investment
banks.[1] They flourished without government oversight, transparency, or
limits because proponents contended that "private ordering" of financial
markets, instead of government intervention, was ideal. The champions of
private ordering contended government interference was inappropriate for

sophisticated investors (SIs) who had the expertise and incentives to properly assess risk, and to select and monitor complex investment options.
They believed that by acting in their own interests, SIs would keep the
market safe and ensure the efficient allocation of capital to businesses and
individuals who would make the most productive use of the money. Sophisticated investors include, for example, government, corporate, and
union pension funds, mutual funds, hedge funds, endowments, broker-
dealers, insurance firms, banks, and sovereign funds. They also include individuals who earn as little as $200,000 per year. While many experts
warned about the dangerous consequences of deregulation,[2] Congress and
regulators accepted the conventional perspective that sophisticated market
participants would police and avoid irrational conduct.[3]

The concept of the SI exception is embedded in our securities laws.
It is a mechanism that allows securities issuers to sometimes bypass legal
requirements intended to protect ordinary people who purchase securities
("retail investors"). The securities laws were designed, initially, to protect
retail investors from confusing, worthless, or high-risk investments.[4] In
other words, "Congress was concerned that the average investor was being
fleeced in the financial markets by inadequate disclosure, misrepresentation, and manipulative schemes."[5] Thus, once an investor is deemed "sophisticated," many investment options can be offered and sold without
many protections.[6] The demarcation between the ordinary and the sophisticated, as noted below, depends wholly upon wealth and not upon any measure of experience or skill. The SI concept spread to other financial laws
and rules. And when new risky instruments emerged, the reliance upon a
market filled with SIs was sufficient to convince lawmakers and regulators
to remove barriers and allow for the expansion of these unregulated or very
lightly regulated offerings.

The SI exception may have been a valid carve-out to the early legal
requirements from the 1930s. However, a few major changes make it no
longer viable. First, unlike earlier securities offerings, financial instruments
have grown far more complex than the capacity of computers to handle, let
alone human brains. Some computer scientists and economists argue that
"even when buyers know all of the relevant information," it is nearly impossible to price even the simplest collateralized debt obligations[7] and that
it would take many days for a powerful computer to establish a price.[8]
As a result, mere humans, including most expert analysts, got lost in the
complexity, fell prey to decision-making biases, and overlooked the absence

of critical data points.[9] In the debt and derivative markets, many of these tradable instruments did not exist in the 1930s, nor did they exist even prior to the 1980s or 1990s. Indeed, even those who constructed these instruments admitted difficulty pricing them. For example, a Goldman Sachs employee who helped build and sell such a structure posed this rhetorical question: "Well, what if we created a 'thing,' which has no purpose, which is absolutely conceptual and highly theoretical and which nobody knows how to price?"[10]

Second, the incentive to maximize short-term personal welfare meant "sophistication" in forecasting and preventing the demise of one's firm and the financial system as a whole was subordinated to short-term profit seeking by senior executives and other employees. Thus, those who expected "self-interest" to prevail forgot the agency problem—that personal self-interest is not the same as the firm's or shareholders' self-interest.

Third, a huge shift in ownership has occurred since the SI exemptions were conceived. In the early twentieth century, "managerial capitalism"[11] emerged, characterized by diffuse shareholders and powerful managers— the separation of ownership from control.[12] However, by the end of the century, we experienced an intermediation revolution.[13] In the 1970s, *individuals* held about 80 percent of U.S. corporate equities;[14] however, currently, giant intermediary *institutions* hold legal title to approximately 70 percent.[15] Also, the vast majority of outstanding corporate and government bonds are held by institutions.[16] While institutions may hold legal title to these investments, they are not the real investors who put their money at risk. Instead, they are often investing the capital of real people whose money is funneled to them through various other intermediaries. For example, in 2009, one class of institutional investor, the mutual fund, held 24 percent of U.S. equities.[17] Institutional investors who make investment decisions without the benefit of proper protections do so on behalf of underlying or "ultimate" investors. These are pension fund beneficiaries, mutual fund shareholders, and other ordinary people who on their own behalf would not be considered sophisticated and thus could not directly make such purchases.

Therefore, when a sophisticated institutional investor makes poor choices, this harms the ultimate investors, the people whom the securities laws were designed to protect. Former president Bill Clinton recently recognized this problem. He explained that the justification for the failure to regulate complex instruments was that: "these things are expensive and sophisticated and only a handful of investors will buy them and they don't need any extra protection, and any extra transparency. . . And the flaw in that argument was that first of all sometimes people with a lot of money make stupid decisions and make [them] without transparency . . . And secondly, the most important flaw . . . was even if less than 1 percent of the total investment community is involved in [these investments] so much money was involved that if they went bad, they could affect 100 percent of the investments, and indeed 100 percent of the citizens in countries."[18] In other words, reliance upon the sophisticated investor ignores reality; the entities the law deems to meet the definition are largely neither sophisticated enough to match the complexity of the instruments or lack of data nor the actual investors who have placed their capital at risk.

Looking back on the global financial crisis, it is clear that reliance upon SIs was misguided. There are numerous examples of how SIs were not able to make good choices. And, these incidents were not on the fringes but central to the crisis. As more information emerges concerning the creation and sale of toxic securities, it is clear that reliance upon SIs provided the rationalization for sharp if not illegal practices. Firms like Goldman Sachs invoked the SI concept while defending against securities fraud allegations that it created and sold some sophisticated clients bonds that were designed to fail while allowing others who helped create the bonds to bet against them. In addition, lobbyists and legislators continue to rely upon the sophisticated investor framework to shield certain financial institutions and instruments from government oversight. In this fashion, the SI concept continues to be trumpeted by those who seek carve-outs from reform efforts.

Despite the reliance on the SI concept, little attention has been paid to the importance of the SI failure. Accordingly, an examination of the incapacity of sophisticated investors to monitor unregulated investment options and of the role sophisticated investors play in creating systemic risk is a necessary prerequisite to restoring financial safety and economic stability.

Causes of the Global Financial Crisis

While common ground exists as to the proximate causes of the crisis, debate persists as to the root causes, the cure, and the preventative steps to avoid a similar catastrophe. It is widely believed that the crisis began in mid-2007 with defaults on subprime mortgages on homes in the United States. These subprime mortgage loans had been sold into shell entities and transformed into mortgage-backed securities (MBS). These securities had been further sold to investors and sometimes into new shells, which in turn sold collateralized debt obligation (CDO) securities. The value of these MBS and CDOs depended upon expected rates of homeowners making their monthly mortgage principal and interest payments in full and on time. When mortgages were originated with borrowers who were increasingly less capable of making payments, defaults skyrocketed. Correspondingly the value of the MBS and CDOs declined.

The origination of these risky mortgages was driven by SIs willing to substitute a rating for good independent judgment. As Alan Greenspan has testified, "there was a remarkably large demand in collateralized debt obligations in Europe which were funded by subprime mortgages. And the reason the demand was so large is the . . . yields were high and the credit rating agencies were giving the tranches of these various CDOs Triple-A."[19]

Although the nationally recognized statistical rating organizations (credit rating agencies) had issued top ratings to huge portions of these issuances, many of these securities were built to fail.[20] This was the case in part out of indifference and in part out of conflict of interest. At the beginning of the toxic securities production chain were mortgage brokers and other lenders who were paid transaction-based fees. They planned to immediately sell the loan and thus cared little about the ability of the borrowers to repay the loans. In the middle of the chain were the investment banks that selected and bought these mortgage loans. These bankers were paid large fees to package the loans into increasingly complex structures. They looked the other way.[21] And in some cases they were allegedly taking large side bets, hoping for the failure of the very instruments they were peddling to their own clients.[22]

While some of the insiders understood the danger ahead, many of the large institutional investors did not. They were targeted by the investment banks to purchase these highly rated instruments so as to support other clients, who were taking the opposite bets. An instrument that helped in the packaging and sale of these MBS and CDOs was the credit default swap (CDS). As discussed below, CDS were initially designed to act as insurance and appeared to some to limit the risk of default on these underlying loans.

Instead, however, credit derivatives magnified the risks. When defaults materialized and underlying mortgaged home values declined, subprime securities investors located in the U.S. and beyond lost money.[23] This contagion spread to other investments. This was the case because owners of these securities, such as the large investment banks, had taken on huge amounts of short-term debt to finance the purchase of these assets that were hard to price and difficult to sell. When the values began to decline, they had to sell other assets to raise capital. Thus, excessive leverage throughout the banking and shadow banking system amplified the rapid asset declines.[24] Investment banks that depended on short-term (often overnight) loans to finance up to 50 percent of their assets saw this funding suddenly dry up. There was a "run on the banking system, by the banking system."[25]

Origins of the Sophisticated Investor Concept

> The securities laws were not enacted to protect sophisticated businessmen from their own errors of judgment.
> —*Hirsch v. DuPont* (1977)[26]

The embedding of the SI concept occurred just after the Great Depression around the enactment of the first federal securities law, the Securities Act of 1933 (the "1933 Act").[27] The 1933 Act governs the initial offering and sale of securities. It requires registration with the SEC of securities before they are sold, controls the nature of disclosures of offers for new securities, and creates criminal and civil liability for false and misleading statements. It responded to the pre-Crash proliferation of securities that were of low to no value. In 1933, an expert from the Department of Commerce who testified at House hearings revealed that of the $50 billion in securities sold during the previous thirteen years, half were "undesirable or worthless."[28]

The emphasis of this law was on full disclosure of material facts—the idea that sunlight would be the best disinfectant—and on liability for false, misleading, or incomplete information in the offering of securities.[29] The purposes of the law were to protect members of the public and also to protect market integrity. Both the Congress and the President articulated that confidence in the financial system as a whole was threatened if investors were preyed upon.[30] President Franklin D. Roosevelt declared that "if the country is to flourish, capital must be invested in enterprise. But those who seek to draw upon other people's money must be wholly candid regarding the facts upon which the investor's judgment is asked."[31] He saw the law as putting an end to "private exploitation of the public's money."[32]

In the original statute, there was an exemption from registration with the SEC for "private" offerings.[33] A problem arose, however, because the law did not express a distinction between what was a private and what was a public offering.[34] The SEC provided some guidance in 1934, suggesting that an offering could not be considered "private" if it was made to more than approximately "twenty-five" persons.[35] In 1953, the Supreme Court in *SEC v. Ralston Purina* eliminated the quantity limit and instead determined that the test as to whether something is a private or a public offering is whether the investors can "fend for themselves" or if they need "protections afforded by registration."[36]

Later, a "safe harbor" was created for those issuers who wanted to avoid the full registration under the 1933 Act and the potential for heightened liability, but wanted some assurance that the SEC would not pursue them for misjudging. Using the Reg. D safe harbor,[37] implemented under regulations including Rule 506, by making an abbreviated filing with very limited disclosure, issuers of securities could avoid complying with the 1933 Act if they offered shares only to what were defined as "accredited investors."[38] An "accredited investor" includes a natural person with $200,000 income or net worth of $1 million.

It's important to note that while this rule allows sales to an *unlimited* number of accredited investors, it also allows issuers to sell unregistered securities to a limited number (thirty-five) of those who don't qualify as accredited, but who "have enough knowledge and experience in finance and business matters to evaluate the risks and merits of the investment . . . or be able to bear the investment's economic risk."[39] This narrow exception is sometimes referred to as the sophisticated investor exception; however, as a practical matter, because it is difficult to judge whether an investor has that knowledge and experience, issuers rely on the "accredited investor" definition and other objective definitions that use an objective measure of assets or income. Accordingly, when industry members refers to investors as sophisticated, they are typically referring to the objective measures of wealth, not the subjective question of actual knowledge or skill.

The SI concept spread to other areas of financial markets regulation. The antipaternalistic logic met up with the efficient market hypothesis and

thus as new instruments developed the tendency was to stretch the definitions of what was private and to brush aside other legal obstacles so as to
allow trading to flourish.

Leverage and the Sophisticated Investor

> Leverage kills. People forgot.
> —Anonymous comment[40]

Bankers, regulators, advocates, and scholars agree that a key ingredient of
the 2008 crisis was excessive borrowing at all levels of the financial system.
Yet leverage (borrowing relative to assets or relative to equity) was approved
by those private gatekeepers who had the skills and experience to know
better. There were many warnings that the days of easy credit would end
and there would be a tremendous, calamitous adjustment. Yet those in the
position to pull back when it mattered or to increase their own capital
cushion so they would not put their own institutions in jeopardy did not
do so.

Just before the crisis, the leverage at major regulated and unregulated
financial entities was extremely high. The firms with the greatest leverage
were broker-dealers and hedge funds at 27 to 1. Next in line were the mortgage government-sponsored enterprises such as Fannie Mae and Freddie
Mac with a ratio of 23.5 to 1.5. At the other end of the spectrum were
commercial banks (9.8 to 1) and savings banks (8.7 to 1).[41] Yet it was not
just the ratios but also the quality of the assets and the nature of their
financing. Much borrowing and other sources of financing, some including
the multi-trillion-dollar repurchase agreement markets, remained off balance sheet, out of the leverage calculations.[42]

Yet, prior to the crash, the majority view at the Federal Reserve Board
in Washington and the Treasury was that financial engineering through
credit derivatives and CDOs had dispersed risk.[43] The General Accounting
Office (GAO) concluded, "The financial crisis has revealed limitations in
existing regulatory approaches that restrict leverage."[44] Ironically, these devices that mainstream thinkers considered protection against leverage created even more market risk.

However, in retrospect, even the bankers understand this was foolish.
The CEO of Goldman Sachs admitted as much in his testimony before the
Financial Crisis Inquiry Commission in 2010. Lloyd Blankfein was asked

by one of the commissioners whether he could identify the "bad lending practices" that led to the crisis. Blankfein agreed with Jamie Dimon, CEO of JP Morgan, who testified to the commission regarding consumer lending that it was foolish to believe that home prices would "go up forever" or that "stated income" was sufficient on mortgage applications.[45] Regarding commercial credit, Blankfein revealed, "You cannot miss the fact that the covenants are getting a little lighter and the leverage is getting bigger. . . . We all rationalized. 'Gosh the world is getting wealthier. . . . Things are more efficient. These businesses are going to do well.' . . . [You] talked yourself into a place of complacency."[46]

Ignoring the high leverage at operating companies was a lot like ignoring the extremely high price-to-earnings ratios at Internet firms during the Internet bubble. In addition to fueling the credit bubble for outside borrowers, the big investment banks also did so internally. They used high leverage to finance their proprietary trading desks and internal hedge fund operations.

They were able to do so because of legal acts and omissions justified by their sophistication. With regard to their own balance sheets, investment banks were able to get more leveraged because of a 2004 SEC rule change and also the failure to recognize some short-term financing as borrowing. Historically, there had been a difference in regulatory treatment of an investment bank holding company (the parent entity) and the U.S. broker-dealer subsidiar(ies). With the enactment of the 1934 Act, broker-dealers (the subsidiaries) were regulated at the federal level. One of the chief drivers for this legislation was Congress's concern about margin—excessive borrowing by investors to finance their transactions. The intent was to protect investors from their own excessive borrowing and also to redirect credit from the financial markets to other more vital areas of the economy.[47]

Until 2004, borrowing levels of the investment bank holding companies had not been regulated by the SEC at all. A holding company is the entity at the top of a corporate structure that typically issues equity shares to the public. The holding company can also borrow. For investment bank holding companies, broker-dealer operations took place in subsidiaries. While the investment bank holding companies had not been supervised, broker-dealers have been heavily regulated since the 1930s, with net capital requirements beginning for them in 1975 with the net capital rule.[48] The net capital rule measured leverage and liquidity. It was designed to ensure that if a broker-dealer failed, it would have enough assets that if sold, could pay off amounts it owed to certain creditors. Net capital was calculated by adding up the market value of all tradeable assets and discounting or applying a "haircut" to the assets based upon market risk—how difficult they might be to sell at full value. The net capital rule established a limit on debt to net capital of 12 to 1.[49] In 2004, the SEC eliminated the net capital rule for the five largest broker-dealers. This was a trade. In exchange, the investment banks became "consolidated supervised entities" (CSEs) and, for the first time, the SEC gained oversight of investment banks at the parent level.[50] Removing the rule allowed these five firms' broker-dealer subsidiaries to use a "voluntary, alternative method of computing net capital" using their own models pursuant to the international Basel standards.[51] As a result the ratio of average assets to net capital doubled.[52] While the banks benefited from taking on the CSE status by gaining the ability to use much more leverage at their broker-dealer subsidiaries, the SEC did very little by way of supervision at the parent holding company level. As SEC chair Mary Schapiro revealed during a 2010 hearing on the failure of Lehman Brothers, the SEC took little action under its new authority. Schapiro indicated that after the top five independent investment banks took on CSE status, the "SEC did not have the staff, the resources . . . or the mindset to be the prudential regulator of the largest financial institutions in the world."[53] Under the leadership of a different chair, she indicated, the SEC assigned only twenty-four people to monitor those five banks. This stood in stark contrast to the staffing at the firms themselves. According to CEO Richard Fuld, Lehman alone had over twenty-eight thousand employees, of which more than one hundred audit, legal, and other staff were responsible for financial statements.[54]

These same five investment bank CSEs were at the center of the crisis. Bear Stearns and Merrill would have failed without government-subsidized rescues. Lehman filed for bankruptcy. Morgan Stanley and Goldman desperately needed to raise capital and ultimately became bank holding companies so that they could have access to Federal Reserve lending and liquidity facilities, historically open only to the commercial banks.[55] These should have been the most sophisticated investors of all. They took part in every aspect of the capital markets, yet regarding their own balance sheets and the prospects of their borrowers, they were either uninformed or intentionally ignored riskst to support their own growing personal wealth. It was the government's trust of their sophistication that encouraged the SEC to move away from the old capital rule standards.

Hedge Funds and the Sophisticated Investor

> One of the underlying principles behind the idea that hedge funds could operate
> with little to no regulatory requirements was that interests in the funds were only
> sold in private offerings to wealthy investors. These investors were thought to be
> sufficiently "sophisticated" to protect their interests, and to be able to engage in
> effective arms-length negotiation in order to achieve fair and equitable terms.
> —Luis A. Aguilar, SEC Commissioner[56]

Highly leveraged hedge funds were key ingredients in the global financial crisis[57] and they still continue to present systemic risk.[58] The convergence of undercapitalized mortgage pools, credit default swaps and leveraged hedge funds created the perfect storm.[59] Hedge funds were willing buyers of risky tranches of subprime mortgage-backed CDOs.[60] In addition, they were big players in the credit default swap market.

The collapse of the two Bear Stearns hedge funds signaled a transformation of the subprime crisis into a much larger credit problem. There is evidence to suggest that more than half of subprime mortgage bonds were created as a result of a single hedge fund named Magnetar. Author Yves Smith revealed that "industry sources believe that *Magnetar drove the demand for at least 35%, perhaps as much as 60%, of the subprime bonds issued in 2006.* And Magnetar had imitators, including the proprietary trading desks at the major dealers; thus their strategy is arguably the most important influence on subprime bond issuance in 2006–2007" (emphasis in original).[61]

This hedge fund, Magnetar, took the necessary act of buying the small equity piece of (sponsoring) the CDOs. Given that equity investors take the greatest risk, it was difficult to find them. When Magnetar was launched, it was thought to be taking very risky positions given growing concerns about the quality of subprime loans. However, secretly, it was actually using credit default swaps to take substantially larger "bets" against the performance of its own pools and those similar to the ones it sponsored.[62] When almost all of the bonds from the Magnetar-sponsored CDOs became worthless, investors lost over $40 billion.[63]

In addition, unregulated hedge funds are a problem because of the harm they can cause to investors and the markets because they cannot withstand market turmoil. The need to deleverage during the financial crisis created broader problems. Most important, the *techniques* used by hedge funds were the cause of this crisis and earlier meltdowns and crashes. Restricting a dangerous behavior makes sense regardless of who the market player is. Excessive leverage was a chief contributor to the collapse and hedge funds have no leverage restrictions.

The concerns associated with hedge funds and other unregulated pools relate to investment practices, conflicts of interest, and operational controls, issues predating the global financial crisis.[64] These problems were common to the hedge fund and mutual fund precursor—the investment trust. As a result of prior abuses, in 1940, Congress regulated most investment trusts (including mutual funds), requiring transparency, accurate valuation and protection of assets, and fiduciary obligations to investors and forbidding managers from engaging in self-dealing or related-party transactions, or taking on excessive leverage and illiquid portfolio holdings. Fiduciary obligations include the affirmative duty to act in the best interests of one's clients.

A hedge fund is quite similar to a mutual fund. They are both investment vehicles used to pool capital gathered from many investors. The manager of either type of fund then invests this cash in securities and other instruments. Prior to the New Deal legislation, these pooled vehicles were known as "investment trusts"[65] and there was not a distinction between a hedge fund and a mutual fund. Then with the Investment Company Act of 1940 (the "1940 Act"),[66] Congress attempted to regulate and control all investment trusts, calling them "investment companies." What we now refer to as a "mutual fund" is by law considered to be an open-end registered investment company.

The "abuse of leverage was a primary concern that led to enactment" of the 1940 Act.[67] Congress created an exemption for "privately" offered funds.[68] As discussed below, hedge funds took advantage of this exemption and in the 1990s benefited from another one. The justification for both is premised upon the SI concept.

The first hedge fund was launched in 1949. It had $100,000 in assets and was designed to achieve market-neutral returns by going long on undervalued equities and short on overvalued ones.[69] By 1968, there were only 216 hedge funds and by the 1990s, there were still only 3,000 hedge funds, with $38 billion under management.[70] Explosive growth followed. At the peak in 2008, there were 18,000 hedge funds; with $1.9 trillion in assets under management worldwide.[71] Notwithstanding the numbers of funds, assets were highly concentrated. Roughly 75 percent of assets were managed by 200 firms with more than $1 billion each.[72] Also, hedge funds play an extremely large role in trading. Prior to the crisis, they accounted for 30 percent of all fixed-income trades, 85 percent of distressed debt, and 80 percent of certain credit derivatives trades.[73]

Hedge funds were able to gather assets and deploy them in an unrestricted manner, threatening both investors and the system because of both a regulatory anomaly and a recent rule change. Money managers are drawn to operate hedge funds, where fees are substantially higher than their regulated counterparts; unlike other money managers, those of hedge funds enjoy the freedom to charge huge fees (1–2 percent of assets under management and 20–50 percent of profits).[74] Hedge fund managers avail themselves of this exception by advising only sophisticated investors.[75] This results from an exemption from key aspects of the Investment Advisers Act of 1940 (the "Advisers Act"). By law, registered investment advisers are prohibited from charging performance fees—or a share of client asset appreciation.[76] In 1970, Congress extended this limit to mutual fund advisers. The rationale was that these types of "performance fees created incentives for advisers to take inappropriate risks in managing a client's account in order to increase advisory fees."[77] However, investment advisers to hedge funds remain exempt. Then, in 1998, the SEC permitted hedge fund managers to expand the base of fee-paying investors and eliminated contractual and disclosure obligations of hedge fund managers.[78]

In addition, prior to the crisis, hedge fund advisers were exempt from many of the other disclosure obligations and investor protections (such as the fiduciary duties) provided for under the Advisers Act. This is because the fund (a legal fiction, a shell) was considered a single client. The investors in the fund were not counted as clients. A financial adviser was only brought into key portions of the statute, including the fiduciary duty obligation, if the adviser had at least fifteen clients.[79] While mutual fund advisers (fund families) have a legally mandated fiduciary duty to fund shareholders,[80] hedge fund managers did not have the same obligation. With the passage of the Wall Street Reform and Consumer Protection Act of 2010, H.R. 4173 (the "Dodd-Frank Act"), the private adviser exemption has been eliminated and advisers to hedge funds that manage hedge fund or private equity assets greater than $150 million are required to register with the SEC. And, among other obligations that flow from the end to this exception, hedge fund advisers are now fiduciaries and will have to put their clients' interests ahead of all other interests, including their own.

As noted earlier, the hedge fund is not regulated as an "investment company" (like a mutual fund) because of loopholes in the 1940 act, the one that existed at the outset and another from 1996. The original exclusion was under section 3(c)(1) for a private investment fund. This was an investment company that had no more than one hundred persons as investors.[81] This carve-out was designed for collective investments such as investment clubs. In order to gather up more money, managers of 3(c)(1) funds would engage in counting games. Instead of treating all of the people who had their money invested as investors, the law permitted the manager to ignore the true investors, if the money was aggregated by a middleman. In other words, a mutual fund (or other intermediary) with thousands of its own investors that invests in a 3(c)(1) fund counts as only one investor, generally speaking. But if it owns more than 10 percent of the underlying fund, then the SEC will "look through" and count those thousands. If it dedicates more than 40 percent of its own assets to one fund, this might also be seen as an evasion and require look through.[82] As a practical matter, these 3(c)(1) hedge funds were typically limited to "accredited investors" (including individuals with $200,000 in income or $1 million in net worth). Hedge fund managers would limit themselves so as to avoid having to register the securities or provide detailed disclosures.[83]

Dissatisfied with the hundred-person limitation, the industry gained its other exemption with the enactment of the National Securities Markets Improvement Act of 1996 (NSMIA).[84] This law created a new way to avoid the intrusive regulations of the 1940 act. This was the Qualified Purchaser exception under section 3(c)(7). The foundational premise for allowing what should have been private offerings to a hundred investors to now reach an unlimited number of investors was that, according to the SEC, " 'Qualified Purchasers' do not need the Act's protections because they are able to monitor such matters as management fees, transactions with affiliates, corporate governance and leverage."[85]

Notwithstanding this purpose, the actual rule defining Qualified Purchaser uses wealth alone, not skill or experience, as its basis. For example, a natural person (or family company) with $5 million in investments qualifies (as does an institution with $25 million—including corporate, union, and public pension plans).[86] Additionally, to avoid registering shares under the Securities Act of 1934, hedge funds often limit sales to no more than 499 persons—again, though, each person could be a feeder mutual fund with unlimited investors of its own.[87] Now this type of fund of hedge fund structure allows merely "accredited" investors to get exposure (just $200,000 in income). So wealth became a proxy for financial sophistication.[88]

It is clear that "in recent years, [hedge fund] growth has been fueled in part by institutional investors, such as endowments, foundations, insurance companies, and pension plans."[89] According to a 2005 study conducted by the Bank of New York and Casey Quirk & Associates, it was estimated that by 2008, institutions would invest over $300 billion in hedge funds. Of this institutional money, around 40 percent came from pension funds.[90] A 2006 report to Congress noted that almost a quarter of all pension funds were invested in hedge funds. The average amount of pension fund assets dedicated to them was 2.1 percent.[91]

Lured by the attractive returns and pressured to achieve absolute returns[92] in order to finance the retirements of an increasing number of retirees, some pension funds had 20–39 percent of plan assets invested in hedge funds.[93] Given the challenges of its underfunded pension liability, it is not surprising that General Motors was one of the first corporations to invest its pension plan in hedge funds. GM had to pay out over $6.5 billion per year to retirees, necessitating a 7 percent annual return to avoid drawing down principal.[94] These funds represent the employees' deferred wages and future retirement security.

At the time, concerns were raised by "consultants and academics [who] question whether hedge funds, with risks that are hard to measure, are appropriate for pension funds, whose sole purpose, by law, is to pay out predetermined benefits to retired workers."[95] Some suggested that it was inappropriate for funds that have to pay retirees on a specific schedule to lock up assets in hedge funds that could suspend withdrawals.[96] Notwithstanding the growing commitments to hedge funds by pension plans, federal pension law did not require plan sponsors to reveal to beneficiaries how many hedge funds their plans invested in or the amount of total assets invested in them.[97] But for the SI presumption, hedge funds would not have been able to grow as large or take on levels of debt, engage in questionably conflicted transactions, or be a repository for poorly structured, overvalued, high-risk securities. In order to protect investors and reduce systemic risk, hedge fund operations and investment strategies should be subject to many of the substantive requirements of the 1940 Act, the law governing mutual funds. These requirements might include leverage restrictions, asset valuation controls, limitations on self-dealing and related-party transactions, and fiduciary duties to fund investors.

As somewhat of a moderate first step, Section 404 of the Dodd-Frank Act requires advisers to maintain records regarding hedge fund attributes including assets and leverage. In addition, this section of the new law requires the SEC to make rules mandating that hedge fund advisers file reports containing information necessary to protect the public interest and investors, and to assess systemic risk.

Credit Derivatives and the Sophisticated Investor

> The use of derivatives and other synthetic instruments must be regulated even if all the parties are sophisticated investors.
> —George Soros[98]

It is also accepted that credit derivatives, in particular the credit default swap, were key causes of the crisis. A credit default swap is like a home insurance policy. With an insurance policy, the buyer pays the seller premiums. In exchange the seller agrees to cover the buyer's losses if some bad event occurs and damages the home covered under the policy. Similarly with a CDS, the buyer pays the seller a premium based upon a percentage of the underlying asset, typically on a quarterly basis.[99] In exchange, the seller will compensate the buyer if there is a bad "credit event" involving a "reference obligation." Typical credit events include the underlying borrower's default, reorganization, or bankruptcy, though contracts vary.

The CDS was an instrument that morphed from a tool to minimize risk to one that created tremendous risk. CDS contracts were created in the mid-1990s.[100] At that time, a small group of parties were involved in the CDS market and the buyers typically owned the corporate or municipal bond (reference credit) for which they bought protection. For example, banks purchased CDS as a way to transfer some of the risk of the loans (assets) on their books to a third party and reduce their required regulatory capital.[101] In 2000, the notional value was around $900 billion.[102] By 2002, the notional value of CDS contracts grew to $2.19 trillion. By the 2007 peak, it was somewhere around to $57.8 to $63 trillion, depending on the source consulted.[103] As described below, this market was largely naked CDS, or credit insurance bought on debt that the insurance buyer did not actually own.[104]

The corresponding legal enabler was the Commodity Futures Modernization Act of 2000 (CFMA), which deregulated CDS and helped solidify legal rights of buyers and sellers of CDS. The CFMA transformed the CDS market from one that minimized risk to one that was used for speculation. First, an entity was allowed to buy "insurance" to cover a default (or other bad credit event) on a bond (or other instrument) the entity did not own. Second, a secondary market for CDS contracts developed, allowing obligations under a single contract to be sold many times. Third, credit "insurance" had initially been sold in reference to corporate bonds where the issuer was a known entity with recognizable products and services and publicly available financial statements. The transformative moment occurred when CDS were sold for bonds that were issued by conduits (or shells) which were privately issued with little transparency or wrapped inside of conduits in a synthetic securitization structure.

As described above, credit-default swaps were used to speculate on the performance of particular mortgage-backed securities as well as the mortgage market generally. Thus, the CFMA is a chief legal enabler of the crisis. The law did more than stay hands-off. It actually enabled the growth of a market.

The preamble of the CFMA identifies its purpose as "to reauthorize and amend the Commodity Exchange Act to promote legal certainty, enhance competition, and reduce systemic risk in markets for future and over-the-counter derivatives, and for other purposes."[105] The law explicitly states that "it shall supersede and preempt the application of any State or local law that prohibits or regulates gaming or the operation of bucket shops."[106] The need for this language reinforces the reality that CDS were "a form of legalized gambling that allows you to wager on financial outcomes without ever having to actually buy the stocks and bonds and mortgages. It would have been illegal during most of the 20th century under anti-gaming laws, but in 2000, Congress gave Wall Street an exemption and it has turned out to be a very bad idea."[107]

In addition, according to UCLA Law School Professor Lynne A. Stout, the CFMA gave counterparties the ability to enforce agreements in court. In other words, this deregulated market grew with government assistance. Prior to that change, there was uncertainty about the enforceability of these swaps. "Common-law judges accordingly viewed derivatives speculation with suspicion. Under the rule against difference contracts and its sister doctrine in insurance law (the requirement of 'insurable interest'), derivative contracts that couldn't be proved to hedge an economic interest in the underlying were deemed nothing more than legally unenforceable wagers."[108]

Stout contends that "the CFMA not only declared financial derivatives exempt from CFTC or SEC oversight, it also declared all financial derivatives legally enforceable. The CFMA thus eliminated, in one fell swoop, a legal constraint on derivatives speculation that dated back not just decades, but centuries. It was this change in the law—not some flash of genius on Wall Street—that created today's $600 trillion financial derivatives market."[109] She calculates that "by 2008, the notional value of the derivatives market—that is, the size of the outstanding bets as measured by the value of the things being bet upon—was estimated at $600 trillion, amounting to about $100,000 in derivative bets for every man, woman, and child on the planet."[110]

After the CFMA, in 2002, when the topic of regulation arose, Alan Greenspan objected: "This market, presumed to involve dealings among sophisticated professionals, has been largely exempt from government regulation. In part, this exemption reflects the view that professionals do not require the investor protections commonly afforded to markets in which retail investors participate. But regulation is not only unnecessary in these markets, it is potentially damaging, because regulation presupposes disclosure and forced disclosure of proprietary information can undercut innovations in financial markets."[111]

In addition, in a recent televised interview, as noted above, former President Bill Clinton shared his regret that he had allowed deregulation of derivatives. While the President initially blamed Treasury Secretaries Robert Rubin and Lawrence Summers for this "wrong" advice, later, he issued a correction in which he claimed it was actually Alan Greenspan who made these arguments.[112] However, notwithstanding Clinton's attempt to rehabilitate his advisers, research shows that perhaps Summers did also justify deregulation on the basis of SIs. The 1999 report on the OTC derivatives markets by the President's Working Group (for which Summers was a signatory) asserts: "The sophisticated counterparties that use OTC derivatives simply do not require the same protections under the CEA as those required by retail investors."[113]

Given that the premise of the sophisticated investor has crumbled, it follows that we should examine the "sophisticated professional." In addition, the question cannot be whether these professionals can take care of themselves. They act on behalf of institutions whose value they threaten when they operate in their own interest. Moreover, they participate in the larger capital markets that should serve the general public, not operate simply to generate fees and bonuses for the gamblers therein.

This supposition is supported by the recent congressional testimony of University of Texas Law School Professor Henry T. C. Hu, to the U.S. House Committee on Agriculture "there are structural reasons why 'sophisticated' financial institutions may misunderstand—or may act as if they misunderstand—the risks of the derivatives they offer. If such decision making errors threaten the survival of the dealer itself, a request for governmental intervention will not be far behind."[114] Hu informed the committee that notwithstanding the intricate models created by genius quantitative analysts to price credit derivatives, certain behavioral factors interfere with accurate risk assessment. These include "cognitive biases" and an incentive system within the derivative trading units of institutions that discourages raising flags. The cognitive bias he mentions is the "tendency to ignore low probability catastrophic events."[115] Polytechnic Institute of NYU Professor Nassim Taleb deemed these "black swan" events.[116]

Hu provided an excellent example of this cognitive bias. In August 2007, well into the subprime mortgage crisis, the head of the AIG financial products division (responsible for CDS sales) said the following: "It is hard for us, without being flippant, to even see a scenario within any kind of realm of reason that would see us losing one dollar in any of those [credit default swap] transactions."[117] In its 2006 10K (annual filing with the SEC made in early 2007), AIG also described the "likelihood of any payment obligation" under AIG CDS as "remote."[118] Notwithstanding this rosy forecast, in January 2008, AIG disclosed that it had $5 billion in losses associated with its CDS exposure in 2007.[119]

This helps illustrate the failure of sophisticated investors to understand risk. Contracts were limited to a variety of sophisticated investors defined in the statute. It also shows the motive to ignore risk—when one is being compensated extremely well up front and only for winning bets. The head of the AIG financial products division, Joseph Cassano, pocketed $315 million[120] growing AIG's CDS exposure to $440 billion. This exposure brought down the firm and required a $186 billion taxpayer-funded bailout. The AIG example also illustrates the problem with relying solely upon a disclosure regime to protect shareholders and the public from risky activities. If the disclosure proves inaccurate or incomplete, the damage is already done. Additionally, if the problems are widespread, as noted below, the vast majority of architects escape liability.

But for the SI presumption, credit derivatives would not have been deregulated. At best, we would forbid any "naked" credit default swaps—insurance bought on a debt instrument the buyer does not own. At the very least, they would have been required to be traded and cleared on exchanges, where collateral would have to be posted by "sellers" up front and on a regular basis to ensure orderly clearing and reduce market risk. In addition, as the SI presumption prevails, there are still proponents of keeping a good portion of swaps traded over the counter.

While some argue that the ability to bet against debt instruments one does not own helps to avoid bubbles, in fact, this proved not to be the case in the recent crisis. The chief example is the Magnetar hedge fund and its imitators. "Magnetar's approach had the opposite effect—by helping create investments it also bet against, the hedge fund was actually fueling the market. Magnetar wasn't alone in that: A few other hedge funds also created CDOs they bet against. And, as the *New York Times* has reported, Goldman Sachs did too. But Magnetar industrialized the process, creating more and bigger CDOs."[121]

Subprime Mortgage Securitization and the Sophisticated Investor

> Somehow we just missed that home prices don't go up forever and that it's not sufficient to have stated income [on home mortgage applications].
> —Jamie Dimon[122]

> Mr. Chairman, all these [mortgage] loans what we did in that business was underwrite to again the most sophisticated investors who sought that exposure.
> —Lloyd Blankfein[123]

> To the most sophisticated investors in the world, they were wrongly viewed as a "steal."
> —Alan Greenspan[124]

Securitized loans, in particular subprime mortgage pool securities, were the coveted asset that drove the exuberance and the crash. This catalyst also relied on a vehicle designed to disperse risk, but which morphed into a risk creator. This was the CDO. The first publicly traded MBS was launched in the early 1970s.[125] Innovation followed in 1983 when a new structure known as the collateralized mortgage obligation (CMO) was developed. As with a plain vanilla MBS, mortgage loans were pooled and certificates were issued. However, with a CMO, the cash flows were carved up. The pool (sometimes called a conduit) would issue different classes of certificates called "tranches." Each tranche represented a different payment stream. These certificates were considered debt obligations or "bonds." In other words the conduit borrows from the bond purchaser and must pay back principal and interest.

By 1991, 42 percent of all home mortgage debt was securitized.[126] Initially this market was dominated by loans to prime borrowers. Between 2001 and 2006, subprime mortgage origination and securitization skyrocketed. In 2001, $190 billion in subprime loans were originated and $87 billion in bonds for pools of subprime loans were issued. Five years later, there was $600 billion in subprime origination and $448.6 billion in issuance.[127] In contrast, there was a substantial decline in conventional mortgage origination and issuance. As noted earlier, subprime origination and its entire supply chain was ground zero of the disaster.

At the beginning of this supply chain were predatory mortgage lenders. Many borrowers who were eligible for prime loans were pushed into adjustable-rate mortgages and other unsuitable loans with higher fees. At the other end of the chain were investors—with a large appetite for these mortgages.[128] The mortgage-backed bonds paid higher interest rates than corporate bonds that had the same ratings issued by the major rating agencies.[129] In addition, they were treated the same for purposes of bank capital requirements, as a prime mortgage.[130]

While the sponsor of a conduit is supposed to investigate (or exercise "due diligence" on) the practices of originators and mortgage brokers, sponsors often deliberately looked the other way when faced with substantial evidence to support widespread fraud and predation. In addition, they hid this information from investors and rating agencies. "Investment banks that bundle and sell home mortgages often commissioned reports showing growing risks in subprime loans to less creditworthy borrowers but did not pass much of the information to credit rating agencies or investors."[131]

A large contributor to the rapid origination and sale of subprime mortgage-backed bonds was hedge funds, though some hedge fund managers were wise enough to stay away or place positions "betting" against these securities. Investment banks, like Merrill, however, loaded up on these risky securities, perhaps comforting themselves with the sophisticated quantitative models. As noted by investor Ed Thorp:

> The quants on Wall Street . . . simply take the math . . . and they build a machine which, in their imaginary world, must work just fine and must be safe and sound. But in fact, with the securitized pools that were put together to underlie these things, terrible, unsound mortgages were put into the pools, and that's not directly the fault of the quants, except that the quants should, if they were poking around and curious, have known how unsound these things were. It's more the fault of the sell side, who didn't care what was in there and figured they would sell it off, and they wouldn't be caught holding the bag, and of the regulators in government who simply looked the other way.[132]

In addition, sometimes the mortgage pools described above did not contain actual mortgage loans, but instead CDS contracts. In other words, the money from investors in synthetic CDOs would be channeled into a pool that itself was a "naked" seller of CDS on certain mortgages. The pool would not own these mortgages. The pool would receive ongoing premiums from buyers of the credit insurance and would lose money (and thus impact the investors) when the reference mortgages defaulted. Stated differently, a synthetic CDO is one "backed by derivative obligations, rather than by instruments yielding direct cash flows such as asset-backed securities."[133]

These synthetic CDOs and also CDOs squared (pools that own securities of other CDOs) and other varieties could not have existed but for a 1992 rule change by the SEC. And this rule change was justified by the SI presumption. In 1992, the SEC adopted Rule 3a-7 under the 1940 Act.[134] This greatly expanded the ability of asset-backed conduits to avoid being classified as an "investment company." While mortgage-backed securities were explicitly exempt from the requirements of the 1940 Act, pursuant to section 3(c)(5), many other asset securitizations had to fit into the aforementioned "hedge fund" exception under section 3(c)(1). The SEC provided some guidance to the structured finance industry, but made it clear with this "exemptive rule" that pools of mortgage-related bonds, including synthetics, could operate free of the onerous 1940 Act and its accompanying regulations.

The SEC supported this rule change with the comfort that "institutional investors, including banks, savings and loans, pension funds, insurance companies and money managers" were buyers of asset-backed securities, and they were "relatively safe" due to the high ratings offered by the ratings agencies.[135] But for the SI presumption, these CDOs would have had more oversight. In addition, the underlying mortgage loans might have been treated under the securities laws, like the investments that they truly are.[136]

Real-Life Performance of the Sophisticated Investors

> AIG was a AAA-rated company, one of the largest and considered one of the most sophisticated trading counterparts in the world.
> —Goldman Sachs annual report, 2009[137]

It is worthwhile to consider the performance during the crisis of sophisticated investors on which our deregulated system depends. Unlike the theoretical expectations for SIs, actual performance shows that SIs fell short. The failure of SIs is notable with regard to each of the key instruments. This section provides examples of these significant shortcomings regarding subprime securitization, credit default swaps (and other derivatives), hedge funds, and investment banks. It also highlights how, given the complexity of investment options, sophisticated investors often cannot distinguish between a fraudulent offer and a legitimate one.

Numerous types of SIs failed to protect themselves or their own investors and as a result collectively damaged the broader economy. Part of the problem, as noted in the introduction, is that no institution, even with a high-speed computer, is sophisticated enough to understand the complex instruments being offered. According to a Princeton University study of complex securities, "Studies suggest that valuations for a given product by different sophisticated investment banks can be easily 17% apart and that even a single bank's evaluations of different tranches of the same derivative may be mutually inconsistent."[138] Another contributor to the problem was the requirement that many SIs had to purchase instruments that received a AAA rating from a recognized rating agency. The general consensus today is that these SIs relied too heavily on such ratings and did not perform any meaningful independent assessments.

Michael Lewis noted that "the sorts of investors who handed money to [investor bankers], and thus bought the triple-A-rated tranche of CDOs—German banks, Taiwanese insurance companies, Japanese farmers' unions, European pension funds, and, in general, entities more or less required to invest in triple-A-rated bonds—did so precisely because they were meant to be foolproof, impervious to losses, and unnecessary to monitor or even think about very much."[139]

A specific example of an unsophisticated SI is the German bank IKB, known best for its role in the SEC's complaint against Goldman Sachs. In April 2010, the SEC sued Goldman, arguing that it had committed fraud in the structuring and sale of a CDO, the Abacus CDO, in 2007. Specifically, the SEC alleged that Goldman failed to disclose to IKB that a hedge fund manager, John Paulson, had handpicked the subprime-mortgage-backed bonds to be used as references. IKB had been assured in the offering materials that an independent agent had made the selections. In fact, the SEC alleged, Paulson identified the ones he believed were most likely to default, so that he could place a successful bet against certain bonds of the CDO.[140] By 2008, 95 percent of the loans referenced in the Abacus CDO were in default. Paulson's hedge fund purportedly earned $1 billion. Goldman initially defended its actions, claiming that IKB was one of the most sophisticated investors in the market for these exotic instruments.[141] Interestingly, in addition to losing $1 billion on the Abacus deal, IKB was a large investor in the Magnetar-sponsored CDOs. Eventually, IKB had to be bailed out by the German government.[142]

This example helps illustrate how investment banks like Goldman Sachs and hedge funds like Magnetar appeared to engage in SI arbitrage. In other words, it seems that they understood that there are two types of SIs: (1) those with skills equal to their own, meaning the truly sophisticated, and (2) those institutional investors and real people who qualified under the law as "sophisticated" but who were quite easy to fool. This can be seen in the testimony of Goldman Sachs investment banker Fabrice Tourre during hearings before a Senate subcommittee. In his prepared written remarks, from which he read, Tourre defended his role in selling the Abacus bonds. "I was an intermediary between highly sophisticated professional investors—all of which were institutions. None of my clients were individual, retail investors," he explained.[143] However, during the question-and-answer period of the hearings, Senator Susan Collins challenged this assertion, reading from an e-mail that Tourre sent in December 2006, in which he expressed disappointment with the list of target investors. He wrote: "This list might be a little skewed towards sophisticated hedge funds with which we should not expect to make too much money since (a) most of the time they will be on the same side of the trade as we will, and (b) they know exactly how things work and will not let us work for too much $$$, vs. buy-and-hold rating-based buyers who we should be focused on a lot more to make incremental $$$ next year." In the senator's view, "This sounds like a deliberate attempt to sell your products to less sophisticated clients who would not understand the products as well so that you can make more money."[144]

Part of the Goldman public defense can be found in a letter submitted to Phil Angelides, Chair of the separate Financial Crisis Inquiry Commission, but included as an exhibit for the Senate subcommittee hearings. The firm said that "Goldman Sachs and most investors simply did not predict or anticipate how severe the contraction in the housing market would become." However, it provided relevant information to potential purchasers and "this information enabled the sophisticated investors that purchased these instruments to run their own models and make their investment decisions based on their views of relevant macroeconomic factors, market and housing trends, as well as the apparent credit of the borrowers whose mortgages backed the securities."[145] In July 2010, Goldman agreed to settled the case for $550 million, however, the case against Tourre continued.[146]

Another example is the case of the Harvard endowment. The endowment grew from around $25.9 billion in 2005 to a peak of around $36.9 billion in June 2008, falling to $26 billion in June 2009. The investments in question were largely "private equity," that is, from a securities law perspective largely indistinguishable from hedge funds. Both are unregulated, private investment pools.[147]

At Harvard, even the most sophisticated of gatekeepers (former Treasury secretaries Lawrence Summers and Robert Rubin) were at an informational disadvantage vis-à-vis hired money managers. Apparently, Jack Meyer, the head of Harvard Management Company, left under criticism regarding remuneration and strategy. Some of his managers were paid "eight-figure salaries" and both Summers and Rubin questioned his aggressive strategies. However, when he left, the chief risk officer, chief operating officer, and chief technology officer along with thirty portfolio managers and traders followed. Meyer was seen to have damaged the institution, which was now "like a Ferrari without the engine."[148]

Perhaps employees did not sufficiently communicate with their peers or replacements and huge losses resulted. For example, mistakes were made with certain derivatives contracts: "The swaps were put in place under former Harvard president Larry Summers in the early 2000s to protect the university against rising interest rates on all the money it had borrowed. Instead, interest rates plunged. Yet for reasons no one can seem to explain, the university simply forgot to (or chose not to) cancel its swaps [after he was gone]. The result was a $1 billion loss."[149]

Another sophisticated investor was Tremont Holdings, Inc. Tremont is part of the Oppenheimer Funds unit of Massachusetts Mutual Life Insurance Co. Tremont lost over $3 billion in client assets after acting as a major "feeder" to Bernard L. Madoff Investment Securities' Ponzi scheme. Apparently, at least half of Tremont's assets were invested (via assorted feeder funds) with Madoff. Tremont attempted to refund money to clients by liquidating other assets; however, it was blocked by many "gates" and other restrictions on withdrawals from both private equity and hedge fund positions.[150] Clients have sued, claiming that Tremont should have known about the fraud. Tremont has denied the allegations. It stands to reason, then, that if Tremont is liable, it failed in its responsibilities as a sophisticated investor. If Tremont is not liable, then it shows that sophisticated investors are incapable of monitoring.

Without such allegedly sophisticated middlemen, Madoff could not have thrived.[151] There were easy flags that should have been seen by the sophisticated middlemen who channeled money from their own investors to Madoff. These included that Madoff apparently used a three-person accounting firm operating out of a suburban strip mall to audit his funds' financial statements.[152]

Given how poorly these sophisticated middlemen selected and monitored investments, it is surprising how much their clients paid for the privilege of hiring them. Through Ascot Partners LP, J. Ezra Merkin earned as much as 1.5 percent of assets under management. This amounted to around $40 million per year for his three funds, Ascot, Ariel, and Gabriel (which either invested all or a good portion with Madoff).[153] The representations made in the offering memorandum of more than fifty pages were meaningless in retrospect. The limited partners (investors) learned in a short, three-paragraph letter that the $1.8 billion they had entrusted him with had been entirely invested with Madoff.[154] In the letter, Merkin described himself as a "victim of this fraud."[155] Yet Merkin was himself not only sophisticated by SEC standards but also a graduate of Columbia University and Harvard Law School.[156]

Merkin's own hedge fund clients were "a large swath of sophisticated New Yorkers. As a result, many charities and schools that invested with him are now holding worthless investments and trying to explain to their constituents why the money was lost."[157] His clients included fifteen non-profit institutions.[158] Among the sophisticated Merkin investors was a real estate developer and publisher who claimed losses of $40 million personally and from a charitable trust.[159] Additionally, institutions of higher learning, presumably bastions of sophistication, also suffered under Merkin, including one university that claimed to have lost $110 million and another $24 million.[160]

The offering memorandum that governed Merkin's investment mandate reveals why so-called private ordering or private contract is a weak substitute for substantive regulations. The standard language informed the limited partners that investments were "speculative," and that "there can be no assurance that any of the hoped-for benefits of the foregoing approach will be realized."[161] Indeed, up front on page 2, it informed them that Merkin had the right to hand over assets to a third-party manager. Merkin and his legal counsel may well have believed that the offering memorandum gave him enough leeway to invest all assets with Madoff. Moreover, if both Merkin and Madoff had been subject to some of (or lighter versions of) the 1940 Act requirements, this could not have occurred. Too much board oversight, substantive protections, and controls are part of the law that would be much more difficult to circumvent.

Another theory, that self-interest will somehow help middlemen do a better job of protecting clients, is undermined by these examples. Family members who owned an entity that acted as a large feeder to Madoff apparently had "a very substantial part of each family member's personal assets . . . invested with Bernard Madoff alongside those of our investors."[162] Either the annual fees were enough incentive to overlook the warning signs, or as noted above, sophisticated investors are outmatched by fraudsters.

Some might argue that susceptibility to fraud is different from a lack of sophistication in understanding complex investments. And they might contend that Madoff is different from investment banks, credit rating agencies, and hedge funds that helped peddle worthless securities. However, in fact, University of Missouri–Kansas City Professor of Economics and Law and former bank regulator William K. Black has identified "control fraud" at the heart of the crisis. "Control fraud" occurs where a seemingly reputable organization is used by its managers as an instrument of fraud, with accounting the "weapon of choice."[163] According to Nobel Prize-winning economist George Akerlof and economist and Stanford University Senior Fellow Paul Romer, the existence of widespread control frauds can inflate financial bubbles.[164] In addition, the asymmetry of information in the financial market creates what Akerlof called a "lemons market," where the party who has superior information misleads customers into believing what they are buying is of greater value than it actually is.[165] Evidence from the crisis supports this view. Credit rating agency Fitch finally examined subprime loan files in 2007 after the wave of defaults and after origination of such loans had ceased. It then revealed that the "result of the analysis was disconcerting at best. There was the appearance of fraud or misrepresentation of fraud in almost every file."[166]

Conclusion

> There seems to be evidence that these "sophisticated investors" may not have fully appreciated the risks they were taking. Perhaps it may make sense for the definitions of who qualifies as "sophisticated" under our rules to be reconsidered. For example, maybe the criteria for sophistication should focus on more relevant attributes such as focusing on actual investment experience.
> —Luis A. Aguilar, SEC Commissioner[167]

To address the SI failures, we should borrow from the recent example of credit-rating-agency reform. We should remove the SI exceptions from the applicable laws and regulations where we discover SIs cannot protect themselves, their investors, or the markets. This would be analogous to the legal change made in response to the failure of credit rating agencies to properly identify the true risk of complex investments. Like SIs, rating agencies were thought to have the expertise and incentives to gauge the credit quality of securities they were hired to rate. However, notwithstanding their access to tremendous amounts of information, and to advanced computer models, the credit rating agencies were not able to perform as expected. As with the SIs, the most recent examples of rating agency failures were part of a longer history. This included the failure to downgrade Enron's bonds until just before its collapse and the propensity of rating agencies to engage in "ratings inflation" for complex securitizations as well as the failure to incorporate sufficient historical data into their models. And a justification for very limited to no government oversight was the existence of these rating agencies, private actors, supposedly able to police the markets and protect investors.

In response to the failure of credit rating agencies, the Dodd-Frank Act removes most statutory references to credit rating agencies. This change would, effective in two years, amend laws including, among others, the Federal Deposit Insurance Act, the Federal Housing Enterprises Financial Safety and Soundness Act of 1992, the 1940 Act, and the 1934 Act.[168] In addition, Dodd-Frank requires federal regulatory agencies within one year, to review and modify existing regulations so as to avoid treating a credit rating as a substitute for actual credit worthiness. In this way, the law attempts to remove the government sanctioned "seal of approval" that high ratings by the credit rating agencies have represented.[169]

By analogy, if an act of deregulation or failure to regulate was once justified in the legislative history, regulatory releases, working group reports, or other relevant studies by the premise that SIs were the chief or only investors affected, and if evidence shows that SI failure prevailed, harming ultimate investors or destabilizing markets, then those areas should be fixed so that the presumption is that the investors are not sophisticated at all. Then the laws and rules would be updated so that the standard tools including disclosure, oversight, and structural controls would be applied to protect investors and markets.

Chapter 10

The Role of Investment Consultants in Transforming Pension Fund Decision Making: The Integration of Environmental, Social, and Governance Considerations into Corporate Valuation

Eric R. W. Knight and Adam D. Dixon

Introduction

The global financial crisis of late 2007 and beyond is arguably the most severe financial crisis since the Great Depression. A number of the world's leading financial institutions have either gone bust or been bailed out by government, global capital markets remain in a climate of unease and limited confidence, and governments around the world had to return to Keynesian pump-priming fiscal policies to stimulate domestic economies into action and salvage the financial sector.

The scope and scale of this crisis has encouraged academics to reflect on what went wrong. While it is popular for journalists to lay blame on the generic figure of the City Banker, this view does not given sufficient credit to the fact that the world's largest asset owners themselves have suffered deep blows from this crisis. Indeed, the shortcomings of financial markets appear to be more complex than the big bonuses of bankers alone.

In order to delve beneath the surface, this chapter therefore examines the investment processes around the world's largest asset owners: pension funds. Given their long-term time horizons and their exposure to multiple geographies and sectors, pension funds have been described as "universal owners."[1] With command of US\$ 28.2 trillion of the US\$ 74.3 trillion global fund management industry, pension funds have a vested self-interest in the stability of global financial markets.[2] In the context of a global financial crisis, universal ownership should, in principle, make pension fund managers conscientious participants in systemic reforms to the economy. Yet it is questionable whether most pension funds are actually capable of effectively employing their strength as universal owners.

In order to examine this we adopt an economic geography approach to examine the relationships between actors and institutions engaged in the investment process of pension fund money. We extend on the literature on pension fund governance by specifically examining the role of investment consultants.[3] Investment consultants act as intermediaries between pension funds and asset managers. As such, their relational geography in the investment process gives them a conflicted role: they are "thought leaders" driving innovation in investment management practices while also being contractually committed to the demands of their client.

We use the emerging concept of environmental, social, and governance (ESG) considerations as a lens through which to examine the relational geography of investment consultants. ESG considerations are a valuable analytical tool in the context of the financial crisis, as we argue that the failure to incorporate ESG considerations into investment analysis is a contributing factor to the current crisis facing financial markets. We develop our arguments from a series of six case studies collected from questionnaires sent to leading global investment consultants with the assistance of the Asset Management Working Group of the United Nations Environment Programme Finance Initiative. The six investment consultants relied upon are headquartered in the U.K., the U.S., and Japan. However, their operations are spread across other markets (e.g., Canada and the Netherlands) with large funded occupational pensions.[4]

This chapter proceeds in the following manner. The second section sets out what we perceive to be the geographical conundrum at the heart of the global financial crisis. The subsequent section then examines the emergence of ESG integration as an effort to bring investors closer to the local conditions facing their investments. We note that this chapter does not assert the merits of ESG as an investment tool but rather is interested in its penetration and uptake within the pension fund investment process. The fourth section locates investment consultants within the relational geography of pension fund investment management. The fifth section discusses the data used in the chapter to examine these issues and the sixth presents the results of consultants' views on ESG integration techniques and principles in detail. The final section discusses the implications of these results in terms of the difficulty of driving new alternative methods of investment analysis.

The Recent Global Financial Crisis

There has been much speculation as to the underlying causes of the recent global financial crisis. Ostensibly, the trigger for the crisis in late 2007 was the gap between U.S. housing prices and the traded value of subprime mortgage derivatives on global financial markets. When housing prices collapsed in late 2007 and job stability decreased, the growing default rate on mortgages illuminated an asset bubble in the subprime mortgage market.

The specific shortcomings in the subprime mortgage market may be attributed to various factors including failures in asset pricing, risk disclosure, and credit rating.[5] Indeed, many investors after the onset of the crisis pointed the finger at credit rating agencies that had inaccurately graded the risk profile of mortgage-backed financial products. However, these events arguably signal a far deeper malaise in the operation of global financial markets. What this crisis revealed is the gap in financial markets between the asset price traded by global investors and the on-the-ground risks and opportunities facing local companies (and indeed homeowners) in the real economy. As much as financial models and mathematical sophistry attempts to recreate real-world risk through complex modeling, it is only ever an approximation of the real thing. It is the gap between the *global* investor and the *local* investee that often lies at the heart of the world's asset pricing bubbles.[6]

Disclosure of financial information plays a crucial role in attempting to narrow this gap. According to the efficient market hypothesis of financial markets, asset prices fully reflect all publicly available information in the market. In practice, however, only a fraction of information relevant to the likelihood of success or failure of a particular company is reflected in balance sheet disclosures under standard accounting practice. What is missing is a wealth of information surrounding the operational and macroeconomic challenges facing a prospective investment. This ranges from the failure to gauge the macroeconomic risk of default on Russian government bonds, which led to the collapse of Long Term Capital Management, to poor estimates of the future income stream of home mortgagees in outer-suburban Detroit, which triggered the subprime mortgage crisis.

An important move to fill this gap has been the push toward greater information disclosure and analysis of ESG considerations. ESG considerations encompass a wide spread of issues from the corporate governance regulations facing an investee company to the social and environmental challenges impacting market conditions in the future. An example of an issue falling within the environment subset of ESG issues is climate change. Climate change represents an external uncorrelated variable that has not been fully priced into current financial modeling. As such it has been described by Sir Nicholas Stern as potentially the greatest market failure in human history.[7]

Disclosing information on climate change and feeding this into investment analysis is therefore an attempt to build a bridge between the global investor and the local environmental challenges facing a particular business.[8] However, the failure to do so perpetuates the shortcomings of existing asset pricing models illuminated by the recent global financial crisis.

ESG Integration as Investment Tool

The integration of ESG information as a tool in investment analysis (referred to here as ESG integration) needs to be clearly distinguished in the academic literature from the field of socially responsible investment (SRI). The fundamental distinguishing feature between these two approaches is motivation. Whereas SRI is essentially motivated by ethical imperatives and aims to actively shape the market, ESG integration is motivated by economic imperatives and is a risk-analytics tool aimed at capturing the effects of environmental, social, and corporate governance considerations on the risk-adjusted return of portfolios. In this regard, ESG integration is arguably a more tangible and effective method of addressing such issues given conventional investment practice, which relies heavily on quantitative measures and standardized benchmarks.[9]

The SRI literature has a long history stretching back to the 1980s, when it had strong uptake among European funds such as the Stewardship Fund in the United Kingdom and Varldnaturfonden in Sweden.[10] The attempt behind these early funds was to focus investment in assets that were regarded by those investors as "socially responsible." From the practitioner perspective, sell-side analysts were engaged in constructing portfolios that satisfied a particular appetite for nonfinancial goals. Within the academic literature, however, defining which investment goals are "socially responsible" has been contested based on different moral, ontological, ideological, and functional definitions of social responsibility.[11] SRI has been used to describe investment portfolios that achieve a sufficient level of financial return as well as offering social, environmental, and other nonfinancial benefits.[12] This definition of SRI is fundamentally politicized because each investor, as a consumer of financial products, demands its own mix of nonfinancial goals and outcomes, making the construction of a commonly agreed upon "SRI portfolio" practically impossible.[13]

Separately to this prerogative, a body of literature has developed on the *economic* consequences (as opposed to the ethical consequences) of social, environmental, and corporate governance variables for the financial performance of the investments. This literature has spawned many streams of academic research in finance, law,[14] and management.[15] On the one hand, quantitative research has been carried out trying to use social,[16] environmental,[17] or governance[18] variables to explain shareholder returns. This literature at times has faced methodological challenges by virtue of the fact that environmental, social, or corporate governance data has often been located within SRI-related products, either in an aggregated fashion or in the form of self-assessed qualitative metrics. This has given reason to qualify the conclusions of much of this quantitative research. On the other hand, the literature has focused on the ability of ownership rights and shareholder activism to change corporate management. This literature has mainly focused on changing company's governance in light of Jensen and Meckling's (1976) agency theory.[19] Whatever limitations may be placed on the conclusions reached by this research, it is clear that the underlying economic motivations of this research stream fundamentally distinguish it from the ethical overtones of the SRI literature.

ESG integration has emerged as an investment tool that clearly falls within this latter economic-focused literature. Championed to a large extent by the United Nations Environment Programme Finance Initiative and major sell-side investment houses around the world such as Goldman

Sachs, UBS, and JP Morgan, ESG integration is a new investment tool which is focused on risk analytics and identifying long-term "alpha" drivers (above benchmark returns). In other words, it is about more precisely determining the impact of environmental, social, and corporate governance considerations on asset pricing and the future cash flow of businesses. As such, it is a split from the primarily ethical/market-transforming mandate of the SRI community and as such has caused some consternation for academics within this community.[20]

By way of example, the relevance of ESG integration in more accurately making asset pricing estimations is evident in the growth of so-called new paradigm firms.[21] New paradigm firms describe businesses where a significant proportion of their market valuation is attributable to intangible assets such as goodwill, corporate reputation, and brand valuation. This means that market valuation for these businesses is often at a significant premium to the book value of the physical assets of these firms. This is in contrast to "classical model" firms that dominated the early twentieth century. Here, market valuation was closer to book valuation because the firm's assets were primarily physical and tangible assets such as plant and equipment.[22]

Traditionally, new paradigm firms might have been restricted to media companies or consumer retail (such as GAP Inc.), where fashion and style are crucial to making sales. However, more recently intangible assets make up a remarkably large proportion of market valuation. For instance, the book value of assets in the S&P 500 account for only 20–25 percent of corporate valuation. This highlights the importance for investors of understanding how ESG issues are driving the local operation of their investments.

In the context of consumer concern about climate change, mainstream businesses in the utilities, resource, and automobile sectors are increasingly exposed to risks around their environmental reputation. For example, the success of General Electric over the last five years has in part been attributable to sales from its "Eco-magination" product line across 2007–2009. Similar Toyota Motor Corporation has been able to outcompete American car companies in part on the growth of consumer demand for hybrid cars. Another instance where environmental considerations have impacted future cash flow has been in the case of energy company Royal Dutch Shell. It has been argued that Royal Dutch Shell lost a large amount of goodwill following the Brent Spar incident in 1995.[23]

The importance of ESG integration in financial analysis is therefore closely related to the shortcomings of financial markets to connect local issues with the mathematical models built by physically distant global investors. ESG is thus intimately connected with improving corporate valuation as opposed to achieving ethical objectives per se.[24]

The Conflicted Role of the Investment Consultant

Financial markets are more than a combination of mathematical models and information. Behind every investment decision are a complex interpersonal process and set of personal relationships that integrate available information into a buy/sell/hold decision for investors. The extent to which ESG considerations feature in investment analysis depends on how this knowledge feeds into the relational geography of investment decision making. Relational geography is simply concerned with the "social interactions between economic agents."[25] It is alert to complexity and reactivity in economic systems that qualify the pure application of mathematic models to economic decisions.

The literature on the relational geography of pension fund decision making to date has mainly focused on governance architectures in pension fund trustee boards.[26] Ambachtsheer, Capelle, and Lum, for example, argue that board-level competence is a serious limitation in the flow of pension fund capital.[27] As a result, trustee boards widely rely on investment consultants for financial advice, effectively making them crucial actors in the investment decision-making process.[28] Yet despite such an important role, it is questionable whether investment consultants are effective at driving an investment agenda that includes ESG integration. This chapter extends this literature by focusing on the behavior and practices of investment consultants in particular. Before doing this, it is necessary to situate investment consultants within the pension fund investment process.

Although the structure of pension fund investment management can vary by jurisdiction, the organizational structure of the investment process is arguably fairly standardized. For the sake of exposition, we focus primarily on illustrating this structure through the case of trust-based pension jurisdictions. In these jurisdictions—where the vast majority of global pension assets exist—employers or employees make contributions to a fund, which is held in a trust and overseen by a trustee board. Depending on the actual size of the pension fund, administration can be either internal or external, or various degrees thereof depending on the particular administrative task. Large pension funds, given scale effects, often have separate physical pension management organizations. Smaller funds, by contrast, generally delegate most day-to-day management processes to external providers. These tasks range from benefits management and reporting all the way to actual fund management.

Regardless of size, the board of trustees sits at the center of the investment process and is ultimately responsible for the actions of the administration of the fund. Often, mainly with larger funds, members of a board will also sit on an investment committee together with other experts to make recommendations to the board on the allocation of assets, choice of investment managers, and other financial matters—with smaller funds, separate investment committees generally do not exist. In making decisions regarding the choice of investment managers and asset allocation, trustee boards often employ the advice of external investment consultants. This is particularly the case with smaller funds, given limited or nonexistent internal resources for researching investment managers and devising an optimal asset allocation given the fund's risk parameters. Yet even larger funds employ outside consultants to aid in making decisions. A stylized rendition of this organizational structure is visualized in Figure 10.1.

From a slightly stylized though empirically grounded perspective on best-practice investment consulting, the principal responsibilities for which investment consultants are called on to consult encompass three overlapping areas: organizational coherence, people, and process.[29] Regarding "organizational coherence," investment consultants assist with the formation and clarification of a pension fund's organizational strategy and mission. This is more detailed than simply articulating the goal of maximizing beneficiaries' financial returns, which is a trustee's legal obligation. It also involves clarity around the selection of benchmarks, identifying a long-term strategy, and drafting mission statements and statement of investment principles.[30]

Consultants' responsibilities also include assisting trustees in the recruitment of competent fund managers and administrators to provide financial planning advice and advice on asset allocation. This is the "people" aspect of the pension fund investment chain. Investment consultants facilitate the negotiation of investment policy statements between asset owners (funds) and investment managers, so that both parties to the contract have clearly mandated objectives. In this respect, the extent to which a fund has an interest in focusing on short-term or long-term investment horizons and the

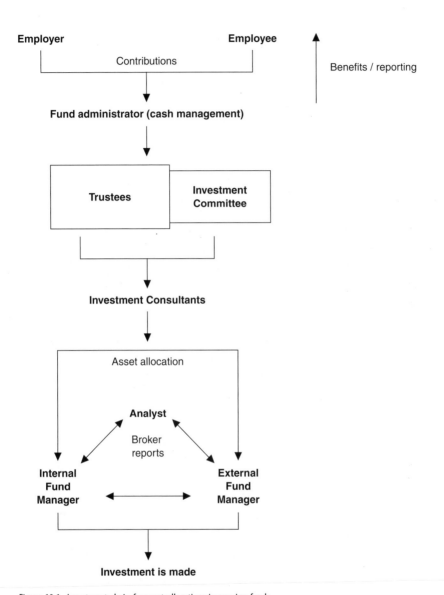

Figure 10.1. Investment chain for asset allocations in pension funds
Adapted from Gordon L. Clark, *Pension Fund Capitalism* (New York: Oxford University Press, 2000)

decision to adopt particular investment methodologies, such as ESG, is largely decided by trustees *with* the assistance of investment consultants.

In certain cases consultants may also become responsible for managing the ongoing relationship between asset owners and managers and the investment process broadly. They evaluate the performance of investment managers on a regular basis and make recommendations for hiring new managers based on which managers have demonstrated a strong performance in asset classes and methodologies that align with trustees' mission and risk appetite. They may also be required to structure products for the pension fund to invest in directly where there is no external expertise available.

Given the intimate role investment consultants have in trustee decision making, they have been described by some practitioners as the gatekeepers of pension fund investment management.[31] Although the term "gatekeeper" arguably overstates the supervisory aspect and functional capacity of investment consultants, they can still play a pivotal role in board operations and are one of the first stops for advice and thought leadership when trustee boards need assistance. They could be more rightly characterized as sophisticated filters of information, or as one consultant suggested to us, "important digits in the combination" that unlocks investment management.

The flip side to the consultants' privileged position is that they are also the subjects of client demand. The dynamics of the financial services industry are such that consultants are required to follow clients' orders. The tension between these two positions—as adviser and as service provider—means that consultants may find themselves in a compromising position. They may be prevented from exercising their leadership at the very moment when it is most needed because a client misunderstands them, is ignorant, or ignores the advice given to them (but likewise, it is entirely possible that consultants themselves may display irrational behavior either because they are actively hostile, stubborn, or ignorant or because they perceive a threat to their business relationship with the client). As we demonstrate below, this fundamental characteristic is a significant barrier to ESG integration.

Data and Methodology

The findings in this chapter draw on the responses of a number of leading international investment consultancies to a detailed questionnaire sent out by the United Nations Environment Programme Finance Initiative's

(UNEPFI) Asset Management working group in 2008 (see the Appendix). The group contacted twenty investment consulting firms in the U.S., Canada, the U.K., France, Germany, Sweden, and Japan and asked recipients to provide detailed responses to nineteen open-ended questions. These questions covered a number of topics broadly categorized within the following topics: fiduciary duties in the management of pension fund assets; evaluation procedures for investment managers' performance; investment practices used to monitor investment managers, such as requests for proposals and analyzing their proxy voting track record; attitudes toward ESG in investment research; and the legal language used to define the relationship between pension funds, consultants, and investment managers.

The response rate to the questionnaire was relatively low: responses were received from six of the twenty consultants contacted. Notwithstanding this low response rate (30 percent), those who did respond represent some of the largest and most important global investment consultants by size of assets under advisement and international reputation. Except for one Japanese consultant with a domestic practice, these consultancies represent the world's largest and arguably the most influential global investment consulting firms with global institutional, tax-exempt assets under advisement of US$ 8 trillion collectively as of June 2008. This represents approximately 30 percent of the world's pension funds assets at the time the questionnaire was completed. Individually, the consultancies varied in worldwide institutional tax-exempt assets under advisement of less than US$ 700 million to almost US$ 3.6 trillion as of June 30, 2008, as set out in Table 10.1.[32]

These respondents were spread across three geographies, with responses received from two offices in each of the U.K., U.S., and Japan respectively. In each case, principals (very senior consultants) within these firms completed the questionnaires, which were cross-checked with team managers in international offices to ensure that they represented the general view of the consultancy as far as possible. Notwithstanding the global coverage of the consultants who responded to the questionnaire, these responses are not intended to cover the entire field of investment consulting globally or indeed regionally. This is one of the limitations of our data set given the low response rate. Rather they provide insight into the views held by consultancies that advise pension funds day to day on the issue of ESG integration. These case studies therefore provide scope to reflect on the institutional uptake of ESG integration in pension fund investment management within developed financial markets.

Table 10.1: Description of Investment Consultant Respondents

Descriptor	Consultant 1	Consultant 2	Consultant 3	Consultant 4	Consultant 5	Consultant 6
Level of ESG experience	"Market leading"	"Market leading"	"Moderately experienced"	"Moderately experienced"	"Least experienced"	"Least experienced"
Firm scope	Global	Global	Global	Global	Global	National
Respondent's office	U.K.	U.S.	U.K.	U.S.	Japan	Japan
Seniority of respondent	Principal	Principal	Principal	Principal	Principal	Principal
Type of respondent	Specialist	Specialist	Mainstream	Specialist	Mainstream	Mainstream
Verification of survey	Cross-checked across global practice	Cross-checked across global practice	Cross-checked within national office	Cross-checked across global practice	Cross-checked within national office	Cross-checked within national office
Worldwide assets under advertisement as of June 30, 2008[a]	Tier 1	Tier 1	Tier 2	Tier 1	Tier 2	Tier 3

[a]These categorizations have been used to maintain the anonymity of the respondents: (1) Tier 1 = over US$1 trillion; (2) Tier 2 = US$500 billion to US$1 trillion; (3) Tier 3 = less than US$500 billion.

We individually evaluated the level of expertise in ESG integration among the respondents and placed them in one of three categories in Table 10.1. In evaluating these categorizations we took into account the number of staff employed on this issue, years of experience in advising on ESG, and the depth and breadth of the responses given. The respondents we considered to be most experienced in ESG integration (hereafter, "market leading consultants") were housed within the responsible investment teams of the U.K. and U.S. offices respectively of two international consultancies, which were world leaders in terms of their depth of market power, geographical scope, and total worldwide, tax-exempt institutional assets under advisement as of June 30, 2008, which were in excess of US$2 trillion. The moderately experienced respondents in ESG integration (hereafter, "moderately experienced consultants") were principals housed in the U.K. and U.S. offices respectively of two international consultancies with strong market presence predominately in Europe and the U.S. and with total worldwide, tax-exempt institutional assets under advisement as of June 30, 2008, between US$1 trillion and US$2 trillion. Finally, the least experienced respondents in ESG integration (hereafter, "least experienced consultants") were principals housed in the Japanese offices of an international and domestic consultancy respectively. These consultancies advised on total institutional assets of less than or equal to US$1 trillion.

It is important to acknowledge that there may be some scope of bias in the results. For example, larger investment consultants may have more capacity and experience to advise on ESG integration because they may have a larger budget to hire this expertise rather than a genuine commitment to the importance of the issue. Furthermore, experienced firms may have a financial incentive to overstate the significance of ESG integration in order to attract more demand among the pension fund client base. The fact that these responses were provided in connection with a public UNEPFI report means that there is some scope for respondents to have a financial or marketing agenda. However, the fact the respondents were told up front that their responses would remain anonymous helps balance this biased effect.

Investment Consultants as Agents for ESG Integration in Investment Thinking

In this section we analyze the responses to the questions asked in the questionnaire, disaggregating them by *organizational coherence, people* and *process*, as per the three principal areas of the consulting relationship discussed in the third section. Although the questions were not framed along these three responsibilities in the questionnaire, we have structured our analysis using this framework as it provides a useful tool for in-depth examination of investment consultants' behavior and investment practices.

Our analysis of the questionnaire responses indicated that the ability of investment consultants to lead change in investment thinking around ESG integration appears to be influenced by the degree of expertise and knowledge the consultant is able to bring to the client regarding the subject. Higher levels of expertise create situations in which the consultant can take a strong position in the consultant-client relationship by providing institutional clarity to trustee boards, offering direction on the selection of the best fund manager, and guiding clients out of a myopic short-term strategy and a culture of limited index-backed mandates. However, where consultants lack expertise the survey responses provide examples of how consultants can be dominated by the client and take a subservient position with respect to investment advice.

Organizational Coherence of ESG

The market leading consultants with the most specialized knowledge of ESG were confident about relating ESG to their clients in economic terms. They had the language to explain how ESG considerations can have a material impact on corporate financial performance and therefore on portfolio performance, as the following response indicates: "An increasing body of evidence exists to show that ESG factors can impact investment performance. . . . We believe ESG factors fall within the purview of fiduciary duty where they are or may be material to long term capital preservation. ESG factors may also contribute to the growth of investments as related opportunities are sought." The strength of these connections varies across sector, geography, investment strategy, and asset classes, and market leading consultants are able to position themselves in relation to clients as "leaders" who could guide their client through this complex terrain. For example, one market leading consultant revealed that ESG integration was more important in asset classes exposed to long-term trends such as long-term, long-only equities. Thus, investment strategies that are highly geared toward short-term returns will fail to integrate these long-term dynamics into their allocations and will therefore be exposed to higher long-term risk profiles.

This leadership position and knowledge directly translated into a more active involvement in pension fund governance. For example, the two leading consultants both maintained global investment manager databases, which included information on ESG integration capacity within the investment manager community. These consultants were therefore able to provide benchmarking services to rank managers for their clients. They also had boilerplate templates for investment management contracts and investment policy statements, which could be amended to offer ESG capabilities to the client. They also expressed comfort in exercising active engagement strategies with company management as well as a variety of other tools such as voting rights and ownership strategies.

Lack of knowledge and expertise on ESG among moderately experienced and less experienced consultants, however, positioned these consultants as "followers" with respect to their clients. They were willing to address ESG issues only on an ad hoc basis and then only when the client had raised these issues first. This placed them in a weaker position with respect to the client and meant that they were subservient to client demand, as the following response suggests: "It is at the discretion of clients to ensure ESG criteria are relevant to their particular fund objectives, investment beliefs and governance arrangements." This meant that they were unable to offer advice on fund managers with ESG capabilities until the client gave permission for a request for proposal to be issued. They also expressed greater reluctance to incorporate ESG-related considerations into the investment management contracts and investment policy statements

The lack of expertise not only placed the consultant in a weaker position in the client relationship but was also consistent with conceptual confusion about what ESG integration actually meant. Specifically, as suggested by the following response, these consultants confused ESG with SRI, which meant that they conceived of ESG in ethical rather than economic terms: "In terms of institutional investors, the circumstances where investment decisions are designed to be closely linked to the institutional mission and objectives are most conducive to deep consideration of ESG considerations." Here "institutional mission" is a reference to mission-related investing, which is a distinctive approach to ethically motivated investment decisions. The miscategorization of ESG as an ethical concept was most pronounced among the least experienced consultants in our data, who were based in

Japan. For them, ESG integration was synonymous with ethical investing and was thought to apply only to environmental polluters, human rights abusers, and other "antisocial forces movements [*sic*]." Although it is not possible to generalize these conclusions Japan-wide, there is certainly emerging empirical evidence to suggest that the meaning of terminology such as SRI, corporate social responsibility (CSR), and responsible investment (PRI) is highly conflated among Japanese pension funds and that there is substantive confusion on the distinction between the ethical and economic issues at play. This confusion indicates that the investment cultures within the Japanese setting deserve further research.[33]

By miscategorizing the issue as ethical rather than economic, investment consultants may lead clients away from considerations that in fact have a very tangible impact on financial returns. Empirical research on trustee board decision making has shown that when issues are framed in terms of ethical responsibility, trustees are less responsible than average members of the public.[34] The lack of knowledge around ESG integration appears to be most pronounced around environmental and social issues as opposed to corporate governance, which has a deeper history in the academic literature.[35] One comment by a moderately experienced consultant indicated that when an ESG issue is apprehended in financial terms, then the consultant is willing to promote its importance in investment management: "We believe that examining the corporate governance of companies is an essential aspect of investment management. However, the impact of environmental and social policies is not currently considered essential." Knowledge and expertise therefore appear to be crucial commodities in negotiating consultants' relationship with pension fund boards. Greater levels of knowledge influence the level of leadership consultants feel comfortable to exercise over clients, and the extent to which they are able to provide more robust professional services. Lack of knowledge, by contrast, can lead to situations of active harm where conceptual confusion means that considerations material to portfolio returns are not brought to clients' attention.

People

In a professional-service-based industry such as investment consulting, the depth of human talent within an organization is an important measure of the organization's experience. This is no different for ESG integration because firms with the most sophisticated understanding of ESG integration tools also employed the largest number of full-time staff. The market leaders had full-time staff focused on ESG integration in offices around the world, primarily the U.K. and the U.S. This compared with less experienced firms in which consultants dealt with ESG considerations on an ad hoc basis depending on client demand.

As discussed above, investment consultants can play an important role in building relationships between asset owners and asset managers around areas of common interest. However, a challenge in establishing these networks has been the lack of expertise within fund managers. Market leading consultants felt that sell-side firms still had a long way to go before ESG integration services were widely available when investors needed them: "Not all managers, across geographies, asset classes and styles have the inclination or ability to abide by such [ESG] language and it might be dangerous to include it [in investment management contracts] otherwise [sic]." The lack of expertise at the fund manager level has been acknowledged by leading industry groups such as Fair Pensions, although they have noted improvements over the last five years.[36] Jaworski also supports the above findings with a survey of 88 sell-side and 240 buy-side institutions in Europe, which indicate that there is weak dialogue and networking between buy-side investors and sell-side analysts around ESG considerations.[37] This lack of expertise in the financial community appears to be an impediment for some investment consultants' ability to form networks of communication around ESG integration. For example, the market leading consultants indicated that they are reluctant to draft legal clauses into investment management contracts between trustees and fund managers with respect to ESG integration because there may be a lack of fund managers who would be able to carry through with this obligation.

Notwithstanding the difficulties in forming networks of communication around ESG integration, leading consultants are beginning to develop tools to assist asset owners to form and evaluate relationships with asset managers. For example, leading consultants have begun to rate fund managers based on their ESG competency in parallel with overall investment rating. Evaluation takes place routinely and takes into account both quantitative and qualitative data such as "idea generation, portfolio construction, management and implementation." This information is compiled into global databases about global investment managers in a comparable and standardized manner. Processing information and applying evaluative metrics can be understood as the first step toward taking leadership for clients on these issues. This is consistent with Lowenstein's contention that financial agents are able to manage only what they can measure.[38]

Moderately experienced consultants by contrast are to a larger extent reliant on the client to express an interest in ESG integration before expertise is forthcoming. Indeed these consultants provide ESG integration advice only on demand and have no full-time institutional capacity in this issue. The short supply of expertise may also be correlated with poor-quality advice, as when one consultant appeared to confuse ESG integration's economic motivations with SRI's ethical motivations: "We have an organized group of investment consultants, research consultants, and analysts who focus on the spectrum of issues in mission investing/ESG/SRI strategies." Although these respondents acknowledge that consultants have some role in raising the issue with clients, they are more likely to wait for trustees with the assistance of employers to take the first initiative. These insights complement the analysis of organizational coherence above but again highlight the importance of knowledge and expertise for fostering effective relationships around ESG integration. The willingness of some consultants with deep knowledge to apply evaluative metrics to fund managers' performance is the first step toward building strong webs of knowledge around pension fund trustee boards.

Process

The ability of investment consultants to transform pension fund governance through knowledge and leadership may be restricted by barriers within the investment culture of consultants themselves, which are overhangs from the client-focused nature of the industry. One such barrier is the strong culture of short-term investing within finance. Short-termism in financial markets is a problem that has been identified among pension fund executives and refers to the tendency to place more weight on immediate issues than on actively dealing with future uncertainties and opportunities.[39] This manifests itself in quarter-to-quarter or half-yearly reporting that tracks performance over a short time rather than over longer time frames, such as three to five years. These longer time frames are typically more suited to ESG integration because there is a significant turnaround time before, for example, new strategies in green product innovations come into play and affect a company's performance.

The market leading consultants have identified this barrier and have actively sought to advise clients to adopt long-term time frames for their investment strategy. This means, for example, hiring and retaining managers on the basis of long-term performance rather than quarter-to-quarter benchmarks. However, some of the less experienced consultants did not believe that time frames featured as a barrier to ESG integration into clients' portfolios. This is because manager performance was evaluated in terms of execution of a particular strategy rather than returns after a period of time. This view again reflected a perception of ESG integration as an ethical investment strategy. The key point is that where asset owners are focused on meeting short-term financial performance objectives, then their portfolios are more likely to be inadvertently and negatively exposed to long-term influences such as ESG issues. It falls to consultants to advise asset owners away from a shortsighted view of performance such as this.

This problem is compounded by a second barrier, which is the use of tracking error limits and index-referenced mandates as benchmarks for financial performance. The use of these benchmarks as targets for fund financial performance penalizes the integration of ESG into portfolio construction. This is because the majority of companies currently do not fully take advantage of the ESG value drivers within their business operation over the long term. This means that marketwide indexes are in general composed of companies focused on short-term gains rather than long-term growth. Since ESG integration requires a firm to make an investment or judgment call on the future, the cash flow benefits to the company will be realized over a longer time than is reflected in quarterly market indexes.

One strategy to overcome this barrier is for asset managers to seek absolute returns rather than market returns. This means that funds set a target for an acceptable positive financial return over a nominated time period (for example 5 percent per year) rather than tracking the market. Indeed, the market leading consultants noted that they observe a trend among their clients away from strict limits toward structures and policies that are friendlier toward absolute return strategies. However, they acknowledge that this trend faces significant cultural barriers. For example, many institutional investors continue to rely on tracking error to minimize their portfolios' deviation from the market rate of return. This is perceived to be an important risk-mitigation mechanism.

The hurdle that this may pose for ESG integration was highlighted by an international consultancy based in the U.K. in the context of defined-benefit pension schemes. Its respondents pointed out that if a fund with an integrated ESG policy performs more poorly than the index and that scheme enters the U.K. pension protection fund, then trustees might be in breach of their fiduciary duty even if the majority (but not all) of the membership are in favor of the ESG-related screen. The fundamental difficulty here is that although the ESG integration strategy is intended to lead to financial outperformance of the portfolio over the long term, it may result in lower performance or higher volatility in the short run as firms in the market capitalize on short-term gains. This is less of a problem in defined-contribution pension schemes because beneficiaries directly take on the investment risk for ESG integration.[40]

Finally, the incentive structure for managers can compound the barriers created by an investment focus on short-term returns and therefore penalize ESG integration. The market leading consultants argued that fixed or capped management fee structures had a neutral effect on ESG-integration approaches. By contrast, performance-based fees can be structured to incentivize short-term gains. This comment suggests that where fee structures are poorly framed, investment professionals can be motivated by financial incentives that are against the best *long-term* interests of their clients. Thus, if as a consequence of the financial crisis incentive structures become better aligned—either through regulation or more effective pressure from buy-side firms—to outcomes over a longer period (e.g., tying remuneration to performance over a period of, say, three years), this barrier to ESG integration may diminish. Indeed, as remuneration incentives are stretched, ESG issues become more salient. In many ways, then, ESG integration itself can be a way of mitigating misaligned incentives, as the nature of ESG issues calls attention to longer-term problems material to performance.

Implications and Conclusions

Investment consultants have privileged positions in driving the direction of global pension fund investment. In these positions, investment consultants can drive the manner in which investments are made and concern is given to longer-term risks not readily priced and understood in the market. The risks of climate change to corporate profitability over the long term are one such example of an ESG consideration that large long-term investors might arguably need to consider when making investments and deciding on their asset allocation. However, our survey responses provide some examples in which profound gaps of expertise and understanding within the investment consulting community can inhibit the dissemination of ESG integration as an investment tool in financial analysis. Indeed, one potentially strong explanation for the low response rate of the questionnaire is the high degree of skepticism about or lack of knowledge of ESG.

There may be a number of reasons why some consultants may struggle with knowledge gaps around ESG integration. For example, ESG information is often disclosed to the market in an unfamiliar manner, such as corporate sustainability reporting or qualitative judgments made by directors. This may conflict with the mindset of financial market agents who are accustomed to information that is "comparable," "verifiable," and "electronically storable and transmittable."[41]

The accounting challenges associated with ESG integration are significant and are slowly being recognized by the academic and practitioner community. It has been suggested that it may be necessary to identify new approaches to fair accounting in order to capture these new dimensions, such as instituting wider principle-based accounting or instituting new investment procedures whereby investors and investee companies engage in deeper dialogue.[42] Novel regulatory approaches are beginning to emerge around this issue, such as the new ESG reporting obligations under the U.K. Companies Act 2006 and the Accounts Modernization Directive 2001 in Europe, which require greater disclosure on corporate governance and social and environmental impacts.[43]

However, the difficulty in understanding ESG information and deploying ESG integration as a tool is not a reason to ignore it when the cost of doing so may be great.[44] Rather, investment consultants could use their position and power to build networks of collaboration and communication to bridge the knowledge gap. There is no doubt that there have been very substantial improvements in the number and scale of collaborative approaches among financial institutions over the last five years.[45] This includes the emergence of numerous not-for-profit advocacy networks such as the Network for Sustainable Financial Markets, the UNEP Finance Initiative, and the World Business Council for Sustainable Development, as well as private sector sell side advisories such as RiskMetrics, On Values, and the Enhanced Analytics Initiative.

However, there is also some evidence to suggest that consultants face barriers to leading clients on the issue of ESG integration, especially where those consultants are in subservient positions with respect to their clients. Caught between their role as adviser to pension fund boards and their position as servant to the client, investment consultants can be providers of new understanding but may also find themselves ultimately led by the demands of their clients. Although consultants have a clear professional duty to raise substantive issues with their client base, they may ultimately be trapped by systemic ignorance within their client base. Among some least experienced consultants surveyed this leads to a problematic situation in which critical issues are addressed only if the client raises them first. This passivity with respect to the client may constitute negligence in cases where clients are shielded from widely recognized systemic issues because of consultants failing to bring these issues to their clients' attention.

An important tool for building relationships of understanding discussed in this chapter is knowledge, training, and expertise. We find examples where consultants with greater ESG experience and knowledge are more confident and able to take leadership positions for their clients with respect to ESG integration compared with their inexperienced counterparts. Consultants who lacked expertise on ESG integration tended to confuse it as an ethical issue rather than an economic issue. This error is highly problematic in light of the fact that trustee boards have a weak appetite for ethical considerations.[46] Therefore ESG integration presented to trustees in this manner is likely to be dismissed, to the fund's financial disadvantage.

We also find barriers to ESG integration within the investment culture of consultants and fund managers more generally. The prevalence of myopia in investment time horizons is coupled with an incentive structure for remuneration that rewards short-term returns of asset managers. There is also a reliance on index-referenced mandates and tracking error limits that result in portfolios being tracked to short-term markers for financial success. This penalizes the use of ESG integration as an investment strategy to the extent that its dynamics play out over a longer time frame. Wider adoption of absolute return strategies may provide some relief in the future toward this structural barrier.

As the current financial model undergoes a thorough reassessment in light of the global financial crisis, investment consultants are required more than ever to be alert to developments in financial innovation. ESG integration as an investment tool aimed to capturing the effect of systemic environmental, social, and governance considerations on portfolio returns is likely to feature prominently in such innovation. Yet while investment consultants command tremendous delegated authority in investment management from pension fund executives, they are also subject to the restrictions of a client-focused industry. Nevertheless, this predicament may erode as networks of knowledge and expertise around the issue of ESG grow, particularly as advocates continue to stress their case.

Appendix: UNEPFI Asset Management Working Group Survey Questionnaire for Investment Management Consulting Firms

For the sake of completeness and comparability, and in order to facilitate analysis and synthesis, we request that you kindly respond in the following format:

On Fiduciary Duty

Q1. Does your firm have a unit or consultant staff dedicated to working with clients who request ESG integration, have an SRI mandate, or have investment policy guidelines concerning, for example, climate change? If not, how are you prepared to respond to clients with such requests?

Q2. Have you observed an increase in client interest on ESG matters when selecting investment managers?

Q3. Do you consider that integration of ESG matters is a requisite aspect of investment management? Please explain why.

Q4. Do you consider that integration of ESG matters is a requisite aspect of investment management as part of fiduciary duty? Please explain why.

Q5. When considering the interests of the ultimate owners of capital (beneficiaries, insured individuals, mutual fund investors, and so forth), do the interests that ought to be considered by fiduciaries go or do not go beyond purely financial interests? In other words, under what circumstances do you see ESG factors requiring consideration in investment management? Please explain.

Q6. In your view, where does the responsibility for the exercise of ESG integration reside? How does it distribute as between trustees, pension fund managers, investment managers, and consultants? What is the role of each?

On ESG Criteria

Q7. Which ESG issues or criteria do you consider are most relevant for inclusion in your client's investment policy statement? For example, issues or criteria having to do with climate change, resource scarcity, pollution generally, reputation risks, human rights, and so forth.

Q8. In your view, can ESG fiduciary duty be discharged solely or primarily through exercise of voting rights? Please explain.

Q9. In your view, can ESG fiduciary duty be discharged solely or primarily through exercise of engagement and dialogue with company managements? Please explain.

Q10. In your view, does ESG fiduciary duty require taking action on whether one holds or refrains from holding certain stocks or bonds in a portfolio? Please explain.

On Evaluating Competence

Q11. Do you currently evaluate an asset manager's abilities to incorporate ESG factors in valuation or portfolio composition as part of your overall assessment of investment managers, regardless of whether a mandate calls for specific socially responsible investment, environmental investment, ethical investment, sustainable investment, or the like? If so, how much weight do you assign to this as part of your total evaluation or ranking? If not, do you have concrete plans to do so in 2008 or 2009?

Q12. What criteria do you currently use to evaluate competence in ESG integration for purposes of a dedicated socially responsible investment mandate, environmental, ethical or similar mandate? Indicate relative weightings if you wish.

On Proxy Voting

Q13. Do you routinely investigate the proxy voting and engagement record of asset managers as concerns environmental and social issues? Or do you only do this if a mandate is specifically SRI, or ethical, or environmental, or the like? Please explain.

On Requests for Proposal (RFPs)

Q14. Do you habitually include questions on ESG policy, form of integration and competence on all RFPs, or only when mandates specifically call for ESG?

On Governing ESG in Mandates

Q15. In your experience, do the typical timeframes for review and evaluation of manager financial performance discourage ESG integration? What improvements would you suggest?

Q16. In your experience, is the prevalent incentive structure for managers neutral towards ESG integration, does it penalize, or does it promote such integration?

Q17. In your experience, is the prevalence of tracking error limits or index-referenced mandates neutral to or does it penalize ESG integration?

On Legal Language

Q18. Should legal language on ESG integration be part of investment management contracts between institutional investors and investment managers? Please explain. If you currently use such language, kindly attach these texts, or an example of text that you see as exemplary or best practice.

Q19. In your view, should language on ESG integration be part of investment policy statements? Please explain. If you have model language, kindly attach such texts, or an example of text that you see as exemplary or best practice.

Open-ended Suggestions

Kindly outline your suggestions for obtaining better operationalization of ESG integration in institutional investment concerning the question areas above or any other areas we may have overlooked.

Chapter 11

Funding Climate Change: How Pension Fund Fiduciary Duty Masks Trustee Inertia and Short-Termism

Claire Woods

Introduction

On January 27, 2010, the U.S. Securities and Exchange Commission (SEC) voted to provide guidance on when public companies should disclose the impact of climate change-related business or legal developments. While the SEC's guidance does not constitute a legal change, it underlines more powerfully than ever that climate change is a risk that investors cannot ignore. Institutional investors, with their broad exposure to systemic risk, should be particularly alert to the implications of this new development. Pension funds control, on average, assets equivalent to 76 percent of the GDP of their respective countries throughout the Western world.[1] In 2006, U.S. pension funds held shares representing approximately one-quarter of U.S. equity markets;[2] U.K. pension funds held shares representing approximately 13 percent of U.K. equity markets.[3] As large shareholders, they have profound potential to influence companies in almost all industries. This chapter focuses on Anglo-American pension funds, because they are similar enough to make comparison straightforward.[4] The advent of two global crises, the global financial crisis and climate change, demands an examination of the investment decisions of pension funds in the face of increasingly complex risk. Are these financial behemoths fulfilling their potential to invest in a better future? Or are they acting myopically, concentrating on quarterly financial performance while funding business in ways that have contributed to and continue to fuel these crises?

At the time of writing, climate change and the global financial crisis present significant challenges to governments around the world.[5] These crises are, to an extent, linked by their genesis in short-termism: in both cases, governments and industry have fostered short-term financial gain without sufficient regard to longer-term social costs of the externalities at play.[6] The *Stern Review* highlights the central importance of environmental sustainability to continued economic growth:

> The evidence shows that ignoring climate change will eventually damage economic growth. Our actions over the coming few decades could create risks of major disruption to economic and social activity, later in this century and in the next, on a scale similar to those associated with the great wars and the economic depression of the first half of the 20th century. And it will be difficult or impossible to reverse these changes. Tackling climate change is the pro-growth strategy for the longer term, and it can be done in a way that does not cap the aspirations for growth of rich or poor countries. The earlier effective action is taken, the less costly it will be.[7]

As for the financial crisis, pension funds have been hit hard. The total assets of all pension funds in the member countries of the Organisation for Economic Co-operation and Development (OECD) declined by US$ 3.3 trillion (that is, nearly 20 percent) from December 2007 to October 2008.[8] If private pension assets are included that figure rises to US$ 5 trillion.[9]

From a broad ethical point of view, it is arguable that pension funds should have a wider ambit of responsibility for promoting a sustainable future, given their financial power and their incursion into service provision once the purview of the state.[10] I argue here that fiduciaries' personal ethical considerations should form a basis for individual investment decisions: the ethical viewpoints of individual trustees and asset managers are too subjective and idiosyncratic to form a proper basis for ad hoc investment decision making. On a wider scale, however, ethics can contribute to our ontological understanding of the role of pension funds. Benjamin Richardson argues that, given their financial significance, institutional investors have an obligation to use their power sustainably by investing in firms whose activities are sustainable.[11] As Stern and others have argued, without environmental sustainability, the financial system ultimately cannot survive.[12]

The primary mandate of pension funds is the creation of financial returns for beneficiaries, but the extent to which this goal is achieved sustainably is a matter for trustees to decide. Pension funds have thus far shown some interest in advocating a change from the short-term focus of the financial system that has fueled the global financial crisis.[13] However, the recent indication of interest is a far cry from action. The financial crisis has revealed that many pension funds are struggling to fulfill their primary mandate of successful financial management on behalf of beneficiaries, let alone to introduce the new variable of sustainability into their management approach.[14] However, by moving toward a longer-term investment paradigm and considering climate change when designing their investment strategies, pension funds have the potential to fulfil their mandate to beneficiaries in a more sustainable manner.

Reflecting on the context of climate change and the global financial crisis, this chapter sets out to demonstrate the theoretical potential of pension funds to drive the reduction of firms' climate change impact, and to expose the practical barriers that stand in their way. It examines first why fiduciary duty is perceived as a barrier to change in investment practices, outlining recent legal developments in the area. It argues that requirements of fiduciary duty have been interpreted too narrowly, and *in theory* should not be perceived as a legal barrier to pension funds' consideration of climate change: fiduciary duty has been flexible enough to evolve with social expectations in the past (and should be able to adapt to the increasing importance of climate change now). However, *in practice*, courts, commentators and trustees themselves have had the tendency to interpret fiduciary duty's requirement of prudence as *what the majority of investors do*. The prudent course of action in this light becomes to maintain the status quo, limiting the potential for innovation in investment strategy toward the inclusion of environmental considerations such as climate change. The uncertainty surrounding the content of fiduciary duty places a practical barrier to investment innovation in this area. Legislative clarification is needed if pension funds are to change their approach toward climate change. Moreover, the focus on fiduciary duty as a barrier to investment innovation in this area masks the behavioral biases toward inertia and short-termism in trustees, which are more insidious and at least as important. These biases, combined with the uncertainty surrounding fiduciary duty, result in a collective action problem: pension funds are unlikely to break with convention unless a significant number of them change their approach simultaneously. Under these conditions, any institutional acceptance of innovation toward a longer-term, more sustainable investment strategy that accounts for climate change will take strong leadership from pension funds themselves.

It is worth noting from the outset that the arguments made here require us to put aside the dichotomy often created between the "financial" and the "social." In examining the overwhelming influence of the status quo on judicial interpretation of "prudence," this chapter attempts to avoid this dichotomy. Instead, the focus here is on the ability of investors and the judiciary to adapt to new social realities; in this case the new social reality is that of environmental issues having a financial impact. At the heart of the argument presented here, therefore, social development requires a revision of what is seen as financial—in other words, the social and the financial are intertwined—and they must be.

This chapter touches upon a range of important issues whose detailed examination is beyond its scope. In particular, it is not the work of this chapter to undertake an empirical analysis of the financial impact of consideration of climate change. This is occurring elsewhere, and comes in addition to the many studies on the financial performance of socially responsible investment (SRI) funds conducted in the past.[15] Furthermore, it does not look in detail at the role of asset managers in managing pension fund investments; instead it explores the work of trustees in the earlier stage of creating investment strategies and in monitoring delegated functions. Finally, this chapter does not look in detail at the ethical arguments for and against pension funds' consideration of climate change.[16] Instead, the focus here remains upon, first, the extent to which, in theory, fiduciary duty presents a barrier to the potential for pension funds to contribute to a more sustainable financial system and in particular to have regard to climate change as a financial risk or opportunity, and, second, on the behavioral barriers that exist in practice.

The Potential for Pension Funds to Alleviate Climate Change

Since the early 1980s, the financial power of pension funds has become ubiquitous across the Western world.[17] In 2007, pension funds in the United Kingdom, the United States, Australia, and Canada controlled assets equivalent to 86, 74, 105, and 55 percent of GDP respectively.[18] The increase in financial importance of pension funds has coincided with a retreat of the state as the primary provider of public infrastructure and governance at the end of the twentieth century.[19] Gordon Clark argues that the influence of pension funds has expanded to enter the governance gap created as the state has retired from its zenith of service provision in the 1930s.[20] As the state has reduced its role in providing both physical and legal infrastructure, a space has grown for corporate and financial self-regulation. Pension funds increasingly provide the essential service of an income stream for retirees—a service that in the recent past was the purview of the state, and in the more distant past the duty of the family. Beneficiaries of pension funds therefore place a great deal of trust in the funds to create and maintain adequate wealth for their postwork years. It is little wonder that pension funds and beneficiaries are wary of any incursion into this function. Nevertheless, as the financial strength of pension funds grows, it is worth considering whether the primary wealth creation mandate of pension funds can fit within a broader agenda of fostering sustainable investment. In outsourcing part of their service provision, governments appear to have lost sight of the whole: a pension system that produces financial benefits for society with the one hand and erodes its ecological foundations with the other cannot be a permanent solution. A rethinking of the purpose and function of pension fund investment is required in order to address this issue.

Before proceeding further, we should note that pension funds do not form a homogenous group. There are a variety of attributes that may alter a pension fund's ability to affect climate change outcomes. First, larger pension funds are undoubtedly in a stronger position to effect industry change. Larger funds have not only a larger degree of corporate control and more resources but also stronger standards of internal competence and investor sophistication. Second, in defined-benefit funds, trustees have more control over how funds are invested, whereas in defined-contribution schemes, beneficiaries have a degree of autonomy to direct their own fund investment. The extent to which beneficiaries avail themselves of this ability is, however, limited, with most beneficiaries failing to opt out of default funds (this is discussed in greater detail in below). Third, traditionally, higher-equity holdings allow funds a greater opportunity for dialogue with firms. While it appears that pension funds' proportion of bond holdings is currently increasing in relation to equity holdings,[21] industry sources suggest that many of the new bond assets are corporate bonds, making any such shift's effect on pension fund behavior less consequential (depending, of course on the nature and class of bond). Finally, investment practices of public and private pension funds may diverge greatly, and care is taken to distinguish between public and private funds where appropriate throughout this chapter. The legal regimes governing public and private pension funds in the U.S. and the U.K. are very similar (at least with respect to fiduciary duty); however, for clarity's sake, both sets of regimes are described where relevant. Readers should bear in mind the diversity in pension fund types while considering the arguments that follow. While different types of pension funds will have varying abilities to effect change, in my view there are enough pension funds with the attributes necessary to make a profound difference in this area.

Growing Power, Growing Responsibility?

The financial power of pension funds has grown steadily over the last fifty years. Given their increasing power to affect social welfare both positively and negatively, does it follow that pension funds have developed a conjunct responsibility? The natural environment is, after all, the underlying resource base of the economy.[22] Drawing on the notion that pension funds have assumed governance[23] responsibilities by virtue of their financial clout, Richardson argues that "where financial institutions manage the assets of millions of people and have the capacity to exert huge economic influence, they must be governed by environmental standards that protect natural systems for the long term. They should be regarded as institutions with special public responsibilities based on ecological ethics."[24] Richardson's argument here is ethical. He notes, correctly, that such ethical obligations are generally unenforceable under existing legal structures.[25] While there is room to argue that pension funds are developing an ethical responsibility to use their burgeoning investment powers in an environmentally sustainable manner, legislative changes would be necessary to make any such ethical responsibility legally enforceable. While the concept is not explored in detail here, it is worth noting that such change is not without precedent: in some jurisdictions, company responsibilities under corporate law have widened in recent years to include some duties to a wider stakeholder group than merely shareholders.[26] In the U.K., for example, the Companies Act 2006 requires directors to have regard to "the impact of the company's operations on the community and the environment"[27] and "the likely consequences of any decision in the long term"[28] when promoting the success of the company.

In *The Rise of Fiduciary Capitalism*, James Hawley and Andrew Williams argue that pension funds are well positioned to encourage companies to produce economy-wide social benefits alongside financial benefits.[29] They argue that as pension funds become universal owners (that is, as they invest across all sectors of the economy), they can derive benefit from social improvements across the economy.[30] Furthermore, they become more vulnerable to systematic financial risks (risks to which the entire economy is exposed). Universal owners have two broad sets of reasons for promoting social welfare as well as focusing on the growth of assets through investment: first, social improvements in all sectors of the economy will be beneficial to the wide range of firms in which they invest.[31] Second, pension funds that are universal owners should have regard to the impact of their investment on factors other than financial value of assets, because negative externalities created by one of their investments in one industry will have an impact on the assets they hold in other industries.[32]

These arguments raise important questions for social policy: should pension funds assume governance roles? Do pension funds owe a duty to stakeholders outside the beneficiary group? In short, is there a wider social role for pension funds? To treat these questions with the completeness they require is beyond the scope of this chapter. The position that this chapter takes is that pension funds generally, with the exception of some large and highly professionally run public pension funds, such as CalPERS, are not ready to assume a broad governance role. Clark et al.'s 2007 study comparing trustee competence with that of Oxford undergraduates showed that although education on financial matters appears to improve trustee competence,[33] on average trustees were less adept than undergraduates at integrating extra financial factors in their investment decision-making process.[34] Furthermore, a wider agenda of sustainability may be ethically preferable, but, as Richardson notes, no such agenda is currently enforceable against pension funds. Any agenda introduced through legislation would have to be careful not to distract trustees from their primary mandate: the creation of retirement benefits for beneficiaries. Broader governance role aside, however, this chapter takes the position that the fulfillment of this primary mandate and the promotion of a more sustainable approach to investment are not necessarily mutually exclusive. Indeed, the fulfilment of the primary mandate is likely to suffer if trustees ignore the long-term consequences of financing environmental degradation.

Climate Change: A Financial Risk and Opportunity

With the increasing financial prominence of pension funds in Western countries comes an increasing potential to encourage the reduction in greenhouse gas emissions across economies. Pension funds could promote reductions in greenhouse gas emissions in two ways while carrying out their investment mandates. First, they could consider carbon footprint as a *risk* that will increase as regulators and markets react to the increasing economic, social, and environmental impact of climate change. Pension funds would then respond to this risk by introducing carbon footprint as an additional metric for assessing each of the assets in their portfolio, and adjusting their investment decisions accordingly. Moreover, pension funds could engage actively with the firms in which they invest on the issue of greenhouse gas emissions. A second approach would be to make specialized investments in firms that are likely to have a particularly positive climate change impact (for instance, renewable energy firms), taking a venture capital approach. This more targeted approach would treat climate change as an *opportunity* to preempt market forces as the demand for greener energy increases. The value of the opportunity may be augmented by government funding[35] and early mover advantage.[36]

More important, pension funds' explicit consideration of climate change could have a broad, lasting influence on the priorities of businesses across economies. If pension funds were to act on climate change, by treating it as a risk, opportunity, or both, they would send a strong signal to businesses about the value that they, as significant shareholders, place on climate change risk and opportunity. The business response to pension fund treatment of climate change could lead to increased attention to climate change risks and opportunities at an individual business level. In carrying out their investment mandates with a conscious regard to the context of climate change, pension funds would make an informal, but potentially highly significant, contribution to climate governance. In short, pension fund investment could help to advance a more carbon-conscious business paradigm.

Why is it, then, that pension funds do not appear to have a strong interest in moving toward a systematic assessment of the risks and opportunities of climate change? While some investment consultancies have argued that carbon footprint must be treated as a risk under the circumstances of climate change,[37] very few pension funds have shown signs of treating the issue in a proactive manner at the investment strategy level.[38] For most funds, climate change goes unremarked, integrated on a haphazard basis into company valuations according to the inconsistent reporting techniques of businesses. Though the risk of global warming has been widely acknowledged since the 1980s,[39] it was until recently[40] largely restricted to the domain of the scientific community. This may explain not only why many pension funds give little or no regard to climate change in their investment strategies but also why little has been written about how pension funds view their own capacity to make a difference with respect to climate change.[41] Still, an analogy can be drawn between pension funds' consideration of climate change and their consideration of other traditionally nonfinancial factors, including environmental factors, which is reasonably well researched.[42] The reason frequently put forward by pension fund trustees, asset mangers, investment advisers, and commentators for the reticence of pension funds toward the consideration of nonfinancial factors is the purported legal barrier created by fiduciary duty.[43]

This chapter proceeds on the basis that given past legal decisions, legislation, and commentary with respect to fiduciary duty and nonfinancial considerations, fiduciary duty is likely to be perceived as posing the foremost legal impediment to fiduciaries' consideration of climate change. The following section explores why fiduciary duty is often perceived as a barrier to fiduciaries' consideration of so-called nonfinancial factors in investment decisions. It argues that the impediment fiduciary duty presents to consideration of nonfinancial factors has been overstated in the past: in reality, fiduciary duty presents little theoretical barrier to fiduciaries' consideration of climate change, to the extent that it poses an investment risk or opportunity.

Fiduciary Duty as a Perceived Barrier to Change

In the trusts law context, fiduciary duty exists to protect the interests of beneficiaries. Fiduciary duty arose in medieval England to protect the property claims of minors against the avaricious intent of guardians; in modern pension funds, it protects beneficiaries' retirement funds from conflicts of interest with the trustees and asset managers who take care of the trust funds, as well as from their imprudence in investment. Paul Finn defines a "fiduciary" as "simply, someone who undertakes to act for or on behalf of another in some particular matter or matters."[44] A person does not owe a fiduciary duty because he is a fiduciary. Rather it "is because a particular rule applies to him that he is a fiduciary or confidant *for its purposes.*"[45] The duty arises out of a relationship of trust and confidence in which a trustee has power to exercise discretion affecting the interests of a beneficiary "in a legal or practical sense,"[46] and it holds the fiduciary to a higher standard of conduct than that expected in normal business transactions.[47]

The origin of the duty in the conscience-based courts of equity, long before it was known by the name "fiduciary duty," gives it an inherently malleable quality. This was particularly so in medieval times—beneficiaries of a trust (or more accurately "use," as it was then known) appealed to the Chancery courts with claims based in ethics or morality where they had no claim in common law (usually because the legal title to their property was in the hands of trustees).[48] In these cases, justice was sought to correct an affront to the conscience, and an appeal was made to the chancellor's moral and theological reasoning. Equity thus complemented the common law by providing justice in situations where the common law, which was restricted by precedent, could not. Those less charitable to the adaptable quality of equity regarded its development as ad hoc, with one prominent jurist complaining that "equity is as long as the chancellor's foot."[49] Fiduciary duty, like the rest of equity, evolved in a somewhat haphazard manner: why is it, asked Ernest Weinrib, two and a half centuries after the seminal case on fiduciary duty,[50] that "certain categories of actors and certain types of acts are singled out for the application of the fiduciary standard and its attendant severe remedies?"[51] The content and application of the duty have become clearer in recent years thanks to the introduction of legislation and academic work,[52] including in the highly legislated area of pension funds and institutional investment.[53] As we will see, however, some significant uncertainties remain about pension fiduciary duty, particularly with respect to the consideration of nonfinancial factors in investment decision making.

This section first outlines fiduciary duty as it applies to pension funds in the U.S. and the U.K., examining the main duties[54] of loyalty and prudence ("Fiduciary Duty in the Context of Pension Funds"). It then explores in detail why fiduciary duty has been found to prevent pension funds' consideration of nonfinancial factors in decision making in the past, considering the U.S. cases *Board of Trustees v. Mayor of Baltimore City*[55] and *University of Oregon v. Oregon Investment Council*[56] and the U.K. case *Cowan v. Scargill*[57] before looking at more recent legal developments in the U.S. and U.K. ("Duty of Prudence"). The section argues that the perceived danger of fiduciary consideration of nonfinancial issues has been construed too widely, setting the scene for the next stage of argument that the consideration of climate change as a risk or opportunity in most circumstances would not conflict with fiduciary duty. Finally, the scope for fiduciary duty to evolve is presented as paradoxical: fiduciary duty is flexible enough to adapt to evolving social expectations over time, but its prudence standard relies on reference to the investment decisions of fiduciaries' peer group, meaning that the prudence standard encourages conformity with convention and stifles innovation in the short term. As a result, it is argued that although fiduciary duty does not present a legal barrier to pension funds' consideration of climate change in most cases, in the absence of legislative clarification, it is likely that any move toward climate change consciousness will happen incrementally, in order to fulfil the conventionality requirements of the duty of prudence ("Pension Fund Fiduciary Duty and Nonfinancial Considerations").

Fiduciary Duty in the Context of Pension Funds

The investment powers of trustees and asset managers of trust funds are limited by their legal obligations to the funds' beneficiaries. Pension funds in the common law world are generally set up as trusts. Pension fund trustees are entrusted with the role of maintaining the fund for the benefit of future pensioners (as beneficiaries). In addition to obligations under legislation, the trust deed, contract, and the common law duty of care, trustees, and in most cases asset managers,[58] are bound by fiduciary duty. Fiduciary duty originates from equity and trusts law, and today exists throughout the Anglo-American legal world in both case law and legislation.

Whereas pension fund trusts are similar in many ways to other trusts,[59] their peculiar intersection with other areas of law, especially employment law,[60] makes pension fund governance particularly complex. Graham Moffatt, writing in 1993, argued that the existence of the pension fund system within two spheres of law (trust law and employment law) led to inconsistencies in its regulation.[61] Scott Donald has gone further, arguing that the regulation of pension funds is somewhat schizophrenic: the funds exist, traditionally, as trusts, but they have a second identity as investment vehicles, where beneficiaries are better conceived of as investors, and a third identity as private welfare providers to beneficiaries/citizens that have filled in a public service function of the retreating state.[62]

In addition to these complexities, the content of pension fund fiduciary duty can vary according to jurisdiction.[63] Bearing in mind these complexities and variations, the following two subsections outline the contents of fiduciary duty in the pension fund context in the U.S. and the U.K. It presents the two central elements of trustee fiduciary duty: the duty of loyalty and the duty of prudence.

Duty of Loyalty: Primacy of Beneficiary Interests

The duty of loyalty establishes that fiduciaries must treat beneficiary interests as paramount in decision making. It requires fiduciaries to act in the sole interests (or best interests, in certain contexts)[64] of the beneficiaries when exercising their discretion with respect to trust funds.[65] P. D. Finn's classic work in formulating general principles on fiduciary duty observes that "the general comments of the judges make it equally clear to what end [the fiduciary] must bend his exertions—the service of his beneficiaries' interests."[66] The duty of loyalty can include (but is not limited to) the following:

- fiduciaries must not put themselves in a position where their interests could conflict with those of a beneficiary;
- fiduciaries must not profit from their position as fiduciaries;
- fiduciaries must not misuse trust property.[67]

Public pension funds in most U.S. states are subject to the Uniform Prudent Investor Act (UPIA). The notes to section 5 of this act assert that "the duty of loyalty is perhaps the most characteristic rule of trust law, requiring the trustee to act exclusively for the beneficiaries, as opposed to acting for the trustee's own interest or that of third parties." UPIA provides that a "trustee shall invest and manage the trust assets solely in the interest of the beneficiaries."[68] A similar conception of the primary purpose of pension funds exists at common law in the various states.[69] Private pension funds in the U.S. are governed by the Employee Retirement Income Security Act of 1974 (ERISA). ERISA provides that "a fiduciary shall discharge his duties with respect to a plan solely in the interests of the participants and beneficiaries and . . . for the exclusive purpose of (i) providing benefits to participants and their beneficiaries and (ii) defraying reasonable expenses of administering the plan."[70]

U.S. law for both public and private pension funds clearly commences with a sole interest test, but a closer examination reveals that the standard can yield, on occasions, to other interests. John Langbein points out that while U.S. law uses the sole interests of beneficiaries as a starting point for the duty of loyalty, the sole interests standard has been whittled away to a "best interests" standard in a number of contexts, in particular commercial contexts.[71] The reasoning behind the increasing number of exceptions to the sole interests standard is that "the trust beneficiary will be better off if the law promotes the mutual advantage of trustee and beneficiary, in the fashion of other commercial relationships, than if it insist that only the beneficiary can benefit."[72] For example, UPIA allows pooled investment vehicles in order to facilitate adequate portfolio diversification, because a singular trust fund is often too small "to diversify thoroughly by constructing its own portfolio of individually selected investments."[73] Similarly, U.S. law allows trustees to be remunerated based on the rationale that "the interest of trust beneficiaries as a class in obtaining the benefits of compensated trust services will more often be served by allowing the intrinsic conflict."[74]

In the U.K., a best interests standard is generally applicable. Under the 2005 U.K. Occupational Pension Schemes (Investment) Regulations, the trustee's foremost duty to beneficiaries is to act in their "best interests," except in the case of a conflict of interest, when they must act "in the sole interest of members and beneficiaries."[75] The common law loyalty requirement in the U.K. is somewhat circular: U.K. trustees must exercise their investment powers "fairly and honestly for the purposes for which they are given and not so as to accomplish any ulterior motive."[76] The purposes of the investment powers are set out in the trust deed and rules.[77] The U.K. Pensions Act 1995 requires trustees to create and maintain a "statement of the principles governing decisions about investments for the purposes of the scheme."[78] In cases involving pension funds, "the best interests of the beneficiaries are normally their best financial interests,"[79] although there is some potential (discussed below) for pension fund trustees to consider nonfinancial factors relevant to beneficiaries' interests.[80]

The U.K. and U.S. positions on the duty of loyalty both secure the interests of the beneficiaries, but in slightly different ways. In the U.S., the law recognizes that in some instances, a slight compromise between interests results in the best outcome for beneficiaries. By contrast, the U.K. approaches potential conflicts of interest by proscribing any compromise of beneficiary interests. The central focus of the duty of loyalty for both jurisdictions remains ensuring that fiduciaries who manage trust funds do not misuse their powers for dishonest gain at the expense of the beneficiaries. While both jurisdictions recognize wealth creation for beneficiaries as the pivotal role of trustees, in neither jurisdiction does the duty of loyalty require the untempered maximization of financial benefit for beneficiaries.[81]

Duty of Prudence: The Modern Prudent Investor

In addition to the duty of loyalty, pension fund fiduciaries have a duty of prudence, or skill, care, and diligence. As this duty will be discussed in detail in the subsection on "Pension Fund Fiduciary Duty and Nonfinancial Considerations," this subsection simply sets out the nature of the duty in the U.S. and U.K.

In the United States, prior to the advent of modern portfolio theory, the classic statement of the prudence test for trustees is found in *Harvard College v. Amory*, which directs that a trustee must "observe how men of prudence, discretion and intelligence manage their own affairs, not in regard to speculation, but in regard to the permanent disposition of their funds."[82]

Since the advent of modern portfolio theory,[83] U.S. pension funds' duty of prudence has been found in variations of the "modern prudent investor rule": in ERISA (for private pension funds) and in UPIA (for almost all public pension funds), and in the Third Restatement of Trusts. Put briefly, the modern prudent investor rule requires prudent investment across a whole portfolio in the best interests of the beneficiaries and for the purposes of the fund.

With respect to private pension funds, ERISA's modern prudent investor rule requires fiduciaries to discharges their duties "with the care, skill, prudence, and diligence under the circumstances then prevailing that a prudent man acting in a like capacity and familiar with such matters would use in the conduct of an enterprise of a like character and with like aims."[84]

Fiduciaries must do so "by diversifying the investments of the plan so as to minimize the risk of large losses, unless under the circumstances it is clearly prudent not to do so,"[85] and must act "in accordance with the documents and instruments governing the plan."[86]

U.S. public pension funds are governed by the laws of their state. Most U.S. states[87] have now adopted UPIA, which is an attempt to codify the common law prudent investor rule in each state jurisdiction. UPIA uses language taken mainly from the Third Restatement of Trusts. UPIA's modern prudent investor rule requires trustees to "invest and manage trust assets as a prudent investor would, by considering the purposes, terms, distribution requirements, and other circumstances of the trust. In satisfying this standard, the trustee shall exercise reasonable care, skill, and caution."[88] In keeping with modern portfolio theory, a "trustee's investment and management decisions respecting individual assets must be evaluated not in isolation but in the context of the trust portfolio as a whole and as a part of an overall investment strategy having risk and return objectives reasonably suited to the trust."[89]

In the U.K., a trustee must manage the trust in the same manner as an ordinary prudent man of business would conduct his own affairs.[90] Under the U.K. Trustee Act 2000, all trustees are required to "exercise such care and skill as is reasonable in the circumstances," having regard to "any special knowledge or experience that he has or holds himself out as having."[91] Therefore, professional trustees and asset managers purporting to have special fund management skills have a higher standard of care.[92]

The Pensions Act 1995 requires pension funds to create a written statement of investment principles.[93] Its subordinate regulations, the Occupational Pension Schemes (Investment) Regulations 2005, specify that pension funds must obtain advice from a qualified person prior to preparing or revising the statement of principles[94] and must ensure adequate portfolio diversification.[95] Pension fund trustees' investment powers must be "exercised in a manner calculated to ensure the security, quality, liquidity and profitability of the portfolio as a whole."[96]

Pension Fund Fiduciary Duty and Nonfinancial Considerations

The fiduciary duties of loyalty and prudence have often been seen as presenting an impediment to the consideration of so-called nonfinancial factors, in particular ethical, environmental, social, and governance (ESG) factors in investment strategy.[97] In reality, it would be more appropriate to think of these "nonfinancial factors" as *not-yet-financial factors*, thus acknowledging that currently nonfinancial factors may become financial as relevant legislation is introduced and public perception develops. This chapter avoids creating a dichotomy between the "financial" and the "social." In examining the overwhelming influence of the status quo on judicial interpretation of "prudence," it focuses instead on the ability of investors and the judiciary to adapt to new social realities; in this case the new social reality is that of environmental issues having a financial impact.

This subsection discusses why so-called nonfinancial factors have been seen as off-limits for pension fund fiduciaries: briefly, the duty of loyalty has on occasion been interpreted as requiring fiduciaries to focus solely on immediate financial returns from investments; courts have at times interpreted the duty of prudence in such a way as to encourage fiduciaries to adhere to the status quo, discouraging innovation in investment (including looking to factors other than traditional financial considerations). Critics oppose the consideration of nonfinancial issues on the basis that such consideration may indulge the political motives of trustees at the expense of financial earnings for beneficiaries.[98] Public pension funds, in particular, may be vulnerable to ill-judged, politically motivated investment decisions.[99] This reasoning, if applied to climate change, paints pension funds' inclusion of climate change in investment strategy as contrary to fiduciary duty, at least insofar as its inclusion is unconventional compared with industry peers.

Part of the reason for the perpetuation of the perception that fiduciaries should not have regard to nonfinancial factors in their investment approach is the lack of recent case law directly on point. The main cases in both the U.S. and the U.K. were decided in the 1980s, and in both places, the questions usually had to do with ethical and political questions regarding investment in then-apartheid South Africa. No case has tested the issue of whether specifically environmental factors may be taken into account in pension fund investment decisions. Certainly, no case has yet dealt with the question of whether pension fund investment strategy may have regard to climate change.

There have been recent attempts to clarify the status of nonfinancial considerations in pension fund investment strategy on both sides of the Atlantic. Unfortunately, neither country has succeeded. In the U.S., recent

Department of Labor Bulletins intended to clarify the department's position have in fact confused the issue further. Some commentators from within the institutional investment industry have interpreted the bulletins as requiring strict avoidance of nonfinancial consideration in investment decision making;[100] many regard them simply as confused, confusing, and contradictory.[101] In the U.K., comments from parliamentary debate in 2008 indicated some support for the view that ESG factors may legally be integrated into pension funds' investment strategies.[102] However, no legislative change was made, and as a result the comments are in no way binding.

For these reasons, the uncertainty surrounding the requirements of fiduciary duty with respect to nonfinancial considerations remains, and creates a perception among trustees that it is safest not to test these waters. Without legislative clarification, it is likely that many pension funds will avoid the issue altogether by ignoring the question of climate change.

U.S. Case Law and Recent Commentary

U.S. cases considering trustees' regard to nonfinancial factors in investment decision making have produced mixed outcomes. In *Board of Trustees of Employee Retirement System of the City of Baltimore v. City of Baltimore*,[103] the City of Baltimore had passed ordinances requiring the city's public pension funds to divest from companies that had business dealings in South Africa. The trustees of the funds sued the City, arguing that the ordinance restricted their ability to properly diversify by reducing their investment universe.[104] This, they argued, unlawfully affected their duty of prudence.[105] The trustees also argued that the ordinances unlawfully affected the common law duty of loyalty by diluting the trustees' focus on the exclusive benefit of beneficiaries through the inclusion of social considerations.[106]

The Court of Appeals found that although the ordinances did reduce somewhat the universe of potential investments for trustees, "a diversified, [South Africa Free] portfolio can be managed consistently with the duty of prudence."[107] Furthermore, the court did "not believe that a trustee necessarily violates the duty of loyalty by considering the social consequences of investment decisions."[108] Instead, the court asserted that "a trustee's duty is not necessarily to maximize the return on investments but rather to secure a 'just' or 'reasonable' return while avoiding undue risk."[109]

By contrast, in *University of Oregon v. Oregon Investment Council*,[110] the Court of Appeals of Oregon refused standing to the University of Oregon student associations that sought a declaration that the state could not invest endowment funds in companies operating in Namibia, South Africa, and Zimbabwe. The students had challenged the Oregon attorney general's view that such divestment amounted to a probable violation of fiduciary duty. The court asserted that the students "do not allege any legally recognized injury, and neither agreement with plaintiffs' opposition to apartheid nor the desirability of encouraging students to become concerned with social and moral wrongs and to seek to right them can turn the alleged 'injuries' into legally recognized ones."[111]

The findings in these two cases (as well as other contemporaneous cases)[112] suggest that whether or not nonfinancial considerations are permissible depends on the specific facts at hand. Surprisingly, there have been no significant recent U.S. legal decisions to shed further light on these questions.

Contradictory views about the status of nonfinancial considerations also appear in U.S. commentary surrounding the issue of nonfinancial considerations in pension fund investment. The comments to section 5 of UPIA, which applies to public pension funds in almost all states, say that "no form of so-called 'social investing' is consistent with the duty of loyalty if the investment activity entails sacrificing the interests of trust beneficiaries—for example, by accepting below-market returns—in favor of the interests of the persons supposedly benefited by pursuing the particular social cause."[113] The UPIA comment suggests that there can be no trade-off between financial and nonfinancial gains in pension fund investment strategies. By contrast, the U.S. Department of Labor's position vis-à-vis nonfinancial considerations by private pension funds is less clear. In 1998, the department said that fiduciary duties under ERISA do not preclude consideration of collateral benefits, such as those offered by a "socially-responsible" fund, in a fiduciary's evaluation of a particular investment opportunity. However, the existence of such collateral benefits may be decisive only if the fiduciary determines that the investment offering the collateral benefits is expected to provide an investment return commensurate to alternative investments having similar risks.[114]

Then, on October 17, 2008, the department released two interpretive bulletins that further muddied its stance on nonfinancial considerations in institutional investment. The first bulletin provides "supplemental guidance relating to fiduciary responsibility in considering economically targeted investments"[115] (the *ETI Bulletin*). The second bulletin provides clarification on "the exercise of shareholder rights and written statements of investment policy, including proxy voting policies or guidelines"[116] (the *Shareholder Rights Bulletin*). The bulletins are intended to reiterate and clarify the Department of Labor's "longstanding view that workers' money must be invested and used solely to provide for retirements and not for political, corporate or other purposes."[117]

The *ETI Bulletin* indicates that ERISA "establishes a clear rule that in the course of discharging their duties, fiduciaries may never subordinate the economic interests of the plan to unrelated objectives, and may not select investment on the basis of any factor outside the economic interest of the plan."[118]

However, where two or more alternative investments "are of equal economic value," fiduciaries are permitted to "choose between the investment alternatives on the basis of a factor other than the economic interest of the plan."[119] The bulletin highlights the Department of Labor's belief that fiduciaries who rely on noneconomic factors to make investment decisions will find it difficult to prove compliance with ERISA "absent a written record demonstrating that a contemporaneous economic analysis showed the investment alternatives were of equal value."[120]

The *Shareholder Rights Bulletin* asserts that the fiduciary duties described in ERISA require that "in voting proxies, regardless of whether the vote is made pursuant to a statement of investment policy, the responsible fiduciary shall consider only those factors that relate to the economic value of the plan's investment and shall not subordinate the interests of the participants and beneficiaries in their retirement income to unrelated objectives."[121]

The *Shareholder Rights Bulletin* also reinforces that all proxy voting guidelines in statements of investment policy must comply with fiduciary duty. As such, these "may not subordinate the economic interests of the plan participants to unrelated objectives."[122]

While Department of Labor bulletins are binding only on pension funds that are governed by ERISA and do not affect general trust law, they are nonetheless likely to influence judicial interpretation.[123] Shortly after the publication of the bulletins, the Social Investment Forum wrote an open letter to the department criticizing inconsistencies and ambiguities in the bulletins' language.[124] The bulletins appear to have confused, rather than clarified, the U.S. Department of Labor's views with respect to the inclusion of financial factors in decision making.

In short, U.S. legal cases, legislation, and Department of Labor commentary present pension funds with unclear guidance about their obligations with respect to the consideration of nonfinancial issues in investment strategy.

U.K. Case Law and Recent Commentary

The case that has had the greatest influence, somewhat undeservedly, on the issue of nonfinancial considerations in pension fund investment decisions in the U.K. is *Cowan v. Scargill*.[125] In that case, the five board-appointed trustees of the Mineworkers' Pension Scheme sued the other five (union-appointed) trustees over their refusal to agree to an investment plan unless it was amended "so as to prohibit any increase in overseas investment, to provide for the withdrawal of existing overseas investments at the most opportune time, and to prohibit investment in energies which are in direct competition with coal."[126] The court found that the union trustees were in breach of their fiduciary duty in refusing to accept the diversified investment plan. Justice Megarry held that "when the purpose of the trust is to provide financial benefits for the beneficiaries, as is usually the case, the best interests of the beneficiaries are normally their best financial interests."[127]

He went on to explain that trustees must put aside their social, political, and moral views when making investment decisions on behalf of the trustees:

> In considering what investments to make trustees must put on one side their own personal interests and views. Trustees may have strongly held social or political views. They may be firmly opposed to any investment in South Africa or other countries, or they may object to any form of investment in companies concerned with alcohol, tobacco, armaments or many other things. In the conduct of their own affairs, of course, they are free to abstain from making any such investments. Yet under a trust, if investments of this type would be more beneficial to the beneficiaries than other investments, the trustees must not refrain from making the investments by reason of the views that they hold.[128]

Pension funds have often cited this case as demonstrating that the "best interests" of beneficiaries coincide with their financial interests and that nonfinancial considerations are likely to breach fiduciary duty. Therefore, the belief that trustees must seek to maximize profit at the expense of all other considerations has held currency with many institutional investors.[129] However, this interpretation has been challenged.

A number of commentators, including Justice Megarry himself, have argued that the *Cowan v. Scargill* decision has been overly influential and has been interpreted too widely. Writing in an academic essay in 1989, Megarry expressed surprise at the amount of attention his decision had received[130] (that was twenty years ago, and the decision is still the primary case on the matter). This view was reinforced in *Martin v. City of Edinburgh District Council*,[131] in which Lord Murray said, "I cannot conceive that trustees have an unqualified duty . . . simply to invest trust funds in the most profitable investment available."[132]

Under the Occupational Pension Schemes (Investment) Regulations of 2005, a pension fund's statement of investment principles must detail "the extent (if at all) to which social, environmental or ethical considerations are taken into account in the selection, retention and realisation of investments."[133] On October 7, 2008, Parliament debated whether legislation should go further and establish a general rule that certain nonfinancial issues could inform pension fund investment decision making. In speaking about a proposed amendment to the Pension Bill, Lord McKenzie argued that "there is no reason in law why trustees cannot consider social and moral criteria in addition to their usual criteria of financial returns, security and diversification."[134] Lord McKenzie went on to say that "it follows from this that it may be appropriate for trustees to engage in these considerations with companies in which they invest. This may include disinvesting from such companies if, acting in accordance with their fiduciary duties and the objects of their trust, they consider that this is right and in the best interests of their members."[135]

These comments were not, however, followed by any legislative clarification of the issue in the U.K. Indeed, they were intended to demonstrate that no legislative sanctioning of socially driven investing was necessary, with Lord McKenzie going on to say, "It would not be appropriate for the Government or Parliament to impose any guidelines that might restrict the trustee's independence in carrying out its overriding duty to members, although governments have a role in engendering a climate which fosters ethical investment and in ensuring that legislation does not act as a barrier to those who are committed to this."[136]

In 2005, the United Nations Environment Programme Finance Initiative (UNEPFI) released a report that examined the issue of institutional investors' treatment of ESG factors in investment decision making. The report surveyed the legal landscape in both common law and civil law jurisdictions and came to the conclusion that "it is not a breach of fiduciary duties per se to have regard to ESG considerations while pursuing the purposes of the trust. Rather, in our opinion, it may be a breach of fiduciary duties to fail to take account of ESG considerations that are relevant and to give them appropriate weight, bearing in mind that some important economic analysts and leading financial institutions are satisfied that a strong link between good ESG performance and good financial performance exists."[137]

Despite the sanguine views of UNEPFI, neither recent case law nor legislation has appeared to confirm or deny either its assertions or those of Lord McKenzie. Nor has the U.S. Department of Labor's recent commentary been tested. With the recent entrance of the Obama administration, it is possible that the commentary will undergo further change before there is an opportunity for it to be tested. Therefore, the legal position with respect to pension funds' consideration of nonfinancial factors in investment strategy remains unclear in both the U.S. and the U.K. As the law currently stands, the inclusion of climate change as a factor in investment decision making may be perfectly acceptable. On the other hand, it may put pension funds at risk of violating their fiduciary obligations: until legislation or case law clarifies the point, funds will not know. And until the advent of either a legal case or legislation confirming that environmental considerations such as climate change may form part of pension funds' investment decision making, pension funds will be wary of amending their investment strategies. It is this uncertainty, rather than fiduciary duty itself, that acts as an impediment to the consideration of nonfinancial factors at present.

Fiduciary Duty's Paradox: Incrementally Flexible

The above section has demonstrated that the uncertainty surrounding pension funds' obligations with respect to nonfinancial factors in investment decision making presents a practical barrier to consideration of environmental factors, including climate change, in both the U.S. and U.K. contexts. It is clear that part of the problem is the lack of both current case law and consistent legislative commentary on the topic. However, the problem runs deeper than that—it is tied to the nature of fiduciary duty itself. This subsection examines what it is about fiduciary duty that makes it ill suited to adapt to changing social circumstances in anything other than an incremental manner. The urgent nature of climate change makes this situation all the more poignant.

Fiduciary duty is a ramshackle concept. In early case law it arose, organically, out of certain relationships of trust. Whether a particular relationship was fiduciary, and what duty it entailed, was often difficult to predict.[138] Indeed, it is difficult to escape the perception that in early times the finding of fiduciary duty, and its content, was rather arbitrary.[139] The preceding subsections have demonstrated that although the nature of pension fund fiduciary duty has been clarified in both the U.S. and the U.K. by successive pieces of legislation, uncertainties remain, particularly with respect to nonfinancial factors in investment decisions. And as Langbein has argued, elements of the duty continue to evolve, both through legislation[140] and through curial interpretation.[141] In short, pension fund fiduciary duty remains, to an extent, "a concept in search of principle."[142]

In order to deal with the changing social and environmental realities associated with climate change, fiduciary duty must be able to accommodate certain investment innovations—in particular to allow the consideration of climate change. It must be able to recognize the transition of climate change from a nonfinancial factor to a financial factor, as legislation (e.g., on emissions trading) and markets are gradually doing. However, this subsection argues that while this type of innovation in fiduciary duty is possible, without legislative change it will be incremental—and too slow to meet the urgent changes required by climate change.

This subsection explores the paradoxical nature of fiduciary duty with respect to investment innovation: the duty can evolve—history has seen it adapt to emerging social expectations—but the tendency for courts to judge fiduciaries' prudence by reference to existing investment norms means that any innovation in investment is bound to be incremental—any change in fiduciary duty must fight against considerable inertia. As a result, while the past flexibility of fiduciary duty suggests that the investment innovation of considering climate change is acceptable in theory, the past also suggests that innovation in the courts (that is, absent legislation) is incremental. Change, when introduced too quickly, has been equated by courts with imprudence in the past. The following subsections visit fiduciary duty's incrementally adaptable nature, showing how it has adapted to evolving financial and social norms in the past (the first subsection), but also discussing its tendency toward inertia (the second subsection). The final subsection discusses what the nature of fiduciary duty means for pension funds' attitudes toward climate change.

Adapting to Changing Social Expectations (both Financial and Nonfinancial)

Fiduciary duty in an investment context has adapted slowly to changing social expectations about finance over the years. If we trace the development of trustees' fiduciary duty since Victorian times, the change in expectations of investment is striking. In the eighteenth and nineteenth centuries, English law took a prescriptive, risk-averse approach to the investment of trust funds. In *Learoyd v. Whitely*,[143] Justice Watson explained the principle as follows: "Business men of ordinary prudence may, and frequently do, select investments which are more or less of a speculative character; but it is the duty of the trustee to confine himself to the class of investments which are permitted by the trust and likewise to avoid all investments of that class which are attended with hazard."[144]

According to John Langbein, early English legal attitudes toward investment of trust funds were deeply affected by the South Sea Bubble: in 1719, Parliament allowed trustees to invest in the South Sea Company, whose shares promptly dropped by 90 percent.[145] In the aftermath, the chastened Parliament instigated a conservative approach to investment of trust funds that began with the Bubble Act 1720[146] and would not disappear completely until the Trustee Act 2000. Under this risk-averse approach, trustees were permitted to invest only in assets specifically authorized in legislation.[147] These generally included consolidated bank annuities, gilts, and mortgages of real property.[148]

The prescriptive nature of these legislative lists was gradually relaxed over time: under the Trustee Investment Act 1961, trust funds were required to be divided into "narrower range' and "wider range" investments,[149] with wider-range investments including U.K. securities and some shares.[150] It was not until the repeal of the 1961 act with the Trustee Act 2000 that the prescriptive approach to investment disappeared from English legislation, allowing trustees to invest in any asset class.

The law with respect to investment of trust funds in the U.S. followed a similar trajectory. U.S. law inherited the English system of prescribing suitable investments for trustees.[151] It began to move away from the prescriptive approach in 1830 with the seminal case *Harvard College v. Amory*, which introduced the classic U.S. statement of the more flexible prudent man test: "All that can be required of a trustee to invest, is, that he shall conduct himself faithfully and exercise a sound discretion. He is to observe how men of prudence, discretion and intelligence manage their own affairs, not in regard to speculation, but in regard to the permanent disposition of their funds, considering the probable income, as well as the probable safety of the capital to be invested."[152]

While there was some resurgence of the process of requiring trustees to invest only in assets included on a "legal list" of investment options for trustees following the New York case *King v. Talbot*,[153] legislative initiatives gradually broadened trustees' investment opportunities throughout the nineteenth and twentieth centuries.[154] In particular, the advent of modern portfolio theory in the 1940s led to the legislative introduction of the modern prudent investor rule.[155] The large amount of legislative change regarding the investment of trust funds in the U.S. is testament to the flexibility of fiduciary duty. As Langbein notes, "the trust of today bears only a distant relationship to the trust of former centuries. The trust that we know is mainly a creature of the twentieth century; accordingly, common law processes of incrementalism were no more suitable for today's trust law than for the regulation of nuclear power plants."[156]

Today, under the modern prudent investor rule, trustees in the U.S. may invest in any asset that is appropriate to the fund portfolio, taking into account the risk and return objectives of the trust and its beneficiaries.[157]

The need for fiduciary duty to entertain new social and economic expectations surrounding investment was such that the adoption of such an obligation had to be facilitated by legislation. In this light, the past flexibility of fiduciary duty with respect to the investment of trust funds is demonstrated by its rapid adaptation to new financial standards. The potential for fiduciary duty to adapt to new investment approaches is therefore clear. Taking these points one step further, the next paragraphs argue that fiduciary duty also has the flexibility to adopt a broader view of investment by allowing the consideration of certain nonfinancial issues in investment decision making.

Changing societal expectations have affected fiduciary duty's approach to investment in subtler ways than risk averseness. Fiduciary duty has had the flexibility to evolve with respect to nonfinancial factors in trustee decision making in the context of changing attitudes toward women in the work place. Although dealing with trustees of a council rather than those of a pension fund, *Roberts v. Hopwood*[158] provides a vibrant illustration of how fiduciary duty can evolve in a social context. In this case, a local authority used its powers under statute[159] to increase wages for its workers to above the national average and to pay men and women equally. The district auditor found that the council's wage increase was unreasonable and ordered its reversal.[160] The council appealed and the case progressed to the House of Lords. The House of Lords found that the council had breached its fiduciary duty by aiming to be a model employer instead of paying the minimum wage. Justice Atkinson argued that "the council would, in my view, fail in their duty if, in administering funds which did not belong to their members alone, they put aside [minimum wage indicators] and allowed themselves to be guided in preference by some eccentric principles of socialistic philanthropy, or by a feminist ambition to secure the equality of the sexes in the matter of wages in the world of labour."[161]

Atkinson LJ regarded the council's decision to increase wages for both men and women as a symptom of "the vanity of appearing as model employers of labour" and of the council becoming "such ardent feminists as to bring about, at the expense of the ratepayers whose money they administered, sex equality in the labour market." In this case, the council's consideration of nonfinancial factors in determining how to invest ratepayers' money was found to violate its fiduciary duty to ratepayers.

With the growth of the antidiscrimination movement throughout the twentieth century, the decision to grant wage parity between sexes no longer appears to be the fanciful indulgence of "some eccentric principles of socialistic philanthropy." Some sixty years later, in *Pickwell v. Camden London Borough Council*,[162] the court affirmed the fiduciary duty of a council to its ratepayers, but also noted the council's entitlement to ensure the welfare of its workers, asserting that the council "must therefore often be involved in balancing fairly these interests which may frequently conflict."[163] The court referred to the decision of the House of Lords in *Roberts v. Hopwood* and said "looking back, as we do, over 60 years of progress in the field of social reform and industrial relations some of their Lordships' observations may, with the benefit of this hindsight, appear unsympathetic. . . . What has changed over those years is our attitudes to what should be regarded as pure philanthropy."[164]

In other words, whereas wage parity was once seen as philanthropy, it is now seen as a legitimate consideration potentially consistent with fiduciary duty. The court's comments with respect to *Roberts v. Hopwood* indicate an acknowledgment of the flexibility of fiduciary duty to yield in accordance with evolving social forces as well as commercial forces.[165] The development of fiduciary duty here was ancillary to the commercial context: just as the duty has adapted to evolving expectations in the investment context, it has also adapted to admit considerations once considered to be nonfinancial. It is therefore possible that fiduciary duty could adapt to changing social expectations about the environment, and in particular climate change. It is important to remember that fiduciary duty, no matter how immutable it appears to be at a single moment in time, is and always will be the object of interpretation; how it will be interpreted will vary with evolving investment and social standards. It is the *rate* of its evolution that is uncertain, an idea that is discussed below.

Inherent Inertia: Prudence Tends Toward the Status Quo

While the content of fiduciary duty clearly can evolve over time, change is often slow. It took more than 250 years for the investment conservatism engendered by the South Sea Bubble to give way to the concept of diversified investment portfolios. In particular, the law lagged significantly behind the finance industry (and, it must be said, financial reality) in adopting modern portfolio theory.[166] I argue here that legal inertia with respect to fiduciary duty and pension fund investment is linked to the prudent man standard.

What is prudence? According to the U.K. pensions regulator, "prudence is difficult to define in general terms and will apply differently to different circumstances."[167] Prudence is so difficult to define precisely because it is circumstantial. When judges are faced with deciding whether a particular trustee's decision was prudent, both U.S. law and U.K. law requires them to look at what other trustees in a similar position would do—they must look to the conventional behavior in the pension fund industry. In 2000, Hawley and Williams argued that "the safest course of action for a professional owner is to take *only* those actions generally accepted as prudent—which historically has led institutions to adopt a conservative view of their responsibilities as owners."[168] The prudent course of action in this light becomes the status quo, slowing innovation in investment decision making. Therefore, although fiduciary duty in the investment context is flexible, it is, paradoxically, susceptible to significant inertia. This is of great consequence for pension fund trustees, as it reinforces preexisting behavioral biases within the industry (this problem is discussed below). This inertia comes from several quarters: legislation, incremental judicial interpretation, and the behavior of the pension fund industry itself.

In the U.S., a formula urging fiduciaries to perpetuate the status quo in investment behavior is built into the modern prudent investor rule. Under the rule as it is formulated in ERISA, trust funds must be managed "with the care, skill, prudence, and diligence under the circumstances then prevailing that a prudent man acting in a like capacity and familiar with such matters would use in the conduct of an enterprise of a like character and with like aims."[169] When determining how a prudent man in an investment context might act, it seems logical that investors should look to the investment behavior of their peers—or at least to the behavior of their peers that has not attracted criticism for imprudent investment. Fiduciaries are therefore encouraged to base their investment judgements essentially on the prevailing investment conventions at any one time.

In the U.K., a trustee must manage the trust in the same manner as an ordinary prudent man of business would conduct his own affairs.[170] Professional trustees and asset managers professing to have special fund-management skills have a higher standard of care.[171] The standard of care for both professional and other trustees is, like the U.S. standard, self-referential. The prudence standard is once again associated with *what other investors do*. As such, U.K. pension fund trustees are expected to associate prudence with a conventional approach to investment.

A preference for maintaining the status quo in investment behavior can be seen in the historical reluctance of many courts to accept modern portfolio investment as prudent. Prior to the introduction of the modern prudent investor rule, courts across the Anglo-American legal world required fiduciaries to be able to demonstrate that each individual investment is "prudent"—any single investment failure could amount to imprudence on the part of the fiduciary. This legal stance resulted in risk-averse decisions by pension fund trustees, but also in returns that were significantly lower than they could have been.[172] The introduction of the U.S. modern prudent investor rule, and its equivalent diversification rule in the U.K., allowed fiduciaries to make investments that were more beneficial for the beneficiaries. The ability of pension funds to adapt to the realities of climate change is similarly restrained by the prudence standard's hostility to anything other than incremental change.

Judicial interpretation of the standard of prudence presents a further pressure on trustees to invest according to the convention of their day. Fratcher points out that "there is a tendency on the part of the courts even in the absence of a statute to lay down definite subsidiary rules on what is and what is not a prudent investment. When a certain investment is held in one case to be improper, the courts are likely to treat the case as a precedent holding that no investment of that type is proper."[173]

It is this tendency that has made palpable the fear of pension fiduciaries of considering factors traditionally seen as nonfinancial in investment decision making; it is this tendency that allowed the judgment in *Cowan v. Scargill* to grow to the (undeservedly) legendary proportions it has reached.

In the U.S., the testimony of experts in financial affairs is usually admissible for determining whether a fiduciary has acted prudently.[174] This self-referential feature is likely to propagate conventional wisdom, rather than to encourage trustees to innovate. The practical consequence of requiring investors to base their actions on the actions of their peers is that the status quo tends to prevail. For this reason, Keith Johnson and Frank Jan de Graaf have described the prudence standard as a "lemming standard."[175] In their view, "pension funds are often reluctant to pursue prudent strategies not being widely used by other pension funds for fear of exposure to liability."[176] In circumstances such as the present, where investors are typically driven by short-term performance, prudent investment becomes short-term investment.

The situation in the U.K. is similar. A report published by the U.K. Department of Social Security in 1997 used in-depth interviews with trustees of forty-eight self-administered private sector occupational pension schemes to examine trustee investment practice. The report found that the main objective for trustees in administering their funds was to provide a good return on assets, and that trustees sought to achieve this aim by "appointing expert advisers and fund managers with successful track records and monitoring their performance; adopting what they perceive as cautious investment policies; and providing guidelines and benchmarks for fund managers for investing schemes' assets."[177] In the U.K., trustees who are unsure of their duty may take advice from experts, including those within the finance industry.[178]

There have been some moves made toward encouraging pension fund trustees to act independently of their peers if their fund is different to the norm. In 1990, the Committee of Enquiry Report into Investment Performance Measurement recommended that "trustees should consider whether their own fund has special characteristics which indicate that it should be invested differently from the generality of funds."[179] However, this does nothing to encourage innovation in a fund that does not have "special characteristics."

The Outcome for Climate Change

The evolution of fiduciary duty, from restricting investment to specific low-risk categories until the second half of the twentieth century to embracing the modern prudent investor rule, reflects a change in social attitudes toward investment. Statutes in both the U.K. and the U.S. are helping to keep fiduciary duty up to date—this is particularly true of the statutory shift from prescriptive lists of investment options for fiduciaries toward the modern prudent investor rule. However, even the statutory developments of the last two decades are insufficient to enable pension funds to move toward a more sustainable investment paradigm.[180] The incrementalism central to the maturation of fiduciary duty in the past cannot facilitate the urgent action required by climate change. Nor does it, more importantly, encourage a deep philosophical change of the kind necessary to look at the long-term sustainability of investments.

An aggravating factor exists here in the question of whether, and to what extent, a court would consider climate change a "nonfinancial" issue. Until such a case is heard or relevant legislation enacted, it will be difficult to displace fiduciaries' anxiety with respect to the consideration of climate change within investment decision making. It is reasonable to predict that courts will decide by reference to convention: if most pension funds view climate change as a nonfinancial issue, then courts are likely to see this position as the prudent one. While almost all governments and major companies around the world now see climate change as a financial issue, as well as an environmental and social one, few pension funds have demonstrated this view. In a way, therefore, pension fund inaction on climate change is likely also to be self-perpetuating without legislative clarification.

There is no intrinsic reason for fiduciary duty to prevent pension funds from adopting a forward-looking approach to investment that includes the consideration of factors (such as climate change) that are coming to be recognized as financial but that have not traditionally informed investment decisions. In theory, fiduciary duty should adapt to new economic realities engendered by climate change, but change, as noted earlier, is likely to be incremental (just as it was with respect to modern portfolio theory and equal opportunity in the past). Left up to pension fund trustees and courts, it is likely that the concept of prudence will lag behind as legislative changes correct the market failures of climate change. In practice, the tendency for prudent behavior to be equated with conventional behavior means that most pension funds will not move beyond the status quo in terms of investment strategy.

Pension fund trustee caution with respect to uncharted financial territory is not surprising, given the uncertainty surrounding fiduciary duty. However, the focus of pension fund trustees on fiduciary duty as the main reason for eschewing change in investment approach obscures significant behavioral impediments to sustainable investment: ingrained short-termism regarding both financial performance and environmental impact, and institutional inertia. These impediments, when combined with the prudence standard's constant reference to the status quo, create a collective action problem: in order for climate change to become an accepted consideration for pension fund trustees, a group of trustees must act in unison.

Ingrained Inertia, Short-termism, and Collective Inaction

Fiduciary duty is an oft-cited cause for resistance to innovation in investment culture, but it must not be mistaken for the only or even most important one. While trustees' fears relating to fiduciary duty and environmental impact are understandable given conservative interpretation of the prudence standard in the past, the influence of fiduciary duty is overstated. This chapter has argued that there is no inherent conflict between pension funds' fiduciary duty and the consideration of climate change as a risk or opportunity, in circumstances where climate change is likely to have a demonstrable financial impact over the long term. The inherent flexibility of fiduciary duty, although incremental, is such that it should be able to adapt to the demands of a climate change economy over time. Clarification by legislators could go a long way toward reducing the confusion-induced inaction on environmental issues attributed to fiduciary duty. In the meantime, the prominence of fiduciary duty as an explanation for stagnation in pension fund investment culture dissembles the more insidious reasons: the behavioral phenomena of institutional inertia and short-termism, which feed into a collective action problem.

This section argues that short-termism and inertia with respect to financial performance and environmental impact are central reasons for pension funds' slow reaction to change, and specifically, to climate change. While much has been said about how behavioral biases can affect financial performance, much less studied is how these biases can prevent innovation in the wider sense. In reality, these behavioral biases mean that the pension fund industry is slow to conduct self-examination, slow to diagnose its systematic shortcomings, and slow to treat them. It is asserted here that strong leadership from within the pension fund industry is needed to combat these problems.

Initiating change is an enduring problem for institutions. This problem becomes all the more pertinent as today's increasingly complex financial, economic, and environmental conditions require not only change but urgent change to the way that financial institutions operate. Studies in psychology and economics have shown that behavioral inertia exists at an individual level, and that this individual behavior is carried into group decisions within institutions. As a result, fiduciary duty's tendency to limit investment innovation is matched by resistance to change within the boards of pension funds. Pension fund trustees, this section argues, have a strong preference for the status quo when faced with decision making. Moreover, pension fund trustees generally find it difficult to integrate unfamiliar variables, such as climate change, into their decisions about investment. These limitations to trustees' ability to innovate investment processes in the context of climate change need to be recognized: even when legislation clarifies the reach of fiduciary duty, pension funds themselves will need to address their tendency toward inertia in investment strategy development.

Individuals generally are resistant to behavioral change. William Samuelson and Richard Zeckhauser demonstrate that when making a decision, people are biased toward maintaining the status quo.[181] They suggest that status quo bias exists largely because individuals want to avoid the cost of changing their behavior, and because people tend to prefer the certainty of the status quo to the uncertainty of change. This behavioral trait may be linked to a second trait: loss averseness.[182] People generally prefer accepting a lower, but more certain, gain than taking a risk for a higher, but more uncertain, gain.[183] Therefore, the status quo is not only less costly but also more certain.

This preference for the status quo has been demonstrated in the decision making of pension fund trustees.[184] It is perhaps somewhat counterintuitive that pension fund trustees are subject to behavioral biases in their trust fund management capacity, given that in their role as trustees they are investing other peoples' money. However, Clark et al. have shown that trustees are often even more careful with trust funds,[185] reflecting perhaps a desire to respect the parameters of fiduciary duty and a reverence toward the higher stakes involved, and their potential personal liability. Their study finds that "trustees believe that their beneficiaries would not, all things being equal, assume any risk if they could avoid it."[186] It should be noted that status quo bias also appears to affect beneficiaries when faced with similar decisions in defined-contribution funds. In these funds, beneficiaries have some ability to direct the investment management of their own fund benefit. However, the majority of such beneficiaries in the U.S. and U.K. retain the default plan, rather than opting for a tailored plan.[187] As a result, defined-contribution funds are unlikely to differ much in practice from defined-benefit funds when it comes to tackling the problem of climate change: since beneficiaries usually choose to leave decisions up to trustees, trustee's voices still remain crucial to the investment strategy of most defined-contribution funds.

The addition of novel contextual layers, such as the consideration of unfamiliar variables, to decision making may weaken the ability of pension fund trustees to make sound investment decisions. Clark et al.'s 2007 study indicates that pension fund trustees, who are generally men in their fifties,[188] while more competent than Oxford undergraduates "when asked to solve a problem that drew upon specific knowledge derived from the context of their roles and responsibilities,"[189] are less competent at integrating new contextual layers into their decision making than Oxford undergraduates. It was found that the inclusion of new "normative issues" expanded decision-making requirements "well beyond trustees' roles and responsibilities."[190]

The addition of the new considerations surrounding climate change tests pension fund trustee decision making in just this way: it adds a novel contextual layer to decision making. Because pension fund trustees prefer to avoid changing their current investment processes, the addition of a novel contextual element to the process makes it harder for pension fund trustees to make rational decisions. The context of climate change is likely to be difficult for pension fund trustees to accommodate under their current decision-making frameworks. Status quo bias is therefore a major challenge for pension funds adjusting to innovative investment strategies in a climate change economy.

It is worth noting that a higher degree of professional qualification in trustees appears to *increase*, rather than decrease, their aversion to innovation in investment strategies.[191] This may indicate that professional training in trustees reinforces existing bias toward inertia within the industry.

The second behavioral bias restricting pension fund innovation in the context of climate change is institutional myopia, or short-termism. That humans discount the value of the future is well established in psychology and economics.[192] What matters here is the extent to which this phenomenon also affects pension fund trustees in their capacity as fiduciaries: most institutional investors focus on short-term performance to such an extent that investee corporations act to promote short-term gains at the expense of long-term performance.[193]

While pension funds usually have long time horizons (to provide retirement income to current workers in the future), the Myners Report investigating short-termism in U.K. institutional investment found that the reward system of pension funds is structured to favor short-termism.[194] In particular, bonuses for asset managers are awarded on an annual basis, and investee company performance is monitored quarterly. Moreover, while short-term performance is easily measured, long-term value can only be predicted. The practical shortcomings in the methods available for measuring long-term performance are difficult to overcome. A potential solution for measuring long-term value is to assess the soundness of the investment *process* itself, rather than continuous reference to share price, but this method does not provide the quick and easy answer found in share price.

In this context, the tendency for fiduciary duty to encourage the maintenance of the status quo reinforces pension funds' ingrained preference for short-term performance over long-term value. It does more than merely reinforce these preferences, however. It also provides a smokescreen behind which these behaviors may escape scrutiny. To the extent that pension fund trustees and asset managers attribute their inaction to fiduciary duty, the concept of fiduciary duty obscures a capacity for change that is not only real but also, increasingly, necessary.

When combined with the tendency of the trustees and courts to judge prudence by reference to conventional behavior, these behavioral biases (especially inertia) create a problem of collective action within the pension fund industry. As this chapter has argued, courts, legislation, and trustees themselves all refer to conventional behavior in order to determine what prudent investing is. As short-term-focused, narrowly construed strategies are conventional for pension funds, these are widely seen as prudent missions. Independently of this, pension funds prefer to behave in accordance with conventional investment culture, which emphasizes short-term financial performance, because they have behavioral biases toward cultivating, and then maintaining, short-termism on the one hand, and toward maintaining the status quo (that is, not challenging convention) on the other. Under these conditions, a collective action problem arises to hinder investment innovation: the adoption by a small number of pension funds of a climate-change-conscious investment strategy will be seen as imprudent, because these innovative funds will be bucking convention in the minority. In order for change to occur, it will require the participation of a larger number of funds, or at least a number of respected, leading pension funds—in short, it will require a change of convention, so that courts and other funds will find climate change to be a prudent consideration.

This chapter has argued that the uncertainty surrounding the requirements of fiduciary duty (and most relevantly here, the duty of prudence), could be alleviated through legislative clarification. However, legislative clarification would only go part of the way toward facilitating the adaptation of pension funds to a climate change economy. In order to overcome the behavioral biases that sustain short-termism and inertia and fuel a collective action problem that nurtures an unhealthy dedication to convention, change needs to come from within the pension fund industry itself. The best way for funds to address these biases is to implement considered governance practices.[195] Pension funds that believe in the need to innovate investment strategies with respect to environmental and social issues, and climate change in particular, need to promote change through strong leadership.

Conclusion

Pension funds, with their staggering financial holdings, have the capacity to bring climate change to the forefront of business agendas. By including climate change risk and opportunity explicitly in their investment strategies, pension fund trustees stand not only to improve the long-term financial performance of their funds but also to contribute to a more sustainable economy. Furthermore, given their prominence as service providers in the vacuum created by the retreat of the state, it is arguable that pension funds have a *responsibility* to look beyond the financial impact of their decisions. However, very few pension funds have chosen to do so thus far. For most pension funds, climate change, like other issues trustees see as tangential to financial performance, remains beyond the scope of investment strategy.

Pension funds' reluctance to expand their investment strategies beyond their conventional barriers into the consideration of environmental issues is frequently attributed to trustees' fiduciary duty. For many years, trustees have interpreted this duty as preventing the consideration of nonfinancial issues in investment decision making. Climate change, whose potential economic effects have only recently become widely accepted, is perceived as one of these. This chapter has argued that this interpretation of fiduciary duty, based on outdated case law, is too narrow. Moreover, to the extent that climate change presents a real financial concern that is likely to increase as further legislation affects the price of carbon, pension funds' consideration of climate change in devising their investment strategy should not, *in theory*, conflict with even a narrow interpretation of fiduciary duty.

In practice, however, the lack of recent case law and unclear commentary on fiduciary duty has created uncertainty for pension funds wishing to adapt to a climate change economy. Pension funds' concerns about fiduciary duty are to an extent justified. Past legal analyses have supported the classification of environmental issues as "nonfinancial" issues, which, together with ethical, political, and social issues, should not influence a fiduciary's investment strategy. As it stands, fiduciary duty in both the U.S. and the U.K. provides a reason for pension funds to delay changing their investment policies to accommodate the more complex investment approach demanded in a climate change economy. Although fiduciary duty has a proven ability to adapt to changing social circumstances, this adaptation is incremental, and ill suited to the rapid changes required to meet the challenges of climate change. Clarification through legislation would help to alleviate the uncertainty surrounding fiduciary duty.

The advent of the financial crisis has given us a moment of pause to examine the state of finance and what it represents. For the work presented here, it represents both an end and a beginning. First, an end: the financial crisis heralds the demise of the efficient markets hypothesis. With its end, the colorful realities of human behavior are suddenly more apparent against the hitherto black-and-white background of economic theory. These realities of human behavior, in particular biases of inertia and myopia, are the greatest barrier to the pension fund industry's shift toward more sustainable investment strategies. The truth is, this chapter has argued, fiduciary duty is only part of the problem. An unclear notion of fiduciary duty feeds into these biases, making them crippling. When these biases combine with prevailing pension fund view that prudence equates to conventional behavior, a collective action problem results: pension funds are unlikely to break with convention unless a significant number of them change their approach simultaneously. Any institutional acceptance of innovation toward a longer term, more sustainable investment strategy will take strong leadership from pension funds themselves. It is fortunate then that the financial crisis also represents a beginning: it provides an opportunity for reevaluation, and a chance to improve the sustainability of the financial system.

The implications to be drawn from this chapter are threefold. First, the uncertainty surrounding pension fund fiduciary duty and environmental considerations, in particular climate change, should be clarified through legislation. Without this clarification, pension fund trustees will have all the impetus they need to shy away from changes they are already reluctant to make. Second, pension funds must reexamine their approach to investment, as they once did at the advent of modern portfolio theory—any move toward a more sustainable investment approach will require funds to act on their own behalf. An adoption of best-practice governance measures will help pension funds to surmount the behavioral barriers to innovation. Finally, a broader point: this chapter has allowed a brief, and rather dismal, glimpse at how Anglo-American courts interact with the institutional investment industry—in short, they appear to reinforce the industry's existing behavioral problems and mutual uncertainties about the application of fiduciary duty in an investment context. In this light, the specter of fiduciary duty becomes a means to ensure that existing financial norms, of the sort that fueled the present financial crisis, remain untouched.

Notes

Chapter 1. Introduction

1. See, for example, John C. Bogle, *The Battle for the Soul of Capitalism* (New Haven, Conn., 2005); Gordon L. Clark, *Pension Fund Capitalism* (New York, 2006); Peter A. Gourevitch and James Shinn, *Political Power and Corporate Control* (Princeton, N.J., 2005); James P. Hawley and Andrew T. Williams, *The Rise of Fiduciary Capitalism* (Philadelphia, 2000); Robert A. G. Monks, *The New Global Investors* (Oxford, 2001); and Michael Useem, *Investor Capitalism* (New York, 1996).

2. Hawley and Williams. Examples of UOs are CalPERS, CalSTRS, and TIAA-CREF in the U.S.; USS and Hermes in the U.K.; FRR in France; and the Norway Pension Fund-Global. While there are likely hundreds of UOs globally, only a few explicitly and publicly call themselves UOs. (Those that do include CalSTRS and TIAA-CREF; USS and Hermes; the Norway Pension Fund-Global; and FRR.)

3. The conference was held on the campus of Saint Mary's College of California. It was convened by the Elfenworks Center for the Study of Fiduciary Capitalism of Saint Mary's College; the Millstein Center for Corporate Governance and Performance of Yale University; and the Principles of Responsible Investment. The conference was additionally funded by the IIRC Institute (for research support) and Hermes Equity Ownership Services (U.K.) (for operating expenses). Paper proposals were solicited and reviewed and some were selected by a panel of six experts, three academics and three practitioners.

4. TIAA-CREF, *Responsible Investing and Corporate Governance: Lessons Learned for Shareholder from the Crises of the Last Decade*, February 2010. In the U.K., Hermes Equity Ownership Services is an important exception as well, having issued a public statement on governance and risk in the late fall of 2008. Informally, many UOs have been questioning not only their risk models but also the models on which these models are built: MPT, EMH, the capital asset pricing model (CAPM), and economic general

equilibrium theory. Few have made these internal conversations public, nor have various institutional investor trade organizations, as of this writing, held formal discussions or panels or put these issues on their meeting agendas. This has been noted by two important U.K. government reports: "The Turner Review" (March 2009) and *A Review of Corporate Governance in UK Banks and Other Industry Entities* ("Walker Report") (July 2009).

5. These critical studies include those by the Yale economist Robert Shiller, one of the early and most trenchant critics of the EMH and MPT in articles such as Robert J. Shiller, "Consumption, Asset Markets and Macroeconomic Fluctuations," *Carnegie-Rochester Conference Series on Public Policy*, 1982, 17: pp. 203–238, and Robert J. Shiller, "From Efficient Markets Theory to Behavioral Finance," *Journal of Economic Perspectives*, 2003, 17: pp. 83–104. For a summary of recent research in behavioral finance, see Justin Fox, *The Myth of the Rational Market: A History of Risk, Reward and Delusion on Wall Street* (New York: Harper Business, 2009), pp. 175–210, 247–264.

Chapter 2. Beyond Risk

1. See Paul Mason, *Meltdown: The End of the Age of Greed* (London: Verso, 2009), for a detailed account of this crisis and its repercussions, notably pp. 37–55.

2. For an excellent discussion of the evolution of the principal concepts of modern portfolio theory, see Peter L. Bernstein, *Capital Ideas: The Improbable Origins of Modern Wall Street* (Hoboken, N.J.: John Wiley & Sons, 2005). It contains a discussion of Markowitz and diversification, pp. 41–60; a discussion of Sharpe and the relationship between risk and rewards, pp. 75–88; a discussion of the Fama and the efficient market theory, pp. 126–145; and a discussion of Black and Scholes and option pricing, pp. 203–230.

3. Justin Fox, *The Myth of the Rational Market: A History of Risk, Reward, and Delusion on Wall Street* (New York: HarperBusiness, 2009), p. 54.

4. Peter L. Bernstein, *Capital Ideas Evolving* (Hoboken, N.J.: John Wiley & Sons, 2007), pp. 37–43.

5. For a discussion of the debate between behavioral economists and advocates of the efficient market hypothesis, see Bernstein (2007), pp. 19–33, and Daniel Kahneman and Amos Tversky, "Prospect Theory: An Analysis of Decision Under Risk," *Econometrica* March 1979: 263–292.

For an extended discussion of the efficient market hypothesis and its critics, see Fox. Typical of Fox's claims is, "As far back as the 1970s, dissident economists and finance scholars began to question this rational market theory, to expose its theoretical inconsistencies and lack of empirical backing. By the end of the century they had knocked away most of its underpinnings" (p. xv).

For a discussion of the limitations of MPT's assumption that stock market returns are evenly distributed on a bell curve, see Nassim Taleb, *The Black Swan: The Impact of the Highly Improbable* (New York: Random House, 2007), pp. 229–252.

For one of many discussions by economists of the limitations of markets in creating sound economies, see Joseph E. Stiglitz, *The Roaring Nineties* (New York: W. W. Norton, 2003). In the book's introduction Stiglitz notes, "This book is intended to explain why I believe that while markets are at the center of the success of our economy, markets do not always work well by themselves, why they do not solve all problems, and why government will always be an important partner to them" (pp. xi–xii). For another such discussion, see David Korten, *When Corporations Rule the World* (San Francisco: Berrett Koehler, 1995). Typical of his position is, "Although business often complains that government interferes unduly with its affairs, most calls for freeing the market ignore a basic reality: the efficient function of a market economy depends on a strong government. This need is well established in contemporary market economic theory and has been demonstrated in practice" (p. 95).

For a discussion of the impracticalities of putting modern portfolio theory into practice, see Bernstein, *Capital Ideas Evolving*, pp. 100–109.

6. For a discussion of modern financial engineering by unethical practitioners, see Gillian Tett, *Fool's Gold: How the Bold Dream of a Small Tribe at J.P. Morgan Was Corrupted by Wall Street Greed and Unleashed a Catastrophe* (New York: Free Press, 2009). Typical of Tett's observations is, "Most of the former J.P. Morgan team considered pointing the finger at derivatives utterly unfair. 'This crisis has *nothing* to do with innovation. It is about excesses in banking,' Winters observed" (p. 212).

For a discussion of how modern financial engineering has introduced excessive risk into the system, see Richard Bookstaber, *A Demon of Our Own Devising: Markets, Hedge Funds, and the Perils of Financial Innovation* (Hoboken, N.J.: John Wiley & Sons, 2007). Typical of Bookstaber's argument is, "In the face of progress and technological advances that have resulted in stability on many fronts, financial markets, designed to provide a mechanism for managing and addressing economic risk, have developed a structure that has made them inherently more risky" (p. 147). Also see Fox, "The act of managing risk in such an environment alters that environment, creating a never-stable feedback loop. The crash of 1987 was the first alarming demonstration of the inherent instability of mathematical risk-management models in finance. It was not to be the last" (p. 229).

For a discussion of how portfolio insurance failed to work in the crash of 1987, see Bookstaber, pp. 7–31.

7. Harry M. Markowitz, "Crisis Mode: Modern Portfolio Theory Under Pressure," *Investment Professional*, New York Society of Security Analysts, vol 2, no. 2, Spring 2009. Available at http://www.theinvestmentprofessional.com/vol_2_no_2/crisis-mode.html.

8. Certain theorists of the financial markets have in fact noted this connection. For example, according to Justin Fox, in 1938 Frederick Macaulay had pointed out that "the errors made by investors and speculators betting on the future via financial

markets weren't random, though. They were 'systemic' and 'constant,' the inevitable result of the 'emotions, lack of logic and insufficiency of knowledge' that characterized all human decision making but especially decision making about the future. These systematic errors, Macaulay argued, were the main cause of the 'violent social disturbances' known as the business cycle. The cure he prescribed was more government planning of economic activity, so the future might hold fewer surprises" (Fox, pp. 27–28).

9. Bernstein, *Capital Ideas*, pp. 120–121.

10. Defenders of MPT's risk-control techniques argue that systemic risk control is also possible. For example, "tail insurance" to control for market-level risk has been proposed by some as a measure to prevent future crises. El-Erian, for example, advocates "tail insurance," arguing that institutional investors "should supplement [traditional risk-management approaches] by spending time and resources identifying what your left tails are and aggressively hedging them in a responsive and cost-effective manner." See Mohamed A. El-Erian, "Managing the Previously Unmanageable: Lessons from the Leverage Unwinds," *CFA Conference Proceedings Quarterly* March 2009, vol. 26, no. 1: 1–4, qtd. on 3.

11. Bruce L. Jacobs, "Tumbling Tower of Babel: Subprime Securitization and the Credit Crisis," *Financial Analysts Journal* March–April 2009, vol. 65, no. 2: 17–29; 1.

12. Mason, p. 77.

13. John Cassidy, *How Markets Fail: The Logic of Economic Calamities* (New York: Farrar, Straus and Giroux, 2009), p. 21. Quoting Raghuram G. Rajan, "Has Financial Development Made the World Riskier?" presented at the Federal Reserve Bank of Kansas City Economic Symposium, Jackson Hole, Wyo., August 25–27, 2005.

14. Michael Musuraca, "The Perfect Storm, Take Two," presented at "Capital Matters: Managing Labor's Capital Conference," Harvard University, April 30, 2009.

15. See Taleb, 241, 271.

16. One implication of this argument might be, for example, that those practicing MPT have contributed to the poor returns of the stock markets in the United States over the past decade. The annualized return of the Standard & Poor's 500 stock index from August 1999 to August 2009 was -0.79 percent, in part because of two dramatic crashes in stock price due to bubbles produced by irrationally exuberant investors. During the period, the economy as a whole grew, so the growth of the economy did not result in returns to investors, as MPT has led us to believe. Moreover, it is unclear how much more the economy as a whole might have grown over this period had it not been for these crashes. Further study would be necessary to demonstrate a causal relationship between MPT and an increase in the likelihood of fat-tail events.

17. Bernstein, *Capital Ideas Evolving*, p. 40.

18. "Mainstreaming Responsible Investment," paper delivered at the World Economic Forum meeting in Davos, Switzerland, January 2005.

19. See Bookstaber, pp. 12–15, and Fox, pp. 227–232.

20. James P. Hawley and Andrew T. Williams, *The Rise of Fiduciary Capitalism* (Philadelphia: University of Pennsylvania Press, 2000).

21. This assumption about government is broad and implicitly controversial. Alternative conceptions abound as to what constitutes legitimate government, how those governing should define justice and sustainability, what government's role is in wealth creation and distribution, and what the proper role of government is in the maintenance of financial markets. Any full-blown theory of finance must contend to some degree with issues of this sort. This chapter adopts without elaboration the position that governments should be primarily concerned with issues of justice and sustainability, with the understanding that the fuller exploration of such an assumption is part of the task of those concerned with a theory and practice of investment. Ultimately finance cannot be separated from politics and it is important that the political context in which financial theory evolves and financial markets operate be as clearly articulated by investors as possible.

22. Steven Lydenberg, "Building the Case for Long-Term Investing in Stock Markets: Breaking Free from the Short-term Measurement Dilemma," in Henri-Claude De Bettignies and François Lépineux, eds., *Finance for a Better World: The Shift Toward Sustainability* (Basingstoke, U.K.: Palgrave Macmillan, 2009), pp. 168–186.

23. Chistian Grollier and Alain Leclair. "Pourquoi l'ISR a-t-il besoin de recherche unversitaire? Regards croisés," *Revue d'Économie Financière* no. 8: 11–18.

24. Amy Domini, "Financial Markets: For Whose Benefit?" *OECD Observer* June 2009; available online at http://www.oecdobserver.org/news/fullstory.php/aid/3040/Financial_markets:_for_whose_benefit_.html.

25. James Fallows, "Be Nice to the Countries That Lend You Money," *Atlantic* December 2008: 62–65.

26. John M. Keynes, *The General Theory of Employment, Interest and Money* (Cambridge, U.K.: Palgrave Macmillan/Cambridge University Press, 1936), chapter 12.

27. James Buchan, *The Authentic Adam Smith: His Life and Ideas* (New York: W. W. Norton, 2006), p. 61.

28. CalPERS 2010, "Facts at a Glance," available at http://www.calpers.ca.gov/eip-docs/about/facts/general.pdf, accessed February 27, 2010.

Chapter 3. The Quality of Corporate Governance Within Financial Firms in Stressed Markets

1. For example, an investor can hedge credit risk by purchasing credit default swaps to buy credit protection. See J. Ralfe, "Reasons to Be Hedging—1, 2, 3," *Risk* 9 (7) (1996), pp. 20–21. See also M. Crouhy, D. Galai, and R. Mark, "Credit Risk Revisited," *Risk Supplement* (March 1998), pp. 40–44.

2. Gap revenue can be generated by profiting from interest rate sensitivity mismatches between the financial firm's assets and liabilities. For example, if the firm has

a three-year interest rate sensitive asset funded by a one-year interest rate sensitive liability, then the interest rate sensitive gap can either be left open or hedged by a three-year fixed floating interest rate swap.

3. The Black-Scholes model is a financial model used to predict the value of a European-style option. See F. Black and M. Scholes, "The Pricing of Options and Corporate Liabilities," *Journal of Political Economy* 81 (1973), pp. 637–654. The Merton model is a financial model used to predict the probability of default. See R. C. Merton, "Theory of Rational Options Pricing," *Bell Journal of Economics and Management Science* 4 (1) (1973), pp. 141–183.

4. Convexity is a mathematical measure that quantifies the sensitivity of an asset to large changes in price or yield. In option contracts convexity (commonly termed "gamma") measures the change in delta for a change in the price of the underlying asset; in fixed-income products it measures the change in duration for a change in yield or interest rates. Mathematically, convexity is the first derivative of a change in value with respect to duration/delta, or the second derivative of a change in value with respect to yield/underlying asset. See F. R. Macauley, *Some Theoretical Problems Suggested by Movements of Interest Rates, Bond Yields, and Stock Prices in the U.S. Since 1856* (New York: National Bureau of Economic Research, 1938).

5. EVA works to balance return versus risk considerations where EVA = NOPAT − WACC × Operating Capital. NOPAT refers to the net operating profit after taxes.

6. For example, return on assets and return on equity .

7. For example, a business unit is incented to increase FCF while risk management (in concert with the CFO) strives to reduce the WACC (e.g., by reducing Rs and Rd).

8. VAR is a statistical measure that estimates how much a portfolio of assets and liabilities might lose in a given period as a result of a risk. VAR, which can be implemented through the variance/covariance, historical, or simulation methods, is based on assumptions related to liquidation period, shape of the statistical distributions, desired confidence level, and volatilities and correlations between portfolio contracts. See E. Derman, "Model Risk" in *VAR—Understanding and Applying Value-at-Risk* (London: Risk Books, 1997).

9. R. Mark, "Integrated Credit Risk Management," in *Derivative Credit Risk*, 2nd edition (London: Risk Books, 1999).

10. R. Mark and D. Krishna, "How Risky Is Your Risk Information?" *Journal of Risk Management in Financial Institutions* 1, no. 4 (2008), pp. 439–451. Also see A. Bansal, R. J. Kauffman, R. M. Mark, and E. Peters, "Financial Risk and Financial Risk Management Technology," *Information and Management* 24 (1993), pp. 267–281.

11. W. Sharpe and G. J. Alexander, *Investments* (Englewood Cliffs, N.J.: Prentice-Hall, 1990).

12. MCS is an analytical technique in which a large number of simulations are run using random quantities for uncertain variables and the distribution of results is examined to infer which values are most likely.

13. H. M. Markowitz, "Portfolio Selection," *Journal of Finance* 7 (1952), pp. 77–91.

14. H. M. Markowitz, *Portfolio Selection: Efficient Diversification of Investments* (New York: John Wiley and Sons, 1959), p. 8.

15. W. F. Sharpe, "Capital Asset Prices: A Theory of Market Equilibrium under Conditions of Risk," *Journal of Finance* 19 (1964), pp. 425–442.

16. An investment strategy based on the Kelly philosophy can be utilized to protect the investor against financial ruin in stressed markets. For example, let's say you have a choice of using only one of three investment strategies that call for making an investment every week. Assume the first strategy has the highest geometric mean and the third strategy has the highest arithmetic mean. Assume also that the second strategy is the only one where you can be wiped out on any given weekly investment. The Kelly criterion focuses on maximizing the geometric mean, and therefore the investor would put money on the first strategy. The worst case, in the Kelly philosophy, is the second. That's because it has 0 as one of its outcomes. Any long-term investor who keeps investing money weekly on the second strategy must eventually go bust since the second strategy's geometric mean is 0. Assume the variance and the arithmetic mean of all the investments increase from the first strategy to the third strategy. Markowitz theory refuses to decide among these three cases, since all are legitimate choices. See William Poundstone, *Fortune's Formula* (New York: Hill and Wang, 2005).

17. See Sharpe.

18. Beta equals the standard deviation of the asset multiplied by the correlation of the asset with the market portfolio (M) divided by the standard deviation of M. In other words, beta is a measure of the covariance between that asset's return and the return on the market, divided by the market variance.

19. See Sharpe and Alexander.

20. The CAPM is used to set the hurdle rate for institutions utilizing a RAROC approach. RAROC balances the risk and return trade-offs against a desired hurdle rate. For example, superior risk governance calls for firms to use RAROC to measure performance. RAROC equals the risk-adjusted net income divided by economic capital. An investment is rejected if RAROC does not exceed the hurdle rate. (See the Appendix.)

21. For example, if it is implemented in a spreadsheet or a C + + computer code.

22. The vetter can stress test the model by looking at some limit scenario in order to identify the range of parameter values for which the model provides accurate pricing. This is especially important for implementations that rely on numerical techniques.

23. Organized by the Elfenworks Center for the Study of Fiduciary Capitalism, October 5–7, 2009.

24. Funding-liquidity risk relates to a firm's ability to raise the necessary cash to

roll over its debt; to meet the cash, margin, and collateral requirements of counterparties; and (in the case of funds) to satisfy withdrawals.

25. For example, French insurance companies had to buy large amounts of French government bonds at certain points on the yield curve; Japanese banks had large needs to receive a fixed rate and pay a floating rate in yen-denominated swaps; and when the Federal Reserve Bank raised U.S. interest rates in 1994, European investors became large sellers of futures on providing liquidity to meet these institutional demands. See A. F. Perold, "Long-Term Capital Management Case Study," Case No. 200–007, Harvard Business School, 1999. See also Crouhy, Galai, and Mark, *Essentials of Risk Management* (New York: McGraw Hill, 2006), which is the principal syllabus material for PRMIA's Associate Professional Risk Manager certificate.

26. For example a postmortem shareholder report on UBS's write-downs indicates that shortcuts were taken to speed up the production of risk reports. But these shortcuts were systematically gamed so that risks were structured in such a way they did not show up at all in the calculations of risk.

27. See Lawrence D. Brown and Marcus L. Caylor, "Corporate Governance and Firm Performance," Georgia State University, December 7, 2004, available at Risk Metrics, http://papers.ssrn.com/sol3/papers.cfm?abstract_id = 586423.

28. See Millstein Center for Corporate Governance and Performance, http://millstein.som.yale.edu/.

29. A portfolio with assets in the same industry (or country) is more exposed to systematic risk. A key aim of risk governance in stressed markets is to properly assess the global, regional, and industrial sector considerations used as input factors to drive industry and country systematic risk. Systemic risk is a form of risk that is common to all companies, assets, or markets and that cannot therefore be reduced or eliminated through diversification.

30. These may include up to seven risk categories such as interest rates, foreign exchange rates, equity prices, commodity prices, credit spreads, swap spreads, and vega (volatility). In the case of interest rates, for example, the methodology might define six stress shocks to accommodate both changes in the level of rates and changes in the shape of the yield curve. In the case of credit spreads and equities, there may be only one stress shock, i.e., the widening of credit spreads and the fall of equity prices

31. The cost of credit, like other business costs, is priced into the transaction in the form of a spread over funding cost. There is no need for risk capital as a buffer to absorb this expected risk. See Crouhy, Galai, and Mark, "A Comparative Analysis of Current Credit Risk Models."

32. For example, one such mechanism is charging the business unit for any funding cost incurred by its activities.

33. We want $N - \text{Hurdle Rate} \times EC > 0$. If we insert the components of risk into EC then we want $N - \{MRC + CRC + ORC + BRC + FRC + SRC - PE \text{ (Portfolio Effect)}\} \times \text{Hurdle Rate} > 0$. See F. Modigliani and M. H. Miller, "The Cost

of Capital, Corporation Finance, and the Theory of Investment," *American Economic Review* 48 (1958), pp. 261–297.

34. The cost of common equity (Re) is determined via a model such as CAPM. CAPM is such that Re = Rf + Be × (Rm − Rf) where Rf is the risk-free rate, Rm is expected return on the market portfolio, and Be is the firm's common equity market beta.

35. The cost of preferred equity(Rp) is simply the yield on the firm's preferred shares.

36. The after-tax RAROC is N/D where N = ($90 − $9 − $60 − $10 + $5.25) × (1 − 0.3) and D = $75. Observe that $90 million is the expected revenue, $9 million is the operating cost, $60 million is the interest expense (6 percent of the $1 billion borrowed fund), $10 million is the expected loss, and $5.25 million is the return on economic capital. Recall that economic capital must be invested in risk-free securities rather than being used to fund risky activities.

Chapter 4. Chasing Alpha

1. The City of New York and the U.S. Senate, *Sustaining New York's and the U.S.'s Global Financial Services Leadership*, 2007, subsequently cited as *Sustaining New York's and the U.S.'s Global Financial Services Leadership*, 2007.

2. Ibid., pp. 19, 33, 34, 44, 72. International Financial Services London, *International Financial Markets in the UK*, May 2007.

3. H.M. Treasury, *UK International Financial Services—The Future*, 2009, p. 19. H.M. Treasury, *Reforming Financial Markets*, 2009, p. 18.

4. Speech by Gordon Brown to Mansion House, London, June 16, 2004, hm-treasury.gov.uk.

5. Julian Barnes, "The Deficit Millionaires," *New Yorker*, September 20, 1993.

6. Will Hutton, *The State We're In* (Vintage, 1996), p. 5.

7. *Sustaining New York's and the U.S.'s Global Financial Services Leadership*, 2007, p. 80.

8. Financial Services Authority, *Principles of Good Regulation*, fsa.gov.uk.

9. Financial Services Authority, *Annual Report*, 2006–2007, p. 15.

10. Hector Sants, "The FSA's Retail Agenda: Working with the Industry," speech at the Association of Independent Financial Advisers (AIFA) conference, November 21, 2007, www.fsa.gov.uk,

11. *Sustaining New York's and the U.S.'s Global Financial Services Leadership*, 2007, p. 84.

12. Quoted in Philip Augar, *Chasing Alpha* (Random House, 2009), p. 48. Republished as *Reckless: The Rise and Fall of the City, 2007–08* (Vintage, 2010).

13. *Chasing Alpha*, p. 49.

14. *Chasing Alpha*, p. 42.

15. Centre for the Study of Financial Innovation, *Sizing Up the City,* 2003, p. 14.

16. Chairman Alan Greenspan, "Regulation, Innovation and Wealth Creation," speech at Lancaster House, London, September 25, 2002, federalreserve.gov.

17. Speech by Gordon Brown to Mansion House, June 21, 2006, hm-treasury.gov.uk.

18. Paul Vallely, "Enemies of the People," *Independent,* July 4, 2000.

19. House of Commons Treasury Committee, *Banking Crisis: Dealing with the Failure of the UK Banks,* seventh report of session 2008–2009, p. 3.

20. Treasury Committee, "Banking Crisis: Reforming Corporate Governance and Pay in the City," news release, May 12, 2009, parliament.uk.

21. Author interviews, 2008.

22. Financial Services Authority, *The Turner Review: A Regulatory Response to the Global Banking Crisis,* March 2009, p. 80.

23. Michiyo Nakamoto and David Wighton, "Bullish Citigroup Is 'Still Dancing' to the Beat of the Buy-out Boom," *Financial Times,* July 10, 2007.

24. Interview with Johnny Cameron , March 1, 2007, RBS website. rbs.co.uk.

25. Jane Croft, "Sir James Leaves HBOS on a High Note," *Financial Times,* July 28, 2006.

26. Greenspan, speech.

27. Christopher Fildes, *London Evening Standard,* October 1, 2008.

28. Alex Brummer, *The Crunch* (Random House Business Books, 2008), p. 91.

29. Ibid., p. 88.

30. Hans Christian Andersen, *Fairy Tales* (Penguin, 2004), p. 91.

Chapter 5. Corporate Governance, Risk Analysis, and the Financial Crisis

Many thanks, as always, to Andy Williams for his helpful suggestions and criticisms. Additional thanks to Carlos Joly, Steve Lydenberg, and Mike Musaraca for their helpful feedback.

1. A universal owner is a large institutional investor that by virtue of its large size has a highly diversified portfolio across a number of asset classes. UOs' typical portfolios contain over a thousand and often several thousand equity holdings. In effect, it owns a representative cross section of the economy (increasingly the global economy) as a whole. Hence, "universal." Examples are CalPERS in the U.S., FRR in France, USS and Hermes in the U.K., and the Norway Pension Fund-Global.

2. James P. Hawley and Andrew T. Williams, *The Rise of Fiduciary Capitalism* (Philadelphia, 2000), pp. 175–177.

3. Michel Crouhy, Dan Galai, and Robert Mark, *The Essentials of Risk Management* (New York, 2006). The authors note at least seven general types of risk (e.g., market, credit, legal/regulatory) and at least thirteen specific types of financial risks (e.g., foreign exchange, interest rate, counterparty, transaction) (p. 26).

4. Ibid. The authors note regarding firm/security risk that "an asset's beta represents that portion of an asset's total risk that cannot be neutralized by diversification in a portfolio of risky assets, and for which some compensation must be demanded. . . . By investing in higher-beta securities, the higher risk and also the higher expected future return of the portfolio [are expected]" (p. 26).

5. See ibid., pp. 323–324. The authors in 2006 concluded, as many others had as well, that credit derivatives create massive opportunities, which "they bring for both transferring and assuming credit risk. [A] . . . disaster will surely come, particularly if the boards and senior managers of banks do not invest time to understand exactly how these . . . work" (p. 324).

6. This network can be accessed at http://www.sustainablefinancialmarkets.net.

7. In the context of retirement savings and investment as the long-term goal, what constitutes "sustainable investment" (economically, financially, and environmentally) was a muted debate prior to 2007.

8. Most important here is the Principles of Responsible Investment (PRI) organization. Formed in 2006 the PRI in 2009 had assets of about US$21 trillion, with almost two hundred end-asset owner signatories (http://www.unpri.org/signatories/). A 2009 survey of "mainstream" and "sustainable" investors suggested that there is no discernable difference between them regarding views on various aspects of the financial crisis or in terms of precrisis behavior and analysis. (Huge Wheelan, "An Anonymous Survey of Investor Concerns Might Be the Basis for Neutral Dialogue," available at http//www.responsible-investor.com/home/article/wisdom of crowds/.)

9. See for example, Crouhy, Galai, and Mark, *The Essentials of Risk Management*.

10. *A Review of Corporate Governance in UK Banks and Other Financial Industry Entities*, July 16, 2009, not paginated, section 5.9. See section 5 for a discussion of engagement, stewardship, collective action, and governance, available at http://www.hm-treasury.gov.uk/d/walker_review_consultation_160709.pdf. The U.K. chancellor of the exchequer, Alistair Darling, made similar comments: "shareholders clearly didn't ask the right questions. They didn't take their stewardship seriously. There are huge questions to be asked about the role of the shareholders in these [failed banks]." (Patience Wheatcroft, "UK's Darling Blasts Banks' Investors," *Wall Street Journal*, November 13, 2009, p. C2.)

11. TIAA-CREF, *Responsible Investing and Corporate Governance: Lessons Learned for Shareholders from the Crises of the Last Decade*," not dated, available at http://www.tiaa-cref.org/about/governance/.

12. Joseph A. Dear, "Written Statement Prepared for: U.S. Senate Banking Subcommittee on Securities, Insurance and Investment Re: Regulating Hedge Funds and Other Private Investment Pools." July 15, 2009, not paginated. The Conference Board notes that large institutional investors remain committed to alternative investments as a means to pursue higher returns and to reduce portfolio volatility. Yet it is not clear how such a commitment speaks to the growing academic, practitioner, or business

journalistic literature that suggests that such investments paradoxically increase systemic volatility as a whole. (The Conference Board, *The 2009 Institutional Investment Report*, p. 5.) CalPERS has pressed hedge funds to reduce terms as well as provide "clawback" fees for underperformance. (Jenny Strasburg and Craig Karmin, "CalPERS Tells Hedge Funds to Fix Terms, or Else," *Wall Street Journal*, March 28–29, 2009, p. B1.) Whether CalPERS's view is typical is not clear. See Leslie Wayne, "Public Pension Managers Rethink Hedge Fund Ties," *New York Times*, April 15, 2009, p. B1.

13. Anne Stausboll, chief executive officer, "Memorandum to California Congressional Delegation," December 9, 2009.

14. Joseph Dear, "Averting Financial Crisis: Regulatory Reform and Corporate Governance," National Press Club "Newsmaker" Speech, November 3, 2009, Washington, D.C.

15. Hermes Equity Ownership Services, *The Way Ahead*, London, November 2008.

16. Amar Bhidé, "In Praise of Primitive Finance," *The Economists' Voice* 6, no. 3, article 8, available at www.bepress.com/ev/vol6/iss3/art8. Feb 2009, p. 2; Frank Knight, *Risk, Uncertainty and Profit* (Boston, 1921).

17. This is captured somewhat differently by a Keynesian and a Bayesian view. The former argued that uncertainty could not be quantified, while the latter believed it could. (Bhidé, "In Praise of Primitive Finance," p. 1.) See Nassim Nicholas Taleb, *The Black Swan* (New York, 2007), and Richard Bookstaber, *A Demon of Our Own Design* (Hoboken, N.J., 2007), for more detailed discussions of uncertainty, risk, "fat tails," and computing power in relation to financial theory and practices. Donald MacKenzie, *An Engine, Not a Camera: How Financial Models Shape Markets* (Cambridge, Mass., 2008), provides an excellent intellectual history of modern financial thought. Crouhy, Galai, and Mark, *The Essentials of Risk Management*, warn of the dangers of fat tails in modeling risk, typically unrecognized and "not accounted for" in theoretical distributions, including the Black-Scholes option pricing model (p. 350).

18. Alpha in common usage is above market (or portfolio-benchmarked) returns for a given level of (supposed) risk. Alternative beta suggests that the search for alpha/ increased yield mostly took the form of alternative investments (e.g., commodities including various financial products, real estate, hedge funds, and private equity) that actually returned market average (supposedly) risk-adjusted rates in the alternative investment space. For alpha discussion see Philip Augar, *Chasing Alpha: How Reckless Growth and Unchecked Ambition Ruined the City's Golden Decade* (London, 2009). See Crouhy, Galai, and Mark, *The Essentials of Risk Management*, p. 113, for a discussion of beta and firm-specific risk.

19. Steve Brull, "Pensions: Washington State's Doubling Down," *Institutional Investor*, February 28, 2008, available at http://www.sib.wa.gov/financial/io.html.

20. Crouhy, Galai, and Mark, *The Essentials of Risk Management*, p. 287.

21. See, for example, Carlos Joly, "Responsible Investment: Can It Regulate Capitalism?" forthcoming in *Corporate Governance*.

22. Stephen Brown, William Goetzmann, Bing Liang, and Christopher Schwarz, "Trust and Delegation," available at http://ssrn.com/abstract = 1456414.

23. This chapter does not develop and discuss the large and rapidly growing literature on financial market instability and crises, but it is strongly influenced by, for example, Hyman P. Minsky, *Stabilizing an Unstable Economy* (New York, 2008), and George A. Akerlof and Robert J. Shiller's recent *Animal Spirits* (Princeton, 2009). See also Keith Ambachtsheer, "Pension Management," in *The Finance Crisis and Rescue* (Toronto, 2009), pp. 139–148, and Andrew Smithers, *Wall Street: Imperfect Markets and Inept Central Bankers* (New York, 2009).

24. Rodney Sullivan, head of publications for the CFA Institute, "The Crisis Is One of Governance," *Financial Times,* August 3, 2009 p. 11.

25. Grant Kirkpatrick, "The Corporate Governance Lessons from the Financial Crisis," *Financial Market Trends*, OECD, February 11, 2009 available at http://www.oecd.org/dataoecd/32/1/42229620.pdf.

26. Ibid., pp. 2, 4–5.

27. Ibid., pp. 12–14.

28. Lucian A. Bebchuk and Holger Spamann, "Regulating Bankers' Pay," Harvard University, John M. Olin Center for Law, Economics and Business, available at http:/ssrn.com/abstract = 1410072. Bebchuk and colleagues specify this argument regarding Bear Stearns and Lehman Brothers. (Lucian A. Bebchuk, Alma Cohen, and Holger Spamann, "The Wages of Failure: Executive Compensation at Bear Stearns and Lehman 2000–2008," working draft, December 2, 2009, available at http://papers.ssrn.com/sol3/papers.ffm?abstractid = 15135222#.) Shareowner alignment with top management in six large banks is argued as well in "Governance in Crisis: A Comparative Case Study of Six U.S. Investment Banks," Nestoradvisors research note, April 2009 (London, 2009). For a more traditional analysis, see Institute of International Finance, *Final Report of the IFF Committee on Market Best Practices*, 2008, available at http://www.iif.com/events/article + 193.php.

29. This is parallel to the problem many institutional owners had with stock options in the 1990s; they were seen by many as a means to align owner and manager interests, but most institutional investors which support granting options ignored the downside risk to debt holders of massive leveraged option issues. (Author's unpublished interviews with large institutional owners, 1997.)

30. VAR time frame is far too short, often extending no more than a few years, and often far less. Additionally, VAR assumes a multivariate normal distribution. Crouhy et al. conclude that VAR "must be supplemented by [other] methodologies . . . stress testing and worst-case scenarios." (Crouhy, Galai, and Mark, *The Essentials of Risk Management,* pp. 163, 173.) Internal VAR usage by banks permitted them to reduce capital by between 20 and 50 percent (p. 67).

31. More fundamentally as Martin Wolfe wrote in the *Financial Times*: "A business that is too big to fail cannot be run in the interests of the shareholders, since it is no longer part of the market [since it is de facto insured by the state]." ("Reform of

Regulation Has to Startt by Altering Incentives," June 24, 2009.) I would add "too big in scale or scope, or too interconnected" to fail.

32. Lord Meghnad Desai, "Act Now to Prick Oil Bubble," *Financial Times*, June 6, 2008.

33. Michael Mackenzie, Gillian Tess, and Aline van Duyn, "As Consumer Prices Climb, Derivatives Find New Favor," *Financial Times*, June 18, 2008, p. 7. The article makes the point that commodities are a major focus of an inflation hedge. Ironically, if too many act on this, it feeds the very inflation to be hedged against, in addition to creating a potential (actual?) bubble in the very asset that is seen as a hedge. Especially important contributors are insurance companies and pension funds, but generally hundreds of billions of dollars have flowed into the commodities markets in the last five years, and with the expanding sources of funds have also come financial instruments and indexes previously absent from those markets, e.g., exchange-traded funds. (Diana B. Henriques, "Lieberman Seeks Limits to Reduce Speculation," *New York Times*, June 12, 2008, p. C4.) (This is a classic example of complex financial market systems and herding behavior negating the original reason to hedge; see below.)

34. Masters's testimony before the Permanent Subcommittee on Investigations, Committee on Homeland Security and Governmental Affairs, U.S. Senate, May 20, 2008. Available at http://www.deepgreencrystals.com/images/Michael%20Masters%2-0Written%20Testimony.pdf.

35. Ibid.

36. In our book, Andrew Williams and I pointed out that if UOs hold equity long term in index or indexlike portfolios, it drives corporate governance engagement (voice being the only option if exit is blocked). In turn, this led to a concern for portfolio-wide externalities and in some circumstances to public policy actions. It would appear that UO actions in commodity markets turn this concern on its head. (Thanks to Andy Williams for this point.)

37. Based on a few anecdotal pieces of evidence, even some of the most committed sustainable institutional investors have not considered undertaking such an analysis. It would be interesting and important to know if any have taken such an analysis, and if so, how it has influenced their investment strategy.

38. In separate actions, U.S. senators Lieberman and Feinstein proposed various restrictions (Feinstein) or the banning (Lieberman) of institutional investors from commodity markets. (Henriques, "Lieberman Seeks Limits to Reduce Speculation"; Zachary Coile, "Bill Would Limit Trading in Energy Markets," *San Francisco Chronicle*, June 14, 2008, p. A3; Joanna Chung, "Limits Imposed on Overseas Oil Trading," *Financial Times*, June 18, 2008, p. 4.

39. Asset Management Working Group of the United Nations Environmental Programme Finance Initiative, *Fiduciary Responsibility*, report, July 2009, p. 41.

40. "Asset Based Investment: Notes Toward an Alternative Theory and Definition of Success," presented at the Elfenworks Center for the Study of Fiduciary Capitalism conference "Institutional Investors, Risk/Return, and Corporate Governance Failures:

Practical Lessons from the Financial Crisis," October 2009, p. 1. It should also be added that MPT is based on the assumptions of the efficient market hypothesis (EMH—in all its variants), one key assumption being that people are entirely rational actors and markets incorporate all available information, thereby making markets "efficient." See Akerlof and Schiller, *Animal Spirits*, among others, for empirical and theoretical critiques of the EMH. See also Hawley and Williams, *The Rise of Fiduciary Capitalism*, chapters 4–5, for critiques of the financial model in corporate governance (based on the EMH). For a nice discussion of behavioral finance, see Lisa Kramer, "Behavioral Finance," in *The Finance Crisis and Rescue*, pp. 125–135.

41. Crouhy, Galai, and Mark, *The Essentials of Risk Management,* p. 110.

42. In turn attempts to control new risk (which is long term), typically using VAR models, required significant guesswork and judgment, which was typically not undertaken either by most "quants" or by CEOs and others at the top level of management. As pointed out previously, VAR is best used for short-term, not long-term, risk measurement. (Justin Fox, *The Myth of the Rational Market* [New York, 2009], pp. 238–239.) Fox quotes Taleb: "Our activities may invalidate our measurements. . . . All markets go down together."

43. Fox, *The Myth of the Rational Market*, p. 249.

44. Ibid., p. 253, and Hawley and Williams, *The Rise of Fiduciary Capitalism*, pp. 18–21.

45. In 2009–2010 Trucost contracted with the PRI to conduct an initial quantitative analysis of selected environmental externalities on a portfolio from a holistic perspective.

46. See Taleb, *The Black Swan*, pp. 15–17. Also see *The Economist* for a good summary of financial risk in "The Gods Strike Back," February 13, 2010.

47. George Soros, *The New Paradigm for Financial Markets* (New York, 2008).

48. Roy E. Allen and Donald Snyder, "New Thinking on the Financial Crisis," *Critical Perspectives on International Business* 5 (12) (2009). pp. 49–51.

49. John Maynard Keynes, *The General Theory of Employment, Interest and Money*, chapter 12 (New York, 2009).

50. The U.S. trade union SEIU, between May and September 2008, did raise a number of flags regarding increasing risk focused on Bank of America, taking proxy actions, and called for congressional hearings on Washington Mutual. This was, to my knowledge, the exception, although it, too, was well into the crisis, though before September 2008 when Lehman collapsed. While more widespread proxy vote support for the proxy action was ultimately forthcoming from a large group of institutional investors, few publicly committed prior to voting. (Various SEIU news releases, 2008.)

51. Suggesting mobilization linked to advocacy (something quite rare among even the most self-conscious UOs) brings to mind CalPERS's actions in the 1990s to amend the California state constitution to make itself more autonomous from the governor's office in order to protect its assets. If that was done in the defense of fiduciary obligation, as I believe it was, then other forms of legislative lobbying and mobilization

on the most serious matters would also be appropriate. See also Joly, "Responsible Investment." Hermes, the U.K. equity ownership services group, a leader in corporate governance, issued both an analysis of the crisis and a program, including significantly stepped-up regulation and enforcement. But this was not until November 2008. (*Imperatives Arising out of the Crisis* [November 2008] and *The Way Ahead.*)

52. Lydenberg, "Asset Based Investment." For Lydenberg this means developing "asset based investment," that is, defining and maintaining specific roles and tasks for various asset classes. See the section above on oil speculation for an example of seeking alpha while risking both beta (the larger market return) and sustainability. Robert Monks has for years also raised the issue of the scope of fiduciary duty, as have Johnson and Jan de Graff. (Keith L. Johnson and Frank Jan de Graff, "Modernizing Pension Fund Legal Standards for the 21st Century," February 2009, Network for Sustainable Financial Markets, available at wws.sustainablefinancialmarkets.net.)

53. There are a variety of social justice and politically based arguments for considering the huge growth of income inequality as an issue, and arguably one that could have some fiduciary implications for pension plans. Additionally, there is a link between consumer spending and debt-driven consumption that has been augmented during the last three-plus decades by stagnant or sinking real incomes in the lowest three or four quintiles. Absent debt, some sectors would have been materially worse off. Further, how an economy supports its consumption sector (about 70 percent of GDP in the U.S.) is related to the issue of what is a sustainable economy.

54. John C. Coffee ("Gatekeepers: The Professions and Corporate Governance"), as quoted by Jennifer Taub, "Enablers of Exuberance: Legal Act and Omissions That Facilitated the Global Financial Crisis," a discussion draft presented at Elfenworks conference, "Institutional Investors, Risk/Return, and Corporate Governance Failures," pp. 21, 23, 32.

55. Taub, "Enablers of Exuberance," p. 24. Lydenberg, "Asset Based Investment," similarly suggests such restrictions. Taub notes an agency issue (p. 50) among institutional investors. They are not putting their own money at risk, but rather that of others. Williams and I point this out, calling them "professional investors." Hawley and Williams, *The Rise of Fiduciary Capitalism.*

Chapter 6. Great Expectations

1. Group of 20 (G20), "Global Plan for Recovery and Reform" (communiqué from the London summit, April 2, 2009); Group of 20, "Leaders' Statement" (Pittsburgh summit, September 24–25, 2009); Committee of European Banking Supervisors (CEBS), *High-Level Principles for Remuneration Policies* (CEBS, 2009); Financial Services Authority (FSA), *Reforming Remuneration Practices in Financial Services: Feedback on CP09/10 and Final Rules*, Policy Statement, 09/15 (FSA, 2009); Organisation for Economic Co-operation and Development (OECD), *Corporate Governance and the*

Financial Crisis: Key Findings and Main Messages (OECD, 2009); Grant Kirkpatrick, *Corporate Governance Lessons from the Financial Crisis* (OECD, 2009); House Committee on Oversight and Government Reform (U.S.), *Supplemental Information on CEO Pay and the Mortgage Crisis* (House of Representatives Committee on Oversight and Government Reform, 2008).

2. Financial Stability Board (FSB) (formerly the Financial Stability Forum, FSF), *FSF Principles for Sound Compensation Practices* (FSB, 2009).

3. Kym Sheehan, "Is the Outrage Constraint an Effective Constraint on Executive Remuneration? Evidence from the UK and Preliminary Results from Australia" (working paper, 2007), http://ssrn.com/abstract_id = 974965; Stephen Davis, "Does 'Say on Pay' Work? Lessons on Making CEO Compensation Accountable," (working paper, Millstein Center for Corporate Governance, 2007); Jeffrey N. Gordon, "'Say on Pay': Cautionary Notes on the UK Experience and the Case for Shareholder Opt-In," *Harvard Journal on Legislation* 46 (2008): 323; Fabrizio Ferri and David Maber, "Say on Pay Vote and CEO Compensation: Evidence from the UK" (working paper, 2008), http://ssrn.com/abstract_id = 1169446; Walid M. Alissa, "Boards' Responses to Shareholders' Dissatisfaction: The Case of Shareholders' Say on Pay" (working paper, 2009), http://ssrn.com/abstract_id = 1412880; Jie Cai and Ralph A. Walkling, "Shareholders' Say On Pay: Does It Create Value?" (working paper, 2009), http://ssrn.com/abstract_id = 1030925; Martin Conyon and Graham Sadler, "Shareholder Voting and Directors' Remuneration Report Legislation: Say on Pay in the UK," *Corporate Governance: An International Review* (2010): 296.

4. Financial Services Authority, *The Turner Review: A Regulatory Response to the Banking Crisis* (FSA, March 2009), 79–81.

5. United Nations Environment Programme Finance Initiative (UNEPFI), *Fiduciary Responsibility: Legal and Practical Aspects of Integrating Social, Environmental and Governance Issues into Institutional Investment* (UNEPFI, 2009), 11.

6. Certain aspects of this work have appeared previously in Kym Sheehan, "The Regulatory Framework for Executive Remuneration in Australia," *Sydney Law Review* 31 (2009): 273.

7. Colin Scott, "Analysing Regulatory Space: Fragmented Resources and Institutional Design," *Public Law* (Summer 2001): 329, 331.

8. Remuneration practice includes setting remuneration policy, writing the remuneration contract, execution of the contract (namely, the executive performs and the company makes payments according to the contract), and termination of the contract.

9. The disclosure of remuneration annually via the remuneration report together with ad hoc disclosures related to remuneration, such as share transactions, margin loans, and company loans.

10. There are two types of engagement: proactive engagement with shareholders by the company and reactive engagement with the company by shareholders.

11. The annual advisory vote on the remuneration report combined with all other remuneration-related resolutions.

12. From Sheehan, "The Regulatory Framework for Executive Remuneration in Australia," 278.

13. Codes of best practice issued by the Corporate Governance Committee of the Financial Reporting Council (FRC, U.K.) *The Combined Code* (FRC, 2008), and ASX Corporate Governance Council (Australia), *Corporate Governance Principles and Recommendations* (ASX, 2007).

14. This good practice is issued collectively through representative organizations, such as the Association of British Insurers (ABI), the National Association of Pension Funds (NAPF), the Australian Council of Superannuation Investors Inc. (ACSI), and the Investment and Financial Services Association (IFSA).

15. Australian Institute of Company Directors (AICD), *Executive Remuneration: Guidelines for Listed Company Boards* (AICD, 2009); Institute of Chartered Secretaries and Administrators (ICSA), *Remuneration Committee—Terms of Reference*, guidance note 071014 (ICSA, 2007).

16. A rule is classified as voting guidance if it states the particular voting outcome that will attach to having the practice and can be issued by either proxy advisers or institutional shareholder representative groups.

17. An example of a content rule is "shareholders will have an annual vote on the remuneration report. The effect of this vote is advisory only" (*Corporations Act 2001* (Cth), s 250R(3); *Companies Act 2006* (U.K.) c 46, ss 439(1),(5)). A facilitative rule would be "the shareholder may appoint a proxy to vote on its behalf at the meeting" (*Corporations Act 2001* (Cth), s 250A; *Companies Act 2006*, c 46, s 324).

18. James Kirkbride and Steve Letza, "Regulation, Governance and Regulatory Collibration: Achieving a "Holistic" Approach," *Corporate Governance: An International Review* 12 (2004): 85, 89–90.

19. *Corporations Act 2001* (Cth), s 300A; *Corporations Regulations 2001* (Cth) reg 2M.3.03; *Large and Medium-Sized Companies and Groups (Accounts and Reports) Regulations 2008* (U.K.) SI 2008/410, Schedule 1, paragraph 45.

20. Examples include Association of British Insurers, *Executive Remuneration: ABI Guidelines on Policies and Practices* (ABI, 2007); Australian Council of Superannuation Investors, *ACSI Governance Guidelines: A Guide for Superannuation Trustees to Monitor Listed Australian Companies* (ACSI, 2009); National Association of Pension Funds, *Corporate Governance Policy and Voting Guidelines* (NAPF, 2007); Investment and Financial Services Association, *Executive Equity Pay Guidelines*, guidance note12 (IFSA, 2007); Investment & Financial Services Association, *Corporate Governance: A Guide for Fund Managers and Corporations*, IFSA Guidance NoteNo. 2 (IFSA, 2009).

21. Cass Sunstein, "Social Norms and Social Roles," *Columbia Law Review* 96 (1996): 903, 909.

22. The FRC's *Combined Code* and the ASX Corporate Governance Council's *Corporate Governance Principles and Recommendations*.

23. For example, the Institutional Voting Investment Service offered by the Association of British Insurers utilizes the ABI's own guidelines in screening company

remuneration disclosures. In Australia, the Australian Council of Superannuation Investors offers a proxy advisory service to members based on its own guidelines. RiskMetrics undertakes this analysis for ACSI.

24. Martin Conyon, Simon Peck, and Graham Sadler, "Compensation Consultants and Executive Pay: Evidence from the United States and the United Kingdom," *Academy of Management Perspectives* 23 (2009): 43, 49.

25. Productivity Commission, *Executive Remuneration in Australia: Productivity Commission Inquiry Report No. 49* (Productivity Commission, 2009), 174.

26. Lucian Bebchuk and Jesse Fried, *Pay Without Performance: The Unfulfilled Promise of Executive Compensation* (Cambridge, Mass.: Harvard University Press, 2004), 37; Committee on Oversight and Government Reform, *Executive Pay: Conflicts of Interests Among Compensation Consultants* (Committee on Oversight and Government Reform, 2007), 3–4; Financial Stability Board, David Walker, *A Review of Corporate Governance in UK Banks and Other Financial Industry Entities: Final Report* (HM Treasury, 2009), 123–124.

27. Marc T. Moore, "Whispering Sweet Nothings: The Limitations of Informal Governance in UK Corporate Governance," *Journal of Corporate Law Studies* 9 (2009): 95, 103.

28. ASX Corporate Governance Council, *Corporate Governance Principles and Recommendations* (ASX 2007), 35.

29. Julia Black, "Regulatory Conversations," *Journal of Law and Society* 29 (2002): 163, 170–171.

30. Explanatory Memorandum Corporations Law Economic Reform Program (Audit Reform and Corporate Disclosure) Bill 2000, 170.

31. Department of Trade and Industry (DTI), *Directors' Remuneration: A Consultative Document* (DTI, 2001), 13.

32. Deborah Gilshan and PIRC Limited, *Say on Pay Six Years On: Lessons from the UK Experience* (Railpen Investments and PIRC Limited, 2009), 25; Productivity Commission, *Executive Remuneration in Australia, Discussion Draft* (Productivity Commission, 2009), 215.

33. Igor Filatotchev, Gregory Jackson, Howard Gospel, and Deborah Allcock, *Key Drivers of "Good" Corporate Governance and the Appropriateness of UK Policy Responses* (report prepared for the Department of Trade and Industry, U.K., 2007), 153–154.

34. David Seidl, "Standard Setting and Following in Corporate Governance: An Observation-Theoretical Study of the Effectiveness of Governance Codes," *Organization* 14 (2007): 705, 707–709.

35. Sandeep Gopalan, "Changing Social Norms and CEO Pay: The Role of Norm Entrepreneurs," *Rutgers Law Journal* 39 (2007): 1, 4; Camelia M. Kuhnen and Alexandra Niessen, "Is Executive Compensation Shaped by Public Attitudes?" (working paper, 2009), http://ssrn.com/abstract = 1328572, 16.

36. Geofrey P. Stapledon, *Institutional Investors and Corporate Governance* (Oxford: Oxford University Press, 1991), 127; Richard Lamming, *The Effects of Financial*

Institutions and Investor Behaviour on Management Practice: A Report for the Department of Trade and Industry (University of Southampton, School of Management, 2005), 30.

37. Doreen McBarnet and Christopher Whelan, "The Elusive Spirit of the Law: Formalism and the Struggle for Legal Control," *Modern Law Review* 54 (1991): 848, 850–851.

38. Company Law Review Steering Group, *Modern Company Law for a Competitive Economy: Developing the Framework* (Company Law Review Steering Group, 2000), 61.

39. Ian Ayres and John Braithwaite, *Responsive Regulation: Transcending the Deregulation Debate* (New York: Oxford University Press, 1992), 39.

40. John Core, Wayne Guay, and David Larcker, "The Power of the Pen and Executive Compensation," *Journal of Financial Economics* 88 (2008): 1, 23.

41. *Financial Services and Markets Act 2000* (U.K.) c 8, ss 3–6; *Australian Securities and Investments Commission Act 2001* (Cth), s 1(2).

42. Ravi Singh, "Board Independence and the Design of Executive Compensation" (working paper, 2006), http://ssrn.com/abstract = 673741, 2–3.

43. *Corporations Act 2001* (Cth), s 200B(1), prohibits payments made in connection with retirement from office unless prior shareholder approval is obtained under s 200E(1) for payments that fall outside the exceptions in ss 200F, 200G, 200H. In the U.K., there is *Companies Act 2006* (UK) c 46, ss 217–219, noting the exceptions in ss 220–221;, formerly *Companies Act 1985* (UK) c 6, ss 312, 313.

44. Shareholder approval is required under *Corporations Act 2001* (Cth), s 208(1); *Companies Act 2006* (U.K.) c 46, ss 197(1), 198(1), 200(2), 201(2) and 203(1), formerly *Companies Act 1985* (U.K.) c 6, s 341.

45. ASX, *Listing Rules*, rule 10.14 (ASX, 2002).

46. ASX, *Listing Rules*, rule 7.2, exception 5, and *FSA Handbook, Listing Rules* (2008), LR 9.4.1(2)R.

47. *Companies Act 2006* (U.K.) c 46, ss 213(3), (4) arising from breach of s 197(1), 198(1), s200(2), s 201(2), and s 203(1); ss 222(1)–(5). Termination payments made in breach of *Corporations Act 2001* (Cth), s 200B, will result in the imposition of a constructive trust pursuant to s 200J. Unauthorized related party transactions in Australia attract civil liability for persons involved in the contravention as defined in s 79: s 209(2). Criminal liability can attach for a dishonest contravention of the requirement to obtain prior shareholder approval: s 209(3). A contravention does not invalidate the transaction—s 209(1)—but is a civil penalty provision for which ASIC can seek a pecuniary penalty order (s 1317G) and a compensation order on behalf of the company (s 1317H).

48. FSA, *Reforming Remuneration Practices in Financial Services*, 23–24; European Commission, *Commission Recommendation Complementing Recommendations 2004/913/EC and 2005/162/EC as Regards the Regime for the Remuneration of Directors of*

Listed Companies, 2009/385/EC, OJ L 120 (15.5.2009), 29; DTI, *Directors' Remuneration.*

49. International Corporate Governance Network (ICGN), *ICGN Statement of Principles on Institutional Shareholder Responsibilities* (ICGN, 2007); United Nations Environment Programme Finance Initiative (UNEPFI), *UN Principles of Responsible Investment* (UNEPFI, 2006).

50. International Corporate Governance Network, *ICGN Remuneration Guidelines* (ICGN, 2006), 1.0.

51. ICGN, *ICGN Statement of Principles on Institutional Shareholder Responsibilities,* 7.

52. Ibid., 6.

53. United Nations Environment Programme Finance Initiative, *Principles for Responsible Investment: Report on Progress 2009* (UNEPFI, 2009), 28.

54. United Nations Environment Programme Finance Initiative, *2008 Overview* (UNEPFI, 2008), 8.

55. Iris H-Y Chiu, "The Meaning of Share Ownership and the Governance Role of Shareholder Activism in the United Kingdom," *Richmond Journal of Global Law and Business* 8 (2008): 117, 141. Company Law Review Steering Group, *Modern Company Law for a Competitive Economy,* 90; Institutional Shareholders' Committee (ISC), *Code on the Responsibilities of Institutional Investors* (ISC, 2009); Myners Review of Institutional Investment for HM Treasury (Myners), *Institutional Investment in the United Kingdom: A Review* (Myners, 2001), 91.

56. ICGN, *ICGN Statement of Principles on Institutional Shareholder Responsibilities,* 10.

57. Super System Review, *Clearer Super Choices: Matching Governance Solutions. Phase 1—Preliminary Report* (Super System Review, 2009), 17–18.

58. United Nations Environment Program Finance Initiative, *Principles for Responsible Investment* (UNEPFI, 2006).

59. John Braithwaite and Peter Drahos, *Global Business Regulation* (Melbourne: Oxford University Press, 2003), 16.

60. Catholic Super, *Annual Report 2007* (Catholic Super, 2007); Hesta Super Fund, *Annual Report 2007/2008* (Hesta Super Fund, 2008), 2.

61. Ayres and Braithwaite, *Responsive Regulation,* 56; Dalia Tsuk Mitchell, "Shareholders as Proxies: The Contours of Shareholder Democracy," *Washington and Lee Law Review* 63 (2006): 1503, 1564–1572.

62. American Federation of Labor–Congress of Industrial Organizations, "Executive Paywatch" (American Federation of Labor, 2009), http://www.aflcio.org/corporate watch/paywatch/.

63. The mission statement of the AFL-CIO is "to improve the lives of working families—to bring economic justice to the workplace and social justice to our nation." AFL-CIO, "What We Stand For: Mission and Goals of the AFL-CIO," http://www .aflcio.org/aboutus/thisistheaflcio/mission, accessed April 30, 2010.

64. John Coffee Jr., *Gatekeepers: The Professions and Corporate Governance* (New York: Oxford University Press, 2006), 5.

65. Joseph McCahery, Zacharias Sautner, and Laura Starks, "Behind the Scenes: The Corporate Governance Preferences of Institutional Investors," European Corporate Governance Institute (Financial Working Paper No. 235/2009, 2009), http://ssrn .com/abstract = 1331390, 4–6.

66. John Evans and King Tan, "Drivers of Investment Choice: Some Evidence from Australian Superannuation Participants" (Centre for Pensions and Superannuation discussion paper, November 2007).

67. Albert Verdam, "An Exploration of the Role of Proxy Advisors in Proxy Voting" (working paper, 2007), http://ssrn.com/abstract = 978835; Cindy R. Alexander, Mark A. Chen, Duane J. Seppi, and Chester S. Spatt, "The Role of Advisory Services in Proxy Voting" (working paper, 2006), www.atl-res.com/finance/CHEN.pdf; Jennifer Bethel and Stuart Gillan, "The Impact of Institutional and Regulatory Environment on Shareholder Voting," *Financial Management* 31 (2002): 29; Stephen J. Choi, Jill E. Fisch, and Marcel Kahan, "Director Elections and the Influence of Proxy Advisors" (working paper,2008), http://ssrn.com/abstract_id = 1127282.

68. John Armour, Henry Hansmann, and Reinier Kraakman, "Agency Problems and Legal Strategies," in Reinier Kraakman et al. (eds.), *The Anatomy of Corporate Law: A Comparative and Functional Approach*, 2nd edition (Oxford: Oxford University Press, 2009), 48.

69. Paul L. Davies, *Gower and Davies Principles of Modern Company Law*, 8th edition (London: Sweet & Maxwell, 2008), 787–790.

70. Pamela F. Hanrahan, *The Funds Management Industry in Australia: Officers' Duties and Liabilities* (Chatswood, Australia: LexisNexis Butterworths, 2007), 133–142; Robert Baxt, Ashley Black, and Pamela Hanrahan, *Securities and Financial Services Law*, 7th edition (Chatswood, Australia: LexisNexis Butterworths, 2008), 461–520.

71. Walker, *A Review of Corporate Governance in UK Banks and Other Financial Industry Entities*, 62–63; ISC, *Code on the Responsibilities of Institutional Investors*; Productivity Commission, *Executive Remuneration in Australia*, 321–322.

72. Association of British Insurers and the National Association of Pension Funds, *Joint Statement on Executive Contracts and Severance* (ABI and NAPF, 2008); ACSI, *ACSI Governance Guidelines*, 18–19.

73. For a discussion on inequality of CEO payments in the USA, see Thomas Clarke, "A Critique of the Anglo-American Model of Corporate Governance," Comparative Research in Law and Political Economy Working Paper No. 15/2009 (Osgoode Hall Law School, 2009), 9–13.

74. Sheehan, "Is the Outrage Constraint an Effective Constraint on Executive Remuneration?"

75. PricewaterhouseCoopers and the Department of Trade and Industry, *Monitoring of Corporate Governance Aspects of Directors' Remuneration* (PWC, 1999).

76. Royal Bank of Scotland PLC, *Annual Report and Accounts 2007* (Royal Bank of Scotland, 2008), 114.

77. Royal Bank of Scotland PLC, *Annual Report and Accounts 2008* (Royal Bank of Scotland, 2009), 168.

78. Deloitte & Touche, *Executive Directors' Remuneration* (Deloitte & Touche, 2003), 86; Deloitte, *Executive Directors' Remuneration* (Deloitte, 2004), 74–78; Deloitte, *Executive Directors' Remuneration: Your Guide* (Deloitte, 2005), 79–91; Deloitte, *Executive Directors' Remuneration: Your Guide* (Deloitte, 2006), 83–96; Deloitte, *Executive Directors' Remuneration: Your Guide* (Deloitte, 2007), 77–82.

79. Simon Creedy, "Qantas Shareholders Revolt on Pay," *Australian*, October 10, 2009, 3.

80. Qantas Airways Limited, *Annual Report 2009* (Qantas, 2009), 74.

81. Qantas Airways Limited, *Annual Report 2005* (Qantas, 2005), 64.

82. Qantas Airways Limited, *Annual Report 2006* (Qantas, 2006), 65.

83. The proxy voting outcomes are required to be disclosed by companies under *Corporations Act 2001* (Cth), s 251AA. The percentages were calculated by the author on the basis of votes for as a percentage of total votes cast, excluding abstentions and undirected proxies.

84. Michael Evans, "Bringing up Baby and the Bank," *Sydney Morning Herald*, November 28, 2008, 25.

85. Bebchuk and Fried. *Pay Without Performance*, 104; Mark Maremont, "Latest Twist in Corporate Pay: Tax-Free Income for Executives," *Wall Street Journal*, December 22, 2005, A1; Productivity Commission, *Executive Remuneration in Australia: Discussion Draft*, 290.

86. Sheehan, "The Regulatory Framework for Executive Remuneration in Australia," 302–303.

87. Financial Reporting Council, *Consultation for a Stewardship Code for Institutional Investors* (FRC, 2010), 19–20.

88. Australian Prudential Regulatory Authority (APRA), *Prudential Practice Guide PPG 511 Remuneration* (APRA, 2009), 5; FSA, *Reforming Remuneration Practices in Financial Services*, 23.

89. APRA is able to adjust or exclude a specific prudential requirement in APS 510: APRA, *Prudential Standard APS 510—Governance* (2009), 82; *Banking Act 1959* (Cth), s 11AF(2).

90. *Banking Act 1959* (Cth), s 11CG(1). The requirement to maintain capital adequacy is governed by a separate standard, *Prudential Standard APS 110 Capital Adequacy*. The remuneration policy required under APS 510 must form part of the authorized deposit-taking institution's risk-management system required under *Prudential Standard APS 310 Audit and Related Matters*.

91. *FSA Handbook, Senior Management Arrangements, Systems and Controls* (2010), SYSC 19.2.1R.

92. FSA, *The Turner Review*, 4.

93. Australian Prudential Regulatory Authority, *The APRA Supervision Blueprint* (APRA, 2010).

94. APRA, *Prudential Practice Guide PPG 511 Remuneration*, 5.

95. Kevin Rudd, "Global Financial Crisis" (address to the National Press Club, Canberra, October 15, 2008); "Darling Puts Pressure on Banks," *Sunday Times*, London, September 27, 2009, 1st edition, 1–2; G20, "Leaders' Statement."

Chapter 7. Against Stupidity, the Gods Themselves Contend in Vain

I thank the participants at the 2009 Conference on "Institutional Investors, Risk/ Return, and Corporate Governance Failures: Practical Lessons from the Global Financial Crisis" at Saint Mary's College of California and, in particular, Shyam Kamath for their helpful comments.

1. Based on market capitalization of share price at December 31, 2007, through May 2009; "A.I.G. Lists Banks It Paid with U.S. Bailout Funds," *New York Times*, March 15, 2009, available at http://www.nytimes.com/2009/03/16/business/16rescue .html.

2. See http://www.cbsnews.com/stories/2009/03/05/business/main4845936.shtml.

3. "Citi Federal Aid Deal This Week," *Associated Press*, February 26, 2009.

4. See, e.g., the critique of the role of executive compensation by Lucian A. Bebchuk, Alma Cohen, and Holger Spamann, "The Wages of Failure: Executive Compensation at Bear Stearns and Lehman 2000–2008" (2009), available at http://www .law.harvard.edu/faculty/bebchuk/pdfs/BCS-Wages-of-Fail ure-Nov09.pdf . Under TARP and the Emergency Economic Stabilization Act (EESA) (PL 110–343), executive compensation for certain financial institutions is subject to limitation and the board is required to determine whether the compensation structure for executives creates incentives for the executives to take undue risks. The Dodd-Frank Wall Street Reform and Consumer Protection Act (Dodd-Frank) (PL 111–203), enacted in mid-2010, included a number of corporate governance provisions, which addressed nomination of directors by shareholders, access to the proxy statement by shareholders, and compensation of executives. Other, even more stringent corporate governance requirements had been under consideration prior to the passage of Dodd-Frank. See, e.g., "Shareholder Bill of Rights Act of 2009," available at http://www.corpfinblog.com/uploads/ file/bill-text-shareholdersbill-of-rights-act-of-2009(2).pdf; H.R. 3269, the Corporate and Financial Institution Compensation Fairness Act; and http://www.sec.gov/rules/ proposed/2009/33-9046.pdf.

5. See "Shareholder Bill of Rights," note 4. Dodd-Frank required risk committees for certain financial institutions, but did not require risk committees for all public companies. See Dodd-Frank, note 4.

6. See note 4.

7. See item 402(s) of SEC Regulation S-K.

8. Margaret Blair, *Ownership and Control: Rethinking Corporate Governance for the Twenty-First Century* (Brookings Institution Press, 1995).

9. The Sarbanes-Oxley Act in 2002 (PL 107–204), and related rule making, mandated the independence of certain directors and various aspects of board relationships and relationships of the company and board with auditors. See also the discussion of EESA, Dodd-Frank and related legislation in notes 4–7.

10. *In Re Caremark Int'l Inc. Derivative Litig.*, 698 A.2d 959 (Del. Ch. 1996), pp. 967–968.

11. *In Re Citigroup Inc. Shareholder Derivative Litigation* (Del. Ch., February 24, 2009), available at http://www.delawarelitigation.com/uploads/file/int99(1).pdf, p. 30.

12. Ibid., p. 26 (n. 50).

13. Stephen M. Bainbridge, "The Business Judgment Rule as Abstention Doctrine," 57 *Vanderbilt Law Review*, 83, pp. 114–115 (2004), quoted in *In Re Citigroup*, p. 30.

14. *Aronson v. Lewis*, 473 A.2d 805, p. 811 (Del. 1984).

15. *In Re Citigroup*, pp. 26–27.

16. *Stone v. Ritter*, 911 A.2d 362, p. 370 (Del. 2006), cited in *In Re Citigroup*, p. 23.

17. *In Re Citigroup*, p. 29.

18. John Kenneth Galbraith, *A Short History of Financial Euphoria* (Penguin, 1991).

19. Richard Posner, *A Failure of Capitalism* (Harvard University Press, 2009), p. 100.

20. Testimony of October 23, 2008, to House Oversight Committee, quoted in Congressional Oversight Panel, "Special Report on Regulatory Reform," January 2009, p. 6.

21. Posner, pp. 317–318.

22. Posner, p. 235.

23. Galbraith, p. 16.

24. Galbraith, p. 20. Posner also notes that urging the expenditure of preventive costs for a problem that may arise—but is not a quantifiable certainty—earns decision makers no praise: when the harm is averted, the costs are perceived as costs incurred to prevent something that wasn't going to happen anyway. Posner, p. 138.

25. Posner, p. 111.

26. Posner, p. 147. See also Gregory Zuckerman, *The Greatest Trade Ever* (Random House, 2009), pp. 216–223.

27. In the context of leveraged buyouts in the late stages of the financial boom, Citigroup CEO Chuck Prince was quoted as saying, "As long as the music is playing, you've got to get up and dance," *New York Times*, "Citi Chief on Buyouts: 'We're Still Dancing,'" July 10, 2007, available at http://dealbook.blogs.nytimes.com/2007/07/10/citi-chief-on-buyout-loans-were-still-dancing/. His comment is often repeated as an example of the "all-in" strategy for dealing with asset bubbles.

28. See discussion in chapter text after note 30 number respecting the approach of Goldman Sachs to the late-stage bubble market.

29. See Zuckerman, pp. 216–223 and generally in chapters 12 and 13, for discussions of investors who rightly analyzed the coming crash, but saw no immediate returns (or even near-term losses).

30. Joe Nocera, "Risk Mismanagement," *New York Times*, January 2, 2009, available at http://www.nytimes.com/2009/01/04/magazine/04risk-t.html?pagewanted = 1.

31. Lloyd Blankfein, "Lessons from the Financial Crisis," available at http://blogs .law.harvard.edu/corpgov/2009/04/15/lessons-from-the-financial-crisis-2/.

32. Ibid.

33. Posner, p. 323.

34. *In Re American International Group, Inc. 2008 Securities Litigation* (S. Dist. N.Y., 08-CV-4772-LTS).

35. See *In Re Citigroup.*

36. Facts presented herein are from the pleadings, as recited in the case.

37. *In Re Citigroup*, p. 25.

38. *In Re Citigroup*, p. 26.

39. *In Re Citigroup* p. 30.

40. *In Re Citigroup*, p. 34.

41. C.A. No. 769-VCS, 2009 WL 366613 (Del. Ch. February 10, 2009).

42. *In Re* Citigroup, p. 39.

43. The facts presented herein come primarily from the plaintiffs' brief for *In Re AIG*, for which underlying source material is often excluded. Many allegations are based on news accounts and congressional testimony. At the time this material was prepared, AIG had not filed a response brief and so elements of the facts described herein were not challenged.

44. Over time, AIGFP became a wholly owned operation of AIG, a billion-dollar operation in its own right with hundreds of employees in the U.K. and U.S. For additional information on AIGFP and Cassano, see also Michael Lewis, "The Man Who Crashed the World," *Vanity Fair*, August 2009 available at http://www.vanityfair .com/politics/features/2009/08/aig200908.

45. Lewis's description of the development of CDSs is apt: "Once upon a time Chrysler issued a bond through Morgan Stanley, and the only people who wound up with credit risk were the investors who had bought the Chrysler bond. Now Chrysler might sell its bonds and simultaneously enter into a 10-year interest-rate-swap transaction with Morgan Stanley—and just like that Chrysler and Morgan Stanley were exposed to each other. If Chrysler went bankrupt, its bondholders obviously lost; depending on the nature of the swap and the movement of interest rates, Morgan Stanley might lose, too. If Morgan Stanley went bust, Chrysler along with anyone else who had done interest-rate swaps with Morgan Stanley stood to suffer. Financial risk had been created, out of thin air, and it begged to be either honestly accounted for or disguised. . . . There was a natural role for a blue-chip corporation with the highest

credit rating to stand in the middle of swaps and long-term options and the other risk-spawning innovations. The traits required of this corporation were that it not be a bank—and thus subject to bank regulation and the need to reserve capital against the risky assets—and that it be willing and able to bury exotic risks on its balance sheet. There was no real reason that company had to be A.I.G.; it could have been any AAA-rated entity with a huge balance sheet. Berkshire Hathaway, for instance, or General Electric. A.I.G. just got there first." (Ibid.)

46. When the market collapsed, approximately $10 billion of the losses experienced by AIG were on the speculative CDS instruments.

47. AIG's report on form 10-K for the period ended December 31, 2007, p. 33.

48. Joseph St. Denis, letter to Henry Waxman, chairman of the House Committee on Oversight and Government Reform, October. 4, 2008, available at http://oversight .house.gov/documents/20081007102452.pdf.

49. St. Denis, p. 4.

50. See Blankfein.

51. *In Re Citigroup*, p. 39.

52. Review of case status on PACER for 08-CV-4772-LTS (S. Dist. N.Y.) as of February 19, 2010.

53. See discussion in note 4; Dodd-Frank provided specific enabling authority for the SEC rules providing access to the corporate proxy statement for director candidates nominated by shareholders, and the SEC adopted "proxy access" rules in August 2010. http://www.sec.gov/rules/final/2010/33-9136.pdf.

54. See, e.g., Sarbanes-Oxley, section 404, and SEC Rule 13a-15.

55. See, e.g., SEC Regulation S-K, item 402(b).

56. See John C. Coffee Jr., "Gatekeepers: The Role of the Professions and Corporate Governance" (Clarendon Lectures in Management Studies, 2006).

57. See, e.g., section 14 of the Securities Exchange Act of 1934 (as amended), proxy access discussion in n. 53.

58. See, e.g., sections 13–15 of the Securities Exchange Act and related SEC forms and rule making pursuant to those sections.

59. See Bruce Dravis, *The Role of Independent Directors After Sarbanes-Oxley* (American Bar Association, 2007), pp. 42–44.

60. The court suggested in *In Re Walt Disney Co. Derivative Litig.*, 906 A.2d 27 (Del. 2006), that standards of corporate governance evolve with time and experience, and the standard of care under Delaware law should not be considered static. "Recognizing the protean nature of ideal corporate governance practices, particularly over an era that has included the Enron and WorldCom debacles, and the resulting legislative focus on corporate governance, it is perhaps worth pointing out that the actions (and the failures to act) of the Disney board that gave rise to this lawsuit took place ten years ago, and that applying 21st century notions of best practices in analyzing whether those decisions were actionable would be misplaced. Unlike ideals of corporate governance, a fiduciary's duties do not change over time. How we understand those duties

306 Notes to Pages 162–163

may evolve and become refined. . . . This Court strongly encourages directors and officers to employ best practices, as those practices are understood at the time a corporate decision is taken. But Delaware law does not—indeed, the common law cannot—hold fiduciaries liable for a failure to comply with the aspirational ideal of best practices."

61. See, e.g., Charles Roxburgh, "Hidden Flaws in Strategy," *McKinsey Quarterly*, December 2005, and Renee Dye et al., "Flaws in Strategic Decision-Making," *McKinsey Quarterly*, November 2008. These articles consider such common decision-making flaws as managers who are overconfident in their own abilities and overoptimistic in their forecasting; biases in favor of the status quo; the "anchoring" bias, in which prior results skew the judgment about what (favorably or unfavorably) can be calculated about the future; and "confirmation bias," in which data supporting a desired result are given credence and contrary data are dismissed.

62. Robert Sutton has written regarding a "zero tolerance" rule for bad managers. See http://bobsutton.typepad.com/my_weblog/. From Michael Lewis's description, AIG's Cassano may have been a classic bad manager. "Across A.I.G.F.P. the view of the boss was remarkably consistent: a guy with a crude feel for financial risk but a real talent for bullying people who doubted him. . . . The few people willing to question [Cassano's] judgment wound up quitting the firm. Left behind were people who more or less accommodated [him]" (Lewis).

63. Posner, pp. 86–87.

64. See generally Bebchuk et al. "Even if the excessive risk-taking incentives that executives of Bear Stearns and Lehman had (and the similar incentives that executives of other financial firms had) were not a major driver of risk-taking in the years preceding the financial crisis, such incentives could become so in the future if retained" (p. 5).

65. Posner, pp. 317–318.

66. Posner, p. 324.

67. Blankfein.

68. See, e.g., Congressional Oversight Panel, p. 22; John Gapper, "The Case for Glass-Steagall Lite," March 12, 2009, *Financial Times.com*, available at http://blogs.ft .com/gapperblog/2009/03/the-case-for-a-glass-steagall-lite/.

69. Gapper, p. 22.

70. See generally the discussion in chapter 10 of Posner. "As far as I know, no one has a clear sense of the social value of our deregulated financial industry. . . . The profits were, until the financial crisis . . . enormous, but undoubtedly contained a large amount of economic rent. . . . Obviously a stock exchange and a credit system are enormous public goods . . . but the value added by the vast increases in recent years in the amount of speculative trading is unclear. Until we get a clear idea of what it is, we do not know what the costs would be of adopting a 1960s-style model of the financial system." Posner, pp. 295–296.

71. Fraud Enforcement and Recovery Act of 2009 (PL 111–21).

Chapter 8. Real Estate, Governance, and the Global Economic Crisis

The European Centre for Corporate Engagement (ECCE), and METEOR, the research school of Maastricht University, provided financial support for this research. We thank the participants at the 2009 Conference on "Institutional Investors, Risk/Return, and Corporate Governance Failures: Practical Lessons from the Global Financial Crisis" at Saint Mary's College of California, Shyam Kamath, and two anonymous referees, for their helpful comments.

1. P. M. A. Eichholtz and N. Kok, *The EU REIT and the Internal Market for Real Estate* (Brussels: European Property Federation, 2007).

2. R. Bauer, P. M. A. Eichholtz, and N. Kok, "Corporate Governance and Performance: The REIT Effect," *Real Estate Economics*, 36, 2010: pp. 1–29.

3. M. C. Jensen, "Agency Costs of Free Cash Flow, Corporate Finance, and Takeovers," *American Economic Review*, 76, 1986: pp. 323–329.

4. R. La Porta, F. Lopez-De-Silanes, A. Shleifer, and R. Vishny, "Agency Problems and Dividend Policies Around the World," *Journal of Finance*, 55, 2000: pp. 1–33.

5. S. A. Johnson, T. C. Moorman, and S. Sorescu, "A Reexamination of Corporate Governance and Equity Prices," *Review of Financial Studies*, 22, 2009: pp. 4753–4786.

6. R. Rajan and L. Zingales, "Which Capitalism? Lessons from the East Asian Crisis," *Journal of Applied Corporate Finance*, 11, 1998: pp. 40–48.

7. T. Mitton. "A Cross-Firm Analysis of the Impact of Corporate Governance on the East Asian Financial Crisis," *Journal of Financial Economics*, 64, 2002: pp. 215–241.

8. P. A. Gompers, J. Ishii, and A. Metrick, "Corporate Governance and Equity Prices," *Quarterly Journal of Economics*, 118, 2003: pp. 107–155.

9. W. Drobetz, A. Schillhofer, and H. Zimmermann, "Corporate Governance and Expected Stock Returns: Evidence from Germany," *European Financial Management*, 10, 2001: pp. 267–293.

10. R. Bauer, N. Guenster, and R. Otten, "Empirical Evidence on Corporate Governance in Europe: The Effect on Stock Returns, Firm Value, and Performance," *Journal of Asset Management*, 5, 2004: pp. 91–104.

11. R. Bauer, B. Frijns, R. Otten, and A. Tourani-Rad, "The Impact of Corporate Governance on Corporate Performance: Evidence from Japan," *Pacific-Basin Finance Journal*, 16, 2008: pp. 236–251.

12. J. E. Core, W. R. Guay, and T. O. Rusticus, "Does Weak Governance Cause Weak Stock Returns? An Examination of Firm Operating Performance and Investors' Expectations," *Journal of Finance*, 61, 2006: pp. 655–687.

13. Johnson, Moorman, and Sorescu, "A Reexamination of Corporate Governance and Equity Prices." The increasing recognition of corporate governance as a driver of firm value could explain the contrasting results between early studies on corporate governance and performance and those studies published more recently. However, alternative explanations for the results of Gompers, Ishii, and Metrick are risk and the investment environment surrounding the market, which both influence

stock returns. Gompers, Ishii, and Metrick, "Corporate Governance and Equity Prices."

14. B. Han, "Insider Ownership and Firm Value: Evidence from Real Estate Investment Trusts," *Journal of Real Estate Finance and Economics*, 32, 2006: pp. 471–493.

15. J. C. Hartzell, L. Sun, and S. Titman, "The Effect of Corporate Governance on Investment: Evidence from Real Estate Investment Trusts," *Real Estate Economics*, 34, 2006: pp. 343–376.

16. C. Ghosh, and C. F. Sirmans, "Board Independence, Ownership Structure and Performance: Evidence from Real Estate Investment Trusts," *Journal of Real Estate Finance & Economics*, 26, 2003: pp. 287–318. Z. Feng, C. Ghosh, and C. F. Sirmans, "How Important Is the Board of Directors to Reit Performance?" *Journal of Real Estate Portfolio Management*, 11, 2005: pp. 281–293.

17. J. C. Hartzell, J. G. Kallberg, and C. H. Liu, "The Role of Corporate Governance in Initial Public Offerings: Evidence from Real Estate Investment Trusts," *Journal of Law and Economics*, 51, 2008: pp. 539–562.

18. Bauer, Eichholtz, and Kok, "Corporate Governance and Performance: The Reit Effect."

19. See http://www.issproxy.com for a detailed description of the corporate governance quotient and its underlying scoring system.

20. There are three types of real estate investment trusts: equity REITs, which purchase, own, and manage real estate properties (they may also develop properties); mortgage REITs, which invest in loans secured by real estate; and hybrid REITs, which generate income from rent and capital gains, like an equity REIT, as well as interest, like a mortgage REIT.

21. The NAREIT index is the leading benchmark for listed property companies in the Unites States.

22. Recent market reports have documented price drops of more than 40 percent in the largest commercial property markets (*New York Times*, January 16, 2010).

23. E. Zivot, and D. W. K. Andrews, "Further Evidence on the Great Crash, the Oil-Price Shock, and the Unit-Root Hypothesis," *Journal of Business and Economic Statistics*, 10, 1992: pp. 251–270.

24. E. F. Fama, and K. R. French, "Common Risk Factors in the Returns on Stocks and Bonds," *Journal of Financial Economics*, 33, 1993: pp. 3–56.

25. M. M.Carhart, "On Persistence in Mutual Fund Performance," *Journal of Finance*, 52, 1997, 57–82.

26. J. D. Peterson, and C. Hsieh, "Do Common Risk Factors in the Returns on Stocks and Bonds Explain Returns on Reits?" *Real Estate Economics*, 25, 1997: pp. 321–345.

27. Our results are robust to using the Global Property Research (GPR) Global 250 index.

28. Data obtained from http://mba.tuck.dartmouth.edu/pages/faculty/ken.french/data_library.html.

29. H. White, "A Heteroskedasticity-Consistent Covariance Matrix Estimator and a Direct Test for Heteroskedasticity," *Econometrica*, 48, 1980, pp. 817–838. Karafiath evaluates the performance of OLS, weighted least squares, feasible generalized least squares (FGLS), and corrected least squares using Monte Carlo simulations, for cross-sectional regression that use abnormal returns. He finds that the OLS estimator of abnormal returns is well specified and performs as expected if the sample size is larger than seventy-five observations. I. Karafiath, "On the Efficiency of Least Squares Regression with Security Abnormal Returns as the Dependent Variable," *Journal of Financial and Quantitative Analysis*, 29, 1994: pp. 279–300.

30. We also estimate the model including and controlling for delisted companies. The results are robust for existing REITs. The governance quality has no significant effect in these estimations, either.

31. Bauer, Eichholtz, and Kok, "Corporate Governance and Performance: The Reit Effect."

32. Market equilibrium may be another explanation for the lack of a relation between governance and performance. However, given the flux in real estate markets preceding the crisis, this seems unlikely.

33. Mitton, "A Cross-Firm Analysis of the Impact of Corporate Governance on the East Asian Financial Crisis."

34. Bauer, Eichholtz, and Kok, "Corporate Governance and Performance: The Reit Effect."

35. Johnson, Moorman, and Sorescu, "A Reexamination of Corporate Governance and Equity Prices."

36. Gompers, Ishii, andMetrick, "Corporate Governance and Equity Prices."

37. Core, Guay, and Rusticus, "Does Weak Governance Cause Weak Stock Returns? An Examination of Firm Operating Performance and Investors' Expectations."

38. M. Cremers, and V. B. Nair, "Governance Mechanisms and Equity Prices," *Journal of Finance,* 2005, 60: pp. 2859–2894.

39. The ownership concentration data are collected for 2006 in order to have the last point of observation before the crisis, following Mitton, "A Cross-Firm Analysis of the Impact of Corporate Governance on the East Asian Financial Crisis."

40. Ghosh and Sirmans, "Board Independence, Ownership Structure and Performance: Evidence from Real Estate Investment Trusts."

41. Mitton, "A Cross-Firm Analysis of the Impact of Corporate Governance on the East Asian Financial Crisis."

42. Bauer, Eichholtz, and Kok. "Corporate Governance and Performance: The Reit Effect."

43. D. Brounen, H. Op 't Veld, and V. Raitio, "Transparency in the European

Non-Listed Real Estate Funds Market," *Journal of Real Estate Portfolio Management,* 2007, 13: pp. 107–118.

Chapter 9. The Sophisticated Investor and the Global Financial Crisis

Note to epigraphs: "Legal Matters with Charles T. Munger," *Stanford Lawyer,* Spring 2009 (interview of Charles Munger by Joseph Grundfest), p. 16, available at http://www.law.stanford.edu/publications/stanford_lawyer/issues/80/pdfs/sl80_mun ger.pdf.

1. Jennifer S. Taub, "Enablers of Exuberance: The Legal Acts and Omissions That Facilitated the Global Financial Crisis," September 2009, available at http://papers.ssrn .com/sol3/papers.cfm?abstract_id = 1472190, and James Crotty, Jane D'Arista, Gerald Epstein, and Jennifer S. Taub, "Regulations to End 'Too Big to Fail Investment Banking,'" *SAFER Policy Note, No. 14,* January 12, 2010, available at http://www.peri.u mass.edu/fileadmin/pdf/other_publication_types/SAFERbriefs/SAFER_note14.pdf.

2. James K. Galbraith, "Who Are These Economists, Anyway," *Thought and Action* 25 (Fall 2009), p. 85, citing Paul Krugman, "How Did Economists Get It So Wrong?" *New York Times Magazine,* September 2, 2009.

3. Report of the President's Working Group on Financial Markets, "Hedge Funds, Leverage and the Lessons of Long-Term Capital Management," April 2009 ("in our market-based economy, market discipline of risk taking is the rule and government regulation is the exception") p. 26, available at http://www.treas.gov/press/releases/ reports/hedgfund.pdf.

4. Stephen J. Choi, "Regulating Investors, Not Issuers: A Market Based Proposal," *Berkeley Program in Law and Economics Working Paper Series 2000–1* (1990), p. 2.

5. C. Edward Fletcher III, "Sophisticated Investors Under the Federal Securities Laws," *Duke Law Journal* 6 (1988), p. 1133.

6. The protections that remain are prohibitions against fraud. See Donald C. Langevoort, "The SEC, Retail Investors and the Institutionalization of the Securities Markets," *Virginia Law Review* 95 (2009), p. 1025.

7. Colin Rowat, "Let's Be Realistic About Sophistication," *Financial Times,* April 23, 2010.

8. James Crotty and Gerald Epstein, "Avoiding Another Meltdown," *Challenge* 52:1 (2009), p. 9.

9. Ed Thorp, "'The Quants': It Pays to Know Your Wall Street Math," *Fresh Air,* NPR, February 1, 2010, available at http://www.npr.org/templates/transcript/tran script.php?storyId = 123209339.

10. Steve Eder and Karey Wutkowski, "Goldman's 'Fabulous' Fab's Conflicted Love Letters," Reuters, April 26, 2010, available at http://www.reuters.com/article/ idUSTRE63O26E20100426.

11. Alfred D. Chandler, Jr., *The Visible Hand: The Managerial Revolution in American Business* (Cambridge, Mass., 1977), p. 10.

12. Adolf A. Berle and Gardiner C. Means, *The Modern Corporation and Private Property* (New York: 1932).

13. Jennifer S. Taub, "Able but Not Willing: The Failure of Mutual Fund Advisers to Advocate for Shareholders' Rights," *Journal of Corporation Law* 34:3 (2009), p. 105.

14. James P. Hawley and Andrew T. Williams, *The Rise of Fiduciary Capitalism: How Institutional Investors Can Make Corporate America More Democratic* (Philadelphia: 2000), p. 1.

15. Stephen Davis, Jon Lukomnik, and David Pitt-Watson, *The New Capitalists: How Citizen Investors Are Reshaping the Corporate Agenda* (Boston: 2006), p. 4; Also see Langevoort, citing *Securities Industry and Financial Markets Association Fact Book*, 2007, p. 65.

16. U.S. Census Bureau, table 1164, Equities, Corporate Bonds, and Treasury Securities—Holdings and Net Purchases by Type of Investor: 2000 to 2008, available at http://www.census.gov/compendia/statab/2010/tables/10s1164.pdf.

17. Investment Company Institute, Investment Company Fact Book, 50th ed. (2010), p. 12, figure 1.5, available at http://www.ici.org/pdf/2010_factbook.pdf (as of year-end 2009)..

18. Quoted in Jake Tapper, "I Was Wrong to Listen to Wrong Advice Against Regulating Derivatives," April 17, 2010, available at http://blogs.abcnews.com/political punch/2010/04/clinton-rubin-and-summers-gave-me-wrong-advice-on-derivatives-and-i-was-wrong-to-take-it.html.

19. Dr. Alan Greenspan, testimony before the Financial Crisis Inquiry Commission hearing, "Subprime Lending and Securitization and Government-Sponsored Enterprises," April 7, 2010, official transcript, available at http://fcic.gov/hearings/pdfs/2010-0407-Transcript.pdf.

20. Jesse Eisinger and Jake Bernstein, "The Magnetar Trade: How One Hedge Fund Helped Keep the Bubble Going," ProPublica, April 9, 2010, available at http://www.propublica.org/feature/the-magnetar-trade-how-one-hedge-fund-helped-keep-the-housing-bubble-going.

21. For a detailed exposition of the conflicts of interest and indifference to risk in the mortgage origination and distribution process, see the Financial Crisis Inquiry Commission hearing, "Subprime Lending and Securitization and Government-Sponsored Enterprises," April 7–9, 2010, available at http://fcic.gov/hearings/04-07-2010 .php, including the testimony of Richard Bitner, Richard Bowen, Patricia Lindsay, and Susan Mills.

22. Securities and Exchange Commission, "SEC Charges Goldman Sachs with Fraud in Structuring and Marketing of CDO Tied to Subprime Mortgages," news release, April 16, 2010, available at http://www.sec.gov/news/press/2010/2010-59.htm.

23. U.S. GAO Report, *Financial Markets Regulation: Financial Crisis Highlights*

Need to Improve Oversight of Leverage at Financial Institutions and across System, July 22, 2009, p. 1, available at http://www.gao.gov/new.items/d09739.pdf.

24. Richard Bookstaber, "Blowing up the Lab on Wall Street," *Time*, August 6, 2007; GAO Report , citing David Greenlaw, Jan Hatzius, Anil K. Kashyap, and Hyun Song Shin, "Leveraged Losses: Lessons from the Mortgage Market Meltdown," U.S. Monetary Policy Forum Paper No. 2, Rosenberg Institute, Brandeis International Business School, and Initiative on Global Markets, University of Chicago Graduate School of Business, 2008; "The Bet That Blew Up Wall Street: Steve Kroft on Credit-Default Swaps and Their Central Role in the Unfolding Economic Crisis," *60 Minutes*, CBS, October 26, 2008, available at http://www.cbsnews.com/stories/2008/10/26/60minutes/main4546199.shtml.

25. Interview with Gerald Epstein, "Obama Takes on Wall Street? Part 2," *Real News Network*, January 22, 2010, available at http://therealnews.com/t2/index.php?option = com_content&task = view&id = 31&Itemid = 7&jumival = 4746; also see Gary Gorton and Andrew Metrick, "Securitized Banking and the Run on Repo," *Yale ICF Working Paper*, November 13, 2009.

26. *Hirsch v. DuPont*, 553 F.2d 750, 763 (2d Cir. 1977), cited by Fletcher p. 1083.

27. Securities Act of 1933, 15 U.S.C. Sec. 77a,, and Homer Cherrington, *The Investor and the Securities Act* (Washington, D.C.: 1942), pp. 132–133.

28. "National Affairs: Caveat Venditor," *Time*, April 10, 1933, available at http://www.time.com/time/magazine/article/0,9171,929518,00.html.

29. Ibid.

30. Fletcher, p. 1133, quoting Senator Sam Rayburn (D-Tex).

31. "Roosevelt Signs the Securities Bill," *New York Times*, May 27, 1933.

32. Ibid.

33. See the 1933 Act, section 4(2) ("transactions by an issuer not involving a public offering").

34. Cherrington, p. 109.

35. Ibid., referencing the SEC letter to the Corporation Trust Company, April 27, 1934.

36. *SEC v. Ralston Purina*, 346 U.S. 119 (1953).

37. Regulation D, 17 C.F.R. Secs. 230.501–508 (2007); for more details, see http://www.sec.gov/answers/rule506.htm.

38. Securities and Exchange Commission, "Rule 506 of Regulation D," available at http://www.sec.gov/answers/rule506.htm.

39. Securities and Exchange Commission, "Q&A: Small Business and the SEC: A Guide to Help You Understand How to Raise Capital and Comply with the Federal Securities Laws," available at http://www.sec.gov/info/smallbus/qasbsec.htm.

40. Remark made during a panel at the Yale Governance Forum, New Haven, Conn., June 11, 2009 (the author attended this conference; however, due to Chatham House Rules, whereby neither the identity nor the affiliation of a speaker may be revealed, this quote is not attributed).

41. Congressional Oversight Panel, "Special Report on Regulatory Reform," January 29, 2009, p. 24 ("COP Report"), available at http://cop.senate.gov/reports/library/report-012909-cop.cfm.

42. Erik R. Sirri, director, Division of Trading and Markets, U.S. Securities and Exchange Commission,"Remarks at the National Economists Club: Securities Markets and Regulatory Reform," April 9, 2009, available at http://www.sec.gov/news/speech/2009/spch040909ers.htm.

43. Gillian Tett, *Fool's Gold: How the Bold Dream of a Small Tribe at J.P. Morgan Was Corrupted by Wall Street Greed and Unleashed a Catastrophe* (New York, 2009), p.152.

44. GAO Report, unnumbered "Highlights" page.

45. Jamie Dimon, CEO of JP Morgan, testimony before the Financial Crisis Inquiry Commission hearing, January 13, 2010, p. 60, official transcript, available at http://www.fcic.gov/hearings/pdfs/2010-0113-Transcript.pdf. Note that the official transcript ends this sentence with "prices," but from the televised testimony on CSPAN, it is clear he is speaking about mortgage loan applications.

46. Lloyd Blankfein, CEO of Goldman Sachs Group, Inc., testimony before the Financial Crisis Inquiry Commission hearing, January 13, 2010, pp. 63–64, official transcript, available at http://www.fcic.gov/hearings/pdfs/2010-0113-Transcript.pdf.

47. Fletcher, p. 1134.

48. For explanation of Rule 15c3–1 prior to the amendment, see Securities and Exchange Commission, "Final Rule: Alternative Net Capital Requirements for Broker-Dealers That Are Part of Consolidated Supervised Entities," 17 CFR Parts 200 and 240, Release No. 34–49830, File No. S7–21–03, August 20, 2004,("Amended Net Capital Rule") available at http://www.sec.gov/rules/final/34-49830.htm.

49. Julie Satow, "Ex-SEC Official Blames Agency for Blow-Up of Broker-Dealers," *New York Sun,* September 18, 2008.

50. Amended Net Capital Rule.

51. Robert L. D. Colby, acting director, Division of Market Regulation, U.S. Securities and Exchange Commission, testimony before the U.S. House Subcommittee on Financial Institutions and Consumer Credit hearing, "Prudential Supervision of U.S. Securities Firms," September 14, 2006, available at http://www.sec.gov/news/testimony/2006/ts091406rldc.htm.

52. John Plender, "Financial Crisis Served Up with Relish," *Financial Times*, February 1, 2010.

53. Mary Schapiro, SEC Chair, testimony during the question-and-answer session after prepared remarks before the House Committee on Financial Services hearing, "Public Policy Issues Raised by the Report of the Lehman Bankruptcy Examiner" ("Lehman Hearing"), April 20, 2010, archived webcast, available at http://www.house.gov/apps/list/hearing/financialsvcs_dem/hrfc_04202010.shtml.

54. Richard Fuld, testimony during the question-and-answer session after prepared remarks, Lehman Hearing.

55. Andrew Ross Sorkin and Vikas Bajaj, "Shift for Goldman and Morgan Marks the End of an Era," *New York Times*, September 21, 2009, available at http://www.ny times.com/2008/09/22/business/22bank.html.

56. SEC Commissioner Luis A. Aguilar, "Hedge Fund Regulation on the Horizon: Don't Shoot the Messenger," presented at the Spring 2009 Hedgeworld Fund Services Conference, New York, June 18, 2009, available at http://www.sec.gov/news/speech/2009/spch061809laa.htm.

57. Paul Tustain, "Bear Stearns and MBS Hedge Funds: What are the Real Risks Today?" *Safe Haven*, June 22, 2007, available at http://www.safehaven.com/article-7812.htm.

58. Andrew W. Lo, *Hedge Funds: An Analytic Perspective*(Princeton, N.J.: 2008), p. 302.

59. Bookstaber.

60. Tustain.

61. Yves Smith, *ECONned: How Unenlightened Self Interest Undermined Democracy and Corrupted Capitalism* (New York: 2010), p. 260.

62. Jesse Eisinger and Jake Bernstein, "Magnetar Gets Started," *ProPublica*, April 9, 2010, http://www.propublica.org/feature/magnetar-gets-started.

63. Eisinger and Bernstein, "The Magnetar Trade."

64. Robert Metz, "Market Place: Big Guys Lost in Hedge Fund," *New York Times*, March 16, 1972 (more than thirty-five years ago, a story that "echoes" the present-day scandals).

65. *The SEC, Investment Trusts, and Investment Companies*, H.R. Doc. No. 707, 75th Cong., 3d Sess. Pt. 1 (1939); *The SEC, Investment Trusts, and Investment Companies*, H.R. Doc. No. 70, 76th Cong., 1st Sess. Pt. 2 (1939); *The SEC, Investment Trusts, and Investment Companies*, H.R. Doc. No. 279, 76th Cong., 1st Sess. Pt. 3 (1939) (the "Investment Trust Study").

66. Investment Company Act of 1940, 15 U.S.C. §80a-1(b)(7) and (b)(8).

67. Memorandum from the Division of Investment Management to Arthur Levitt, SEC Chairman, regarding mutual funds and derivative instruments (September 26, 1994) ("derivatives memo"), p. 20, available at http://www.sec.gov/divisions/investment/imseniorsecurities/immemo092694.pdf (referencing the Investment Trust Study).

68. Thomas P. Lemke, Gerald T. Lins, Kathryn L. Hoenig, and Patricia S. Rube, *Hedge Funds and Other Private Funds: Regulation and Compliance 2008–2009 Edition* (2008), p. 90.

69. Aguilar.

70. Roger Lowenstein, *When Genius Failed: The Rise and Fall of Long-Term Capital Management* (New York: 2000), p. 26, and Aguilar.

71. Peter Lattman and Jenny Strasburg, "Clients Flee Cerberus, Fallen Fund Titan," *Wall Street Journal*, August 29, 2009.

72. Managed Fund Association, FAQ, available at http://www.managedfunds.org/hf-hf-adviser-faqs.asp.

73. John P. Hunt, "Hedge Fund Regulation: The President's Working Group Committees' Best Practices Reports—Raising the Bar but Missing Risks," June 2008, p. 1, available at SSRN: http://ssrn.com/abstract = 1279870.

74. Lemke et al., p. 2.

75. Ibid., pp. 41–42.

76. 1940 Act, 15 U.S.C. §80b-5(a) (prohibits "compensation to the investment adviser on the basis of a share of capital gains upon or capital appreciation of the funds or any portion of the funds of the client").

77. Division of Investment Management, U.S. Securities and Exchange Commission, "Protecting Investors: A Half Century of Investment Company Regulation" ("Half Century Study") (1992), p. 237.

78. Securities and Exchange Commission, "Final Rule: Exemption to Allow Investment Advisers to Charge Fees Based upon a Share of Capital Gains upon or Capital Appreciation of a Client's Account," 17 CFR Part 275, Release No. IA-1731, File No. S7–29–97, effective August 20, 1998, available at http://www.sec.gov/rules/final/ia-1731.htm.

79. Investment Advisers Act, 15 U.S.C. §80b-3(b)(3).

80. *SEC v. Capital Gains Research Bureau, Inc.*, 375 U.S. 180 (1963).

81. Half Century Study, p. 103.

82. Lemke et al., pp. 96–98 and 103. Prior to an amendment, the test was two-part and look through would happen only if the investing fund had 10 percent of its assets invested in the hedge fund and held 10 percent of the hedge fund's voting securities.

83. Ibid., p. 85.

84. The National Securities Markets Improvement Act of 1996, Pub. L. No. 104–290 (1996) (NSMIA is codified in various sections of the United States Code).

85. Half Century Study pp. 104–105.

86. Securities and Exchange Commission, "Final Rule [on 3(c)(7)]:Privately Offered Investment Companies," 17 CFR Part 270, Release No. IC-22597, International Series Release No. 1071, File No. S7-30-96, effective June 9, 1997, available at http://www.sec.gov/rules/final/ic-22597.txt.

87. Lemke et al., p. 114.

88. For a recent example, consider Wallis K. Finger, "Unsophisticated Wealth: Reconsidering the SEC's 'Accredited Investor' Definition Under the 1933 Act," *Washington University Law Review* 86 (2009), p. 733.

89. Aguilar.

90. Riva D. Atlas and Mary Williams Walsh, "Pension Officers Putting Billions into Hedge Funds," *New York Times*, November 27, 2005.

91. William Klunk, actuary, Domestic Policy Division, *Pension Funds Investing in Hedge Funds*, CRS Report to Congress, June 15, 2007.

92. Fiona Stewart, "Pension Fund Investment in Hedge Funds," *OECD Working Papers on Insurance and Private Pensions* (2007).

93. Atlas and Walsh.

94. Ibid.

95. Ibid.

96. Ibid.

97. Klunk.

98. George Soros, "America Must Face Up to the Danger of Derivatives," *Financial Times*, April 22, 2010, available at http://www.ft.com/cms/s/0/707ef202-4e3d-11df-b48d-00144feab49a.html.

99. Richard R. Zabel, "Credit Default Swaps: From Protection to Speculation," *Pratt's Journal of Bankruptcy Law* (September 2008), available at http://www.rkmc.com/Credit-Default-Swaps-From-Protection-To-Speculation.htm.

100. Ibid.

101. Nomi Prins, *Other People's Money: The Corporate Mugging of America* (New York: 2004), pp. 108–109.

102. Zabel.

103. Houman B. Shadab, "Guilty by Association? Regulating Credit-default Swaps," *Entrepreneurial Business Law Journal*, 4, no. 2, 2010, p. 433, available at http://ssrn.com/abstract = 1368026, citing Bank for International Settlements, "OTC Derivatives Market Activity in the Second Half of 2008," May 2009, p. 7.

104. An estimated 80 percent of the CDS market consisted of "insurance" policies on instruments the buyers did not own. Matthew Leising and Alan Bjerga, "Peterson Says 'Naked' Credit Default Swap Ban Not Permanent," *Bloomberg*, February 3, 2009.

105. The Commodities Futures Modernization Act, H.R. 5660 (CFMA), available at http://www.cftc.gov/stellent/groups/public/@lrrulesandstatutoryauthority/documents/file/ogchr5660.pdf.

106. CFMA Sec. 117 "Preemption."

107. "The Bet That Blew Up Wall Street."

108. Lynne A. Stout, "How Deregulating Derivatives Led to Disaster, and Why Re-Regulating Them Can Prevent Another," *Lombard Street*,1.7 (2009), p. 6, available at http://www.finreg21.com/files/finreg21-finreg21/Lombard%207.pdf.

109. Ibid., p. 7.

110. Ibid., p. 5.

111. Alan Greenspan, chairman, "Regulation, Innovation, and Wealth Creation," presented to the Society of Business Economists, London, September 25, 2002, available at http://www.federalreserve.gov/boarddocs/speeches/2002/200209252/default.htm.

112. Joshua Zumbrun, "Clinton Calls Advice He Got on Derivatives, 'Wrong', Update 1," *Bloomberg News*, April 19, 2010, available at http://www.bloomberg.com/apps/news?pid = 20601070&sid = aN7MOt1sroPc.

113. Report of the President's Working Group on Financial Markets, "Over-the-Counter Derivatives Markets and the Commodity Exchange Act," November 1999, p. 16, available at http://www.ustreas.gov/press/releases/reports/otcact.pdf.

114. Henry T.C. Hu, "Credit Default Swaps and the Financial Crisis: 'Interconnectedness' and 'Beyond,'" testimony before the U.S. House Committee on Agriculture hearing, "The Role of Credit Derivatives in the U.S. Economy," October 13, 2008, p. 2, referencing Henry T.C. Hu, "Misunderstood Derivatives: The Causes of Informational Failure and the Promise of Regulatory Incrementalism," *Yale Law Journal* 102 (1993), pp. 1457–1513.

115. Hu, "Credit Default Swaps," p. 4.

116. Nassim Nicholas Taleb, *The Black Swan: The Impact of the Highly Improbable* (New York: 2007).

117. Hu, "Credit Default Swaps," p. 5, citing Gretchen Morgenson, "Behind Insurer's Crisis, Blind Eye to a Web of Risk," *New York Times* September 27, 2008.

118. Hu, "Credit Default Swaps," p. 5.

119. Andrew Ross Sorkin, *Too Big To Fail* (New York: 2009), p. 160.

120. Michael Daly, "Pin AIG Woes on Brooklyn Boy: Joseph Cassano Walked Away with $315 Million While Company Staggered," *New York Daily News*, March 17, 2009.

121. Eisinger and Bernstein, "The Magnetar Trade."

122. Dimon, p. 60.

123. Blankfein, p. 107.

124. Greenspan, testimony.

125. Half Century Study, p. 5.

126. Ibid.

127. Adam B. Ashcraft and Til Schuermann, "Understanding the Securitization of Sub-prime Mortgage Credit," *Federal Reserve Bank of New York Staff Report No. 318*, March 2008, table 1, p. 2.

128. Greenspan, testimony.

129. Ashcraft and Schuermann, p. 29.

130. Plender. In reviewing Robert Pozen, *Too Big to Save? How to Fix the U.S. Financial System* (Hoboken, N.J.: 2010), Plender notes that "the Basel I capital adequacy regime did, after all, give the same 4 per cent capital requirement to a prime mortgage with a 30 per cent down payment as to a subprime mortgage with a minimal down payment. Its treatment of mortgage-backed securities was absurdly lax."

131. Patrick Rucker, "Wall Street Often Shelved Damaging Subprime Reports," *Reuters*, July 27, 2007.

132. Thorp.

133. Richard E. Mendales, "Collateralized Explosive Devices: Why Securities Regulation Failed to Prevent the CDO Meltdown, and How to Fix It," *University of Illinois Law Review* 2009, no. 5 (2009), p. 1397.

134. Securities and Exchange Commission, "Adopts Rule 3a-7 under the Investment Company Act of 1940," 17 CFR Part 270, Release IC-19105, File No. S7-12-92, November 19, 1992, available at http://content.lawyerlinks.com/default.htm#http://content.lawyerlinks.com/library/sec/sec_releases/ic_19105.htm.

135. Half Century Study, p. 20.

136. Jonathan Macey, Geoffrey Miller, Maureen O'Hara, and Gabriel D. Rosenberg, "Helping Law Catch Up to Markets: Applying Broker-Dealer Law to Subprime Mortgages," *Journal of Corporation Law* 34.3 (2009), pp. 790–839.

137. Goldman Sachs, *Annual Report*, 2009, p. 7.

138. Sanjeev Arora, Boaz Barak, Markus Brunnermeir, and Rong Ge, "Computational Complexity and Information Asymmetry in Financial Products," Princeton University, working paper, October 19, 2009, p. 1.

139. Michael Lewis, *The Big Short: Inside the Doomsday Machine* (New York: 2010), p. 141.

140. SEC, "SEC Charges Goldman Sachs with Fraud in Structuring and Marketing of CDO Tied to Subprime Mortgages."

141. Zachary A. Goldfarb, "SEC Confident on IKB Part of Goldman Lawsuit," *Washington Post*, Ezra Klein WonkBook, April 24, 2010, available at http://www.washingtonpost.com/wp-dyn/content/article/2010/04/23/AR2010042305223.html.

142. Eisinger and Bernstein, "Magnetar Gets Started."

143. Fabrice Tourre, testimony before the Senate Permanent Subcommittee on Investigations hearing, "Wall Street and the Financial Crisis: The Role of Investment Banks" ("Wall Street Hearing"), April 27, 2010, available at http://hsgac.senate.gov/public/index.cfm?FuseAction = Hearings.Hearing&Hearing_id = f07ef2bf-914c-494c-aa66-27129f8e6282.

144. "Wall Street Hearing," April 27, 2010, exhibit 61, p. 7, available at http://hsgac.senate.gov/public/_files/Financial_Crisis/042710Exhibits.pdf.

145. Letter to Chairman Phil Angelides, "Wall Street Hearing," March 1, 2010, exhibit 148.

146. Sewell Chan and Louise Story, "Goldman Pays $550 million to Settle Fraud Case," *New York Times*, July 15, 2010.

147. "Endowment Value Declines 29.5% as Investment Return is Negative 27.3%," *Harvard Magazine*, September 10, 2009, available at http://harvardmagazine.com/breaking-news/sharp-endowment-decline-reported.

148. Nina Munks, "Rich Harvard, Poor Harvard," *Vanity Fair*, July 2009, available at http://www.vanityfair.com/online/daily/2009/06/harvard.html.

149. Munks.

150. Jenny Strasburg, "A Madoff Feeder Will Auction Assets," *Wall Street Journal*, August 15, 2009.

151. Eric Konigsberg, "In Fraud Case, Middlemen in Spotlight," *New York Times*, December 16, 2008.

152. Stephen Gandel, "The Madoff Fraud: How Culpable Were the Auditors?" *Time*, December 17, 2008.

153. Leslie Wayne, "Inquiry Started of Financier Who Invested with Madoff," *New York Times*, January 15, 2009.

154. Alison Leigh Cowan, "Firm That Trusted a Disgraced Investor," *New York Times*, December 15, 2008.

155. Cowan.

156. Wayne.

157. Ibid.

158. Ibid.

159. Karen Freifeld and Patricia Hurtado, "Mort Zuckerman's Fraud Claim Against Ezra Merkin over Madoff May Proceed," *Bloomberg*, May 7, 2010, available at http://www.bloomberg.com/news/2010-05-07/mort-zuckerman-s-fraud-claim-against-ezra-merkin-over-madoff-may-proceed.html.

160. Wayne.

161. Cowan.

162. Konigsberg.

163. William K. Black, "Epidemics of 'Control Fraud' Lead to Recurrent, Intensifying Bubbles and Crises," presented at the University of Massachusetts, Amherst, Political Economy Research Institute, March 9, 2010.

164. Ibid., citing George Akerlof and Paul Romer, "Looting: The Economic Underworld of Bankruptcy for Profit," in: Brainard, W., Perry, G. (Eds.), *Brookings Papers on Economic Activity* 2: 1–73 (1993).

165. Ibid., citing George A. Akerlof, "The Market for 'Lemons': Quality Uncertainty and the Market Mechanism," *Quarterly Journal of Economics* 84.3 (1970), pp. 488–500.

166. William K. Black, "The Two Documents Everyone Should Read to Better Understand the Crisis," *Huffington Post*, February 25, 2009.

167. Aguilar.

168. Wall Street Reform and Consumer Protection Act of 2010, H.R. 4173 (the "Dodd-Frank Act"), Section 939, available at http://frwebgate.access.gpo.gov/cgi-bin/getdoc.cgi?dbname = 111_econg_bills&docid = f:h4173enr.txt.pdf.

169. Dodd-Frank Act, Section 939A.

Chapter 10. The Role of Investment Consultants in Transforming Pension Fund Decision Making

1. James P. Hawley, and Andrew T. Williams, "Universal Owners: Challenges and Opportunities," *Corporate Governance* 15 (3) 2007: 415–420.

2. Fund Management 2008, International Financial Services London Research, City of London, U.K. Department of Trade and Investment.

3. Gordon L. Clark, *Pension Fund Capitalism* (New York: Oxford University Press, 2000).

4. The geography of pension funds is quite diverse. Countries with large occupational pension funds relative to GDP include the U.S., U.K., Canada, Australia, the

Netherlands, Switzerland, and Japan. Although funded pension arrangements are increasing in other countries through reform of public pension systems, actual assets under management remain small.

5. George Soros, *The New Paradigm for Financial Markets: The Credit Crisis of 2008 and What It Means* (New York: Public Affairs, 2008).

6. Gordon Clark, Adam Dixon, and Ashby Monk, introduction to *Managing Financial Risks: From Global to Local*, edited by Clark, Dixon, and Monk (Oxford: Oxford University Press, 2009).

7. Nicholas Stern, "Climate Change, Ethics and the Economics of the Global Deal," Manchester: Royal Economic Society public lecture, 2007.

8. UNEP Finance Initiative, *The Materiality of Social, Environment, and Corporate Governance Issues to Equity Pricing*, UNEPFI, 2004.

9. Sarah Forrest, Anthony Ling, and Waghorn Lanstone, *Enhanced Energy ESG Framework*, Goldman Sachs Investment Research, 2006.

10. Céline Louche and Steven Lydenberg, *Socially Responsible Investment: Differences Between Europe and United States*, Vlerick Leuven Gent Working Paper Series 2006/22, 2006.

11. Joakim Sandberg, Carmen Juravle, Ted Martin Hedesström, and Ian Hamilton, "The Heterogeneity of Socially Responsible Investment," *Journal of Business Ethics* 87 (4) 2009: 519–533.

12. Russell Sparkes and Christopher J. Cowton, "The Maturing of Socially Responsible Investment: A Review of the Developing Link with Corporate Social Responsibility," *Journal of Business Ethics* 52 2004: 45–97.

13. John Hendry, Paul Sanderson, Richard Barker, and John Roberts, "Responsible Ownership, Shareholder Value and the New Shareholder Activism," *Competition and Change* 11 (3) 2007: 223–240.

14. Bernard S.Black and John C. Coffee, "Hail Britannia? Institutional Investor Behavior Under Limited Regulation," *Michigan Law Review* 92 (7) 1994: 1997–2087.

15. Gerald F, Davis and Tracey A Thompson, "A Social Movement Perspective on Corporate Control," *Administrative Science Quarterly* 29 1994: 141–173.

16. Marc Orlitzky, Frank L. Schidt, and Sara L. Rynes, "Corporate Social and Financial Performance: A Meta-analysis," *Organisation Studies* 24 (3) 2003: 403–441.

17. Rob Bauer, Jeroen Derwall, Nadja Guenster, and Kees Koedijk, "The Eco-efficiency Premium Puzzle," *Financial Analysts Journal* 61 (2) 2005: 51–63.

18. Rob Bauer, Robin Braun, and Gordon L. Clark, "The Emerging Market for European Corporate Governance: The Relationship Between Governance and Capital Expenditures, 1997–2005," *Journal of Economic Geography* 8 (4) 2008: 441–469.

19. Michael C, Jensen and William H. Meckling, "Theory of the Firm: Managerial Behavior, Agency Costs and Ownership Structure," *Journal of Financial Economics* 3 (4) 1976: 305–360. See also Gordon L. Clark and Tessa Hebb, "Pension Fund Corporate Engagement: The Fifth Stage of Capitalism," *International Relations* 59 (1)

2004:142–171. Also, Tessa Hebb, *No Small Change: Pension Funds and Corporate Engagement* (Ithaca, N.Y.: Cornell University Press, 2008).

20. Benjamin Richardson,"Sustainability Should Be regulated into Fiduciary Duty," *Responsible Investor* January 11, 2009, available at http://www.responsible-investor.com/home/article/richardson

21. Baruch Lev, *Intangibles: Management, Measurement and Reporting* (Washington, D.C.: Brookings Institute Press, 2001).

22. Gordon L. Clark and James Salo, "Corporate Governance and Environmental Risk Management: A Quantitative Analysis of 'New Paradigm' Firms," in *Pensions at Work: Socially Responsible Investment of Union-Based Pension Funds*, edited by J. Quarter, I. Carmichael, and S. Ryan (Toronto: University of Toronto Press, 2008).

23. Daniel Esty and Andrew Winston, *Green to Gold: How Smart Companies Use Environmental Strategies to Innovate, Create Value, and Build Competitive Advantage* (New Haven: Yale University Press, 2006). See also Neil Gunningham, Robert Kagan, and Dorothy Thornton, *Shades of Green: Business, Regulation and the Environment* (Stanford, Calif.: Stanford University Press, 2003).

24. Gordon L. Clark and Eric Knight, "Implications of the UK Companies Act 2006 for Institutional Investors and the Corporate Social Responsibility Movement," *University of Pennsylvania Journal of Business Law* 11 (2) 2009: 259–296.

25. Jeffrey S. Boggs and Norma M. Rantisi, "The 'Relational Turn' in Economic Geography," *Journal of Economic Geography* 3 2003: 109–116.

26. Gordon L. Clark and Roger Urwin, "Making Pension Boards Work: The Critical Role of Leadership," *Rotman International Journal of Pension Management* 1(1) 2008: 38–45, available at http://utpjournals.metapress.com/content/m12443103k07/?p = 58f2cb39da534f9d80ea043edc414706&pi = 1.

27. Keith Ambachtsheer, Ronald Capelle, and Hubert Lum, "The Pension Governance Deficit: Still with Us," *Rotman International Journal of Pension Management* 1 (1) 2008:14–21. See also, Gordon L. Clark, Emiko Caerlewy-Smith, and John C. Marshall, "Pension Fund Trustee Competence: Decision Making in Problems Relevant to Investment Practice," *Journal of Pension Economics and Finance* 5 (1) 2006: 91–110.

28. We note that not all pension funds operate in trust-based legal environments, particularly those in civil law countries. However, other jurisdictions, such as the Netherlands, have comparable fiduciary systems of investment oversight (for the Netherlands see Rene Maatman, *Dutch Pension Funds: Fiduciary Duties and Investing* [Amsterdam: Kluwer Legal Publishers, 2005]). Ultimately, investment consultants are typically involved at some point during the investment decision-making process.

29. Gordon L. Clark and Roger Urwin, "Making Pension Boards Work: The Critical Role of Leadership," *Rotman International Journal of Pension Management* 1 (1) 2008:38–45.

30. Carmen Juravle and Alan Lewis, "Identifying Impediments to SRI in Europe: A Review of the Practitioner and Academic Literature," *Business Ethics: A European Review* 17 (3) 2008:285–310.

31. Stephen Davis, Jon Lukomnik, and David Pitt-Watson, *The New Capitalists* (Boston: Harvard Business School Press, 2006).

32. Pensions & Investments, Consultants by Total Worldwide Advisory Assets, 2008, available at www.pionline.com.

33. Kyoko Sakuma and Celine Louche, "SRI in Japan: Its Mechanisms and Drivers," *Journal of Business Ethics* 82 (2) 2008: 425–448.

34. Emiko Caerlewy-Smith, Gordon L. Clark, and John C. Marshall, "Agitation, Resistance, and Reconciliation with Respect to Socially Responsible Investment: The Attitudes of UK Pension Trustees and Oxford Undergraduates," *Environment and Planning A* 38 (9) 2006: 1585–1589.

35. Bauer, Braun, and Clark..

36. Pensions & Investments.

37. William Jaworski, *Use of Extra-financial Information by Research Analysts and Investment Managers*, ECCE Working Paper, 2007.

38. Louis Lowenstein, "Financial Transparency and Corporate Governance: You Manage What You Measure," *Columbia Law Review* 96 (5) 1996:1 335–1353.

39. Angela J. Black and Patricia Fraser, "International Comparisons on Stock Market Short-termism: How Different Is the UK Experience," *The Manchester School of Economic Studies Supplement* 68 2000: 38–50.

40. What may be needed is a change in investment culture, which allows for a greater deviation from the index for periods of time where less conventional investment strategies are adopted. In addition, it may be helpful to more widely implement specific ESG-integrated indexes as benchmark for performance for the management of pension funds assets over the long term. These kinds of indexes have been around for some time now with the Dow Jones Indexes, STOXX Limited and SAM Group launching the Dow Jones Sustainability Indexes in 1999. The real barrier is therefore translating this into the investment culture.

41. Allen N. Berger, Nathan H. Miller, Mitchell A. Petersen, Raghuram G. Ragan, and Jeremy C. Stein, *Does Function Follow Organizational Form? Evidence from the Lending Practices of Large and Small Banks*, National Bureau of Economic Research Working Paper 8752, 2002.

42. UNEP Finance Initiative, *Fiduciary Responsibility: Legal and Practical Aspects of Integrating Environmental, Social and Governance Issues into Institutional Investment*, 2009.

43. Clark and Knight.

44. Matthew Kiernan, "Universal Owners and ESG: Leaving Money on the Table," *Corporate Governance* 15 (3) 2007: 478–485.

45. Danyelle Guyatt, *Identifying and Mobilizing Win-Win Opportunities for Collaboration Between Pension Fund Institutions and Their Agents* (Toronto: Rotman International Center for Pension Management, 2007). See also Danyelle Guyatt, "Pension Collaboration: Strength in Numbers," *Rotman International Journal of Pension Management* 1 (1) 2008: 46–52.

46. Caerlewy-Smith, Clark, and Marshall.

Chapter 11. Funding Climate Change

I would like to thank Gordon Clark, Robin Ellison, John Evans, Dorothee Franzen, Taylor Gray, Jim Hawley, and Benjamin Richardson for their helpful comments on an earlier draft of this chapter. Any mistakes are of course my own. This work was completed with the support of the University of Oxford Clarendon Fund Scholarship.

1. Organisation for Economic Co-operation and Development (OECD), "Special Feature: Private Pensions and the 2008 Turmoil in Financial Markets," 5 *Pension Markets in Focus*, 3, 12 (2008); see also Keith Johnson and Frank Jan de Graaf, *Network for Sustainable Financial Markets, Consultation Paper No. 2: Modernizing Pension Fund Legal Standards for the 21st Century*, 3–4 (2009).

2. See Conference Board, news release, "U.S. Institutional Investors Boost Ownership of U.S. Corporations to New Highs" (September 2, 2008) 1: "public pension funds have increased their share of equity markets from 2.9 percent in 1980 to 10 percent 2006. . . . Private pensions funds' share declined from 15.1 percent in 1980 to 13.6 percent in 2006."

3. U.K. Office of National Statistics, "Share Ownership," available at http://www .statistics.gov.uk/cci/nugget.asp?id = 107.

4. See generally Gordon L. Clark, *Pension Fund Capitalism* (2000). English and American pension funds have many similarities in terms of governance, funding, and regulation.

5. See, e.g., World Economic Forum, *World Economic Forum Annual Meeting: The Power of Collaborative Innovation 2008*, 3–17 (2008).

6. Cf. Nicholas Stern and Joseph Stiglitz, Opinion, "Obama's Chance to Lead the Green Recovery," *Financial Times*, March 2, 2009 (arguing that the financial crisis and climate change may have common solutions), available at http://www.ft.com/cms/s/0/ 7c51644a-075b-11de-9294-000077b07658.html.

7. Nicholas Stern, *Stern Review: The Economics of Climate Change—Long Executive Summary* ii (2006).

8. OECD, supra note 1 at 3.

9. Ibid.

10. See Clark, supra note 4 at 16–42 (on pension funds and the retreat of the state); see Benjamin Richardson, "Putting Ethics into Environmental Law: Fiduciary Duties for Ethical Investment," 46 *Osgoode Hall Law Journal* 243, 247–248 (2008) (on the ethical obligations of institutional investors).

11. See Richardson, supra note 10.

12. See Stern, supra note 7. See also Kenneth Arrow et al., "Economic Growth, Carrying Capacity, and the Environment," 15 *Ecological Economics* 91, 92–93 (1995).

13. For example, the Marathon Club, a group of institutional investors who promote long-term investment, has released a report highlighting lessons for institutional investors from the credit crunch. See generally Marathon Club, *Behavioural Aspects of Investment Management: Lessons from the Credit Crunch* (2008).

14. See, e.g., "The Effects of Recent Turmoil in Fin. Markets on Ret. Sec.: Hearing Before the H. Comm. on Educ. and Labor," October 7, 2008 (statement of Peter R. Orszag, director, Congressional Budget Office), available at http://www.cbo.gov/ftp docs/98xx/doc9864/10-07-RetirementSecurity_Testimony.pdf.

15. On the financial impact of climate change, see, e.g., Sonia Labatt and Rodney R. White, *Carbon Finance: The Financial Implications of Climate Change* (2007); cf. Rob Bauer et al., "Socially Responsible Investing: The Eco-Efficiency Premium Puzzle," 61 *Financial Analysts Journal* 51 (2005). For meta-analyses of SRI and financial performance see, e.g., Marc Orlitzky, Frank L. Schmidt, and Sara L. Rynes, "Corporate Social and Financial Performance: A Meta-Analysis," 24 *Org. Studies* 403 (2003); see also Benjamin Richardson, *Socially Responsible Investment Law* 173–176 (2008) (for a brief review of various studies conducted). Despite the volume of analysis on performance of SRI funds compared to the market as a whole, there is no consensus about the financial outcome of SRI. This lack of consensus is due partly to variations in research methodology, as well as the varying meanings given to SRI funds. Further confusion is added by scholars offering different ways to *measure* performance: if part of the purpose of SRI funds is to create positive social externalities, then financial performance becomes one of several performance measures, rather than the only one: see Abigail McWilliams and Donald Siegel, "Event Studies in Management Research: Theoretical and Empirical Issues," *Academy of Management Journal* 626–657 (1999).

16. For a brief analysis of ethical arguments for sustainable investment, see Richardson, supra note 10 at 259–266.

17. See Clark, supra note 4 at 17.

18. See OECD, supra note 1 at 12.

19. See Clark, supra note 4 at 16–42; James Hawley and Andrew Williams, "Shifting Ground: Emerging Global Corporate-Governance Standards and the Rise of Fiduciary Capitalism," 37 *Environmental and Planning A* 1995, 1998 (2005).

20. See Clark, supra note 4 at 16–42.

21. See, e.g., David Litterick, "Market Falls Add £40bn to UK Pensions Deficit," *Daily Telegraph* (March 25, 2008).

22. See Stern, supra note 7; Arrow et al., supra note 12.

23. The term *governance* is here used in the broad sense, as described by Jan Kooiman in *Governing as Governance* 4–8 (2003).

24. See Richardson, supra note 10 at 247.

25. Ibid. (where Richardson argues that neither appeals to conscience nor market forces alone will be sufficient to bring about a more ethical approach to investment; instead, certain regulatory reforms are required).

26. See Claire Woods and Roger Urwin, "Putting Sustainable Investing into Practice: A Governance Framework for Pension Funds," *Journal of Business Ethics,* Special Issue: *The Next Generation of Responsible Investing* (Forthcoming, 2010) (who note a parallel development in some sectors of the pension fund investment industry following the financial crisis).

27. Companies Act (2006) (U.K.) s. 172(d).

28. Ibid. s. 172(a).

29. James P. Hawley and Andrew T. Williams, *The Rise of Fiduciary Capitalism* (2000).

30. Ibid.

31. Ibid. at xv–xxvii, 3–7.

32. Ibid. at 3–7.

33. Gordon L. Clark, Emiko Caerlewy-Smith, and John C. Marshall, "The Consistency of UK Pension Fund Trustee Decision-Making," 6 *Journal of Pension Economics and Finance* 67, 75 (2007).

34. Ibid. at 82.

35. The U.S. Department of Energy had an enacted budget of $26.4 billion for the financial year 2010. It has requested a budget of $28.4 billion for 2011. This is in addition to an allocation of $38.7 billion under the Recovery Act dedicated to clean energy projects: see U.S. Department of Energy, *Budget of the United States Government, Fiscal Year 2011*, 69–72 (2009). Similarly, the U.K. has committed around £60 billion to renewable energy and the low-carbon sector from 2009 to 2011: see HM Treasury, *Budget 2009: Building Britain's Future*, 133–335 (2009).

36. See Watson Wyatt, *Macro Factors: The Update* 6 (2005).

37. See generally Mercer Investment Consulting for the Carbon Trust and the Institutional Investor Group on Climate Change, *A Climate for Change: A Trustee's Guide to Understanding and Addressing Climate Risk* (2005).

38. See Benjamin Richardson, "Climate Finance and Its Governance: Moving to a Low Carbon Economy Through Socially Responsible Financing?" 58 *International and Comparative Law Quarterly* 597, 600 (2009) ("Although the financial sector is publishing numerous studies that warn of the impact of global warming on its self-interest, so far tangible changes in investment practices are hard to discern" [citations omitted]), at 617 (citing instances where investors *have* responded to climate change risk). See also Institutional Investor Group on Climate Change (IIGCC), *Investor Statement on Climate Change Report 2008*, 8 (2008): the IIGCC has twenty-two signatories (representing around £2 trillion in assets) to its statement committing to a proactive response to climate change. The Norwegian Government Pension Fund-Global, though strictly speaking a sovereign wealth fund, has an ethical mandate: see Gordon Clark and Ashby Monk, "The Legitimacy and Governance of Norway's Sovereign Wealth Fund: The Ethics of Global Investment," 3–4 (September 15, 2009). Available at SSRN: http://ssrn.com/abstract = 1473973.

39. The Intergovernmental Panel on Climate Change was established in 1988: see Labatt and White, supra note 15 at 5.

40. The *Stern Review* (see supra note 7) shed a new, interdisciplinary light on the problem of climate change by assessing its economic effects.

41. The concept of climate change was highly contested in the business community until recently. While the view that governments and business must address the

problem of climate change is now accepted by the vast majority of governments and most businesses (for a contrarian view, see generally Bjorn Lomborg, *Cool It: The Skeptical Environmentalist's Guide to Global Warming* [2007]), it is not surprising that aftershocks of the initial controversy continue to retard and confuse trustee decision making on the topic. It is arguable, however, that any remaining controversy surrounding climate change is less contentious an issue for trustee decision making than the breakdown of established financial wisdom following the financial crisis: see, e.g., "What Went Wrong with Economics," *Economist,* July 18, 2009, at 11; Adair Turner, "How to Tame Global Finance," Features, *Prospect* Magazine, August 27, 2009.

42. See, e.g., United Nations Environment Programme Finance Initiative, *Fiduciary Responsibility: Legal and Practical Aspects of Integrating Environmental, Social and Governance Issues into Institutional Investment,* 32–46, 75 (2009); see generally UN-EPFI, *A Legal Framework for the Integration of Environmental, Social and Governance Issues into Institutional Investment* (2005); Paul Palmer et al., *Socially Responsible Investment: A Guide for Pension Schemes and Charities,* 97–103 (Charles Scanlan, ed., 2005); Richardson, supra note 15.

43. See Axel Hesse, *Long-Term and Sustainable Pension Investments: A Study of Leading European Pension Funds* (2008) (presenting results of surveys and interviews with trustees and asset managers of a number of leading pension funds, which showed that most of these funds see fiduciary duty as a significant barrier to the inclusion of ESG factors in pension fund investment decision making); see also John Langbein and Richard Posner, "Social Investing and the Law of Trusts," 79 *Michigan Law Review,* 72, 88–91, 96–104 (1980) (arguing that making investments for social or ethical reasons is generally contrary to pension funds' mandates); see also Rosy Thornton, "Ethical Investments: A Case of Disjointed Thinking," *Cambridge Law Journal* 396, 397–399, 415 (2008) (arguing that SRI is "of doubtful legality"); UNEPFI, *Legal Framework,* supra note 42 at 7–8 (describing the perception of fiduciary duty regarding ESG issues in the U.K.).

44. P. D. Finn, *Fiduciary Obligations* 201 (1977).

45. Ibid. at 2.

46. *Hospital Products Ltd v. United States Surgical Corporation* 156 CLR 41, 96–97 (1984) (Austl.) (Mason J).

47. See *Meinhard v. Salmon* 164 N.E. 545 (N.Y. 1928) at 546 (opinion of Cardozo J) ("Many forms of conduct permissible in a workaday world for those acting at arm's length, are forbidden to those bound by fiduciary ties. A trustee is held to something stricter than the morals of the market place. Not honesty alone, but the punctilio of an honour the most sensitive is then the standard of behavior").

48. See Donovan Waters QC, "The Trust: Continual Evolution of a Centuries-Old Idea," 14 *J. Int'l. Trust and Corp. Plan.,* 257, 258 (2007).

49. Ibid.

50. *Keech v. Sandford* 25 ER 223 (1726) (in this case, the defendant was required to hold a lease in constructive trust for an infant beneficiary).

51. Ernest J. Weinrib, "The Fiduciary Obligation," 25 *U. Toronto L.J.* 1, 1 (1975).

52. See, e.g., Finn, supra note 44.

53. John Langbein outlines the introduction of large amounts of legislation relating to fiduciary duty in the U.S. investment context during the second half of the twentieth century: see John Langbein, "Why Did Trust Law Become Statute Law in the United States?" 58 *Alabama L.R.* 1069, 1069–1071 (2007). Similarly, in the U.K. context, a number of acts have clarified fiduciary duty in the investment context; see, e.g., the Pensions Act 1995 and the Trustee Act 2000.

54. *Bristol and West Building Society v. Mothew* Ch. 1 (CA) (1998) at 18 per Millett LJ; see also Robert Flannigan, "The Fiduciary Obligation," 9 *O.J.L.S.* 285, 310 (1987).

55. *Board of Trustees v. Mayor of Baltimore City* 317 Md. 72, 562 A.2d 720 (1989).

56. *University of Oregon v. Oregon Investment Council* 82 Or. App. 145 (1987), 728 P.2d 30.

57. *Cowan v. Scargill* Ch. 270 (1985).

58. In the U.K., the Trustee Act 2000 provides that agents are subject to the same duties as trustees when exercising trust powers. When it comes to asset management, trustees are required to detail the agency agreement with asset managers in writing (s. 13[1]) and to prepare a "policy statement," which records how agents (e.g., asset managers) are required to exercise the powers that have been delegated to them (s. 13[2]). In the U.S., see ERISA, which provides that a person is a fiduciary with respect to a plan to the extent (1) he exercises any discretionary authority or discretionary control respecting management of such plan or exercises any authority or control respecting management or disposition of its assets, (2) he renders investment advice for a fee or other compensation, direct or indirect, with respect to any moneys or other property of such plan, or has any authority or responsibility to do so, or (3) he has any discretionary authority or discretionary responsibility in the administration of such plan: 29 U.S.C. s. 1002(2l)(A)(i)–(iii).

59. *Cowan v. Scargill* [1985] Ch. 270 at 290 (judgment of Megarry VC).

60. *Imperial Group Pension Trust Ltd v. Imperial Tobacco Ltd* 1 WLR 589 [1991] at 597 (judgment of Browne-Wilkinson VC).

61. See Graham Moffatt, "Pension Funds: A Fragmentation of Trust Law," 56 *M.L.R.* 471, 488 (1993).

62. See Scott Donald, "Beneficiary, Investor, Citizen: Characterising Australia's Super Fund Participants," 8 *Univ. N.S.W. Legal Research Series* (2009) at 3.

63. See Flannigan, supra note 54 at 310.

64. See John Langbein, "Questioning the Trust Law Duty of Loyalty," 114 *Yale L.J.* P 929, 963–987 (2005), and for the U.K. context, see Occupational Pension Schemes (Investment) Regulations Cl. 4(2).

65. See generally Langbein, supra note 64.

66. Finn, supra note 44 at 15.

67. See Flannigan, supra note 54 at 311.

68. Uniform Prudent Investor Act (UPIA) (1994) s. 5.

69. *Restatement (Third) of Trusts* (1992).

70. ERISA (1974) 29 USC s.1104(a) (setting out the prudent standard of care).

71. See Langbein, supra note 64 at 968–978.

72. Ibid. at 969.

73. UPIA s. 3 cmt.

74. See Langbein, supra note 64 at 977.

75. Occupational Pension Schemes (Investment) Regulations Cl. 4(2).

76. *The Duke of Portland v. Lady Topham* 11 HL Cas 32 (1864) at 54.

77. See *Harries v. Church Commissioners for England* 1 WLR 1241 [1992] at 1246.

78. See section 35.

79. *Cowan v. Scargill* 1 Ch. 270 [1985] at 287 (judgment of Megarry VC).

80. See *Martin v. City of Edinburgh District Council* SLT 329 [1988]. In this case, Justice Murray questioned Justice Megarry's strong statement for purely financial considerations, saying, "I cannot conceive that trustees have an unqualified duty simply to invest trust funds in the most profitable investment available. To accept that without qualification would, in my view, involve substituting the direction of financial advisers for the discretion of trustees." Similarly, in *Harries v. Church Commissioners for England* 1 WLR 1241 [1992] at 1242, it was found that trustees "must not use property held by them for investment purposes as a means for making moral statements at the expense of the charity of which they are trustees," but that this did not prevent them from acting as "responsible shareholders."

81. This is discussed in the section on "Duty of Prudence" below.

82. *Harvard College v. Amory* 26 Mass. (9 Pick.) (1830) at 461.

83. See UPIA, comment to s. 5.

84. ERISA 29 USC s. 1104(a)(B).

85. ERISA 29 USC s. 1104(a)(C).

86. ERISA 29 USC s. 1104(a)(D) ("insofar as such documents and instruments are consistent with the [other] provisions" of ERISA).

87. At the time of writing of this chapter, forty-eight U.S. states (all except Delaware and Mississippi) as well as the District of Columbia had adopted UPIA. See Michael E. Hunter, *Prudent Investor Rule—Risk Management Update*, available at http://prudentinvestor-trustee.com/jurisdictions.html.

88. UPIA s. 2(a).

89. UPIA s. 2(b).

90. *Speight v. Gaunt* 9 App Cas 1 (1883) (HL) at 19 (judgment of Lord Blackburn) (approving 22 ChD 727 at 739–740, CA, per Jessel MR); Re Whiteley, *Whiteley v. Learoyd* (1886) 33 ChD 347 (CA) at 355 (Lindley LJ).

91. Trustee Act (2000) s. 1(1)(a).

92. See also *Barlett v. Barclays Bank Trust Co Ltd* Ch. 515 [1980] at 534.

93. Pensions Act (1995), ss. 35–36.

94. See Occupational Pension Schemes (Investment) Regulations 2005 Cl. 2(2)(a).

95. Cl. 4(7).

96. Cl. 4(3).

97. See Palmer et al., supra note 42 at 79; Richardson, supra note 15 at 206; see also Hesse, supra note 43; see also Langbein and Posner, supra note 43 at 96–104.

98. See, e.g., Jon Entine, *U.S. Investment Funds and Fiduciary Irresponsibility, Ethical Corporation,* January 16, 2004; Andrew Sheen, "Walk the Line," *Global Pensions,* November 26, 2008 (citing the example of Connecticut public pension funds' decision to invest in a large but ailing local employer, Colt, in 1990, to save the company from bankruptcy; the plans lost $21 million of a combined $25 million investment within two years).

99. See Sheen, supra note 98.

100. See Peter Kinder, *"Rigid Rule" on Economically Targeted Investments: New ERISA Regulations on a Plan's "Economic Interests," KLD Blog,* November 25, 2008, available at http://blog.kld.com/uncategorized/"rigid-rule"-on-economically-targeted-investments-new-erisa-regulations-on-a-plan's-"economic-interests"/.

101. Lisa Woll, CEO, and Cheryl Smith, board chair, Social Investment Forum, letter to Bradford P. Campbell, assistant secretary, Employee Benefit Security Administration, U.S. Department of Labor, December 19, 2008, Available at http://www.socialinvest.org/news/releases/pressrelease.cfm?id = 129.

102. Lord McKenzie of Luton, *Hansard,* House of Lords, October 10, 2008, column 917.

103. *Bd. of Tr. of Employee Ret. Sys. of City of Baltimore v. City of Baltimore* 317 Md. 72 (1989); 562 A.2d 720.

104. *Bd. of Tr. of Employee Ret. Sys. of City of Baltimore v. City of Baltimore* 317 Md. 72 (1989) at 103.

105. *Bd. of Tr. of Employee Ret. Sys. of City of Baltimore v. City of Baltimore* 317 Md. 72 (1989) at 103.

106. *Bd. of Tr. of Employee Ret. Sys. of City of Baltimore v. City of Baltimore* 317 Md. 72 (1989) at 102.

107. *Bd. of Tr. of Employee Ret. Sys. of City of Baltimore v. City of Baltimore* 317 Md. 72 (1989) at 104.

108. *Bd. of Tr. of Employee Ret. Sys. of City of Baltimore v. City of Baltimore* 317 Md. 72 (1989) at 109.

109. *Bd. of Tr. of Employee Ret. Sys. of City of Baltimore v. City of Baltimore* 317 Md. 72 (1989) at 107.

110. *Univ. of Oregon v. Oregon Inv. Council* 82 Or. App. 145 (1987), 728 P.2d 30.

111. *Univ. of Oregon v Oregon Inv. Council* 82 Or. App. 145 (1987), 728 P.2d 30 at 150.

112. See, e.g., *Blankenship v. Boyle,* 329 F. Supp. 1089 (D.D.C. 1971); *Withers v. Teachers' Ret. Sys. of City of N.Y.,* 447 F. Supp. 1248 (S.D.N.Y. 1978).

113. UPIA, comments to s. 5. UPIA's comments to s. 5 refer in turn to Langbein and Posner: see supra note 43.

114. Letter from the Department of Labor to William M. Tartikoff, senior vice president and general counsel of Calvert Group Ltd. (May 28, 1998) (Calvert letter).

115. Employee Benefits Security Administration, *Interpretive Bulletin Relating to the Fiduciary Standard Under ERISA in Considering Economically Targeted Investments*, 29 CFR s.2509.08–1 (*ETI Bulletin*).

116. Employee Benefits Security Administration, *Interpretive Bulletin Relating to Exercise of Shareholder Rights*, 29 CFR s.2509.08–2 (*Shareholder Rights Bulletin*).

117. Employee Benefits Security Administration, news release n. 08–1448-NAT, "U.S. Department of Labor Updates Fiduciary Guidance on Exercising Shareholder Rights and Investing in Economically Targeted Investments," October 16, 2008.

118. *ETI Bulletin*, supra note 115.

119. Ibid.

120. Ibid.

121. *Shareholder Rights Bulletin*, supra note 116.

122. Ibid.

123. See Kinder, supra note 100.

124. See Woll and Smith, supra note 101.

125. *Cowan v. Scargill* Ch. 270 [1985].

126. *Cowan v. Scargill* Ch. 270 [1985] at 276–277.

127. *Cowan v. Scargill* Ch. 270 [1985] at 287.

128. *Cowan v. Scargill* Ch. 270 [1985] at 287–288.

129. UNEP FI, *Legal Framework*, supra note 42 at 3, 6, 9, 27–28, 82, 88.

130. Robert Megarry, "Investing Pension Funds: The Mineworkers' Case," T. G. Youdan (ed.), *Equity, Fiduciaries and Trusts* 115 (1989).

131. SCLR 90 [1988].

132. SCLR 90 [1988] at 334.

133. Cl. 3(b)(vi).

134. Lord McKenzie of Luton, supra note 102.

135. Ibid.

136. Ibid.

137. UNEPFI, *Fiduciary Responsibility*, supra note 42 at 100.

138. See, e.g., Richard Clements and Ademola Abass, *Equity and Trusts: Texts, Cases, and Materials* (2008) ("The most common fiduciary relationships exist between trustees and beneficiaries, agents and principles, directors and companies and partners and co-partners"); L. S. Sealy, "Fiduciary Relationships," 69 *Cambridge L.J.*, 73 (1962) (outlining four categories of fiduciary duty).

139. See Kirsten Edwards, *Essential Equity and Trusts*, 88 (2005, 2nd ed.) (arguing that fiduciary duty was plagued by uncertainty for a number of reasons, including "wide indicia for finding a fiduciary relationship, the necessity of flexibility in the approach of courts and the subjective notions of public policy and good conscience which underlie decision making"); see also Sealy, supra note 138 at 73.

140. See Langbein, supra note 53 at 1070–1071, 1077–1078.

141. Ibid. at 968–971.

142. Sir Anthony Mason, "Themes and Prospects," in P. D. Finn (ed.), *Essays in Equity* 246 (1985).

143. *Learoyd v. Whitely* 12 AC 727 (1887). In this case the trustees lost a significant sum of trust money by investing in the mortgage of a brickfield that went broke.

144. *Learoyd v. Whitely* 12 AC 727 (1887) at 733.

145. John Langbein, "The Uniform Prudent Investor Act and the Future of Trust Investing," 81 *Iowa L. R.* 641, 643 (1996).

146. 6 Geo. Ch. 18 (Eng.). The Bubble Act prevented fiduciaries from investing in anything but consul bonds (government-backed bonds). See Randall H. Borkus, "A Trust Fiduciary's Duty to Implement Capital Preservation Strategies Using Financial Derivative Techniques," 36 *Real Prop., Probate and Trust J.* 127, 130 (2001) (noting that Parliament's restriction of trust investment to government bonds had the added attraction of ensuring that English trust funds stayed within England).

147. The earliest of these was the Law of Property (Amendment Act) (Eng.) "Lord St Leonard's Act" 1859, which was followed by further acts, including the Trust Investment Act 1889 and the Trustee Act 1925.

148. Paulo Panico, "Trustee Investment Powers in International Trust Law," 15 *Trusts and Trustees* 96, 97 (2009).

149. Trustee Investment Act (1961), s. 2.

150. Ibid. sched. III.

151. Langbein, supra note 53, at 1077–1078.

152. *Harvard College v. Amory* 26 Mass. (9 Pick.) (1830) at 461.

153. *King v. Talbot* 40 N.Y. 76 (1869). The New York courts interpreted the investment powers of trustees narrowly, restricting them to statutory lists: see Mark L. Ascher, *Scott and Ascher on Trusts* s.19.1.2. (2007, 5th ed.).

154. See Fredric J. Bendremer, "Modern Portfolio Theory and International Investments under the Uniform Prudent Investor Act," 35 *Real Prop. Prob. and Tr. J.* 791, 797 (2001); Langbein, supra note 145 at 643.

155. Langbein, supra note 145 at 644.

156. John Langbein, supra note 53 at 1071.

157. See UPIAs. 2(e) ("A trustee may invest in any kind of property or type of investment consistent with the standards of this [act]").

158. *Roberts v. Hopwood* AC 578 [1925].

159. Metropolis Management Act (1855), s. 62.

160. *Roberts v. Hopwood* AC 578 [1925] at 590–591.

161. *Roberts v. Hopwood* AC 578 [1925] at 591–592.

162. *Pickwell v. Camden London Borough Council* QB 962 [1983].

163. *Pickwell v. Camden London Borough Council* QB 962 [1983] at 987 (judgment of Forbes J).

164. *Pickwell v. Camden London Borough Council* QB 962 [1983] at 986 (judgment of Forbes J).

165. It is possible that a similar change in the pension fund context would be more difficult to achieve than in the council context, because statutory requirements mean that councils have a wider stakeholder group than pension funds: see *Pickwell v. Camden London Borough Council* QB 962 [1983] at 987 (judgment of Forbes J).

166. See Frank Finn and Peter Ziegler, "Prudence and Fiduciary Obligations in the Investment of Trust Funds," 7 *Austl. L. J.* 329, 337 (1987) (with respect to U.K. and Australian contexts). See Langbein, supra note 145 at 643–645.

167. Pensions Regulator (U.K.), Media Centre, *Questions and Answers: Scheme Specific Funding,* available at http://www.thepensionsregulator.gov.uk/mediacentre/events/sfWorkshop/ssfQAansw ers.aspx.

168. Hawley and Williams, supra note 29 at 168.

169. See ERISA 29 USC s.18.1104.

170. *Speight v. Gaunt* 9 App Cas 1 at 19 (1883), HL, per Lord Blackburn (approving 22 ChD 727 at 739–740, CA, per Jessel MR); Re Whiteley, *Whiteley v. Learoyd* 33 ChD 347 (1886) at 355, CA, per Lindley LJ.

171. *Bartlett v. Barclays Bank Trust Co Ltd* Ch. 515 (1980) at 534.

172. See Borkus, supra note 146, *and.* 127, 129; see *also* Stephen P. Johnson, Note, "Trustee Investment: The Prudent Person Rule or Modern Portfolio Theory, You Make the Choice," 44 *Syracuse L. R.* 1175, 1177 (1993).

173. William Fratcher, *The Law of Trusts* (*Scott on Trusts*), 434–435, s. 227 (1988, 4th ed.).

174. Ascher, supra note 153, at 1396 s.19.1.2.

175. Johnson and De Graaf, supra note 1 at 5.

176. Ibid. at 5.

177. C. Pratten and S. Satchell, *Pension Fund Scheme Investment Policies,* DSS Research Report No. 82 (1998).

178. *Learoyd v. Whiteley* 12 App Cas 727 (1887), HL, at 734 per Lord Watson.

179. Pratten and Satchell, supra note 177.

180. Also an insufficient catalyst for change is any move toward greater democratization of pension fund governance: cf. Benjamin Richardson, supra note 15 at 246–254. Given the behavioral biases described below, as well as the barriers Richardson acknowledges, the idea that beneficiaries may be a viable means of imposing discipline on funds is no more than a liberal dream.

181. William Samuelson and Richard Zeckhauser, "Status Quo Bias in Decision Making," 1 J. *Risk and Uncertainty* 7, 47–48 (1988).

182. Daniel Kahneman and Amos Tversky, "Prospect Theory: An Analysis of Decision Under Risk," 47 *Econometrica* 263, 284–289 (1979).

183. Ibid.

184. See Clark et al., supra note 33; see also Gordon L. Clark, Emiko Caerlewy-Smith, and John C. Marshall, "Pension Fund Trustee Competence: Decision Making in Problems Relevant to Investment Practice," 5 *J. Pension Econ. and Fin.* 91 (2006).

185. Clark et al., "Pension Fund Trustee Competence," supra note 184, at 101–102.

186. Ibid. at 102.

187. Alistair Byrne et al., "Default Funds in UK Defined-Contribution Pension Plans," 63 *Fin. Analysts J.* 40, 40 (2007) (noting findings from a survey of plans that 48–81 percent of U.S. defined-contribution plan assets and over 80 percent of such assets in the U.K. were invested in the default fund).

188. See Clark et al., supra note 33 at 73.

189. Ibid. at 82.

190. Ibid.

191. Emiko Caerlewy-Smith, Gordon L. Clark, and John C. Marshall, "Commentary, Agitation, Resistance, and Reconciliation with Respect to Socially Responsible Investment: The Attitudes of UK Pension Fund Trustees and Oxford Undergraduates," 38 *Env. and Plan. A* 1585, 1586 (2006).

192. See, e.g., George Lowenstein and Richard Thaler, "Anomalies: Intertemporal Choice," 3 *J. Econ. Perspectives* 181 (1989).

193. See, e.g., Clark et al., "Pension Fund Trustee Competence," supra note 184 at 97–99.

194. Paul Myners, *Institutional Investment in the United Kingdom: A Review* (2001).

195. See Gordon L. Clark and Roger Urwin, "Best-Practice Pension Fund Governance," 9 *J. Asset Mgmt.* 12 (2008); see also Gordon L. Clark and Roger Urwin, "Making Pension Boards Work: The Critical Role of Leadership," 1 *Rotman International Journal of Pension Management* 38, 40–44 (2008).

Contributors

Philip Augar, financial writer, Cambridge, England

Adam D. Dixon, Lecturer at the University of Bristol, England

Bruce Dravis, corporate and securities law attorney and former co-chair of the California Corporations Committee

Piet Eichholtz, Professor of Real Estate Finance, Chair of the Finance Department, Maastricht University, the Netherlands

James P. Hawley, Professor, Graduate Business Programs, Saint Mary's College of California and Director of the Elfenworks Center for the Study of Fiduciary Capitalism

Shyam J. Kamath, Professor, Graduate Business Programs and Associate Dean, Saint Mary's College of California

Eric R. W. Knight, doctorate candidate in Economic Geography, University of Oxford, Oxford, England and Solicitor admitted to Supreme Court of New South Wales, Australia

Nils Kok, Assistant Professor in Finance and Real Estate, Maastricht University, the Netherlands

Steve Lydenberg, Chief Investment Officer, Domini Social Investments, New York, New York

Robert Mark, Founder and Chief Executive Officer, Black Diamond Risk Enterprises

Kym Sheehan, Lecturer, Ross Parsons Centre of Commercial Corporate and Taxation Law, Faculty of Law, University of Sydney, Australia

Jennifer S. Taub, Lecturer and Coordinator of Business Law Program within the Isenberg School of Management at the University of Massachusetts, Amherst

Andrew T. Williams, Professor, Graduate Business Programs, Saint Mary's College of California and Associate of the Elfenworks Center for the Study of Fiduciary Capitalism

Claire Woods, doctorate candidate in Economic Geography, University of Oxford, Oxford, England and Solicitor admitted to Supreme Court of Victoria, Australia

Erkan Yonder, doctoral candidate, Maastricht University, the Netherlands

Index

Acknowledgments

The editors gratefully acknowledge the support of the School of Economics and Business and the Elfenworks Center for the Study of Fiduciary Capitalism at Saint Mary's College of California for organizing the conference at which the chapters in this volume were originally presented. We also deeply appreciate the cooperation of the co-conveners of the conference: the Principles for Responsible Investment and the Millstein Center for Corporate Governance and Performance, Yale University. Our heartfelt thanks goes to Hermes Equity Ownership Services, Ltd. for sponsoring the conference and to the Investors Responsibility Research Center Institute for providing crucial support to the authors and presenters. The editors are especially grateful for the crucial assistance of Stephen Davis, Executive Director of the Millstein Center for Corporate Governance and Performance; Jon Lukomnik, Program Director for the IRRC Institute; James Gifford, CEO Principles of Responsible Investment; Colin Melvin, Chief Executive Officer, Hermes Equity Ownership Ltd.; and Roy Allen, Dean of the School of Economics and Business Administration at Saint Mary's College. Each provided timely, insightful, and much appreciated suggestions as the conference took shape. Many thanks to Erin Graham, our editor at the University of Pennsylvania Press, for her prompt answers to our many questions and for her guidance and patience as this volume progressed to publication. We are deeply grateful to the contributors to this volume and the participants for taking part in this innovative conference and for the results they brought about. The former were generous with their time and expertise and prompt but patient with our requests and suggestions for revision, while the latter contributed to an engaging conversation and offered key insights on the topics of the conference and the papers that were presented. Finally, the editors would like to acknowledge a special debt of gratitude to Cherrie Grant for cheerfully and efficiently providing administrative support for the conference; support that extended far beyond reasonable expectations and, therefore, without whose help the conference simply would not have been possible.

WITHDRAWN
UTSA LIBRARIES